CHURCHILL'S GENERALS

CHURCHILL'S GENERALS

EDITED BY

John Keegan

WARNER BOOKS

A WARNER BOOK

First published in Great Britain in 1991 by
Weidenfeld & Nicolson

This edition published by Warner in 1992

A CIP catalogue for this book
is available from the British Library

ISBN 0 7515 0049 6

Printed in England by Clays Ltd, St Ives plc

Warner
A division of
Little, Brown and Company (UK) Limited
165 Great Dover Street, London SE1 4YA

CONTENTS

List of Illustrations   vii

List of Contributors   ix

INTRODUCTION   1
John Keegan

1   IRONSIDE   17
Brian Bond

2   GORT   34
Brian Bond

3   DILL   51
Alex Danchev

4   WAVELL   70
Ian Beckett

5   ALANBROOKE   89
David Fraser

6 ALEXANDER 104
Brian Holden Reid

7 AUCHINLECK 130
Philip Warner

8 MONTGOMERY 148
Michael Carver

9 WILSON 166
Michael Dewar

10 O'CONNOR 183
Barrie Pitt

11 CUNNINGHAM, RITCHIE and LEESE 200
Michael Craster

12 HORROCKS 225
Alan Shepperd

13 HOBART 243
Kenneth Macksey

14 PERCIVAL 256
Keith Simpson

15 WINGATE 277
John W. Gordon

16 SLIM 298
Duncan Anderson

17 CARTON DE WIART and SPEARS 323
G. D. Sheffield

Index 351

ILLUSTRATIONS

Alexander (*Popperfoto*)

Wavell (*Popperfoto*)

O'Connor after his return from captivity (*Imperial War Museum*)

Wilson (*Popperfoto*)

Ritchie, Norrie and Gott in the Western Desert (*Imperial War Museum*)

Cunningham in East Africa (*Imperial War Museum*)

Montgomery and Alanbrooke in Italy (*Imperial War Museum*)

Montgomery with war correspondents in Normandy (*Robert Hunt Library*)

Hobart (*Imperial War Museum*)

Percival (*Popperfoto*)

Slim (*Popperfoto*)

Wingate in Burma (*Popperfoto*)

Churchill with the Anglo-American high command in North Africa (*Imperial War Museum*)

CONTRIBUTORS

DUNCAN ANDERSON is a Senior Lecturer in War Studies at the Royal Military Academy Sandhurst. He has a Master's in War Studies from Queen's University Ontario and a doctorate in History from the University of Oxford. An Australian by birth, he has researched various aspects of the war in the Pacific and contributed to several books on the subject.

IAN BECKETT is a Fellow of the Royal Historical Society and Senior Lecturer in War Studies at the Royal Military Academy Sandhurst. He was born at Whitchurch, Buckinghamshire and educated at Aylesbury Grammar School and the Universities of Lancaster and London. He is the author of a number of books, General Editor of the Manchester University Press *War, Armed Forces and Society* series and Secretary to both the Council of the Army Records Society and the Buckinghamshire Military Museum Trust. He is married with two children and lives in Wiltshire.

BRIAN BOND was educated at Worcester College, Oxford and lectured in history at Exeter and Liverpool Universities (1961–6). Since then he has taught in the Department of War Studies at King's College,

London and is now Professor of Military History. His books include *The Victorian Army and the Staff College* (1972), *Liddell Hart* (1977), *British Military Policy Between the Two World Wars* (1980), *War and Society in Europe 1870–1970* (1984) and *Britain, France and Belgium, 1939–1940* (1990). He is currently a Council Member of the Army Records Society and the Society for Army Historical Research, and is President of the British Commission for Military History. He lives at Medmenham in Buckinghamshire.

FIELD-MARSHAL LORD CARVER started his military career in 1935 in the Royal Tank Corps. In the Second World War he commanded a tank battalion and an armoured brigade while still in his twenties. After the war he commanded an infantry brigade and division, and held many important posts on the staff before becoming Commander-in-Chief Far East in 1967, Chief of the General Staff in 1971, and Chief of the Defence Staff between 1973 and 1976. His most recent books are *The Seven Ages of the British Army, Dilemmas of the Desert War, Twentieth Century Warriors* and *Out of Step*.

MICHAEL CRASTER was educated at Wellington College, RMA Sandhurst and Balliol College Oxford. Commissioned into the Argyll and Sutherland Highlanders, he transferred to the Grenadier Guards in 1970, and returned to Oxford to command the Officers Training Corps in 1985. Most recently he has just completed a tour as the Defence Attaché in Vienna. Author of *15 Rounds a Minute*, an account of the 2nd Battalion Grenadier Guards in 1914, he has also been responsible for a number of articles in military journals.

ALEX DANCHEV is Lecturer in International Relations at the University of Keele, and Alistair Horne Fellow of St Antony's College, Oxford, 1990–91. He has held Fellowships in the Department of War Studies, King's College, London, and the Woodrow Wilson Centre, Washington, DC. He is the author of two books on Anglo-American relations during the Second World War, *Very Special Relationship* (1986) and *Establishing the Anglo-American Alliance* (1990). His forthcoming work includes an edited collection of international perspectives on the Falklands conflict, *A Matter of Life and Death*, and a study of the philosopher-statesman Oliver Franks, *Founding Father*.

COLONEL MICHAEL DEWAR was commissioned into the 3rd Green Jackets, the Rifle Brigade in 1962 and served with his regiment in Cyprus, Borneo, Germany, Northern Ireland, Berlin, Malaya and the United States. In 1985 he was appointed to command the Light Division Depot in Winchester before becoming, on promotion, Colonel Defence Studies between 1987 and retirement from the Army in 1990 to take up the appointment of Deputy Director of the International Institute for Strategic Studies. He has written extensively on defence issues: his books include *Brush Fire Wars – Minor Campaigns of the British Army since 1945* (1984), *The British Army in Northern Ireland* (1985) and *The Art of Deception in Warfare* (1989).

GENERAL SIR DAVID FRASER was commissioned in the Grenadier Guards in 1941 and served with the 2nd Battalion in northwest Europe and thereafter in Malaysia, Egypt, Cyprus, West Africa and Germany, commanding a battalion, a brigade and a division. He was Vice Chief of the General Staff, British Military Representative to NATO and Commandant of the Royal College of Defence Studies before retiring in 1980. Biographer of Alanbrooke (1982) and military historian (*And We Shall Shock Them*, 1983), he is also a novelist (the *Treason in Arms* series, five vols, 1985 *et seq*, and *The Hardrow Chronicle*, four vols, 1990 *et seq*).

JOHN W. GORDON is Professor of History at The Citadel, Charleston, South Carolina, and has served as visiting professor at the US Military Academy, West Point. He served in Vietnam in 1967–8 and has since, in the US Marine Corps Reserve, been a battalion commander and both a group and brigade operations officer. He received his doctorate in history from Duke University, is the author of *The Other Desert War: British Special Forces in North Africa, 1940–1943* (1987), and serves as a member of the adjunct faculty, US Marine Corps Command and Staff College.

JOHN KEEGAN was for many years Senior Lecturer at the Royal Military Academy Sandhurst and is now Defence Editor of *The Daily Telegraph*. His books include *The Face of Battle, Six Armies in Normandy, The Mask of Command* and *The Second World War*. He was Lees Knowles Lecturer in Military History at Cambridge 1986–7 and he is a Fellow of the Royal Historical Society and the Royal Society of Literature.

KENNETH MACKSEY, MC, RTR, served in the Royal Armoured Corps and Royal Tank Regiment from 1941 until retirement in 1968 when he became a full-time military historian and author. Educated at Goudhurst School, at Sandhurst and at the Staff College, Camberley, he saw military service in northwest Europe and various parts of the Far East. Since 1980 he has been a consultant to the Canadian Army in the writing of interactive military scenarios, of which *First Clash* is the first of a series. He is the author of thirty-five books, including *Armoured Crusader: Major-General Sir Percy Hobart*; *Guderian: Panzer General*; *Kesselring, Maker of the Luftwaffe* and *Rommel, Campaigns and Battles*; besides histories of the Royal Tank Regiment and Royal Armoured Corps.

BARRIE PITT served in both the European and Mediterranean theatres in the Second World War. He edited the enormous partwork *History of the Second World War* and was also editor-in-chief of *Ballantine's Illustrated History of World War II*. His books include *1918 – The Last Act*, *Churchill and the Generals*, and the massive account of the desert campaigns, *The Crucible of War*.

BRIAN HOLDEN REID is Lecturer in War Studies, King's College, London, and since 1987 has been Resident Historian at the British Army Staff College, Camberley. He is the first civilian to work on the Directing Staff for over 100 years and helped set up the Higher Command and Staff Course. A Fellow of the Royal Historical Society and Royal Geographical Society, from 1984 to 1987 Dr Reid was Editor of the *RUSI Journal*. He is the author of *J. F. C. Fuller: Military Thinker* (1987), and has edited (with John White), *American Studies: Essays in Honour of Marcus Cunliffe* (1991) and (with Colonel Michael Dewar), *Military Strategy in a Changing Europe: Towards the Twenty-First Century* (1991).

G. D. SHEFFIELD was educated at the University of Leeds and King's College, London and now lectures in the Department of War Studies at RMA Sandhurst. His books include *Warfare in the Twentieth Century: Theory and Practice* (co-editor, 1988) and *From Vimy Ridge to the Rhine* (co-editor, 1989). He is working on a doctoral thesis on Officer-Man Relations, Morale and Discipline in the British Army, 1914–18. He is Secretary of the British Commission for Military History.

LIEUTENANT-COLONEL G. A. SHEPPERD entered the Army from Sandhurst in 1931, joining The Manchester Regiment and served in the West Indies, Egypt and Palestine. During the War he attended the Staff College, and after a period as Brigade Major he was sent to the RAF Staff College, later returning there on the Directing Staff. In the invasion of Normandy he was serving on HQ 3rd British Division, and was severely wounded. After the War he joined the Directing Staff of the Staff College, Camberley; but retired in 1947 to join the Staff of the newly opened Royal Military Academy Sandhurst. Here he stayed for twenty-nine years. His books include *The Italian Campaign 1943-45*, *Sandhurst*, *The Royal Military Academy* and *France 1940, Blitzkrieg in the West*.

KEITH SIMPSON was educated at the University of Hull and King's College, University of London. He was a Senior Lecturer in War Studies and International Affairs, Royal Military Academy Sandhurst 1973–86; Head of the Foreign Affairs and Defence Section of the Conservative Research Department 1986–8 and then Special Adviser to the Secretary of State for Defence 1988–90. He is now director of the Cranfield Security Studies Institute. His books include *The Old Contemptibles* (1981); *History of the German Army* (1985); as editor with Ian Beckett, *A Nation in Arms: A Social Study of the British Army in the First World War* (1985) and, as editor, *The War the Infantry Knew 1914–1919* (1987).

PHILIP WARNER joined the Army in 1939 after graduating from Cambridge and served until 1945, mainly in the Far East. Subsequently he was an Assistant Principal in the Treasury, a Lecturer for the British Council in Spain, and a Senior Lecturer at the RMA Sandhurst, where he founded the Communication Department. He is the author of forty-five books, mainly on military history, including *Auchinleck: The Lonely Soldier* (1981), *Kitchener: The Man Behind the Legend* (1985), *Horrocks: The General Who Led from the Front* (1984), *Passchendaele* (1987), *World War II: The Untold Story* (1988) and *The Battle of France 1940* (1990). He is currently working on a biography of Field-Marshal Earl Haig.

INTRODUCTION

JOHN KEEGAN

Churchill was a soldier. He had been commissioned from the Royal Military College into the 4th Hussars, had charged with the 21st Lancers at Omdurman, served in the South African Light Horse, held a commission in the Queen's Own Oxfordshire Hussars Yeomanry and commanded the 6th Royal Scots Fusiliers in the trenches of the First World War. 'They evidently will like vy much to have me', he wrote home of his first evening in command. 'The general – Furse – is extremely well thought of here and is a thoroughly frank & broadminded man. ... Most of the staff have met me soldiering somewhere or other, & we had a pleasant evening.'[1]

Much of the British army *had* met Churchill soldiering – in India, on the North-West Frontier, in Egypt and the Sudan, in South Africa, on manoeuvres in England – and were familiar with the sight of him in khaki. It was not, however, as a soldier that his brother officers thought of him. He had been a minister and had sat in the Cabinet. He remained a Member of Parliament. Above all, however, he had been a war correspondent, a trade he had begun while still a subaltern. It had caused resentment at the time, resentment which Churchill had returned when he was denied facilities to write as he chose. In 1897 *The Daily Telegraph* appointed him its correspondent with the Indian Army on the North-

I

West Frontier. Shortly afterwards he wrote home to his mother,

The Simla authorities have been very disagreeable to me. They did all they could to get me sent down to my regiment. I ... invite you to consider what a contemptible position it is for high military officers to assume – to devote so much time and energy to harrying an insignificant subaltern. It is indeed a vivid object lesson in the petty social intrigue that makes or prevents appointments in this country.

With entirely unconscious irony he added, 'Talk to the prince about it'; by 'the prince' he meant the future King Edward VII.[2]

There was the nub of the military establishment's attitude to young – and middle-aged – Winston. He relished the military life, revelled in action, romanticized the profession of arms, thought of himself as a soldier, treading in the footsteps of his ancestor the great Duke of Marlborough, yet nevertheless expected that as a junior officer he should be allowed, as his biographer William Manchester puts it, 'to praise or deprecate his seniors ... to write for newspapers while wearing uniform' and generally to behave as if he were, like Marlborough, a strategist and a warlord, without having borne any of the responsibility that high command brings in its train. No wonder that a contemporary of his wrote of Churchill in his Indian years that he was 'widely regarded in the Army as super-precocious, indeed by some as insufferably bumptious'.[3]

By the time the Second World War broke out, Churchill had added greatly to his output of military writing but had also transformed his reputation. *The World Crisis*, his history of the First World War, was criticized for its egocentricity but was also recognized as a stirring and powerful account of the conflict. His life of *Marlborough* had won nothing but praise. It was a great biography, a major contribution to the historiography of the War of the Spanish Succession and an education – for the author as much as his readers – in the arts of command and diplomacy. His personal standing had also been changed utterly. The appeasers in the Conservative Party might bear an unspoken grudge that he had been proved right in his unflinching opposition to Hitler; they no more dared voice it than did the backwoods Tories their disapproval of his youthful desertion of the party for the Liberals. Churchill's party loyalty might have been compromised in the past. His patriotism had never been in doubt and, now that circumstances had driven the country to war with the dictators against whom he had railed so long as a lonely voice, he had become *the* patriot, awaiting only the moment when circumstances would bring the victory in which he could rejoice or the setback which would carry him to national leadership.

The moment came on 10 May 1940, the day on which Hitler's *Wehrmacht* opened its attack in the West. On the previous day Conservative dissatisfaction with Chamberlain's conduct of the Norwegian campaign had boiled over into an angry display in the chamber of the House of Commons, which the Prime Minister had left to shouts of 'Go! Go!' Chamberlain, persuaded that he no longer commanded the confidence of his own party, and informed that neither the Liberals nor Labour would join a National Government under his leadership, advised the King that he must send for Churchill. On his return from Buckingham Palace that afternoon, Churchill sent for the handful of men with whom he proposed to form a War Cabinet. Martin Gilbert, his official biographer, recalls the letter he had written to his wife from the trenches on having almost been killed by a German shell twenty-four years earlier, which epitomized the spirit in which he set forth on his task: '20 yards more to the left & no more tangles to unravel, no more hatreds and injustices to encounter: joy of all my foes ... a good ending to a chequered life, a final gift – unvalued – to an ungrateful country – an impoverishment of the war-making power of Britain which no one would ever know or measure or mourn.'[4] How gifted was Churchill to command the war-making power of Britain at the supreme crisis in the nation's life?

Although Churchill had held all three service ministries, and the Admiralty twice, had been a member of Lloyd George's and Chamberlain's War Cabinets, and had fought as a combatant on the North-West Frontier, in the Sudan, in South Africa and on the Western Front, the only campaigns in which he had been closely involved in the direction of operations were Antwerp and the Dardanelles. The first had been a brief and peripheral episode in 1914, but may be judged a success; it had prevented the Germans capturing the Channel ports in the course of their advance on Paris. The second had been a protracted and tragic failure, which had forced Churchill to leave office and had overshadowed his reputation and his own thinking for years after. He continued to believe that the attempt to force the Straits by an amphibious assault had been frustrated by a series of mishaps, and that Gallipoli might have driven the Turks out of the war in 1915. His, however, was an increasingly personal judgement. As the Gallipoli vision faded, more and more observers concluded that it had been a doomed enterprise.

Antwerp and Gallipoli are significant indicators of Churchill's strategic cast of thought, as is his deep involvement in the Marlburian epic. He saw Britain's 'war-making power' as essentially amphibian, even though he was wise enough to perceive that the essence of war in his own time was attritional. The tension between his emotional, romantic vision of war as an escapade and his sombre, realistic appreciation of the relentless material character it had assumed in the modern age was to dominate his direction of operations and later his strategic diplomacy throughout the Second World War. His heart was fired by daring lunges at the enemy's weak points: by O'Connor's offensive into Italian Libya, by the expedition to Greece, by the torpedo attack on the Italian fleet at Taranto, by Wingate's penetration of the Japanese positions in Burma, by the idea of a drive towards Vienna through the river valleys of Yugoslavia. His head told him that the power of the German Reich had to be broken by other means: the defeat of the U-boats, the strategic bombing of German cities, the invasion of north-west Europe. Throughout the war his conduct of operations was to oscillate between the romantic and the realistic; he could rarely resist an adventure but was consistently drawn back into the mainstream of strategy by the promptings of his own common sense, reinforced, of course, by the arguments and advice of his staff officers, of whom Alanbrooke, as David Fraser describes in his chapter on the CIGS, was to prove the most influential.

There are two other salient characteristics of Churchill's strategic outlook. The first was his fascination with intelligence. Because of Britain's success – building on the achievements of the Polish and French cryptographic services – in decrypting the German Enigma radio traffic at an early stage of the war, its high command enjoyed an unprecedented and, for a time, unique advantage in its ability to read the enemy's 'secure' communications. The Prime Minister accorded the cryptographic organization, the Government Code and Cipher School at Bletchley, every facility it required; and, at the outset, he insisted on seeing its 'raw' product for himself. Only after he accepted that decrypts unannotated or uninterpreted by experts were of limited value to decision-makers did he agree that he should receive 'Ultra' messages in their processed form. He nevertheless insisted on his daily quota of Ultra material throughout the war (continuing to call it 'Boniface', an early covername, long after 'Ultra' had come into general use), and rightly so; by reading the most important of the daily decrypts, he made himself better informed about the progress of the war than any other of the major war leaders of whose routine we have detailed information.[5]

Churchill's other fascination was with 'special operations'. 'Now set Europe ablaze' was his instruction to Hugh Dalton on 22 July 1940, the day he set up the Special Operations Executive.[6] SOE had two functions: first, to conduct sabotage and subversion in the occupied territories of Europe; second, to raise the conquered peoples of Europe in guerrilla warfare against Hitler. Churchill had direct and extensive experience of irregular warfare. He had fought Afghans on the North-West Frontier, charged against Sudanese on the Nile, reported Spain's war against the Cubans, negotiated with the leaders of the Irish Republican Army and, above all, campaigned against the Boers, 'the most good-hearted enemy I have ever fought against in the four continents in which it has been my fortune to see Active Service'. His experience in the Boer War had been formative. It had persuaded him that a people in arms could disrupt the purpose of even the mightiest empire, and from that conclusion he drew the belief that what the Boers had done the Poles, Czechs, Belgians, Dutch and French might do likewise.

It was in that belief that he most clearly revealed his tendency to romanticize war-making. For the truth was, of course, that the British had been as 'good-hearted' as the Boers in their conduct of the campaign in South Africa. They had, admittedly, confined the Boer women and children in what they unfortunately called 'concentration camps', where disease had run rife. They had, however, eschewed deliberate atrocity and punished soldiers guilty of it. The army's good behaviour had been in part guaranteed by the operation of a free press and the readiness of 'pro-Boers' at home to publicize and castigate infractions of the law. Ultimately, however, it had depended upon what the French call 'le fair-play britannique'. The British themselves called the Boer War 'the last of the gentleman's wars', a tribute as much to themselves as to the enemy. What Churchill failed to grasp was that the Germans under Hitler were not prepared to play the gentleman. They were constructing an empire in a hurry, freely invoked the continental laws of 'state of siege' and conventions of right of conquest to impose their authority, and even more freely broke all laws and conventions against those who challenged it. Arbitrary arrest, imprisonment without trial, summary execution, hostage-taking and, finally, mass murder were all methods that the Germans were prepared to use. Except in Yugoslavia and the rear areas of the Eastern Front, where terrain and recent traditions of lawlessness favoured the guerrilla, they proved entirely successful in suppressing disorder. A 'Europe ablaze' was to remain, throughout the war, a strategic chimera, despite the enormous resources which SOE, at Churchill's bidding, devoted to encouraging conflagration.

The principal instrument of Churchill's waging of war on land was therefore to be the British Army and his principal agents its senior officers. The machinery for directing military operations was quickly and efficiently rationalized by Churchill as soon as he assumed the premiership. Before 10 May 1940, there had been three bodies charged with strategic decision-making: the War Cabinet, the Standing Minis-terial Committee for the Co-ordination of Defence, and the Chiefs of Staff Committee. Churchill retained the first and the third, but abolished the second, of which he had been chairman since April, replacing it with the office of Minister of Defence, who was himself. The new Minis-ter had no ministry; instead Churchill appointed, to work to him and the War Cabinet, two new committees: the Defence Committee (Oper-ations) and the Defence Committee (Supply). The Defence Committee (Operations) was the key agency. It consisted of the Deputy Prime Minis-ter, Attlee, the three Service ministers – Admiralty, War, Air – and later the Foreign Secretary, but was always attended by the Chiefs of Staff.

Churchill, as Minister of Defence, therefore stood at 'the focal point at which the military and political elements of the High Command were fused'.[7] He often attended the meetings of the Chiefs of Staff Committee, saw them again when they attended the Defence Committee (Operations) and had instant access to them also through his own personal Minister of Defence's office, formed from the military wing of the War Cabinet secretariat, whose chief, General 'Pug' Ismay, was both a member of the Chiefs of Staff Committee and chief of staff to the Prime Minister.

In practice, as time wore on, the War Cabinet was content to leave the conduct of the war to the Prime Minister and the Chiefs of Staff and did not wish to be brought into strategic discussions. The formal Defence Committee eventually came less and less into the picture, and was later superseded by what Churchill called 'Staff Conferences': meet-ings of a few ministers with particular interests, together with himself and the Chiefs of Staff.[8] Thus Martin Gilbert, Churchill's biographer, on his method of making war. The picture is filled out by comments from two of those closest to the Prime Minister during the war, General Sir Leslie Hollis, Ismay's deputy, and Sir John Peck, one of Churchill's private secretaries. The old system, represented by the Committee of Imperial Defence which dated from before 1914, had seemed to Churchill to represent, Hollis said, 'the maximum of study and the minimum of action'. It was all very well 'to say that everything had been thought of. The crux of the matter was – had anything been done?' Churchill's famous marginal minute, ACTION THIS DAY, exactly represented his preference between thought and action. He nevertheless accorded the greatest weight to correct thinking. Despite Alanbrooke's notorious judgement that 'Winston had ten ideas every day, only one of which was good, and he did not know which it was', Churchill was a formidable strategic brain.

I have the clearest possible recollection [Peck wrote] of General Ismay talking to me about a meeting of the Chiefs of Staff Committee at which they got completely stuck and admitted that they just did not know what was the right course to pursue; so on a purely military matter they had to come to Churchill, civilian, for his advice. He introduced some further facts into the equation that had escaped their notice and the solution became obvious. The point of the story is that one of the reasons for the success of the working relationship between Churchill and the Chiefs of Staff was their deep respect, even on the frequent occasions when they disagreed with him, for his *military* talents if not genius.[9]

The difference between Churchill's and Hitler's methods of exercising command scarcely needs emphasis. Hitler operated quite deliberately a system of divide and rule. He kept ministers separate from service chiefs, the service chiefs separate from each other and they in turn separate from his own operational headquarters, the *Oberkommando der Wehrmacht* (OKW), so that no man in the Reich but he could claim to have a comprehensive view of Germany's strategic situation. Indeed, he did not attempt to conceal the principle by which he commanded: *Führerprinzip* was the political philosophy of the Nazi state and, in disputes with his generals – Guderian and Manstein were the most disputatious – he consistently dismissed objections to his decisions with the rejoinder that they were ignorant of the relevant economic or diplomatic context, which only he perceived. Churchill, by contrast, worked by free debate between colleagues who shared full access to the widest sources of information; access to Ultra had, for security reasons, to be strictly limited but the Chiefs of Staff were among those who had it.

What sort of men were Churchill's generals? In age, background, education, training and experience they were remarkably similar, typical products of their class and age. All those who held high command or staff appointments had been born in the same decade, give or take a year. Ironside, the oldest, was born in 1880, Slim in 1891. Almost without exception they had been trained at the Royal Military College, Sandhurst or the Royal Military Academy, Woolwich, the latter the cadet school for gunners and engineers. All but Slim had been educated at public schools – and a limited number of public schools with strong military traditions at that: two at Eton, two at Wellington and two at Cheltenham. None had been to university, although several spoke at least one foreign language: Ironside spoke seven, Alanbrooke and Spears were bilingual in French, Percival spoke Russian, Alexander spoke German and some Russian, Horrocks spoke French, German and some Russian, and Auchinleck and Slim spoke, of course, Urdu, the official language of the Indian Army; Slim also spoke Gurkhali and Auchinleck, a gifted linguist, a number of north Indian dialects. Wavell kept up the classical languages he had learnt at Winchester, anthologized poetry and wrote a little of his own, as well as a number of thoughtful essays on the profession of arms; Slim supplemented his income between the wars by *nom de plume* journalism, at which he was successful; Alexander, who had won the art prize at Harrow, painted occasionally and appreciated pictures: he made the well-known landscape artist, Edward Seago, his camouflage officer as a means of attaching him to his headquarters in Italy during the Second World War.

The British generals of the First World War have been categorized, a little loosely, as 'cavalry generals'. Those of the Second were almost exclusively infantrymen or gunners, a reflection of the character of the First World War in which they had all served. Some had served extensively on the staff – Montgomery, for example, after having been gravely wounded as a platoon commander in 1914. A high proportion, however, had fought in the trenches and been highly decorated for bravery: Gort had the VC, DSO and two bars and MC, and Alexander was widely thought to have earned a VC; O'Connor had the DSO and bar and the MC and had been nine times mentioned in despatches; even Percival, upon whom obloquy descended after Singapore, could not be accused of lack of physical courage: he had won the DSO and bar and MC in North Russia in 1919. Many of them had been wounded at close quarters. The story of Montgomery's wounding was particularly poignant. Shot through the chest, he had been saved by a solder from his platoon who had been killed dressing his wound and whose body had then shielded him from most of the bullets a German sniper continued to fire at him.

In their professional lives the experience of Churchill's generals was also closely similar, as was to be expected of regular officers in the small army of a great empire. The majority had been students at the Staff College and later Directing Staff (instructors); Montgomery, exceptionally, had been a student and DS at the Staff College, Camberley and then a DS at the Staff College, Quetta, the Indian Army's senior training establishment; Slim, reversing the pattern, had been a student at Quetta and a DS at Camberley. Alexander had been a late student at Camberley, when Montgomery was a DS (and later claimed to have thought little of his over-age pupil), but had then gone to the new Imperial Defence College, a war school for senior officers founded in 1922, at the appropriate stage; most of Churchill's other generals were also IDC graduates.

The value of the British staff colleges in the interwar years, it must be recognized, however, was social rather than educational. They brought together the most promising officers of their generation, ensuring that they knew each other well thereafter; but, even in the two years that the courses at Camberley and Quetta lasted, they taught far less than the Prussian Kriegsakademie would have done (and the disguised Reichsheer staff college was teaching) and taught what they did teach less well. The aim of the Camberley and Quetta courses was to fit an officer to serve as a Brigade-Major, the lowest level of operations officer in the military hierarchy. The Kriegsakademie, by contrast, set out to produce divisional chiefs of staff (the 'ia', or Eins A, as the German Army knew them), who would be qualified to rise to the highest staff appointments thereafter. The spirit of the German course was intellectual rather than procedural, concerned not to teach routines, 'staff duties' as the British called them, but to inculcate powers of analysis and a cast of mind that would ensure that all graduates should react congruently when confronted by a similar military problem. The Kriegsakademie system, based upon replication of staff tasks, rigorous mutual critique, 'staff rides' and battlefield tours, and deep study of military history, had been imitated by all other staff colleges, of which it was the *maison mère*; as imitators, however, none had achieved its standards of excellence. They were certainly not characteristic of either Camberley or Quetta in the interwar years.

British officers, by contrast, had a far wider range of experience, military and non-military, than their German contemporaries or those of any other army, an advantage which went far to compensate for the defects in their formal training. The small wars of empire gave them frequent practice in the command of troops in action; the politics of empire, which underlay such wars, accustomed them to co-operating with imperial civil servants in the implementation of strategies which, though small in scale, were often complex in nature; while the varied terrain and climate of the empire itself, and the absence of resources and difficulties of supply in remote campaigning-grounds imposed an excellent practical training in logistics.

One among Churchill's generals escaped categorization by training or experience: Alan Brooke – or Alanbrooke as he became known after assuming that title in the peerage, whom David Fraser, a friend and subordinate of the field-marshal, takes as the subject of his chapter. Alanbrooke had both a mind and a character of exceptional quality; significantly, he was the only brother officer whom the intractable Montgomery could bring himself to admire. Montgomery knew that Alanbrooke was more able than he, because Alanbrooke was demonstrably the most able man in Churchill's military entourage. He was a superb military technician, who had mastered the intricacies of artillery tactics in the most complex artillery battles ever fought, those of the Western Front of 1916–18. He was, however, far more than a technician. He was also a large-minded strategist, who comprehended both the essentials of Britain's interests in the waging of the Second World War and the limits which Britain's strengths and weaknesses imposed on the strategic choices which had to be made. He disapproved of 'sideshows', so often Churchill's enthusiasm because sideshows, on paper, appeared adventurous and romantic; on the other hand, he stoutly supported Churchill in his objection to a premature launching of the cross-Channel invasion, because he recognized how injurious failure would be to a Britain weakened by three years of war which the United States had not undergone.

We have now reached a stage [he wrote in his diary in July 1943] when all three Services, and industry supplying them, are living beyond their means. ... Cuts must be made; unfortunately, while recognising that cuts must be made, Winston won't face up to reducing formations. It is useless retaining emaciated formations which we cannot maintain, and I refuse to do so, and that leads to differences of opinion of the severest nature with Winston.[10]

Such differences he disguised from the Americans, however, thus acting perfectly correctly as a shield to his master but a supporter of his policies in the public forum.

Alanbrooke was seen at his best in his reaction to Churchill's suggestion that he should assume command in the Middle East in the summer of 1942, after Churchill had rightly concluded that Auchinleck was no longer fitted to command the Desert Army. Alanbrooke longed to accept Churchill's offer of the command for himself. He nevertheless rejected it. He had been Chief of the Imperial General Staff, in succession to Dill, only since the previous November, but had already recognized that he had a peculiar ability to protect Churchill from his worst strategic excesses, those potentially most damaging to Britain's interests.

'I could not put the real reasons to Winston' for declining the appointment, he wrote in his diary on August 6 and went on:

Whether I exercised any control or not, I knew by now the dangers to guard against. I had discovered the perils of his impetuous nature. I was now familiar with his method of suddenly arriving at some decision as it were by intuition, without any kind of logical examination of the problem. I had, after many failures, discovered the best way of approaching him. I knew that it would take at least six months for any successor, taking over from me, to become as familiar with him and his ways. During those six months anything might happen. I would not suggest that I could exercise any real control over him. I never met anybody that could, but he had grown to have confidence in me, and I had found that he was listening more and more to any advice I gave him.[11]

At this point, however, Churchill did not accept Alanbrooke's advice to appoint Montgomery to command of Eighth Army. His preference was for General 'Strafer' Gott, and it was only Gott's death the following day, shot down by a German fighter, that brought Montgomery to the post. As commander-in-chief Middle East Churchill had already nominated Alexander who, after commanding 1st Division in the Dunkirk campaign, had just supervised the miseries of the retreat from Burma. Montgomery may not have conformed to the Churchillian military ideal; Michael Carver, who served under Montgomery, makes clear how unorthodox he was. Alexander, in contrast, personified orthodoxy. Handsome in person, graceful in manner, gracious in character, he was also celebrated among his contemporaries for his physical courage, and Churchill admired physical courage above almost all other qualities. Some men held that the brave could do no wrong in his eyes; Auchinleck was brave and Churchill had confided to Alexander a few days after dismissing him the emotional trouble it had caused him. 'You know', he said, 'it was like killing a magnificent stag.'[12] Alexander, for reasons that Brian Holden Reid makes plain, was to try Churchill's patience by his conduct of the Italian campaign but no thought of dismissing him ever seems to have entered Churchill's head. He felt something of the same indulgence towards Gort, that paragon of courage, and even thought of appointing him CIGS, though prudence checked him at the last moment. Of Freyberg, another VC and a hero of the Dardanelles, he would hear no criticism at all; he called him 'the Salamander', because like the mythical creature he could live in fire, and forgave him even the loss of Crete, which may have been taking indulgence too far. All these were warriors 'that every man at arms would wish to be', or that Churchill in his romantic mood would wish to have been; that they were not very good generals was a truth to which he could blind himself.

Wavell was a moderately good general who failed to click with the Prime Minister. Ian Beckett depicts how different the two men were in temperament. Wavell was clever, thoughtful, well read; he escaped the criticism levelled by Churchill at admirals as a breed: 'I do not think that a sailor is well qualified for a command of this character [the tri-service appointment in South-East Asia] ... they rarely have the time or opportunity to study military history and the art of war in general.'[13] Wavell had studied military history and written about the art of war, notably in his Lees Knowles lectures at Cambridge on 'Generals and Generalship'. But that was perhaps the trouble; his generalship smelt of midnight oil, and his personality had the faint, musty odour of the bookish Wykehamist. He lacked dash and was naturally cautious; events thrust him into campaigns, like the intervention in Greece, where caution was a desirable quality but dash would have looked better. He never had adequate forces, except for the brief period when he opposed only the Italians in the Western Desert; Churchill perhaps unconsciously reproached him for not being a Rommel, a general who also disposed of inadequate forces but maximized their potential. On 3 June 1942, Churchill complained to his former private secretary, Jock Colville, of Wavell's 'excessive caution and inclination to pessimism [which] he finds very antipathetic'.

Churchill ought also to have found Montgomery antipathetic. The Prime Minister was cavalier, the future field-marshal Cromwellian – both these loose words have meaning in their case. The soldier had devoted his life to bringing his instincts under the command of his will, until he allowed himself almost no room at all for friendship, for imagination or for family feeling. The politician had tempered his instincts until he could find his moment, when they had burst forth in a tempest of inspired activity, passionate, rhetorical and dramatic. In some strange way, however, the two personalities were to mesh by antithesis. Churchill was fond of saying that it was the role of the political leader to organize 'creative tension' between subordinates. No more creative tension existed in his war leadership than that between himself and his leading general. Both were men of high self-consciousness, of deep emotion. Both found it easy to believe that they were right and others wrong. Churchill found no difficulty in praising Montgomery in victory. Montgomery found it very difficult to accept Churchill's when victory hung in the balance. The most notorious conflict of will between them occurred during the preparation for D-Day, on 19 May 1944, over the administrative arrangements for the landing.

One by one [records Nigel Hamilton, Montgomery's official biographer] Monty ran through the battles he had won in the past two years: Alamein, Tripoli, Mareth, Wadi Akarit, the assault upon Sicily, the invasion of the Italian mainland – all under the overall leadership of the Prime Minister. The invasion of Normandy was all set; the men were confident they would succeed. Did the Prime Minister wish to shake that confidence, to come between a general and his men, his own staff in fact? 'I could never allow it – never', Monty pronounced. 'If you think that is wrong, that can only mean you have lost confidence in me.'[14]

In another version of this incident, Montgomery took Churchill into his study and sat at his desk, which seemed 'a proper arrangement'. The Field-Marshal told the Prime Minister that he could not address his staff. 'He became tearful and gave in'.[15] This is dramatic stuff. The only trouble is that the witness of events in both cases is Montgomery himself. Churchill, when he became aware of the accounts that were circulating, wrote that 'This interview has been misrepresented'. It is widely known that Churchill was given to tears. The likelihood that he cried in frustration before his own appointee to high command reeks of improbability.

It makes nevertheless for stirring biography. There were few other dramatic relationships in Churchill's direction of high command. Wingate, his personal choice to lead the 'deep penetration' Chindit expeditions behind Japanese lines in Burma, was an unlikely candidate for a senior appointment. He had been raised in the Plymouth Brethren, had become converted to Zionism while serving in Palestine during the Arab Revolt of 1936–9, had attempted suicide on one occasion and was quite unclubbable; his military contemporaries regarded him as a loner and an outsider. Churchill hoped to make a second Lawrence of Arabia of him, but the truth was that he lacked, among other qualities, Lawrence's intellect and imagination. There was no 'creative tension' between Churchill and Wingate; the relationship was that of master and pupil.

With Slim, the Montgomery of the Far East, Churchill might have established a creative relationship had the two men come to know each other; Duncan Anderson's character portrait makes that clear. Distance denied them the chance to become intimate. Slim was the opposite of Auchinleck, a British officer who became one of the Indian Army. Once transferred, he was virtually lost to sight by his contemporaries at home and made his career by his own achievements against the Japanese. Churchill, in any case, and though he kept the thought to himself, had a low opinion of the British forces in the east. After the humiliation of Singapore and the agony of the retreat from Burma, he associated them with defeat. Only slowly did he recognize that in Slim he had found a man of sterner mettle than Wavell or any of the other generals who commanded on the road to Mandalay.

The worst of the eastern generals was, of course, Percival, whom Churchill never forgave for his surrender of Singapore; the photograph of Percival walking under the white flag to negotiate with his Japanese opponent remains perhaps the most humiliating image of British defeat ever to confront the public in the nation's history. Percival should not have been appointed to high command; as Keith Simpson, who has studied his career in detail, makes clear. He was an able staff officer, nothing more. He owed his elevation to Dill, then Chief of the General Staff, whose talents were also those of a staff officer. Dill was appointed by Churchill to succeed Ironside – emphatically not a staff officer, though he might have made a magnificent commander of some desperate venture in the field – because Ironside had not only failed in his job but behaved incautiously in his private life. There was absolutely nothing incautious about Dill. Quite the contrary; Churchill's nickname for him, Dilly-Dally, cut very close to the bone. Alex Danchev, who has written the official biography of Dill, sympathizes with his subject but nevertheless accepts the justice of Churchill's attitude. Dill was, in many ways, akin to the generation of officers at the head of the French Army in 1940, elderly in outlook and bureaucratic by habit. It was not entirely coincidental that he hit it off so well with Marshall, the American Chief of Staff, when he was appointed to head the British liaison staff in Washington after his removal as CIGS. Marshall, too, was a ponderous bureaucrat; what allowed him to journey to the heights of American government was that the United States needed such a man while it was mobilizing its millions for war. Marshall, to do him justice, was a better judge of men than Dill. He singled out Eisenhower for advancement from the start; it seems unlikely that Percival would have recommended himself to him.

Of all Churchill's senior officers, the closest to him in experience of life, in style and in temperament were two who never held high command, though they enjoyed his confidence in positions where political and military responsibilities overlapped: Spears and Carton de Wiart, whose dashing styles Gary Sheffield captures in his chapter. Carton de Wiart was a VC and also a cosmopolitan, a sportsman and an aristocrat. He was an inspired choice (not Churchill's) as head of the mission to Poland, an inspiration to his immediate subordinates in the doomed expedition to Norway, might have been a man of destiny in Yugoslavia, had he not fallen by mischance into enemy captivity, and was an arrestingly eccentric representative of British interests at the headquarters of Chiang Kai-shek. Spears, also a cosmopolitan, was a close and old friend of Churchill's, who admired greatly his dash, intelligence and courage. He was not, however, the right choice to act in liaison with de Gaulle. Though the two men at first got on well, Spears subsequently took it upon himself to act for British interests, particularly in the Middle East, with a robustness that alienated de Gaulle. They became in the end enemies, a state of affairs that speaks for the unwisdom of Churchill's choice in the first place.

The flaw in all Churchill's appointments to high command was that he would, had circumstances permitted, really have preferred to exercise command himself, at all times and in all places. Churchill was a frustrated Marlborough, who itched to be both the general on the field of battle and the presiding genius of the alliance. As it was, Ronald Lewin notes, he succeeded in reducing 'the way of life of a Minister of Defence and Prime Minister to that of an uninhibited eighteenth-century aristocrat, the grotesque dressing gowns, the afternoon sleep and the mandatory baths, the cigars, the brandy, the best of everything'; the saving feature of his style of command was that it was 'for all its extravaganza, actually efficient'.

Churchill had learnt one overridingly important lesson from his Cabinet experience of the First World War: not to try to 'achieve a great enterprise without having ... plenary authority'.[16] Plenary authority he had in full between 1940 and 1942; even after the intervention of the Americans he continued to exercise it over all his generals, with the possible exception of Montgomery. Montgomery enjoyed the advantage of a run of unbroken success which he owed exclusively to his own talents. In the end, however, plenary authority told. Inter-Allied arrangements subordinated Montgomery to Eisenhower on 10 September 1944. Nine months later when victory in Europe came, Churchill was still Minister of Defence, the longest serving of all Hitler's opponents and, by any reckoning, the most implacable and successful of his foes.

NOTES

1 William Manchester, *The Last Lion* (London, 1983), p. 590.
2 Ibid., pp. 259–60.
3 Ibid., p. 260.
4 Martin Gilbert, *Finest Hour* (London, 1983), p. 314.
5 Ronald Lewin, *Ultra Goes to War* (London, 1978), chapter 7, *passim*.
6 J. G. Beevor, *SOE* (London, 1981), p. 12.
7 Ronald Lewin, *Churchill as Warlord* (London, 1973), p. 34.
8 Gilbert, op. cit., p. 234.
9 Ibid., pp. 234–5.
10 Quoted Lewin, *Churchill as Warlord*, p. 203.
11 Ibid., pp. 157–8.
12 Nigel Nicolson, *Alex* (London, 1973), p. 155.
13 Arthur Marder, *Old Friends, New Enemies*, vol. 2 (Oxford, 1990), p. 233.
14 Nigel Hamilton, *Monty*, vol. 2 (London, 1983), p. 592.
15 Lewin, *Churchill as Warlord*, p. 246.
16 Ibid., p. 266.

I

IRONSIDE

Field-Marshal Lord Ironside

BRIAN BOND

In a diary entry written in June 1940, shortly before his retirement, Ironside reflected that his dazzling career prospects had been diminished in the decade 1926–1936 under the discouraging regimes of Milne and Montgomery-Massingberd. The Army was in the doldrums and Ironside felt unwanted; he became irritated at his inability to influence training and organization and lost confidence in his future. Thus, when his belated opportunity came in 1939 Ironside was probably past his best, and moreover he was given an appointment – Chief of the Imperial General Staff – for which he knew himself to be unsuited both by temperament and experience.[1]

Edmund Ironside was born in 1880, the son of a surgeon-major of the Royal Horse Artillery who died when he was still an infant. His mother eked out her pension by regular Continental travel and Edmund showed an early aptitude in foreign languages, in seven of which he became an interpreter. He was commissioned from Woolwich in time to serve in the South African War with the Royal Field Artillery, and shortly afterwards, disguised as a Boer transport driver, he accompanied the German military expedition to South-West Africa where he did useful work for British Intelligence, demonstrating his great resourcefulness and linguistic skill.[2] Six foot four inches tall and correspondingly broad he was inevitably nicknamed 'Tiny'. He was the original of John Buchan's soldier-hero Richard Hannay of *The Thirty Nine Steps*, *Greenmantle* and *Mr Standfast*. Not least among his distinctions Ironside represented Scotland at rugby.

In temperament Ironside was not so much the archetypal 'gentle giant' as a supremely self-confident, forceful and opinionated commander. He was more typical of his generation in being an open-air soldier who intensely disliked the confines of desk work, particularly at the abominated War Office. In general he held a low, if not contemptuous view of politicians and, in the case of Hore-Belisha, was later to admit in his diary that the War Minister's Jewish origins had increased his antipathy.

Nevertheless after the First World War he was generally regarded as an able and progressive officer. He was closely associated with the radical advocate of mechanization and armoured warfare, 'Boney' Fuller, and conducted a regular and remarkably frank correspondence on professional matters with Basil Liddell Hart. This correspondence reveals a lively mind ranging widely over the trends in modern warfare and ideas for improving the Army.[3] As Ironside's career developed, however, Liddell Hart was adversely impressed by his 'trade union' attitude to promotions, evidenced by his keeping (and openly discussing) a large ledger containing the names of all officers above him on the Army List with his and other people's views of their performance, health and prospects. Also, despite his facility with languages, contemporaries such as his fellow gunner Henry Pownall noted his intellectual limitations. Pownall rejoiced prematurely at his impending retirement in June 1938, noting in his diary, 'It's a mercy his soldiering days are over. ... There's always been more bluff and brawn than brain.' This harsh judgement would be more widely endorsed after Ironside's term as CIGS between September 1939 and May 1940.

Ironside passed through the Staff College at Camberley on the eve of the First World War and served throughout on the Western Front. He distinguished himself in successive staff and command appointments culminating in command of 99 Brigade in the 2nd Division in the Spring of 1918. In September 1918 he was appointed Brigadier General Staff to the Allied expedition to Archangel but took over the command shortly after its arrival, becoming General Officer Commanding in North Russia in 1919 with the substantive rank of major-general. This placed him among the three or four youngest major-generals in the Army. From 1922 to 1926 he was an inspiring Commandant at the Staff College with

'Boney' Fuller as his Chief Instructor, and then commander of the 2nd Division at Aldershot. Thereafter, like other precocious contemporaries who had received rapid promotion, he had to mark time – including a disheartening period on half-pay – until his seniors such as Milne, Massingberd, Harington and Deverell eventually retired.

When Ironside was appointed to Eastern Command in 1936 he had more experience of senior command in war than almost any other serving officer and, but for his age, still seemed a strong contender for command of the Field Force in event of war. He found the Army at home in a dire state of unpreparedness. 'We are in no state to go to war', a typical diary entry reads, 'There are no men and there is no money for their equipment and there is no will amongst the Cabinet Ministers to want an Army.... We have nothing with which to fight – literally nothing – and will not have anything for two years.' He concluded that the absence of an Expeditionary Force was a godsend: nobody would dream of sending such a derisory force to the Continent. As late as May 1938 he could write: 'Never again shall we even contemplate a Force for a foreign country. Our contribution is to be the Navy and the RAF.'[4]

It is necessary to devote some space to promotions because an important contention in this essay (as also in that on Gort) is that both officers were given unsuitable appointments – square pegs forced into round holes. This was an unintended consequence of Hore-Belisha's shake-up of the high command in 1937 in the attempt to break up the prevailing system of Buggins' turn and bring forward dynamic, progressive, unorthodox leaders. It is also worth noting, in view of his later criticisms, that Ironside welcomed Hore-Belisha's arrival at the War Office in May 1937: 'We are at our lowest ebb in the Army and the Jew may resuscitate us.... He is ambitious and will not be lazy as some of the others were. He starts in when things are at their worst and will have to show results.' He also greeted Lord Gort's appointment as Military Secretary as 'the best piece of news I had heard for many years'.[5]

Towards the end of 1937 Hore-Belisha determined to remove Deverell as CIGS and faced the critical question of who should succeed him. Ironside was in the running but spoilt his chances by an unimpressive performance as a Commander in the major exercise of 1937. For this he was severely (and Liddell Hart thought unfairly) criticized in public by Deverell from a draft prepared by Alan Brooke – no admirer of Tiny's. It is interesting, however, that even Liddell Hart – Ironside's strong supporter and Hore-Belisha's adviser at this period – thought that he was better suited to be Commander-in-Chief in India with Wavell as CIGS. Unfortunately the taciturn Wavell had made a very poor impression on the War Minister and the appointment eventually went to Gort. Ironically Gort would have preferred to hold a revived appointment as Inspector General of the Forces so as to extend his active career. Hore-Belisha's idea was that Gort would be the dynamic 'front man' in pushing through radical reforms while Sir Ronald Adam as his deputy would supply the brains in the sphere of strategy – a dubious arrangement since it was Gort and not Adam who had to present the Army's case in the Chiefs of Staff committee.[6] Ironside told Hore-Belisha he had chosen the right man and had never really pictured himself as CIGS, for which the War Minister was greatly relieved. Yet within a few months Ironside was privately recording his opinion that Gort was completely out of his depth as CIGS.

Early in 1938 Ironside accepted the appointment of Governor of Gibraltar and assumed it would end his military career. However, Gort and Hore-Belisha both held out the prospect of command in the Middle East in event of war, and since Tiny was convinced that Egypt was the hub of the Empire and the place where Britain's main military effort must be made, this was an added attraction. Hore-Belisha also made the 'preposterous' suggestion that the British Army might well be employed in Spain and he (Tiny) would be on the spot to take command.[7]

In December 1938 Hore-Belisha consulted Liddell Hart about recalling Ironside from his exile on the Rock to be Inspector General of Overseas Forces. Liddell Hart was doubtful because he thought there would be confusion of responsibilities between this post and that of CIGS. Sir John French had been Inspector General of Overseas Forces before 1914 and Commander-in-Chief designate. The danger would be that Ironside would regard himself as the virtual Commander-in-Chief and Gort would be relegated to administrative duties. This was all the more likely given Tiny's dominant character and considerable seniority over Gort. Nevertheless Hore-Belisha went ahead, giving Ironside the appointment in May 1939 and making Walter Kirke Inspector General of Home Forces. As regards demarcation of duties he ruled that both Inspectors would be 'outside the War Office' but able to come inside as and when they needed.[8]

Even if Ironside was not officially informed that he was C-in-C designate, it was a reasonable assumption to make and he behaved accordingly. He continued to believe to the very eve of war that the Middle East was the most likely destination of Britain's small and under-equipped Field Force. Friction with Gort over their respective responsibilities soon occurred and was gleefully recorded by Major-General Henry Pownall, Director of Military Operations and Intelligence at the War Office. On Tiny's appointment Pownall expressed the opinion that he was quite unsuited to be a C-in-C on a modern battlefield. 'He would do alright bush-whacking or knocking the Middle East about but he is *not* intelligent, not enough so to deal with a first-class enemy.' Pownall may have been prejudiced but Sir John Slessor, who had known Tiny at various points in his career, recorded an almost identical view.[9] The only incident in Ironside's brief tenure of the Inspector-Generalship that deserves mention here is his visit to Poland in July 1939 to assess the Poles' military capabilities and intentions. He reported prophetically that no Eastern Front really existed, that France would not attack the Siegfried Line and that Poland would be quickly overrun. He urged that an agreement with Russia was essential, but this advice was anathema to the Prime Minister.[10]

When war with Germany seemed certain at the end of August, Ironside was so confident of being appointed C-in-C that he sent his assistant, Colonel Macleod, to Aldershot to assemble his headquarters staff. After an agonizing wait the bombshell exploded on 3 September: Hore-Belisha appointed Gort commander of the Field Force for France and made Ironside CIGS. The details of this dramatic incident need not be described again here,[11] but the circumstances and momentous consequences deserve some discussion. Gort and Hore-Belisha had been on extremely strained terms and both were delighted at the chance for Gort to leave the War Office and take a command, for which he was more suited. Tiny's chance of the command of the Field Force may have been harmed by French hints that he would not be acceptable – but their preference was for Dill rather than Gort. Hore-Belisha was now stuck with Tiny for, as Sir John Kennedy put it, he had 'raised a regular Frankenstein's monster in bringing Ironside back from the dead'.[12] Ironside had a commanding presence and a popular reputation, and he was strongly supported by Churchill, now recalled to the Admiralty and a member of the War Cabinet. Churchill overcame opposition – from Kingsley Wood and others – and Ironside was made CIGS. This was a bad mistake for, as Ironside honestly admitted, 'I am not suited in temperament to such a job as CIGS, nor have I prepared myself to be such.' Indeed he had never before held a staff appointment at the War Office. Furthermore, one must ask, since he had been passed over as unsuitable in 1937, why (at the age of sixty) was he deemed suitable in 1939? Ironside soldiered on in increasingly irksome conditions but the error in appointing him must be borne in mind when we consider his shortcomings as CIGS.

Eyewitnesses differ on Ironside's performance in the early months of the war and particularly on his relations with Hore-Belisha. Sir John Kennedy paints a generally attractive and positive picture of a rumbustious bull-in-a-china-shop, courageous, self-confident and intolerant of nonsense – political or military. Kennedy retails Tiny's version of his haranguing the War Cabinet but he also records that, far from impressing ministers, Ironside had annoyed them very much. 'His manner with politicians was much too brusque; on the other hand it was a joy to hear him give a straightforward military survey in a military environment.' Francis de Guingand, by contrast, thought that so far from 'nearly reducing H-B to tears', Ironside was very respectful towards the minister and would not have dared to pound the table or harangue him.[13]

Ironside's view of strategic priorities at the outset of war may be summarized briefly. Britain's first task in the West was to build up the French order of battle with the Field Force eventually expanded to some twenty divisions. The initial aim must be to withstand a German offensive which Ironside (correctly) thought Hitler might be willing to risk in the autumn of 1939. He continued to envisage the Middle East as the main theatre in which Britain would ultimately launch an offensive when she had assembled twelve divisions. Ironside described Turkey as 'our front line and our bastion'. 'A door might open in Rumania or Italy; or we might have to send in small forces to put Poland and Czecho-Slovakia back on their feet.' From the outset he was understandably unhappy about the lack of overall direction and the inefficient organization of strategy and policy. After three weeks at war he complained: 'The old gentlemen sitting here in London have no idea of the seriousness of the position. ... How can we get a unified command of operations? How are we to stop those stupid conferences of the Chiefs of Staff and War Cabinets, discussing the little details of the nothings that have happened?'[14] Things would have to get worse in the months before Churchill became Prime Minister, and Ironside scarcely survived long enough to experience the benefits which ensued.

Ironside's lack of balance and gravitas are evident in the remarks about Poland and Czechoslovakia quoted above. He also displayed instability on two important issues in the autumn of 1939. In September Gamelin raised the possibility of an Allied advance from the defences being prepared on the Franco-Belgian frontier to the line of the Escaut (or Scheldt). Ironside wrote to Gort and spoke out in Cabinet against this projected move: there was a danger of being caught in the open by low bombing attacks, and the Escaut Line, unreconnoitred and unprepared, would be linear and ineffective. Yet when Gamelin set out his reasons for the projected advance on 26 September Ironside acquiesced. No firm decision was taken and in the following weeks the General Staff prepared a paper stressing the folly of the advance unless the Allies could be sure of occupying defensive positions before the Germans attacked. Dill and Brooke (the Corps commanders) were unhappy about the project, as were some of the French field commanders. No new arguments were advanced by Gamelin, but on 9 November Ironside and Newall (the CAS) accepted his plan, to the dismay of the General Staff. Ironside explained to the War Cabinet that Gort had been placed under the French command and given the right of appeal to the Government, but since he had not done so they would be ill-advised to intervene.[15] This was a curious line to be taken by the Cabinet's senior adviser on military strategy, particularly as he knew that Gort was determined to play the part of a loyal ally.

The other issue concerned the main role of the RAF's bomber force in the event of a German attack in the West; should it, in short, be concentrated on close-support attacks on the enemy's communications or should it be directed towards 'strategic bombing' of the Ruhr? Ironside was acutely aware of the derisory provision for close Army–Air support and was fighting for the Army to have control of its own aircraft. Yet in discussions with the Air Staff and Churchill, and later with the French war leaders, Ironside vehemently favoured bombing the Ruhr, declaring repeatedly that it would be 'decisive', apparently because he believed the German generals were rigid and inflexible and would be unable to readjust to this chaos in their rear. Slessor remarked that Ironside's assessment went far beyond the Air Staff's claims for the immediate effects of industrial bombing, while Gort was indignant that his CIGS had sold the pass on so contentious an inter-Service dispute.[16]

Ironside was increasingly depressed by the Cabinet's policy of 'wait and see' and the endless, futile discussions. Even Chamberlain, for whom he expressed considerable admiration, was described as 'just a weary, tired old man, dominating at times all the other mediocrities who bear the responsibility with him'. His diary entries on Hore-Belisha become more frequent and more scathing.[17] For his part, the War Minister told Liddell Hart that he wished he had chosen Ironside in the first place rather than Gort. Despite his limitations he had much more drive than any other soldier. He could always get a reasoned opinion from Tiny. On 14 December, with the axe of dismissal poised over his head, Hore-Belisha failed to take Chamberlain's hint that he could have Gort and Ironside replaced if he lacked confidence in them.[18]

Ironside played only a subsidiary role in the notorious 'Pill box affair' which provided the pretext for Hore-Belisha's dismissal from the War Office early in January 1940, so the matter can be covered more fully in the essay on Gort. At the first hint of trouble between the War Minister and the Commander-in-Chief on 19 November, Ironside warned the former to be careful how he dealt with Gort. 'He was put in by the King and must not be monkeyed about.' It seems clear from Tiny's own account that on 28 November he volunteered to go and examine the Field Force's defences for himself. The notion that he had been sent out by the War Cabinet or Hore-Belisha only served to exacerbate the paranoiac atmosphere at GHQ. Whether Ironside went out to France with an open mind may be doubted: he certainly returned a staunch supporter of the GHQ line that Gort had been insulted and that, 'H-B must go'. On 3 December Ironside saw the King, who was angry about the dispute. A fortnight later Tiny noted that in many ways it would be a pity if H-B had to go, but he found him impossible personally. When he heard of H-B's resignation on 6 January he seemed genuinely surprised but felt a sense of intense relief.[19]

Ironside's role in advocating operations in Scandinavia between the end of December 1939 and mid-March 1940 does not enhance his reputation as a sound strategist; indeed it does much to justify Pownall's linking his name with Churchill's as 'the Crazy Gang'. The opportunity for British operations in Scandinavia was of course provided by Finland's gallant resistance against the Russian invasion, but from the outset Ironside saw assistance to Finland as no more than a pretext: the real objectives were the occupation of the Swedish iron ore fields around Gällivare and the distraction of German forces away from western Europe. Pownall was right to link the CIGS's name with Churchill's because both men fretted at Britain's inactivity and longed to seize the initiative. But whereas Churchill favoured the lesser plan of mining the Norwegian leads to force German transport vessels into open waters and perhaps provoke a full-scale reaction, Ironside favoured the major scheme of a military expedition through Narvik along the electric railway into Sweden. Tiny believed that if Finnish resistance could be prolonged it would prevent a German advance in the Balkans. If Germany could be provoked into armed intervention in Scandinavia the Middle East would be kept quiet. An offensive through Narvik to Lulea (the Swedish port on the Gulf of Bothnia from which iron ore was shipped to Germany in the ice-free summer months) would offer the Allies a big return for little expenditure. It presented a chance to seize the initiative and throw confusion into German councils. On 26 December Churchill told Ironside that his own scheme – of mining the leads – would soon receive Cabinet approval. He did not think the Germans would be able to take action against Norway and Sweden before May and only then might Britain have to send a force through Narvik to Lulea.

Ironside thought they had stumbled upon 'the one great stroke which is open to us to turn the tables upon the Russians and Germans'. He saw that Norwegian and Swedish co-operation was vital but assumed that it could be obtained. He accepted that once an operation was started in Scandinavia it was likely to grow into a major campaign, but in that event it must be carried through 'despite all other demands made upon our troops and material'. A few days later, however, he and the other Chiefs of Staff warned the Cabinet against implementing Churchill's plan until their own forces were prepared. 'It is like putting a stick inside a hornets' nest without having provided yourself with a proper veil', he wrote prophetically. Throughout January 1940 he continued to advocate the larger scheme, making the assumptions that 'if we pushed in a brigade to Gällivare' the Germans would be unable to react before May, and also that the enemy was incapable of mounting more than one operation at a time.[20]

At the meeting of the Supreme War Council on 5 February Ironside found Daladier 'genial' and the French delegation delighted at Britain's willingness to shoulder the main burden of the Scandinavian enterprise. Assuming Norwegian and Swedish acquiescence, the essence of the plan was to push a strong force through Narvik and Trondheim:

We are supplying two divisions and two strong brigades, while the French supply a brigade of Chasseurs Alpins, two battalions of the Legion and four battalions of Poles. This will all pass across the Narvik–Lulea line and we shall sit down in strength upon our L. of C., making sure of Gällivare and Boden. I can see a whole host of objections from the Scandinavians, but what I most fear is a passive resistance – a strike amongst the officials of the railway.

If we bring this off we shall have carried out a great coup, which will upset the even tenor of the German preparations. It may bring in Norway and Sweden. I don't doubt that it will have an electrifying effect upon the Germans. They will have to come out in the open and declare themselves for or against the Russians.[21]

Ironside showed awareness of the risks of the plan, but deemed them worthwhile if the German supply of iron ore could be stopped. He took it for granted that France was secure and could only benefit from the German diversion. This hair-raising scenario did not delight GHQ in France. Pownall penned a most devastating critique against 'those master strategists Winston and Ironside': communications and logistics would be a nightmare even if all went well; there was a real risk of antagonizing Russia; the Germans could *easily* mount an attack on the Western Front as well as in Scandinavia or the Balkans; and why should the Norwegians and Swedes allow us to make their countries a battlefield – if they were so pro-ally and anti-German, why did they not stop the ore supply themselves or let us buy it at an enhanced price?[22]

Ironside continued to support the scheme up to the last minute, despite the opposition of other senior army officers involved in the planning such as Kennedy and Ismay, and Newall (the CAS) who described it as 'hare-brained'. Chamberlain, too, was 'horrified' at the political risks involved, but the expedition was set to go ahead on 12 March when Finland's timely collapse caused its postponement.[23]

Making due allowance for Pownall's hostility to Ironside, his anger at the CIGS's failure to keep GHQ informed about the Scandinavian project and its repercussions on the Field Force in France were justified. As Pownall noted on 12 March, part of 5th Division had actually been withdrawn from France with a view to despatching it to Norway, III Corps had been held up in England, and the supply of ammunition to France had totally ceased in February because it was needed elsewhere. Pownall found consolation in the rumour that Ironside would shortly be appointed Commander-in-Chief in India.[24]

When Anglo-French operations in Norway eventually began in early April the circumstances were entirely different to what Ironside had envisaged: in a brilliant combined operation the Germans seized Bergen, Trondheim and Narvik and soon achieved air dominance over the battle zone. Ironside supported the expedition to take Narvik, but he was almost alone among the decision-makers in realizing it would not be a 'walkover'. On 14 April Churchill, who from the outset had dominated the British response, insisted against the CIGS's violent protests that the rear half of the convoy carrying troops to Narvik be diverted to Trondheim. This predictably caused chaos and got the operation to seize Trondheim through a pincer movement from landings at Namsos and Andalsnes off to the worst possible start.

Ironside, whose previous relations with Churchill had been very good, now became exasperated at the First Lord's attempt to supervise all military operations as if he were a company commander. He also found Churchill's see-saw changes of mood hard to cope with. The CIGS justifiably felt that his proper responsibility for military advice could not be exercised due to the frequent rambling discussions of the Chiefs of Staff, the ill-named Co-ordination Committee and the War Cabinet. As he noted on 19 April: 'Strategy is directed by odd people who collect odd bits of information. This is discussed quite casually by everyone.' Two days later he questioned the sanity of trying to run operations by committee with every morning's Cabinet meeting taken up with descriptions in detail of every little incident in the fighting. It was like a lot of children playing a game of chances.[25]

Perhaps Ironside's most important achievement in the Norwegian campaign was to insist on the speedy evacuation of the Central Front (Namsos and Andalsnes) on 26 April. British ministers were relieved, but the CIGS was unhappy that he had felt obliged to force through this decision without consulting the French. On 7 May he fairly summed up the campaign as a muddle in every way. 'Always too late. Changing plans and nobody directing. To bed very upset at the thought of our incompetence.' He was obliged to admit that, contrary to his stereotyped view, the Germans had displayed a remarkable ability to improvise. An even greater shock was impending.[26]

Ironside, like Gamelin, had at times hoped that the Germans would attack on the Western Front in the winter months of 1939–40, and he deluded himself, despite ominous signs, that French morale was sound. As late as 31 March he expressed a poor opinion of German generalship and staff work: an attack on the Western Front would be a terrible gamble for them. In October 1939 he had mentioned the Ardennes as a possible approach route for the Germans, but at that time their main thrust (in planning) was directed at central Belgium and the Netherlands.[27] It seems probable that in May 1940 the CIGS was as surprised as the other Allied war leaders by the bold execution of the Manstein Plan.

Ironside's role in the battle of France was not of great significance. He knew his days as CIGS were numbered when Dill was brought back from France in late April as VCIGS. Gort and Pownall at GHQ had completely lost confidence in him. Lastly, even before he became Prime Minister on 10 May, Churchill was now presiding over both the Chiefs of Staff and the Co-ordination committees as a virtual Minister of Defence. On 19 May, however, Ironside was instructed by the

War Cabinet to go over to France and order Gort to retreat south-west so as to link up with the main French armies supposedly assembling for a counter-attack to smash through the Panzer corridor now stretching tenuously to the Channel coast. Gort and Pownall quickly convinced him that the War Cabinet was hopelessly out of touch with events and that a retreat northward to the Channel ports offered the only faint hope of escape. Ironside also witnessed the French commanders' moral collapse and was sufficiently exasperated to shake General Billotte by his tunic buttons. He believed that only a minute portion of the BEF could escape.[28]

On 27 May Dill replaced Ironside as CIGS. He welcomed the change to a job more to his liking – Commander-in-Chief Home Forces – further sweetened by Churchill's promise of a field-marshal's baton in due course. The War Cabinet rightly believed he would infuse more drive and purpose into defence preparations and, as seemed all too likely, would be the best commander to lead the ill-trained, ill-equipped and totally inadequate forces remaining in the United Kingdom against an invading army.

Ironside understandably, though wrongly, assumed that Hitler would have ordered thorough planning for the invasion, but he was more realistic than the Chiefs of Staff in appreciating that the Germans would be unlikely to attempt an invasion before achieving command of the air. When Ironside took up his command the most vulnerable area of the coastline seemed to lie between the Wash and Folkestone, but after the fall of France the whole of the southern coast was threatened. The number of troops available was superficially impressive but there was a dearth of guns and tanks, training was defective and the means of mobility lacking. Initially therefore Ironside had no alternative to organizing a largely static 'crust' of beach defences, with blocks and stop-lines further inland and a small mobile reserve north and west of London to counter-attack landings in East Anglia or on the south coast. In the first half of June Ironside's difficulties were exacerbated by the removal of some of his best units for the ill-fated second BEF.

Ironside presented his complete plans to the Chiefs of Staff Committee on 25 June. They comprised five main elements. First, an extended 'crust' along the probable invasion beaches whose defenders would fight where they stood to gain time and break up all penetrations. Second, there would be blocks manned by Local Defence Volunteers (later renamed the Home Guard) equipped with 'Molotov cocktails' and other devices to use against tanks. Thirdly, small, local mobile reserves would be mounted in armoured fighting vehicles such as 'Ironsides'. Fourthly, there was to be a strong static defence line constructed to stop any breakthrough from reaching London or the industrial Midlands. Lastly, there was the GHQ Reserve consisting initially of one armoured and the equivalent of three infantry divisions.[29]

On the following day Ironside's scheme was severely criticized by Lord Hankey (Chancellor of the Duchy of Lancaster) and the Vice Chiefs of Staff. They were alarmed at the implication that 'the main resistance might only be offered after the enemy had overrun nearly half the country, and obtained possession of aerodromes and other vital facilities'. They also deplored the plan's lack of attention to the south coast. This scheme they described as 'completely unsound' and 'nothing short of suicidal'.[30]

The Chiefs of Staff were more sympathetic to Ironside's problems and confirmed that his plan of defence was 'generally sound', but they required him to revise his paper clarifying his determination to resist the enemy on the beaches and his intentions regarding the location and use of reserves.[31] Ironside and his chief of staff, General Sir Bernard Paget, were exasperated by repeatedly being summoned to explain their plans; and although Churchill nominally supported the Commander-in-Chief, his memorandum of 28 June caused further confusion. In this paper, in curious contrast to his recent and famous 'We shall fight them on the beaches' speech, he wrote that 'The battle will be won or lost, not on the beaches, but by the mobile brigades and the main reserves.'[32] By the end of June Ironside believed that the Chiefs of Staff were confused about what the priorities for home defence should be or what could reasonably be expected given the limited forces available. He was also aware of criticism from some of the senior commanders, including Montgomery, Auchinleck and, above all, Brooke, who took up Southern Command on 26 June. Brooke felt strongly that more effort should be put into creating a strong reserve for mobile operations; he also believed that the Germans' main thrust would come not across the North Sea but across the Channel against the south coast.[33] On 17 July Brooke seized his opportunity when showing Churchill the south coast defences to convince the Prime Minister that a change of Home Forces Commander was needed and that he was the man for the job.[34] Two days later Ironside's supersession by Brooke was announced. Ironside took his sudden replacement philosophically. Though sometimes irritated by Churchill he had greatly admired his courageous leadership during the prolonged crisis since he had become Prime Minister. Chur-

29

chill in turn appreciated Ironside's performance as Commander-in-Chief Home Forces and the soldierly dignity with which he accepted his supersession. He was promptly promoted field-marshal and in 1941 received a peerage.

Reviewing the *Ironside Diaries* in 1962, A. J. P. Taylor concluded: 'Few men have been less successful as CIGS, and none has been more conscious of it.'[35] Ironside was certainly aware of his shortcomings and he had recognized from the outset that he was far from ideally suited for the post. In conclusion, however, three points may be advanced in mitigation of Mr Taylor's severe judgement. In contrast to the other two services the Army was largely inactive during Ironside's period in office. Similarly, with the notable exception of Churchill, Chamberlain's War Cabinet took a predominantly passive and Micawberish view of grand strategy that was alien to Ironside's restless temperament. Finally, he had to function in a loose structure of decision-making through a plethora of committees with ill-defined responsibilities which were lacking in co-ordination and direction from the top. One may question whether any other CIGS between, say, 1922 and 1945 would have done better in these circumstances.[36]

NOTES

Note. I have not been able to examine the original Ironside diaries which are currently in the custody of his official biographer, Dr Wesley Wark, in Canada. Dr Wark has kindly read and commented on this essay in draft but I remain entirely responsible for its contents. I am also very grateful to Dr David Newbold for permitting me to make use of the section of his doctoral thesis (on Britain's preparations to meet a German invasion on land in World War II) covering Ironside's period as Commander-in-Chief Home Forces.

1 R. Macleod and D. Kelly (eds), *The Ironside Diaries 1937–1940* (1962), p. 365. (Henceforth referred to as 'Macleod'.)

2 Geoffrey Powell, 'John Buchan's Richard Hannay', *History Today*, August 1987.

3 B. H. Liddell Hart, *Memoirs*, vol. I (1965), p. 81. All other references are to Volume II. See also the Liddell Hart–Ironside correspondence in the Liddell Hart Centre for Military Archives at King's College, London.

4 Macleod, pp. 24–5, 57–8.

5 Macleod, pp. 24, 26.

6 Liddell Hart, *Memoirs*, vol. II, pp. 21–3. R. J. Minney, *The Private Papers of Hore-Belisha* (1960), pp. 68–70 (henceforth referred to as 'Minney').

7 Macleod, pp. 38–9, 52–3, 59–60, 64.

8　Liddell Hart, *Memoirs*, II, pp. 74, 239. Minney, p. 210.

9　Brian Bond (ed.), *Chief of Staff: The Diaries of Lieutenant-General Sir Henry Pownall*, vol. I, *1933–1940* (1972), pp. 203, 206, 215–16 (henceforth referred to as 'Pownall'). Pownall speculated that Hore-Belisha had deliberately appointed Ironside in order to provoke Gort into resigning. For Sir John Slessor's unflattering opinion of Ironside, see *The Central Blue* (1956), p. 242.

10　Macleod, pp. 75, 81–2, 85.

11　See Pownall, pp. 222–3 and Macleod, pp. 93–4.

12　Sir J. Kennedy, *The Business of War* (1957), pp. 18–20.

13　Kennedy, pp. 18–25. F. de Guingand, *Operation Victory* (paperback edition 1960), pp. 35–8. Minney, p. 234.

14　Kennedy, pp. 25–6. Macleod, pp. 103–10 passim.

15　Kennedy, pp. 27–31. J. R. Colville, *Man of Valour, Field-Marshal Lord Gort VC* (1972), p. 153 (henceforth referred to as 'Gort'). Macleod, pp. 113, 136, 394. Slessor, p. 251.

16　Macleod, pp. 141–2. Slessor, pp. 246–7, 252. Gort, p. 175.

17　Macleod, pp. 125, 136, 158. Kennedy, pp. 40–1.

18　Liddell Hart, *Memoirs*, II, pp. 264, 269. Minney, pp. 266–7.

19　Macleod, pp. 164–7, 194–6.

20　Macleod, pp. 188–92. Pownall, pp. 280–8.

21　Macleod, pp. 215–16. See also R. A. C. Parker, 'Britain, France and Scandinavia, 1939–40' in *History*, October 1976, pp. 369–87.

22　Pownall, pp. 280–3.

23　Kennedy, pp. 48–9. Macleod, p. 228.

24　Pownall, pp. 288–93.

25　Macleod, pp. 257–9, 265, 268, 273.

26　Macleod, pp. 284–5, 296.

27　Liddell Hart, *Memoirs* II, p. 265. Macleod, pp. 125, 204, 241.

28　Gort, pp. 172–3. Pownall, pp. 323–5. Macleod, pp. 277, 290–1.

29　Cab 79/5 COS(40) 193rd Meeting, 25 June 1940. B. Collier, *The Defence of the United Kingdom* (1957), pp. 129–30.

30　Cab 80/13 COS(40) 490. Letter from Lord Hankey to the COS Committee, 25 June 1940. Cab 79/5 COS(40) 195, 26 June 1940.

31　Cab 79/5 COS(40) 197, 27 June 1940. Cab 80/13 COS(40) 495, Memorandum by the COS, 27 June 1940.

32　Cab 80/13 COS(40) 498, note by the Prime Minister to the COS Committee, 28 June 1940.

33　Sir A. Bryant, *The Turn of the Tide* (the Alanbrooke Diaries, 1957), pp. 189–90. Field-Marshal Viscount Montgomery, *Memoirs* (1958), pp. 68–70. J. Connell, *Auchinleck* (1959), pp. 156–7.

34　Bryant, *The Turn of the Tide*, pp. 194–5. W. S. Churchill, *The Second World War*, vol. II (1949), pp. 233–4.

35 *The Sunday Observer*, 11 November 1962.
36 Many authorities suggest that Dill would have been preferable to Gort as CIGS in 1937 or to Ironside in 1939 but note Sir Alexander Cadogan's diary entry for 29 April 1941: 'Dill is the most unimpressive – if charming – personality I have ever come across. Almost I am persuaded to believe in Ironside!' (D. Dilks (ed.), *The Diaries of Sir Alexander Cadogan 1938–1945* (1971), p. 374).

CHRONOLOGY: EDMUND IRONSIDE

1880, May 6	Born in Edinburgh
1883–7	Tonbridge School
1887–9	Royal Military Academy, Woolwich; commissioned Royal Artillery
1899–1902	South African War (despatches, Queen's Medal with 3 clasps, King's Medal with 2 clasps)
1908	Captain
1909–12	Brigade Major
1913–14	Staff College, Camberley
1914, October	GSO3, 6th Division
1915	GSO2; marries Mariot Ysobel Cheyne (one s, one c); awarded DSO
1916–17	GSO1, 4th Canadian Division; brevet Lieutenant-Colonel
1918	Commands 99 Infantry Brigade, 2nd Division; awarded CMG; promoted brevet Colonel
1918, October– 1919, October	C-in-C Allied Troops Archangel; promoted major-general; knighted (KCB) 1918 (his account, *Archangel 1918–1919*, published 1953)
1920	Commands Ismid Force
1921	Commands North Persian Force
1922–6	Commandant, Staff College, Camberley
1926–8	Commands 2nd Division, Aldershot
1928–31	GOC Meerut District, India
1931–3	Half-pay, Lieutenant, Tower of London
1933–6	Quartermaster-General, India; promoted General, 1935
1936–8	GOC Eastern District; awarded GCB 1938
1938–9	Governor and C-in-C, Gibraltar
1939, May– September	Inspector-General of Overseas Forces
1939, September 3 – 1940, May 27	Chief of the Imperial General Staff

1940, May 27 – July 19	C-in-C Home Forces; promoted Field-Marshal
1941	Created Baron Ironside of Archangel
1959, September 22	Dies in London

2

GORT

Field-Marshal Lord Gort

BRIAN BOND

The late Sir John Colville aptly called his biography of Gort *Man of Valour*, for whatever his subject's limitations of mind and personality, few ever questioned his outstanding courage. When the French Prime Minister Reynaud dared to do so at the height of Anglo-French friction during the Dunkirk evacuation he received a furious rebuke from Sir Edward Spears. Spears himself reflected:

It had never occurred to me nor, I fancy, to any of his contemporaries to describe Gort as intelligent above the average. But, as far as that goes, Foch was not intelligent either ... But he was an undoubtedly great man nevertheless, for he had other qualities, steadfastness, resolution, courage, and so had Gort, who in addition possessed the great virtue of loyalty.[1]

Gort attained the heights of his profession as CIGS and Commander-in-Chief of the Field Force (between 1937 and 1940) and at a comparatively young age, but then suffered the common fate of British commanders at the start of a war, being made the scapegoat for peacetime neglect of the army and relegated to the sidelines.

John Standish Surtees Prendergast Vereker was born in 1886 and succeeded his father as sixth Viscount Gort in the Irish peerage in 1902. He was educated at Harrow and Sandhurst and commissioned into the Grenadier Guards in 1905. In the First World War he performed excellently as a staff officer, particularly in the Operations Branch at GHQ where he played an important part in planning the operations in 1917. But it was as a battalion and brigade commander that he achieved the truly outstanding reputation for bravery which ensured him a distinguished career in the post-war Army. In 1917 he was awarded the DSO and bar when commanding the 4th Battalion Grenadier Guards and was twice badly wounded. In March 1918 he displayed conspicuous bravery at Arras in helping to check the German offensive and was awarded a second bar. But his greatest exploit was on 27 September 1918 when, again badly wounded, he was awarded the Victoria Cross as temporary commander of 3 Guards Brigade in the storming of the Canal du Nord and the Hindenburg Line. He also won the Military Cross and was eight times mentioned in despatches. As Gort's entry in the *Dictionary of National Biography* sums up, he acquired 'a reputation for the rarest gallantry, complete disregard of personal danger and power to keep alive in his troops a spirit of endeavour untamed by loss and strain'.[2]

After the war Gort made steady, if not spectacular, progress. He was an instructor at the Staff College in 1921, was promoted Colonel in 1925, Commander of the Guards Brigade in 1930, Director of Military Training in India 1932, and in 1936 returned to the Staff College as Commandant. In 1937 Gort's career prospects were transformed when Hore-Belisha appointed him, first, Military Secretary at the War Office and, shortly afterwards, the youngest ever CIGS. He skipped the rank of lieutenant-general to become a full general and in so doing passed above many officers senior to him on the Army List including Dill, Brooke and Wavell.

In early life Gort had acquired the ridiculous and inappropriate nickname of 'Fat Boy', but was later known familiarly as 'Jack'. In what would now be termed his 'lifestyle' he was austere and self-denying, indeed he seemed to delight in privations and expected others to do the same. On his appointment to the Staff College in 1936 one colonel remarked: 'He will have all the beds made of concrete and hosed down with cold water nightly.' His suggestion that officers might use their leisure hours at Camberley learning to fly rather than following the drag hunt was not widely appreciated. He also had a schoolboy sense of fun which he never entirely grew out of. In his days as an instructor at the Staff College in the early 1920s he had been a ringleader in various rags, such as squirting hoses under the bedroom doors of those who retired too early on mess nights, and – as will be seen later – he was not above treating the War Minister to similar horseplay in 1939.

Gort had married his cousin Corinna Vereker in 1911 but this did not prove a successful partnership and the marriage was dissolved in 1925. While Lady Gort actually broke up the marriage, Gort himself may have contributed. As his commander in the Shanghai Relief Force in 1927, General John Duncan, revealingly wrote to his own wife:

He is a bit too intense for peacetime soldiering. He is a very fine soldier and extremely able, but he is in a class by himself and works himself to death. It may be the result of his domestic troubles, but if he was like this before I can quite imagine his wife leaving him.[3]

When Gort was rather surprisingly appointed CIGS in December 1937 his biographer assessed his qualities as follows:

there was no more honest man than Gort and if none would have called him brilliant, his integrity, experience, shrewd common sense and that most worthy of all qualities, true simplicity ... were a combination that was certain to attract loyalty and might reasonably be expected to achieve success.

In the opinion of his contemporaries, however, he was regarded as an ideal man to command a division.[4]

In promoting Gort to the highest appointment in the Army, Hore-Belisha hoped he would supply the drive for pushing through overdue reforms while his character would appeal to the troops and enhance the Service's reputation with the public. Sir Ronald Adam as his deputy would supply the brains and adroitness necessary in the Chiefs of Staff Committee and the Committee of Imperial Defence. Sir John Kennedy's opinion, that 'In the War Office this fine fighting soldier was like a fish out of water',[5] may be too severe, but it soon became apparent that Gort was not ideally suited to be CIGS. As we shall see, one of Gort's salient characteristics throughout his life was an obsession with detail, sometimes to the exclusion or neglect of the broader picture.

Nevertheless, Gort became CIGS at a time when the energetic and ambitious Hore-Belisha – greatly aided by international events – was bringing Army reform to the forefront of British politics, and he played an important part in the great improvements that were accomplished before the outbreak of war. This is not the place for a detailed account of Hore-Belisha's reforms,[6] but Gort's most important achievement, helped by his able Director of Military Operations, Major-General Henry Pownall, was to get the Army's continental commitment recognized by the Government (finally achieved in February 1939), with the resultant rush to get its equipment, weapons and transport modernized – and part of the Territorial Army earmarked for development as its eventual Reserve. Though he remained ignorant of the French Army's weaknesses, Gort was convinced that Germany was Britain's most likely enemy, that the Field Force must be made ready for despatch to France and that the pre-1939 plan to send only two divisions was a completely inadequate contribution to an alliance.[7]

Quite apart from the blighting of individual careers, it was a tragedy for the British Army that Gort and Hore-Belisha proved unable to work amicably together. Pownall, a prejudiced, partisan admirer of Gort, thought the two men could never get on: 'a great gentleman and an obscure, shallow-brained charlatan, political Jewboy'. By the summer of 1939 Pownall believed Hore-Belisha was trying to manoeuvre Gort into resignation but he should refuse to budge; the War Minister's Cabinet colleagues were allegedly sick of him and would surely oust him from office after the general election – due in 1940. Gort and Pownall disliked and resented many things about Hore-Belisha, but chief among them were his flamboyant personality, his unorthodox style in conducting Army business – particularly appointments – and his reliance for advice on Captain B. H. Liddell Hart, *The Times*' military correspondent. For his part, it seems unlikely that Hore-Belisha reciprocated Gort's animosity, but the CIGS's distrust and dislike of him clearly penetrated even Hore-Belisha's thick skin. The unfortunate result was that for several months before the outbreak of war Hore-Belisha and his chief military adviser were barely on speaking terms and saw as little of each other as possible. Hore-Belisha dealt increasingly with Gort's deputy, Adam, and with junior staff officers such as Kennedy.

Thus peacetime civil-military relations in twentieth-century Britain reached their nadir in 1939. To judge by the Pownall and Ironside diaries, all the fault was on one side. But Gort's biographer corrects this impression, pointing out that the CIGS offered his political chief no affection or understanding and little credit for his many admirable reforms. A less formal CIGS, capable of overlooking or even laughing at the War Minister's irritating mannerisms and methods, might have gained the latter's confidence and achieved a working relationship. 'Gort stood firmly by his principles and it cannot be denied that he sometimes confused principle and prejudice.'[8]

Clearly the Army's deficiencies on the outbreak of war resulted from years of inadequate funding and political neglect, and Gort as CIGS could only to a very small extent be held responsible for them. Nevertheless he had failed to press the cause of mechanization and the formation of armoured divisions; the handful of tank experts had been dispersed and not given the key appointments either at the War Office or in commands. Perhaps even more deplorable Gort, though a keen supporter of inter-service co-operation, had failed to win any substantial increase of air co-operation squadrons, much less to gain direct authority for the future Commander of the Field Force over the bombers of the Advanced Air Striking Force.

The Government's omission to appoint a Commander-in-Chief of the Field Force before the declaration of war on 3 September 1939, and the resultant confusion among the three possible choices (Dill, Ironside and – least likely – Gort) have already been outlined in the chapter on Ironside and need not be repeated here. Whether or not Gort pressed for the appointment of Commander-in-Chief is uncertain, but he was evidently delighted to escape from Hore-Belisha and the War Office. Gort, like Alexander, made no secret of the fact that he enjoyed the excitement of war. 'Here we go again, marching to war' was his first remark on reaching the Staff College to form his headquarters, and he added 'I can't expect everybody to be as thrilled as I am'. Middle-aged and with daunting responsibilities, his demeanour struck observers as schoolboyish. Gort took Pownall as his chief of general staff, thus, as in 1914, depriving the War Office of the experience of the two officers most fully acquainted with the war plans and arrangements for co-operation with allies.[9]

Gort revered the memory of Marshal Foch for his offensive spirit and his skill in leading the Anglo-French armies in the victorious advance in 1918; he also respected General Georges, commander of the French forces on the Franco-German frontier in 1939. But Gort's command of the French language was poor, and in his determination to be a loyal ally, conscious as he was of Britain's belated and meagre contribution of troops, he tended to be too deferential towards the professorial General Gamelin, Commander-in-Chief of the French Forces. Indeed Gort was so eager to please and do as he was told that the French tended to regard him as 'a sort of friendly and jovial battalion commander'. Spears felt that the British Government should have insisted that Gort be given a place on the Supreme War Council.[10]

As it was, his position in the Allied command structure was a curious one. Gort's headquarters had liaison with Gamelin's, but he was not under Gamelin's orders. The British Field Force was included in the First Army Group under General Billotte but – initially at any rate

– Gort was to receive his orders from Georges. Like his predecessor Sir John French in 1914, Gort was granted the right to appeal to his own Government should he consider that French orders (or, as it turned out, lack of them) might endanger his troops. To make matters even more confused, Gamelin and Georges were on very bad terms throughout the months of the Phoney War and there were frequent rumours that Gamelin would bypass Georges and issue orders direct to Gort.[11]

Gort established his headquarters at the Château of Habarcq, west of Arras. As he wrote to his daughter Jacqueline: 'I am off to a château with no water, no light and no loo.' His staff appeared grossly inflated because Gort had allowed for an eventual expansion to twenty divisions. It was also dispersed over some fifty square miles as a precaution against air attack. As a consequence communications within the Field Force were extremely cumbersome: Montgomery described it as 'an amazing layout'.[12]

The two original Corps commanders, Dill and Brooke, expressed criticisms of the Field Force's equipment, tactics and training, feeling that Gort was too complacent and too obsessed with detail. In their turn Gort and Pownall suspected the Corps commanders of 'bellyaching' and defeatism. Too much of Gort's time was taken up with ceremonial visits to the French and in entertaining a stream of distinguished visitors at GHQ, but in any case he believed in delegating a large measure of responsibility for training to his subordinates. Montgomery made some sharp criticisms of Gort's leadership in his *Memoirs*, but allowed that he had an impossible task in running a great headquarters as well as exercising direct command over the fighting and administrative forces. The plan was for Gort to appoint two Army commanders under him when four corps were assembled, but only three were in place by May 1940.

Montgomery was justly critical of the deplorable signal communications which rendered the complicated command structure even less effective. As a result of the French obsession with security, wireless communications within the Field Force were never efficient; and outside it they scarcely existed. During the battle, harassed commanders were heavily dependent on the civil telephone service which was frequently out of order and always insecure. Montgomery also believed that Gort's failure to hold field exercises or even indoor war games on the sand table resulted in a total lack of any common policy or tactical doctrine.[13]

Numerous sources show that one of Gort's lifelong traits was an obsession with detail which often struck observers as comical. Thus

Sir John Kennedy was taken aback when, at a senior officers' conference with Hore-Belisha present, the first issue Gort raised was whether a tin hat, when it was not on a man's head, should be worn on the left shoulder or the right. Brooke found him tirelessly occupied with tactical questions such as the proper use of hand-grenades and the number a patrol should carry. After a visit to the Maginot Line Brooke tried to discuss the flaws in the French outpost system of defence, but Gort replied, 'Oh, I have not had time to think of it but, look, what we must go into is the proper distribution of sandbags.' Colville noted the officers' puzzlement that a Commander-in-Chief should concern himself with such details as the tear-off igniting paper on rockets, anti-freeze mixture and night-flying pigeons.[14]

On a much more substantial operational issue, Gort was unhappy about Gamelin's proposal to abandon the frontier defences and advance into Belgium to the line of the river Dyle ('Plan D') in event of a German attack. Gort, Pownall and Ironside were all present at Vincennes on 9 November when Gamelin explained his plans and the safeguards against being surprised in the open. None of them objected. Gort suppressed his reservations in the interests of Allied unity: he was under French orders and would advance when told to without reference to his Government. In retrospect this acquiescence in an extremely risky plan was to be widely criticized as a dereliction of duty.[15]

The final rift with Hore-Belisha resulted directly from the minister's visit to the Field Force in mid-November. Sir John Kennedy has left a hilarious but also slightly distasteful account of Gort's schoolboy-like ragging of the fastidious Hore-Belisha who was trying out a pair of fur-lined but, alas, not waterproof boots with a zip fastener up the back. In foul weather Gort insisted that Hore-Belisha climb a very muddy bank and stand shivering in a howling gale while the former explained a First World War battle, and Pownall did the same a little later. When they at last reached shelter in a château Gort opened a window letting in a piercing draught and shouted jovially, 'Isn't it a grand day!' On the way back Hore-Belisha was given bully beef sandwiches and when the minister was eventually offered a decent meal Gort hung around outside making jocular remarks. Even Pownall felt the joke had gone on long enough and was embarrassed. Hore-Belisha endured this ordeal remarkably well and as he was leaving said to Kennedy, 'I think Gort realized that I am out to help him.'[16]

Alas, Gort did nothing of the kind. On his visit Hore-Belisha had asked to see the troops rather than the defences and so did not gather a true picture of the work completed and in progress. He made no criticisms to Gort, but on his return to London complained both in the War Cabinet and the Army Council at the slow rate of construction of pill-boxes. Gort was displeased to hear of this but what infuriated him, a stickler for correct procedure, was that Hore-Belisha conveyed verbal criticisms to Gort via the latter's Chief Engineer at GHQ, General Pakenham-Walsh. By the end of November GHQ was buzzing with Hore-Belisha's 'crimes' against Gort; Pownall listed these 'crimes' in his diary and determined that the War Minister must be removed. On 29 November Pownall confided to his diary:

It's all a disgusting business. A knife in the back of the man who should be free, above all others, to think of beating Germans. We are now here all facing West, to meet the more dangerous enemy there. I have written in full to Grigg, who will know what to do with my letter. We must now await CIGS's visit and the result. Then, assuming a favourable outcome, we must counter-attack on Hore-Belisha. The thing has come to a head and war cannot be carried out thus.[17]

Since our focus is on Gort rather than Hore-Belisha, there is no need to describe in detail the very effective campaign which speedily convinced the CIGS, the King and the Prime Minister that the War Minister was a liability and resulted in his resignation early in January 1940. It seems unlikely that Gort himself intrigued against the War Minister, but he had a trusted 'hatchet' man in Pownall and must have been broadly aware of his clandestine efforts. Hore-Belisha wrote Gort a conciliatory letter on 4 December, and after a visit from the Prime Minister in which he praised the construction of defences, the storm seemed to be abating. On 27 December Gort wrote to reassure Chamberlain that resentment of Hore-Belisha's misplaced criticisms was now over, though he did hint that confidence and trust in the minister might fail at a critical moment if criticism of armies in the field was not couched in sympathetic language. But, in contrast to Pownall who rejoiced, Gort was surprised at Hore-Belisha's resignation and seemed upset that he might be suspected of causing it.[18]

Major-General A. J. Trythall concludes an extremely interesting article on Hore-Belisha with the speculation that Gort and Pownall pushed what should have been a soluble misunderstanding over the pill-box construction to a showdown because they feared that the War Minister intended to dismiss them. Both generals certainly conveyed this impression at the time but it is not certain that this is what chiefly motivated them. If it did, then they were surely mistaken. Hore-Belisha had been monumentally tactless but repeatedly protested that he was really trying to help Gort and the Field Force. Moreover, when Chamberlain gave him an opportunity to remove Gort in mid-December, Hore-Belisha assured the Prime Minister that he had complete confidence in him.[19] The final irony of the pill-box affair is that the frontier defences were irrelevant, since Gamelin's 'Plan D' for an advance into Belgium had been approved by the Supreme War Council three days before Hore-Belisha's visit.

In the early months of 1940 Gort and Pownall were angry and alarmed at the Government's apparent determination to become involved in operations in Scandinavia and its corresponding neglect of the Western Front. Senior officers from the War Office and even the Prime Minister left the impression that they regarded the Western Front as secure and thought no action was likely there in the foreseeable future. A brigade was withdrawn from 5th Division for operations in Norway; the despatch of III Corps to France was delayed and the supply of ammunition virtually ceased. Ironside failed lamentably to keep Gort informed of government decisions, and the Chiefs of Staff even interfered with the Field Force's leave arrangements without consulting Gort.[20]

However, critics such as Dill and Brooke felt that Gort accepted these intolerable slights too equably and did not sufficiently stress the likelihood of a German attack. 'His outlook was essentially that of a regimental officer and a Guardsman at that. He found it repugnant to question an order, express disagreement or complain.' The problem which most urgently affected Gort in April and early May, however, was his precise place in the Allied chain of command. Would Gamelin allow Georges to exercise untrammelled command and would the latter delegate responsibility for the co-ordination of the British and Belgian armies to Billotte? Uncertainties remained until the Germans invaded Belgium in the early hours of 10 May and the allies responded to the plea for assistance by implementing 'Plan D'.[21]

Given Gort's temperament and thirst for action his choice between the roles of a commander-in-chief at headquarters and a field commander actually fighting the battle from forward positions was a foregone conclusion. Taking Pownall and other senior staff officers with him, Gort immediately left GHQ for a Command Post at Wahagnies near Lille. The separation of the Commander-in-Chief from his GHQ for the critical phase of the campaign proved to be an administrative disaster because communications between the shifting Command Post and GHQ broke down almost completely. All reports of German move-ments, for example, were sent to the Operations section remaining at GHQ but it was often impossible to pass the information to the Command Post. Even Gort's faithful lieutenant Pownall complained in his diary on 14 May that his Commander had been away for eight hours that day – 'too long at difficult times' – but he accepted that the Command Post had to be as close to the fighting as possible. On 16 May Gort added to the communications problems by taking the head of his Intelli-gence Staff, Major-General Mason-MacFarlane, and *his* senior staff officer (Gerald Templer) and putting the former in command of 'Mac-force' to protect the right rear of the Field Force. Montgomery later reflected that the distribution of staff duties between GHQ and the Command Post was 'amateur and lacked the professional touch'. The verdict of the Official Historian was equally severe.[22]

On 12 May General Billotte was appointed to co-ordinate the move-ments of the First Group of Armies (including the British and Belgian forces), but in the succeeding critical days he conspicuously failed to do so as the allies first advanced to the Dyle line and then retreated to the Franco-Belgian frontier while the Panzer columns drove westward behind them to the Channel coast. By 17 May Billotte could not commu-nicate directly with Georges, and Gort had no land telephone lines to either the Belgian or French First Army headquarters on either side of him. Gort was obliged to send senior officers to Billotte to discover his plans for the Allied retreat. On 17 May the British liaison officer with French First Army accidentally overheard that, due to indiscipline in the withdrawal, a serious gap had occurred in the French line and there were no reserves to fill it. Gort and Pownall were reluctant to believe reports that the French senior commanders' morale was cracking, but by 18 May the evidence was overwhelming. Gort visited Billotte that day in a vain effort to cheer him up only to discover that his nominal commander had no plan, no reserves and little hope. He could only point to the map, count up to 'huit panzers' and say pathetically, 'Et contre ces panzers je ne peux rien faire'.[23] It was thus not surprising that Gort and Pownall began to lose faith in the French high command and to think about the necessity of saving the Field Force from the impending débâcle.

Such anxieties were strengthened on 19 May when the Panzer advance severed the Field Force's line of communications with its bases in the Biscay ports. Pownall twice telephoned an uncomprehending War Office to warn that a retreat to the Channel ports might be unavoidable. Unfortunately for Gort, Churchill and the War Cabinet were seriously out of touch with fast-moving events and the following day (20 May) Ironside arrived at GHQ bringing orders that Gort was to march south-west towards Amiens to re-establish contact with the main French armies south of the narrow Panzer corridor. The CIGS was quickly persuaded that such a move was impossible. Indeed by now Gort was having to detach further improvised groups (Petreforce, Polforce and others) to try to hold his southern perimeter from Arras along the canal line westward to the coast.[24]

On 21 May Gort ordered a small-scale counter-attack south of Arras to hold up the German advance.[25] French participation in this operation was minimal but for a few hours it made encouraging progress even against SS units and Rommel's 7th Panzer Division. Here was a tantalizing glimpse of what might have been had Gamelin retained a central reserve. Two days later Gort was obliged to withdraw the Arras garrison to prevent it from being cut off, but the French generals, notably Blanchard, interpreted this as an attempt to sabotage the counter-offensive which Gamelin – and now his successor Weygand – were planning to cut the Panzer corridor by a combined drive from north and south. Despite his waning faith in the French high command, Gort was still prepared to make two British divisions (5th and 50th) available for the northern counter-attack, but in view of the increasing pressure on his (and even more the Belgians') eastward-facing front, he felt more and more convinced that the main effort must come from south of the corridor. In view of contemporary and subsequent French criticisms that Gort never seriously contemplated joining in a counter-attack, it is worth noting that Brooke was dismayed at Gort's slowness to recognize the threat to his eastern flank where a Belgian collapse was imminent.[26]

On the evening of 25 May Gort *did* heed Brooke's warning, moved the two available divisions to the threatened sector and, without consulting the French and in defiance of a War Cabinet order, unilaterally cancelled his part in the projected counter-offensive. This was Gort's most critical decision during the campaign – perhaps in his whole career – and it was desperately uncongenial to him, the loyal ally and combative general *par excellence*. Pownall has sympathetically recorded Gort's growing sense of anxiety, exasperation and impotence during the retreat, and his biographer justly notes that, though his physical stamina was unimpaired, 'his ability to exercise cool judgement in large matters was not matched by a capacity to rise above the smaller worries'.[27]

Nevertheless Gort had made the right decision. Blanchard, Billotte's successor as co-ordinator of the First Group of Armies, accepted it the following day, while the War Office gave him permission to withdraw towards the Channel ports. Had the French forces from south of the corridor been advancing, as was repeatedly claimed, Gort would have been charged with ruining the only hope of thwarting a German victory. I see no reason to alter the judgement I made in 1975, namely that:

The Weygand Plan had in fact already been dead for several days before – in French eyes – Gort 'killed' it by his independent decision. Perhaps if any criticism can be levelled at Gort on this score it is that he was doggedly loyal to the ineffectual Blanchard and the French High Command for too long. He might have decided even earlier to make for the Channel ports as Weygand and Reynaud alleged that he had. By delaying this unpleasant decision to the last possible moment he risked the encirclement of the BEF. Thanks to Allied valour in defence – but also to the wrangles and contradictory orders of the German High Command – the great majority of British troops were successfully evacuated.[28]

To the end of the campaign Gort retained his capacity to inject new zest into despairing French generals. One of his liaison officers describes a remarkable interview in which Blanchard talked at length about French plans, after which Gort responded by tapping Cambrai on the map with a pencil and saying slowly and emphatically, 'Oui mon Général, il faut tuer les Boches et il faut les tuer ici.' Later Blanchard was heard to remark to his chief of staff, 'Tiens, il a bien raison, Lord Gort.' Pownall admirably summed up Gort's performance in the campaign on 28 May:

With all his faults and fussinesses, he is a great gentleman and first-class soldier. . . . The most trivial things have always preyed on his mind and now he has a load that he can never shake off all the days of his life. The Commander of the BEF that was driven into the sea in three weeks! So undeserved a fate.[29]

Gort had made up his mind to stay with his troops to face death or capture but Churchill, after consulting Pownall, ordered him to return to England and he did so on 1 June. He never entirely forgave this order, believing that he was being widely criticized for deserting his post for which the Prime Minister was to blame. This suspicion that he was being made a scapegoat was accentuated by an enforced delay in publishing his Despatches. He probably *was* justified in feeling that Dill and Brooke were cool, if not actually hostile, towards him since they left him to fret on the sidelines with the largely honorary appointment of Inspector General of Training.[30]

In April 1941 Gort was made Governor of Gibraltar, usually a terminal appointment for senior officers and one that irked him. Here, at least, his passion for detail could be legitimately indulged, for example in getting the Rock's cavernous defences deepened and the air strip extended. In fact Churchill had not forgotten him or written him off. In November 1941 the Prime Minister toyed with the amazing idea of re-installing him as CIGS in place of the exhausted Dill who was being posted to Washington; and in March 1942 he flirted with the notion – until dissuaded by Brooke – of appointing Gort to succeed Auchinleck in the Middle East Command.[31]

The change when it came (in May 1942, after exactly one year) was less exalted but still important, namely Governor of beleaguered Malta. The island was under relentless air attacks which had pounded the docks to rubble and blocked the harbour with sunken ships. An amphibious attack from nearby Sicily seemed imminent. Yet, with Rommel's final offensive about to begin, it was vital that Malta hold out as the base for attacks on Axis convoys. Shortly after his arrival Gort helped to secure the safe arrival of a consignment of sixty Spitfires; then, by concentrating all available firepower, Gort saved the supply ship *Welshman* by bring down all the Stukas which attacked it. Not least impressive, Gort supervised the distribution of scarce food and water supplies so successfully that at the height of the crisis two hundred thousand people were receiving rations each day. But Gort's outstanding achievement was to impress on the islanders his own indomitable fortitude and cheerfulness in adversity. He became immensely popular. Indeed his entry in the *Dictionary of National Biography* rates the defence of Malta as his outstanding achievement. His reward was a belated promotion to Field-Marshal.[32]

In 1944–45 Gort was briefly High Commissioner and Commander-in-Chief in Palestine. When informed that his predecessor had been fired upon he characteristically remarked that it looked like being fun; but in reality he was terminally ill and had only just begun to gain the respect of both Arabs and Jews, and to reduce terrorist activities, when he was forced to come home. Apart from his daughter's happy marriage to a fellow Grenadier and winner of the VC, William Sidney (later Lord De L'isle and Dudley), Gort's private life had been rather unhappy; his only son had committed suicide in 1941 and at the end of his life he had no home of his own. Just before his death in March 1946 he was awarded an English viscountcy, but this was a doubtful asset since he had no heir and was too ill to take his seat in the House of Lords.[33]

This essay has attempted to bring out Gort's qualities and limitations as a general, but as a portrait of the man it is necessarily incomplete. Several witnesses, for example, attest to his charm and magnetism but these traits are not evident in his photographs and, as little survives in the way of personal papers, have to be taken on trust by those who did not know him. Though he has his supporters, who have praised his performance both as CIGS and C-in-C, this essay inclines to agree with his critics, such as Montgomery and Brooke, that he was promoted above his mental ceiling. Nevertheless he strove to do his best and it is not self-evident that alternative candidates in either post would have done much better. The fairest conclusion may be that had he commanded a division or corps in 1940, he would have done well in command of an Army later in the war. This was the view of a soldier who *did* enjoy this delayed ascent to the highest military command, Field-Marshal Earl Alexander.[34]

Gort's early death and the absence of substantial private papers meant that his reputation – like Dill's – suffered an eclipse during the post-war 'battle of the memoirs' in which his severe critic, Montgomery, was so prominent. But Gort's positive qualities emerged strongly with the publication of the diaries of his staunch admirer, Pownall (*Chief of Staff*, vol. I, 1972), and in the same year he was the subject of Colville's admirable – and on the whole admiring – biography (*Man of Valour*). This essay opened with Spears' rebuke of a French Prime Minister for presuming to query Gort's outstanding virtues of courage and loyalty, so it may fittingly conclude with his acceptance of Weygand's apology on the same score. 'We have a saying in England,' Spears told the General, '"a good man to go tiger shooting with" and Lord Gort is *par excellence* such a one.'[35]

NOTES

1 Sir Edward Spears, *Assignment to Catastrophe* (one-volume edition 1956), pp. 168, 322. (Henceforth referred to as 'Spears'.)

2 Cyril Falls' entry in *D.N.B. Supplement 1941–1950*.

3 J. R. Colville, *Man of Valour: Field-Marshal Lord Gort VC* (1972), pp. 45–69 (henceforth referred to as 'Gort').

4 Gort, p. 77. C. N. Barclay, *On Their Shoulders: British Generalship in the Lean Years 1939–1942* (1964), p. 36 (henceforth referred to as 'Barclay').

5 Sir John Kennedy, *The Business of War* (1957), p. 5.

6 See R. J. Minney, *The Private Papers of Hore-Belisha* (1960) and Brian

Bond, 'Leslie Hore-Belisha at the War Office, 1937–1940', in J. Gooch and I. F. W. Beckett (eds), *Politicians and Defence* (1981).

7 Gort, pp. 88–92, 120–1.

8 Brian Bond (ed.), *Chief of Staff: The Diaries of Lieutenant-General Sir Henry Pownall*, vol. I (1972), pp. 203, 210–11 (henceforth referred to as 'Pownall'). Gort, pp. 136–8. Kennedy, pp. 13–14.

9 Spears, pp. 43–4, 56. Barclay, p. 37. Brian Bond, *France and Belgium 1939–1940* (1975), pp. 38–40.

10 Spears, pp. 43–4, 56.

11 John C. Cairns, 'Great Britain and the Fall of France', *Journal of Modern History*, 1955, pp. 365–409.

12 Gort, p. 149. Viscount Montgomery, *Memoirs* (1958), p. 52.

13 Montgomery, pp. 52–6. Gort, p. 156.

14 Kennedy, p. 36. Gort, p. 156. Sir A. Bryant, *The Turn of the Tide* (1957), pp. 75–80 (henceforth referred to as 'Brooke').

15 Bond, *France and Belgium*, pp. 53–5. Spears, p. 60. Gort, pp. 153–4.

16 Kennedy, pp. 36–7.

17 Pownall, pp. 259ff and especially pp. 262–5.

18 Gort, p. 166. Pownall, p. 279. A. J. Trythall, 'The Downfall of Leslie Hore-Belisha', *Journal of Contemporary History*, 1981, pp. 391–411.

19 Trythall, pp. 405–8. Kennedy, p. 43.

20 Brooke, pp. 75–80. Gort, pp. 172–3.

21 Bond, *France and Belgium*, pp. 103–4. Barclay, pp. 41–2. Montgomery, pp. 52–4.

22 Gort, pp. 190–1. Pownall, pp. 315–16. Montgomery, pp. 57–8. Brooke, p. 94n.

23 Miles Reid, *Last on the List* (1974), pp. 31–2. Bond, *France and Belgium*, pp. 110–11.

24 Gort, pp. 199, 206–7. Barclay, p. 46. Pownall, pp. 323–4.

25 Brian Bond, 'Arras, 21st May 1940' in C. Barnett and others, *Old Battles and New Defences* (1986).

26 Brooke, pp. 122–3.

27 Gort, pp. 214–15.

28 Bond, *France and Belgium*, pp. 136–7.

29 Reid, pp. 43–4. Pownall, p. 352.

30 Reid, p. 58. Pownall, pp. 357–8. Gort, pp. 224, 233, 235–7. Kennedy, pp. 64–5.

31 Brooke, p. 339. Martin Gilbert, *Winston S. Churchill: Finest Hour* (1983), p. 1234.

32 Gort, pp. 247–54.

33 Gort, pp. 261, 267.

34 Gort, pp. 244–5.

35 Spears, p. 188.

CHRONOLOGY: JOHN GORT

1886, July 10	John Standish Surtees Prendergast Vereker born in London
1899–1904	Harrow School (succeeds as 6th Viscount Gort in Peerage of Ireland, 1902)
1904–5	Royal Military College, Sandhurst; commissioned Grenadier Guards
1911	Marries his second cousin, Corinna Vereker (divorced 1925; two s, one d)
1914, August 5	Promoted Captain; to France as ADC to C-in-C I Corps, Douglas Haig
1914–18	Serves continuously in France and Belgium (despatches eight times, MC, DSO and two bars, VC)
1915	GSO3, I Corps
1916	Promoted brevet Major
1917, April	To command, 4th Battalion Grenadier Guards
1918, March	Commands 1st Battalion Grenadier Guards
1918, September 27	Wins Victoria Cross while in temporary command of 3 Guards Brigade at storming of Hindenburg Line
1919–20	Staff College, Camberley
1921	Brevet Lieutenant-Colonel
1921–3	Directing Staff, Staff College
1925	Colonel
1926	Chief Instructor, Senior Officers' School, Sheerness
1927, January–August	GSO1, Shanghai Defence Force
1927–30	GSO1, 4th Division
1930–32	Commands 4 Guards Brigade
1932–6	Director of Military Training, India; Major-General, 1935
1936–7	Commandant, Staff College, Camberley
1937, September–December	Military Secretary
1937, December 3–1939, September 3	Chief of the Imperial General Staff; General; KCB, 1938
1939, September 3–1940, May 31	Commander-in-Chief, BEF
1940–1	Inspector-General of the Forces; GCB, 1940
1941, May 7–1942, May 7	Governor of Gibraltar
1942, May–1944, July	Governor of Malta; Field-Marshal, 1 January 1943

1944, October– 　1945, November	High Commissioner and Commander-in-Chief, Palestine; 1945, Viscount Gort in peerage of the United Kingdom
1946, March 31	Dies in London

3
DILL

Field-Marshal Sir John Dill

ALEX DANCHEV

Field-Marshal Sir John Dill enjoys an unusual distinction. He had a longer, closer and more influential association with Churchill in the central direction of the Second World War than any other general save Brooke (and perhaps, in a different capacity, Ismay). It was throughout, however, an association strikingly lacking in empathy or understanding, etched in fundamental disagreement, and scarred by a mutual disaffection welling up at times into personal distaste.

Dill was appointed Chief of the Imperial General Staff (CIGS) by Churchill himself in the calamitous days of May 1940, on the very eve of the evacuations from Dunkirk, when Churchill had been Prime Minister for barely a fortnight and was by no means politically secure. He needed, and fleetingly esteemed, Dill's 'abilities and strategic knowledge'. This first, critical, period of their association coincided exactly with Britain's darkest and loneliest hour, when Hitler's armies romped through Europe with impunity, excising allies actual and potential, fatally rupturing the Anglo-French alliance, threatening cross-Channel invasion, slicing deep into the Soviet Union – and all before the Americans had declared their hand.

Catapulted into the daily circus surrounding the Prime Minister, Dill's relationship with Churchill, intimate yet uncomprehending, interdependent yet adversarial, necessary yet unsatisfactory, was both rich in paradox and deeply flawed. These proved to be enduring themes. The tone of the relationship and the terms in which it has been remembered were set by Churchill after only a few weeks. As early as July 1940 he sent to Anthony Eden, then Secretary of State for War, an astonishing personal and professional indictment of his chosen CIGS. 'I do not think that we are having the help from General Dill which we hoped for at the time of his appointment ... he strikes me as being very tired, disheartened and over-impressed with the might of Germany.' This already incorporated one of Churchill's most characteristic and frequently repeated criticisms: of a caution, a pessimism, amounting almost to defeatism. He once stigmatized Dill, to his face in Cabinet, as 'the dead hand of inanition'. His memoirs abound with oblique but insistent denigration of Dill's 'pessimism'. There is none of the personal warmth of the references to one of Dill's colleagues on the Chiefs of Staff (COS) Committee, his 'true comrade' Admiral Sir Dudley Pound. Unlike another of the COS, Air Chief Marshal Sir Charles Portal, Dill would never have been a candidate for the Other Club, that tell-tale mark of Churchillian favour. Like Clement Attlee, Dill may have been 'an admirable character', though even that appears to have been called into question, but he was not 'a man with whom it is agreeable to dine' – the exclusive criterion for Other Club membership.

At bottom, Dill was uncongenial to Churchill, who nicknamed him 'Dilly-Dally'. This may have chimed with the Prime Minister's scathing opinion of the War Office as 'hidebound, devoid of imagination, extravagant of manpower and slow', but it also encapsulated a personal judgement about Dill himself. For Churchill the personal and the professional were inextricably linked. Dill's eventual expulsion from the troglodytic inner sanctum of the Cabinet War Rooms was therefore inevitable. With good reason Churchill took some time to act, but by September 1941 one of his private secretaries noted: 'He has now got his knife right into Dill and frequently disparages him.' In November Dill's 'retirement' as CIGS was announced for 25 December 1941, his sixtieth birthday. Churchill intended for him to become Governor of Bombay, 'a position of great honour', luxurious, remote and inconsequential.

Excommunication in Bombay, 'followed by a bodyguard with lances' (Churchill's bizarre promise), was not to be Dill's fate. No sooner had he in practice ceased to be CIGS (1 December) than the Americans entered the war after Pearl Harbor (7 December) and Churchill felt compelled to take Dill with him on his post-haste embarkation to confer with President Roosevelt in Washington (12 December). Dill's much trumpeted sixtieth birthday was celebrated not in retirement in England, nor in Bombay, but at a party given in his honour by the US Army Chief of Staff in Washington. When the British contingent returned home in January Dill remained, in an unprecedented if indeterminate position of enormous potential influence. Churchill's transparent purpose had been frustrated. Dill was indeed removed from London, only to be ensconced in the emerging centre of Allied decision-making. He became Head of the British Joint Staff Mission in Washington and senior British member of the Combined Chiefs of Staff committee, the Anglo-American military body which directed the grand strategy of the war. But the finest irony was also common knowledge in the US capital. Dill's 'secret' role in Washington was as personal representative of the Minister of Defence, and that office was filled by none other than Winston Churchill.

John Greer Dill, for so many the epitome of the perfect English gentleman, was born in 1881 in Lurgan, County Armagh, Ulster, 'where in those days the Pope was not very well spoken of', as he recalled much later for the Pennsylvania Scotch-Irish Society. 'In my youth I have seen Orangemen on side-cars driving down what they called Papish streets spoiling for a fight, and getting it. . . .' Dill's was a lonely youth, uncomfortably foreshadowing later developments. His father, manager of the local branch of the Ulster Bank and descendant of a long and worthy line of scholars and ministers, died early in 1894, when Dill was just twelve; his mother, the daughter of a prominent Lurgan JP, followed him a few months later. Dill and his elder sister Nina (who was also to die prematurely, in 1921) were taken on by an aunt and uncle, the Reverend Dr Joseph Grundy Burton, an energetic campaigner against Home Rule, something of a raconteur, and a diligent parish clergyman. Dill was swiftly despatched to Cheltenham College (1895–1900), where again he made few friends and rose laboriously from the bottom form to Upper V Military, 'more by the effluxion of time in each form than by reaching the top of it', according to a contemporary. He passed into Sandhurst 154th out of 210, greatly relieved that he had so much to spare. At the Royal Military College his conduct was 'exemplary', his marks uniformly mediocre.

On leaving Sandhurst, Dill was commissioned into the 1st Battalion (100th of Foot), The Prince of Wales's Leinster Regiment (1901) – a southern Irish regiment, there being no other vacancies at the time of the Boer War. 'It was a serious thing for a Black Northerner like me to be thrown among a lot of gossoons [boys] from Kings County, but we mixed, we got to love each other.' He soon sailed for South Africa, where he appears to have enjoyed himself. He read Dickens and Thackeray and was periodically concerned to acquire what he euphemistically called 'curios', or more straightforwardly 'loot', but was disappointed to find nothing better than a bed, a jug, a basin and similar items of furniture – 'hardly worth bringing home though it makes one very comfortable out here'.

Boer War service was followed by his only period of regimental duty, as Assistant Adjutant and then Adjutant of the 1st Leinsters (1902–9). It was during this period that he married Ada Maud, daughter of Colonel William Albert le Mottée (late 18th of Foot), in Fermoy, County Cork, the bride's home town. The marriage was precipitate and unsuitable. Maud was a woman of nervous disposition, painfully shy, given to headaches, depression and excessive self-medication. She died, after a long series of paralytic strokes, on 23 December 1940, two days before Dill's fifty-ninth birthday, when he was CIGS. As to how deeply he was affected, testimony is conflicting. Brooke, his protégé, friend and successor, has left a harrowing vignette of Maud's paralysis in 1940: 'Every visit home to his wife in Windsor was a desperate ordeal; she could not make herself understood, he kept guessing at what she could mean, usually unsuccessfully, and finally with a disappointed look in her eyes she used to throw her head back on the pillow.' Yet Dill's immediate reaction to Maud's death betrays a certain stoicism, even relief, and he quickly recovered his equilibrium. As a widower, there was none of Brooke's own unspeakable anguish, nor the driven quality of Montgomery's subsequent regimen.

Then, in spite of the prurient interest, there was a second marriage in October 1941 to a much younger woman: Nancy Furlong (née Charrington), widow of a member of Dill's staff at Aldershot in the late thirties and daughter of a brewery magnate. Even the wedding provoked an argument with Churchill. Dill asked for a week's leave; the Prime Minister preferred one day; they compromised on three. This time Dill made a very happy marriage, in more than one sense. 'I don't think that Nancy dislikes Washington and Washington certainly likes her', he wrote with feeling in September 1942. 'She makes a great difference to my life and keeps me young.'

Meanwhile, a sea-change had taken place in Dill's professional and intellectual development. In 1913 he became a student at the Staff College, Camberley, under Sir William Robertson. This was perhaps the determining experience of his life. It was the impress and ambience of the Staff College, coupled with the immediate praxis of the First World War, which really launched Dill's career. A captain in 1914, he ended the war a temporary brigadier, and on the evidence of the official historian 'the real Operations brain in [Haig's] GHQ' – a time he relived when a British Expeditionary Force once again found the need to establish a GHQ on the Continent.

On the outbreak of war in 1939 Dill, then GOC-in-C Home Command at Aldershot, was given I Corps of the BEF. This was something of a disappointment, the second in two years. In late 1937 he had been interviewed by the reforming Secretary of State for War, Hore-Belisha, for the post of CIGS. There can be little disputing Basil Liddell Hart's post-war assessment that 'on his record, and strategic grasp, he was the outstanding candidate'. Hore-Belisha nevertheless appointed the eminently unsuitable Gort, with whom he was soon scarcely on speaking terms. Dill went instead to Aldershot. For some time it was understood, not least by Dill himself, that he would command any future BEF. In the event Hore-Belisha again preferred Gort, and appointed the equally unsuitable Ironside as CIGS. Dill was phlegmatic. 'I have no real complaint', he wrote. 'I have lived long enough to know that these things have a way of righting themselves if one leaves them alone.' His exposure to Hore-Belisha, however, may well have coloured his first reactions to Churchill. The politician's propensity to meddle, seen by Dill as the fount of the Army's difficulties with Hore-Belisha, took on an altogether new significance with the renaissance of the arch meddler of the Dardanelles.

In a matter of months things did right themselves. In April 1940 Dill was summoned to London. By common consent it was this belated recall to the War Office, initially in the guise of Vice-CIGS, that infused a disorientated department with purpose and authority. Dill wrote to Gort of his first impressions:

The War Office is, as far as I can see, in complete chaos and the situation in Norway as bad as I expected ... I'm not sure that Winston isn't the greatest menace. No-one seems able to control him. He is full of ideas, many brilliant, but most of them impracticable. He has such drive and personality that no-one seems able to stand up to him ... Our Secretary of State [the short-lived Oliver Stanley] is quite charming and has really good judgement but has never been given a chance ...

He had immediately identified the salient issue. 'Standing up to Churchill' would determine not only Dill's war-time effectiveness but also to a considerable extent his post-war reputation.

Dill is held to have been an ineffective CIGS because he allowed himself to be 'worn down' and possibly 'worn out' by Churchill; because he failed to deliver what the faithful Ismay called 'the one thing that was necessary, and indeed that Winston preferred – someone to stand up to him'. These charges have taken deep root. The imputation of congenital failure to stand up to Churchill has blighted Dill's career and obscured his achievement. It is very largely the imputation of Churchill's inner circle, perpetuated in a great outpouring of post-war reminiscence. But it was the Prime Minister himself who framed its terms and propagated the charge in his own war memoirs. To paraphrase Balfour's celebrated remark about Churchill's earlier memoirs, Winston wrote an enormous book about himself and called it *The Second World War*. The seminal quality of this magnificently egocentric enterprise is well established. Its distortions and suppressions are only now being revealed. Not the least of these relate to 'Dilly-Dally'.

In reality Dill did stand up to Churchill, but not in the most effective fashion. The most obvious problem was Churchill's peculiarly personalized forensic approach to any operation which engaged his attention, together with the 'Parliamentary manners' so alienating to some generals. As John Connell has explained, 'Churchill had matured in an atmosphere in which it is taken for granted that one Member may ... abuse another with unrelenting ferocity on the floor of the House and then – his speech ended – walk out arm in arm with his opponent to a drink in the smoking room or bar.' Dill experienced classic difficulties of adaptation. One night in December 1940 he returned to the War Office around midnight after a long meeting (a regular occurrence) and sought out his sympathetic Director of Military Operations.

I saw that he was agitated. He said: 'I cannot tell you how angry the Prime Minister has made me. What he said about the Army tonight I can never forgive. He complained he could get nothing done ... he wished he had [the Greek General] Papagos to run it. He asked me to wait and have a drink with him after the meeting, but I refused and left Anthony [Eden] there by himself.'

This characteristic episode also serves to highlight a less obvious but no less intractable problem. It was Dill's misfortune to join the Chiefs of Staff committee at a time when acquiescent colleagues, impossibly scarce resources and an impetuous Prime Minister combined to make the cautionary advice of the CIGS at once desperately necessary and singularly unpalatable. Cautionary advice was anathema to Churchill. Hence his public taunt of 'inanition' – an exquisite example of Parliamentary manners.

Perhaps the most fundamental issue on which Dill stood up to Churchill was that of strategic priorities. One damaging exchange was triggered by Dill's 'grave pronouncement' on 'The Relation of the Middle East to the Security of the United Kingdom' (6 May 1941). Dill's note, which ran to some 1,000 words, was itself prompted by Churchill's recent admonitions on the signal importance of Egypt to the British war effort. Dill argued that 'the loss of Egypt would be a calamity which I do not regard as likely and one which we should not accept without a most desperate fight; but it would not end the war.'

A successful invasion alone spells our final defeat. It is the United Kingdom ... and not Egypt that is vital, and the defence of the United Kingdom must take first place. Egypt is not even second in order of priority, for it has been an accepted principle in our strategy that in the last resort the security of Singapore comes before that of Egypt. ...

Ismay thought the Prime Minister 'shaken to the core'. On his own testimony Churchill was 'astonished' to receive this note. He replied a week later 'somewhat controversially', not to say contemptuously,

I gather you would be prepared to face the loss of Egypt and the Nile Valley, together with the surrender or ruin of the Army of half a million we have concentrated there, rather than lose Singapore. I do not take that view, nor do I think the alternative is likely to present itself. ...

This was the nub of the strategic differences between them. In early 1942, soon after arriving in Washington, Dill wrote to Wavell: 'It is odd that Winston should want me to represent him here when he clearly was glad to get me out of the CIGS job. We disagreed too often ... among other things, on what we should do for the Far East.' And again, to Brooke: 'How I wish that I had had some support from our S of S [Secretary of State: Margesson] during the last year of my time as CIGS. It might have helped Britain too – Singapore would have been reinforced and raids would have started months and months ago.'

In one of the many suppressions in his memoirs, Churchill's version ran: 'Sir John Dill must have been himself conscious of the consensus of opinion against him on this aspect, and having sounded his note of warning he let the matter drop.' He was wrong on both counts, for two days later, on 15 May, Dill dispatched a lengthy riposte in which he attempted to elucidate his earlier arguments. With regard to strategic priorities, Dill adduced one of Churchill's own memoranda, not a technique best calculated to please the Prime Minister. His immediate concern, however, was that further reinforcement of the Middle East, ardently sponsored by Churchill, would endanger the safety of the United Kingdom. It was in this context that Dill responded to Churchill's taunts: 'I am sure that you, better than anyone else, must realize how difficult it is for a soldier to advise against a bold and offensive plan. ... It takes a lot of moral courage not to be afraid of being thought afraid.' On this occasion Dill was prepared to resign if overruled; and to appeal to the War Cabinet if that were refused. The Prime Minister was induced to retract.

Disputation was Churchill's essential method of work. Dill recognized this well enough and tried to protect commanders everywhere from the consequences of a minatory summons to act or, often more disturbing, to explain. Notoriously, the most unfathomable case was Wavell, as C-in-C in the cauldron of the Middle East. '*Talk* to him, Archie', urged Dill, in vain. 'They are poles apart', he wrote. 'Wavell is very reserved – "withdrawn" is perhaps a better word – whereas Winston even thinks aloud.' One of Wavell's staff officers remembered the reaction after his first, wounding, appearance before the Cabinet in August 1940. 'My Chief said that the PM had asked him down to Chequers for the weekend but he would be damned if he would risk further treatment of the kind to which he had just been subjected.' It was left to Dill to mediate. 'Archie, no one would deny that you have had unbearable provocation. But he is our Prime Minister. He carries an almost incredible burden. It is true you can be replaced. He cannot. You must go to Chequers.'

At the same time Dill defended the Army as a whole and Wavell in particular from 'unjust' and 'damaging' criticism. He and Eden even threatened simultaneous resignation in support of Wavell. Churchill remained unconvinced but was loath to make any change. Dill repeatedly urged the Prime Minister to 'back him or sack him'. Eventually, finding he had 'a tired fish on this rod and a lively one on the other', Churchill exchanged the 'tired' Wavell for the 'lively' Auchinleck in June 1941. Dill's advice to Auchinleck on taking over his command was embodied in a letter of magisterial breadth and surprising candour:

From Whitehall, great pressure was applied to Wavell to induce him to act rapidly. . . . The fact is that the Commander in the field will always be subject to great and often undue pressure from his Government. Wellington suffered from it: Haig suffered from it: Wavell suffered from it. Nothing will stop it. In fact, pressure from those who alone see the picture as a whole and carry the main responsibility may be necessary. It was, I think, right to press Wavell against his will to send a force to Baghdad, but in other directions he was, I feel, over-pressed.

You may be quite sure that I will back your military opinion in local problems, but here the pressure often comes from very broad political considerations; these are sometimes so powerful as to make it necessary to take risks which, from the purely military point of view, may be seen as inadvisable. The main point is that *you* should make it quite clear what risks are involved if a course of action is forced upon you which, from the military point of view, is undesirable. You may even find it necessary, in the extreme case, to dissociate yourself from the consequences.

Only in his own case did Dill deny to Churchill the disputation he craved. He did make unremitting efforts to convince by written exposition, addressing to the Prime Minister a stream of closely argued minutes and explanatory notes. Too often, these efforts left Churchill unmoved. They were poorly calculated to achieve their purpose, not only because Churchill, 'averse to the exegetical', so rarely found a written case convincing, but also because Dill's style entirely left out of account the necessity to engage or enthrall. As Wavell put it, 'Winston is always expecting rabbits to come out of empty hats.' It was not for want of comprehension on Dill's part; he understood Churchill's requirements as well as anyone. 'Finest hours' were beyond the Army's means in 1940–41. Nor was it sheer incapacity. Dill was by no means inarticulate, as Wavell could be impenetrably inarticulate. Rather, it was a matter of temperament. For Dill, disputing with Churchill would have been an unwarrantable act of propitiation. He refused to pander to the Prime Minister. He could contest Churchill and advise others, but in more than one sense he could not help himself.

Dill's achievement as Churchill's CIGS from May 1940 to December 1941 was nevertheless considerable. It was above all Dill who responded to the imperative of the moment and established the wearying but constructive adversarial relationship between Churchill and the Chiefs of Staff on which Brooke, blessed with new allies and augmented resources, so successfully built in 1942 for the duration of the war. In mid-1940 no one knew, and many doubted, whether such a relationship could be made to work. The combination was unprecedented and unpropitious. The need and pain of definition in 1940–41 are often forgotten. Dill's tenure is elided with Brooke's. Churchillian history recognizes the problem, but credits Ismay alone with its solution. Yet the essential forerunner of the matchless combination of Churchill and Brooke was the ill-matched combination of Churchill and Dill. The prerequisite for Brooke's acceptability and longevity as CIGS was Dill's purgatory. Dill accustomed Churchill to the trammelling of professional advice. 'I live a very hectic life', he wrote. 'Most of it is spent trying to prevent stupid things being done rather than in doing clever things! However that is rather the normal life of a Chief of Staff.'

Dill's primary importance as CIGS therefore lay in the realm of contemporary attitudes and expectations. It was Dill who conditioned expectations of the COS under Churchill. In 1942 these expectations crossed the Atlantic to permeate another unprecedented combination, still less propitious for being international: the Combined Chiefs of Staff (CCS) under both Churchill and Roosevelt. Here, too, Dill's very presence was crucial to the establishment and successful operation of a genuine Anglo-American alliance. Building on his experience of Churchill and the COS, Dill found himself in a position to mediate between London and Washington. His greatest service to the alliance was to contain its enormous fissile potential.

Dill's position in Washington was the subject of protracted Anglo-American argument, resolved only in February 1942 with the President's artful suggestion to the Prime Minister of a personal compact. The crux of the matter was Dill's status. 'I have no objection to his representing the Joint Staffs [British COS] in London', wrote Roosevelt, 'but I particularly hope that I can regard him as the representative of you in your capacity as Minister of Defence. Perhaps this latter status could be understood between you and me.' This intriguing suggestion quickly elicited from Churchill an official directive for Dill. Part A was 'to be announced':

1. You are appointed Head of the British Joint Staff Mission in Washington.
2. You will receive from the Chiefs of Staff committee in London their views and instructions on war policy.
3. Assisted by the members of the JSM you will represent these views at the meetings of the Combined Chiefs of Staff....
4. The Heads of the JSM will retain their responsibilities for representing the individual views of the 1st Sea Lord, CIGS, and CAS to their American opposite numbers in so far as these do not conflict with your

instructions. . . .

5. You will sit when and if you choose on the [new Combined] Munitions Assignment Board and be responsible for representing our needs and policy.

Part B was for Dill's 'personal information and guidance', but was by then very much an open secret:

You will in your contacts with the President of the US, with Mr Hopkins and others represent me in my capacity as Minister of Defence. You will from time to time receive from me such guidance as may be necessary to enable you to represent my views; and you are authorized to correspond direct with me as you think fit. . . .

This directive conceded to Dill a measure of the independent authority for which he had been arguing. First, since the CCS met in Washington the British Chiefs of Staff could not be present in person. Each was therefore represented by the head of his Service Delegation at the Joint Staff Mission. Point four of Dill's directive provided for this to continue. Dill himself retained a special link with Brooke as CIGS, but as the Head of the JSM as a whole he represented not a single Service but the collective COS. As senior British member of the Combined Chiefs of Staff he acted as principal spokesman for the British side. Although he no longer formally sat with the COS he, not they, dealt directly with the Americans from day to day and at the regular weekly CCS sessions. When the Chiefs of Staff of both sides did meet in person, at the great allied Conferences, Dill continued to sit with them. Secondly, representation of the Minister of Defence, already known to the US Joint Chiefs of Staff, enhanced his status and utility within the CCS forum and with the Americans individually, at the same time opening alternative channels of influence. For example Dill could deal directly with Admiral Leahy as Chief of Staff to the US Commander-in-Chief, that is, the President. This he did only rarely. Of greater consequence was Harry Hopkins, Roosevelt's frail Sancho Panza and already a firm friend.

Hopkins cut an unlikely figure. 'I seem to turn out a mixture of a Baptist preacher and a race-track tout', he remarked approvingly of a brilliant *New Yorker* profile. Churchill styled him 'Lord Root of the Matter', correctly identifying his greatest gift. His functions were ill-defined; but when access to the President at once conferred and signalled power, Hopkins lived and worked at the White House and acted as Roosevelt's familiar, at least until 1944, when his influence appears to have waned. He and Dill could be of use to each other. In certain respects they fulfilled analogous functions. Each habitually acted as a 'buffer' between Churchill and Roosevelt. Hopkins monitored Churchill at the White House; Dill contributed to Roosevelt's telegrams. Occasionally they concerted their efforts. Each confided in the other with calculated indiscretion, disseminating the confidences judiciously on either side. It may well be that Dill did better out of this than Hopkins, who received frequent and unsolicited communications from Churchill himself. As a result Dill often found himself better informed than the US Joint Chiefs of Staff. In one instance, almost a month after an important letter had been sent by the President to the Prime Minister, the secretary of the Joint Chiefs circulated a copy to the committee with the following admonition:

I have received it very confidentially from the British Staff Mission and am sending it to you for your personal information. ... Sir John Dill has suggested to Mr Hopkins that copies ... should be sent to the US Chiefs of Staff from the White House. *Until that occurs we do not officially have the letter.*

Dill was not slow to perceive the irony in this – nor to exploit the opportunity it gave, especially in his relationship with Marshall.

If there was considerable scope in Dill's position in Washington, there was also a frustrating hollowness at its centre. 'It is not much fun', he reflected privately, 'to be acting as go-between after having recently been one of the principals.' As he remarked to his son, 'I can make suggestions but I can decide nothing. I have plenty of influence but no power.' Dill's power-base purported to be the JSM. A nucleus British Military Mission in Washington had been established after the secret American–British (ABC) Conversations of January–March 1941. It amounted to only a handful of officers. In June 1941 they were reinforced by several dozen 'Military Advisors to the British Supply Council in the US'. The Mission became a 'joint' one in embryo, with a Delegation from each Service. By the end of 1942 the 'Washington Whitehall' of British representatives had mushroomed to over 9,000, of which the JSM constituted almost one third: some 800 in the British Admiralty Delegation; 1,200 in the British Army Staff; 650 in the RAF Delegation; and 100 central staff. The JSM was by far the largest single mission in Washington – Army numbers alone exceeded all save the Supply Mission (1,800) – and quite eclipsed the 1,000 personnel directly tied to the British Embassy.

The members of the JSM were representatives in the Burkean sense of the word. In his famous speech to the electors of Bristol in 1774

Edmund Burke drew a distinction between a delegate, who merely mirrors and records the views of his constituents, and a representative, who exercises judgement according to his own conscience. The JSM represented its 'constituents' in London in this sense. Dill's premiss, as representative of both COS and Churchill, was Burkean.

To be sure, both COS and Churchill were apt to challenge such an interpretation. Churchill made an uneasy constituent. Apart from his reservations about Dill, he always preferred to negotiate personally with the principals, ideally face-to-face. To Marshall, unheralded, came the characteristic exhortations so familiar to Dill as CIGS. 'I think your idea splendid and real war ... I am sure you should come over here at the earliest.' Understandably concerned to forestall any American exploitation of domestic differences between himself and the COS, Churchill developed a morbid fear of the Chiefs of Staff of both nations 'framing up' against him. In his personal Anglo-American relations, reticence and recalcitrance vied with the more familiar ardour and impatience. Dill endeavoured to dispel the former and manage the latter. He did wrest for himself some discretion; but it was contingent on his perceived influence in Washington, above all on the knowledge of his relationship with the man Churchill dubbed 'the senior American officer', the US Army Chief of Staff and *primus inter pares* on the Joint Chiefs of Staff committee, General George C. Marshall.

Dill and Marshall discovered an empathy unparalleled in Anglo-American military relations. It was Marshall, the noblest Roman of them all, who quickly came to embody a 'possible' America for Dill; and Dill, 'the finest soldier and greatest gentleman I have ever known', who embodied a 'possible' Britain for Marshall.

They first met at the Atlantic Conference off Argentia, Newfoundland, in August 1941. There is some evidence to suggest that Dill, like Brooke, found Marshall wanting strategically. There can be no doubt of a mutual and immediate personal attraction; but a clear-eyed awareness of their respective national interests may well have predominated at this stage. There was an obvious need for Dill to court Marshall just as Churchill courted Roosevelt. Marshall was sensitive and broadly sympathetic to Dill's predicament as CIGS; like Roosevelt, he may have felt impelled to offer at least verbal encouragement. Marshall was also acutely aware of manifold US deficiencies, in planning, in organization, in interService co-operation. It cannot have escaped his attention that Dill was uniquely equipped to furnish him advice and information privately, in anticipation of getting further 'mixed up together'. This was to be a continuing theme. For Dill to rely on Marshall was predictable and inescapable, given Britain's progressive impoverishment. For Marshall to rely on Dill was unanticipated and unintended, but no less real. Throughout their Washington association there was a palpable sense of collusion. 'I have so many battles to fight', Marshall dared to joke with Dill, 'I am never quite sure whether I am fighting you, or the President or the Navy!' It was this embattled Marshall who felt he needed Dill, just as Dill needed him.

The day after Dill's return from the Atlantic Conference he wrote in most unusual terms to Marshall. 'I sincerely hope that we shall meet again before long. In the meantime we must keep each other in touch in the frank manner upon which we agreed.' A few days later Marshall responded in the same sense. This exchange inaugurated a regular correspondence, in itself an important channel of the flourishing but still illicit common-law alliance.

They met again, in dramatically changed circumstances, in December 1941 in Washington. Any reservations Dill may have had quickly disappeared. 'Marshall improves greatly on further acquaintance', he advised Brooke. 'His difficulties are immense, but he is straight, clear-headed and undoubtedly dominates the conferences on the American side.' So began almost three years of sustained intimacy – the pivotal period of the world war – in which scarcely a day passed without some form of communication between them. In March 1942 they began lunching together regularly each week, accompanied on occasion only by their wives. Strict confidentiality prevailed. Lunch immediately preceded Combined Chiefs of Staff meetings. Its primary purpose was not social but diplomatic: if possible to settle or diffuse, informally, any intractable or explosive items on the weekly agenda. In this Dill and Marshall enjoyed a quite astonishing degree of success. Lord Halifax, the British Ambassador, rightly noted that CCS meetings tended to be 'formal in character, most of the business being settled off the record beforehand'. The lunches exemplified Dill's methods – private candour as a means to public conciliation; openness to compromise as a prophylactic against a strong ally becoming an overweening one; 'do as you would be done by' (a suggestion to Churchill) as a precept for the combination to work.

Dill was not given to underestimating the difficulties. 'Standing where I do, I sometimes see tendencies on both sides to turn a blind eye to the other's hopes, fears and ambitions.' The educative task he set himself was better Anglo-American understanding within the CCS organization, a task to which Marshall made a vital and reciprocal contribution. The clearest demonstration of their approach was the quantum jump in information available to each side. Dill showed Marshall virtually all the COS telegrams he received, including those 'for his own information'; British staff studies of operations and intelligence; many of the JSM and his personal telegrams sent to London; and sundry private correspondence with, for example, Brooke and Wavell. Churchill's 'hot ones' were immediately discussed together or in Dill's absence simply taken to Marshall's office by the senior secretary of the JSM, rather as if the US Chief of Staff were on the British distribution list. Occasionally Dill even fed him with Presidential communications which Marshall had not yet seen. In this unorthodox manner Marshall was, in his own words, 'kept *au courant* with what was going on'; a British view was regularly inserted into the American policy-making process; unpleasant surprises were avoided, controversies muffled or forestalled.

In return Marshall showed Dill much of his correspondence with the other members of the Joint Chiefs, with the President and Hopkins, and with commanders overseas, notably Eisenhower in Europe and Stilwell in China. Dill was Marshall's sounding-board. Through Marshall, he gained unique access to internal American deliberations. As early as April 1942, the US Secretary for War noted, after inviting them both to dinner: 'Dill and Marshall have become great friends and so ... we could sit and talk over all kinds of things that the representatives of different countries are not apt to talk about so freely.' Through Brooke, Dill gained similar access to British deliberations. Both Brooke and Marshall reposed complete confidence in Dill. Neither had the same confidence in the other. Moreover both were profoundly wary of their political leaders. The nemesis of 'wild ideas', be they prime ministerial or presidential, haunted the military staff on each side. These were the highly personal parameters that gave Dill the scope and the opportunity to function as he did.

Dill is perhaps best seen as an amateur ambassador, complementing and to some extent supplanting Lord Halifax. His unarguable success in this role is the more striking for the absence of what has always been considered essential for a British ambassador in Washington – the confidence of the Prime Minister. So far from enjoying that confidence, Dill was 'retired' as CIGS precisely because he had forfeited it. One of the festering differences between them was removed with the fall of Singapore in February 1942, after which Dill became if anything more ardent for the Middle East than Churchill himself. Brooke naturally took over as Churchill's most intimate adversary in daily (or nightly) strategic debate, and as mediator between the Prime Minister and commanders everywhere. But new issues arose, and tension between Churchill and his ambassador persisted.

The change wrought by Dill's removal to Washington was that the tension became creative. To official America, Dill quickly came to be seen as a guarantor: a guarantor of the British, against their notorious and incorrigible duplicities; a guarantor of Brooke, against his overbearing advocacy; and a guarantor of Churchill himself, against the 'fatal lullaby' of his imperial pretensions and eccentric strategies. A fresh gloss was put on a well-worn role. The essence of Dill's ambassadorial work was attempting to prevent London doing 'stupid things' whilst simultaneously attempting to persuade Washington that they were, in fact, 'clever things'. Of especial concern, would the itch to do *something* prove too strong for Churchill, particularly when he achieved his insistent purpose of caballing with Roosevelt? 'The PM left last night', Dill wrote in relief after one of the allied Conferences. 'His conduct has been exemplary since he came to Washington ... active but never too wild.'

Dill's almost instantaneous emergence as guarantor was fundamental to his influence on the alliance. Not only could Dill be trusted; he could be trusted to deliver. He was efficacious – for the British and American Chiefs of Staff, above all for Brooke and Marshall, uniquely efficacious. It was Dill, in tandem with Marshall, who made the Combined Chiefs of Staff work, in the words of an American observer, 'not as a mere collecting point for individual rivalries between services and nations, but as an executive committee for the prosecution of global war.' This was Dill's inalienable achievement, and the reason he was considered by the Chiefs of Staff of both nations as 'practically irreplaceable'.

For Dill, promotion of the alliance would be of mutual benefit. Problems would be considered, by definition, Anglo-American problems. Nor did this imply inattention to British interests. Just as Churchill preached and Dill practised frankness, so it was for Churchill to promise, but Dill to redeem, the expectant virtue of combination from the British point of view: it 'makes us no longer a client receiving help from a generous patron, but two comrades fighting for life side by side'. The head of the British Admiralty Delegation reinforced the point at the end of his tour in Washington in 1942. The combined system, he argued, gave Britain 'the constitutional *right* to discuss her needs on equal terms, instead of receiving gratefully such crumbs as may be left from the rich man's table'. In the uncertain beginning of 1942, as the Administration contemplated American unreadiness, as the Japanese eviscerated Britain's Far Eastern empire, as British stock slumped – for the many 'anxious to cry us down', Dill remarked, 'Singapore was money for jam' – Dill anchored Churchill and the COS to the new system. The British Joint Staff Mission in Washington was made indispensable to the functioning of the war-time relationship.

The patron–client relationship, however, waxed rather than waned. It undercut the contemporary rhetoric, very largely the Churchillian rhetoric, of partnership or kinship. Even Dill could find his own position 'wearing and sometimes exasperating'. He grew very tired of 'begging from the Americans', as he was wont to put it on such occasions. 'Individually, they are charming and kindness itself, but to get all we want out of them is not easy.' Dill chafed, not so much at relative British weakness, as at personal powerlessness. He felt keenly, and rather exaggerated, the strict limits on his executive authority. Being able to 'make suggestions but decide nothing' was intensely frustrating. In order to get results he was dependent, as it seemed, on others: on the receptiveness of London and Washington.

And yet he mastered that dependency. With characteristic reticence he courted and won Marshall, and to a remarkable degree the rest of official America. Marshall drew attention to Dill's 'translation' of the American point of view to the British. In effect Dill interpreted each side to the other. Hence his exhortations to frankness: to reveal as much as possible of 'how minds are working', as he was fond of saying, in order to remove suspicion and foster mutual understanding. 'Without him', ran the War Office epitaph, 'Britain could not have understood America so thoroughly and quickly, nor America Britain.'

Dill died in harness on 4 November 1944, of aplastic anaemia. Four days later a memorial service was held at Washington Cathedral. The service was conducted by the Episcopal Bishop of Washington; the lesson read by the US Army Chief of Staff. Afterwards a motorized cortège proceeded along a route lined by thousands of troops to Arlington National Cemetery, the American Valhalla. The coffin, folded in a Union Jack, with an unsheathed sword and a Field-Marshal's cocked hat on top, was transferred to a gun carriage drawn by six grey horses. They were led slowly to the crossroads of Roosevelt and Grant Avenues. The US Joint Chiefs of Staff acted as honorary pall bearers. A simple service was held at the graveside. Salutes were fired, the Last Post and Reveille sounded. One witness wrote afterwards: 'I have never seen so many men so visibly shaken by sadness. Marshall's face was truly stricken. ... It was a remarkable and noble affair.'

The Joint Chiefs of Staff sent as a message of condolence to their British counterparts an extraordinary tribute:

[We] feel [we] share equally with you the loss to our combined war effort resulting from the death of Field Marshal Sir John Dill. His character and wisdom, his selfless devotion to the allied cause, made his contribution to the combined British-American war effort of outstanding importance. It is not too much to say that probably no other individual was more responsible for the achievement of complete cooperation in the work of the Combined Chiefs of Staff.

... we have looked to him with complete confidence as a leader in our combined deliberations. He has been a personal friend of all of us. ...

We mourn with you the passing of a great and wise soldier, and a great gentleman. His task in this war has been well done.

BIBLIOGRAPHY

There is no biography of Dill. For a detailed and sympathetic study of his American apotheosis, 1941–44, see Alex Danchev, *Very Special Relationship* (Brassey's, 1986). A revealing picture of Dill and the British Joint Staff Mission in Washington emerges from the diaries of its secretary, Brigadier Vivian Dykes, also secretary to the Combined Chiefs of Staff committee: *Establishing the Anglo-American Alliance* (Brassey's, 1990), edited by the same author.

On Dill as CIGS the most illuminating contemporary sources are the memoirs of his Director of Military Operations, Major-General Sir John Kennedy, *The Business of War* (Hutchinson, 1957) and the extensive documentation incorporated in John Connell's two-volume biography of Wavell: *Wavell* (Collins, 1964 and 1969). The 'Churchillian' view of Dill may be sampled in Ismay's *Memoirs* (Heinemann, 1960) and indeed in volume six of Martin Gilbert's authorized biography of Churchill himself (Heinemann, 1983). Dill's achievement is reassessed by Alex Danchev in 'The Central Direction of War 1940–1941', in John Sweetman (ed.), *Sword and Mace* (Brassey's, 1986), and 'Dilly-Dally, or Having the Last Word: Field-Marshal Sir John Dill and Prime Minister Winston Churchill', *Journal of Contemporary History*, January 1987.

CHRONOLOGY: JOHN DILL

1881, December 25	Born at Lurgan, County Armagh, Ireland
1887, September	Methodist College of Belfast
1895, January	Cheltenham College
1900, August 20	Royal Military College Sandhurst

1901, May 7	Commissioned 1st Battalion (100th Foot), the Prince of Wales's Leinster Regiment (Dover)
1901, September 10	Boer War (South Africa)
1902, November 10	Assistant Adjutant (Fermoy; Shorncliffe; Blackdown) (Lieutenant)
1906, August 15	Adjutant (Blackdown; Devonport)
1907, February 20	Marries Ada Maud le Mottée
1909, August 14	Brigade Signal Officer (Devonport; Birr) (Captain)
1913, January 22	Student, Staff College (Camberley)
1914, August 4	GSO3, Eastern Command
1914, November 5	Brigade Major, 25 Infantry Brigade (France)
1916, January 3	GSO2, 55th Division (Major)
1916, November 1	GSO2, Canadian Corps
1917, January 5	GSO1, 37th Division (temp. Lieutenant-Colonel)
1917, October 29	GSO1 (Training), GHQ France
1917, December 16	GSO1 (Operations), GHQ France
1918, March 27	Brigadier-General, General Staff (BGGS) (Operations), GHQ France (temp. Brigadier)
1919, March 1	BGGS, Staff College (Colonel)
1922, September 1	Commander, Welsh Border (TA) Brigade
1923, November 1	Commander, 2 Infantry Brigade (Aldershot)
1926, November 1	Army Instructor, Imperial Defence College
1929, January 19	GSO Western Command, India (Quetta)
1931, January 8	Commandant, Staff College (Major-General)
1934, January 22	Director, Military Operations & Intelligence (DMO & I) (War Office)
1936, September 8	GOC Palestine & Trans-Jordan (Lieutenant-General)
1937, October 12	GOC-in-C, Home Command (Aldershot)
1939, September 3	Commander, I Corps, British Expeditionary Force (General)
1940, April 22	Vice-CIGS
1940, May 27	CIGS
1940, December 23	Death of first wife
1941, October 8	Marries Nancy Charrington Furlong
1941, November 19	Retirement as CIGS announced; Governor-designate, Bombay; promotion to Field-Marshal (effective 25 December 1941)
1942, January	Head, British JSM Washington; senior British member, Combined Chiefs of Staff
1944, November 4	Dies in Washington DC

4

WAVELL

Field-Marshal Earl Wavell

IAN BECKETT

Archibald Percival Wavell – 'Archie' to his friends and 'The Chief' to his admirers – was a most untypical soldier. Indeed, he once compared himself to Lieutenant-General Sir Francis Tuker, writing of the latter in January 1947 that Tuker had 'many more interests than soldiering, in fact his defect as a soldier is probably the same as mine, that soldiering rather bores him and books and history and art interest him more'. Wavell remarked much the same to Lieutenant-General Sir Henry Pownall in 1942 and always maintained that he had had no particular inclination to be a soldier and had become one through the determination of his father, who reached the rank of Major-General during the South African War. Certainly his headmaster at Winchester believed that the young Wavell had 'sufficient brains to make his way in other walks of life' and Wavell never lost the interest in literature and the classics cultivated at both Winchester and his earlier preparatory school at Oxford.

After the Second World War Wavell became president of the Virgilian Society and he is possibly as well known today as the author of the poetry anthology, *Other Men's Flowers*, as he is as a wartime commander. While *Other Men's Flowers* is an undemanding collection – Wavell knew each by heart – it is still very suggestive of his wider horizons. As a highly original trainer of troops in the 1930s, Wavell's training exercises displayed classical and literary allusions such as 'Golden Fleece' in August 1932, which was prefaced with a brief account of the legend of Jason and the Argonauts. Wavell was Lees Knowles Lecturer at the University of Cambridge in 1939 and might well have been appointed to the Chichele chair in the History of War at Oxford but for the outbreak of war.

Wavell was the author of a study of Allenby's campaigns in Palestine and, later, Allenby's biographer, completing the second volume of the biography while C-in-C in the Middle East. A period of half-pay in the 1920s was alleviated by contributing articles to the *Encyclopaedia Britannica* and most of Wavell's articles, lectures and addresses were published in a series of books after the Second World War. His intellect was also reflected in his attendance at the Staff College at the age of only 26 when most of his fellow students were at least ten years older. While GOC of 2nd Division he was also employed to rewrite volume 3 of *Field Service Regulations*, dealing with strategy, while it is significant that the one appointment he coveted (but did not receive) was that of Commandant of the Imperial Defence College.

Unfortunately, Wavell's undoubted gifts were undermined by what Ronald Lewin has described as his 'shrouded personality'. In company Wavell found congenial he could be light-hearted and amusing but, more often, the impression created was one of grave taciturnity. He appeared a man with little capacity for small talk who became almost legendary for his silences. The detailed expositions of subordinates and superiors alike were frequently met with no more reaction than the characteristically occasional response of 'I see'. The tireless self-sufficiency of Wavell could inspire and the elephantine memory astound but, equally, the near impenetrable mask could arouse suspicion and hostility, especially among politicians. Sir Stafford Cripps was to remark that 'the trouble about Wavell is that he is no politician' and Wavell's relationship with the Attlee Cabinet while Viceroy was to be marked with as much mutual distrust as Wavell's earlier wartime relationship with Churchill. Indeed, there can have been few more disastrous initial meetings between two men than that between Wavell and Churchill in August 1940.

Wavell's official biographer, John Connell, suggested that the animosity derived from Wavell's remembrance of Churchill's role as First Lord of the Admiralty in the Curragh Incident of March 1914 when the army was seemingly placed in the position of choosing whether or not to coerce Ulster into accepting Irish Home Rule. Then a captain at the War Office, Wavell had chosen to stand by his duty and oppose the pressures being put on him to defy government policy. However, as Lewin has pointed out, there is no evidence that these events had any bearing on those in the summer of 1940 when there was simply no meeting of minds between the two men. Ironically, Wavell's third Lees Knowles lecture had dwelt on the troubled relationship of soldiers and politicians. Churchill hardly represented the ideal example of Abraham Lincoln given by Wavell but Wavell also failed to heed his own message that soldiers should be 'pliant' in dealing with politicians, a failing he saw in the British CIGS during the First World War, Sir William Robertson.

By 1939 when Wavell gave the Cambridge lectures he had already enjoyed a distinguished military career, albeit one largely devoid of fighting command after 1915. Wavell had been commissioned in his father's regiment, the Black Watch, in May 1901, his period of training at Sandhurst being truncated by the demand for officers in South Africa. Wavell joined the 2nd Battalion in South Africa in September 1901 but saw little action while serving on column and in garrison until peace was concluded in May 1902. After home leave to recover from an injury to the left arm sustained at battalion football – thereafter he could not lift his arm higher than the shoulder – Wavell rejoined his battalion in India. Known as 'Podgy', the stocky Wavell learned his trade in the exacting school of the frontier, returning to England only in April 1908 to prepare for the Staff College entrance examination. He passed in first for a competitive vacancy and, upon graduation, received one of only two 'A' grades awarded his intake.

Chosen by the then Commandant, Robertson, Wavell then proceeded to Imperial Russia where he spent almost twelve months learning the language and observing Russian manoeuvres. Posted to the War Office as GSO3 in March 1912, his first task was to prepare a handbook on the Russian Army and, after a brief period with the Directorate of Military Training, he returned to the Russian section of the Directorate of Military Operations. He remained there until August 1914, attending Russian manoeuvres in 1912 and 1913 (as he was to do again in 1936). The outbreak of war saw Wavell temporarily placed in command of the MO5 intelligence section at the War Office from whence he took command of the intelligence section at GHQ in France. Notified of appointment as intelligence officer to IV Corps in November 1914, Wavell managed to escape what he regarded as dull routine by adroit manoeuvring with a friend who did want the post. As a result, Wavell got the job of Brigade-Major to 9 Infantry Brigade.

While First World War staff officers generally have attracted criticism, those who filled the appointment of Brigade-Major had a most exacting job in constant touch with troops and the front line, far removed from the image of 'château generalship'. Wavell was often in the trenches and lost his left eye to a shell splinter on 16 June 1915. After convalescence he undertook a series of staff appointments – GSO2 in GHQ; British Military Representative to Grand Duke Nicholas of Russia in the Caucasus; liaison officer between Robertson as CIGS and General Sir Edmund Allenby as C-in-C of the Mediterranean Expeditionary Force in Egypt and Palestine; and on the staff of the Supreme Allied War Council at Versailles. Wavell then returned to Palestine as BGGS to Sir Philip Chetwode's XX Corps in April 1918 and stayed until March 1920.

Promotion prospects were not good in the peacetime army and Wavell was to spend a total of 22 months on half-pay between January and November 1926 and between April 1934 and March 1935. There was no opportunity to command his battalion, in which he had little seniority, and he passed from the regimental list when appointed AAG at the War Office in December 1921. He did not find the work conducive and equally described his following appointment in MO1 in 1923 as a 'depressing period'. But there were compensations, for his appointment as GSO1 to Major-General Jock Burnett-Stuart's 3rd Division in November 1926 gave Wavell the opportunity to participate in the work of the experimental mechanized force placed under Burnett-Stuart's overall direction. Wavell appreciated the value of armoured mobility and was also to become a keen advocate of the value of air power but it was infantry that he regarded as the backbone of an army. His own progressive ideas for infantry training were subsequently implemented in his appointments as GOC to 6 Infantry Brigade from 1930 to 1934 and as GOC to 2nd Division from 1935 to 1937. Wavell's methods, on which he lectured to the Royal United Services Institution, were highly imaginative and stressed both mobility and flexibility for the infantry arm. In 6 Brigade, for example, Wavell experimented with Carden-Lloyd carriers and in 2nd Division carried out the first long tactical advance by infantry utilizing road transport, hiring Green Line buses to carry a brigade from Reading to Petworth.

Wavell was offered the appointment of Director of Military Training in May 1936 but declined as he preferred to remain with his division.

However, in September 1937 he proceeded to Palestine to succeed his friend, Major-General John Dill, as GOC. The Arab Revolt had broken out in the previous year but Wavell's time in Palestine was relatively quiet and its chief significance lies in his selection of a young engineer, Captain Orde Wingate, to raise the Jewish irregular Special Night Squads to collect intelligence and subject Arab guerrillas to active harassment. Wavell always had a penchant for the unorthodox and was to make note of Wingate's efforts. Similarly, he had given Lieutenant Harry Fox-Davies the opportunity of testing raiding theories during 2nd Division exercises. Subsequently, Fox-Davies was summoned to Cairo in 1941 to join the Long Range Desert Group, the formation of which by Ralph Bagnold in June 1940 Wavell encouraged. In much the same way, of course, Wavell sent Wingate to Abyssinia in 1940 and brought him to Burma in March 1942.

Wavell returned home in April 1938, his appointment as GOC of Southern Command having been announced previously. The Secretary of State for War, Leslie Hore-Belisha, sought to reform the Army and War Office and had concluded that only wholesale changes at the top would enable him to do so. Wavell among others was considered for the post of CIGS but was thought more suitable for a command which would provide II Corps for any British Expeditionary Force in future. Wavell was still relatively unknown outside the Army but his reputation was undoubtedly enhanced by his delivery of the Lees Knowles lectures on 'Generals and Generalship' in February 1939, although these do not make for particularly stimulating reading today. The theme that emerged was Wavell's belief that the general required 'robustness' and was 'never to think the battle or the cause lost'. Ironically, while Wavell himself derived wartime inspiration from poetry and literature and carried a pocket edition of Mallory throughout the early part of the Second World War, a German translation of 'Generals and Generalship' was Rommel's constant companion in the desert.

Wavell was not destined to remain long at Southern Command, being appointed to the new post of GOC Middle East in July 1939. Wavell arrived in Cairo on 2 August to exercise a 'watching brief' over British and Imperial forces in Egypt, Palestine, Transjordan, Cyprus and the Sudan. Already covering three million square miles, his sphere of command would automatically extend in wartime to encompass British Somaliland, Aden, Iraq and the Persian Gulf. In concert with the naval and air C-in-Cs, he would be expected to formulate co-ordinated war plans with Britain's allies, which might conceivably include both Greece and Turkey. In his first appreciation Wavell grasped the vital need to dominate the Mediterranean but his total forces throughout the Middle East barely reached 90,000 men. Of these, 27,500 were in Palestine and 36,000 – comprising 7th Armoured Division and two brigades of 4th Indian Division – in Egypt. By contrast the Italians, who were likely to present the most immediate threat if they sided with Germany, had 250,000 men in Libya and a further 290,000 in Italian East Africa. Resources of all kinds were in short supply. Wavell had only five staff officers in addition to an ADC and did not even possess adequate air transport to enable him to travel around his command. In this particular instance it may not have made much difference since Wavell was a 'complete Jonah in the air', with his wartime command punctuated by a succession of aerial mishaps and crash or forced landings.

The first priority was to prepare Egypt as a base for future operations and it was to ask for more resources that Wavell travelled to London in August 1940. The Italians had declared war in June but had failed thus far to make use of their superior numbers, although their forces in East Africa did move against British Somaliland on 3 August. It was a difficult moment for Britain's new prime minister. France had collapsed, with immediate repercussions for the Allied position in the Mediterranean but Britain itself faced possible invasion and the Battle of Britain had begun, with Luftwaffe attacks on Channel shipping in July. Wavell's Western Desert Force under Lieutenant-General Richard O'Connor had immediately instituted aggressive patrolling on the Libyan frontier but Churchill had already become restless with the apparent lack of decisive action in the desert and with Wavell's pleas for further supplies. Neither man really appreciated the difficulties faced by the other and the series of meetings between 8 and 15 August proved disastrous for their future relationship.

Wavell got agreement on tank reinforcements for the Middle East but there were difficulties over whether a convoy should be run straight through the Mediterranean, as Churchill advocated, or routed around the Cape, as Wavell and others counselled. Churchill wanted the West, East and South African forces gathering in Kenya to be employed at once but Wavell believed they should not be used until properly trained and acclimatized, and similar arguments surrounded the use of Australian and New Zealand forces presently stationed in Palestine. At this stage of the war the administrative machinery for its strategic direction was distinctly lacking in London with Dill, who had become CIGS in May, and the other chiefs of staff all but overwhelmed in the midst of what has been described as a 'daily circus' presided over by an imperious and untrammelled Churchill at the peak of his powers. The hapless Dill's plea to Wavell, 'Talk to him, Archie', failed to break an increasingly frosty atmosphere and Wavell's near total silence in face of Churchill's arguments had the worst possible impact on the prime minister. On 15 August Churchill discussed with the Secretary of State for War, Anthony Eden, Wavell's possible replacement. According to Churchill's memoirs he concluded that it was best to leave Wavell in command for the present. Wavell equally realized that he was not removed only because Churchill 'could not find any good reason to do so'.

Wavell returned to Cairo on 15 August and matters quickly deteriorated. British Somaliland had to be evacuated two days later with the loss of 260 Imperial casualties compared to an estimated 1,800 casualties inflicted on the Italians. Churchill instantly demanded the removal of the local British commander, Major-General Godwin-Austen, but Wavell refused, his signalled reply concluding with the statement that 'a heavy butcher's bill' was 'not necessarily evidence of good tactics'. It roused Churchill to greater anger than anything Dill had yet experienced. Further, on 23 August, Wavell received a directive drafted personally by Churchill seven days earlier for the CIGS and Eden, which went into minute detail with regard to Wavell's tasks and deployments. Wavell showed tact in replying in four different telegrams over four days, writing later that 'I carried out such parts of the directive as were practicable and useful, and disregarded a good deal of it.'

Whatever the pressures from London, Wavell had made up his mind to launch an offensive in Libya and he directed preparations to be begun on 11 September at a time when the Italians had actually begun to move forward themselves, although they promptly stopped after four days at Sidi Barrani, a mere 70 miles inside Egypt. The promised new tanks arrived later that month and deception plans – another penchant of Wavell – were put in hand. Wavell also had the advantage of intelligence derived from the interception of Italian codes and cyphers, although it is important to emphasize that such intelligence and that derived from 'Ultra' still required to be interpreted correctly. Moreover, until March 1941 Middle East Command received only a digest of Ultra material and direct transmission to Cairo was not arranged until after Wavell's departure for India. Similarly, at this stage only Luftwaffe and not German Army codes could be read: the latter only became available in September 1941.

At the same time Wavell was concerned for the security of planning in Cairo and resolved to keep his proposed operation – Compass – secret. However, there is little doubt that Wavell also intended to ensure Churchill would not interfere in the operational details and, despite the latter's chafing at the lack of action by the 'Army of the Nile', Wavell kept his silence. Indeed, it was only because Eden, who arrived in Cairo on 15 October, proposed to divert resources to a Greece threatened by imminent Italian attack and a pro-German coup in Romania, that Wavell was forced to reveal his plans. Characteristically, Churchill wanted to know the precise date of Compass, for which he held out greater hopes than Wavell was prepared to concede. A signal from Wavell to Dill on 6 December cautioning, 'Please do not encourage optimism', became known to Churchill, who expressed shock that Wavell might be 'playing small' and 'not hurling on his whole available force with furious energy'.

Wavell kept the secret to the last, O'Connor attacking on 9 December in what was intended initially only as a five-day raid. In fact, it brought immediate success with Sidi Barrani again in British hands within three days. By 9 February 1941 when O'Connor's advance ended at El Agheila, he had overrun the whole of Cyrenaica. With no more than two divisions at any one time, O'Connor had routed ten Italian divisions, advanced 500 miles and taken 130,000 prisoners, 400 tanks and 1,200 guns.

The victory, however, was not without controversy for Wavell had decided even before Compass began that the 4th Indian Division must be replaced by the less experienced 6th Australian Division to free the Indians for the projected operations against Italian East Africa. The switch, of which O'Connor was not informed until 11 December, delayed his advance but Wavell was undoubtedly right in utilizing sea transport momentarily available to send the Indians to East Africa where they made a vital contribution. It seems unlikely that O'Connor could have advanced any further than he did, although it has been suggested that Tripoli might have been attainable. Compass had only been designed to secure Egypt and the Italian invasion of Greece in October had undermined the venture thoroughly. Resources including air cover were being diverted to Greece as early as November and the Cabinet Defence Committee took the decision to afford the Greeks maximum assistance on 10 January 1941. It was only the refusal of the then Greek prime minister, General Metaxas, to accept British aid that enabled O'Connor's advance to continue beyond Tobruk. Once Metaxas died on 29 January and his successor requested British aid, the desert campaign was at an end. On 11 February Dill signalled that Greece must take precedence over any attempt to reach Tripoli.

Greece added to Wavell's concerns for in February Lieutenant-General Alan Cunningham had opened the British campaign in East Africa by striking at Italian Somaliland from Kenya. It was a campaign of which Wavell was to complain later of Churchill's persistent 'barracking'. Nevertheless, what John Connell has described as 'an immensely complicated, delicate series of major operations, spread over a huge area, inhibited by every kind of administrative, communications, transport and climatic difficulty' was an immense success. Fighting continued in Abyssinia until November 1941 but, for all intents and purposes, Mussolini's East African Empire had been destroyed by May. Cryptanalysis played a vital role but so did Wavell's transfer of the 4th Indian Division from Libya and his encouragement of an Abyssinian revolt by responding positively to a suggestion emanating from the Secretary of State for India, Leo Amery, in July 1940 to employ Wingate to assist Colonel D. A. Sandford in raising Abyssinian irregulars. Italian East Africa also provided a significant proving ground for many future British commanders in Burma, including Slim.

It is as well to record the successes over which Wavell presided for the involvement in Greece was to herald the beginnings of almost uninterrupted disaster. It was once assumed that Wavell was pushed into the Greek campaign against his will, but it is now clear that he had few doubts about the need to fight in Greece. Wavell appreciated that Tripoli was unobtainable and, although it was apparent that German reinforcements were arriving there in early February, it was believed that these forces would be too weak to attack until mid-May at the earliest. By all orthodox calculations this might have been correct but for the fact that Rommel, who commanded the reinforcements, was no orthodox general. Similarly, Ultra intelligence suggested that Greece was in imminent danger of German intervention. While the British could send relatively little assistance it was assumed that this would prove sufficient, thanks to an exaggerated view of the value of the Greek Army. Wavell was convinced that forward defence was the only option, whatever the risks involved. His belief that the operation (Lustre) was militarily viable as well as politically and psychologically necessary – Britain had pledged to defend Greece in 1939 – thus steeled the Cabinet for intervention. Eden concurred with Wavell's appreciation and the other Middle East C-in-Cs acquiesced.

Once the German blitzkrieg struck Greece and Yugoslavia on 6 April 1941 the exposed position of the British and Imperial forces committed by Eden and Wavell to the defence of the so-called Aliakmon Line became apparent. The tactical control of the battle was in the hands of General Sir Henry Maitland Wilson but it was Wavell who bore the brunt of Churchill's demands for daily information. It was a hopeless venture from the beginning and evacuation began on 24 April, a proportion of those taken off by the Royal Navy being diverted to Crete as a matter of convenience. By this time, however, yet another crisis had developed. Rommel had unexpectedly begun to advance in Libya on 31 March at a moment when the Western Desert Force – known as XIII Corps since January – was severely depleted by the Greek expedition.

Wavell was not well served by his Cairo staff and not perhaps sufficiently ruthless to sack those who failed him. Thus, when he went to the Libyan front on 3 April he took O'Connor, now GOC in Egypt, to replace Lieutenant-General Philip Neame commanding XIII Corps. But Wavell was persuaded by O'Connor to leave Neame in place with O'Connor merely in a temporary advisory capacity. It was the worst possible compromise and both O'Connor and Neame were then captured on the night of 6/7 April as the British front crumbled. Wavell retrieved something from the ruins by taking the vital decision to try and hold Tobruk.

On 18 April the Chiefs of Staff ruled that restoring the Libyan front should take precedence over evacuation from Greece but it was a measure of Wavell's burdens that when Rommel was making his first attack on Tobruk's hastily improvised defences Wavell himself was urgently required in Athens. Within ten days of the Chiefs of Staff ruling Crete, which had previously been regarded as a 'receptacle of whatever can get there from Greece', became a new priority in view of Ultra intelligence pointing to the imminence of a German airborne attack. Wavell had certainly ignored the island despite repeated suggestions of its importance ever since October 1940 but he did what he could now in the time available. Moreover, it could be argued that the battle for Crete was lost by tactical errors on the ground for which Wavell had no responsibility.

Already alarmed by the discovery that Wavell had contingency plans for the evacuation of Egypt – Wavell's belief in planning for the 'worst possible case' was often interpreted as defeatism – Churchill found Wavell's Cretan preparations lacking in drive. Wavell had also angered Churchill by his reluctance to send troops from Palestine to restore the situation in Iraq after a pro-German coup on 3 April had isolated the British garrison at Habbaniya whereas the C-in-C in India, Claude Auchinleck, had readily offered troops. Eventually the Chiefs of Staff ordered Wavell to mount a relief expedition on 6 May. Equally, Wavell was reluctant to become involved in any campaign in Syria where the Vichy French authorities had allowed German aircraft to use airfields for attacks on Habbaniya. Wavell's signal to Dill on 17 May opposing the commitment of Free French forces with British forces in support was ill received in London. Eleven days earlier Churchill had revived the notion of removing Wavell and on 19 May he told Dill that his mind was made up to exchange Wavell and Auchinleck.

What proved the final breaking point was the further development of the desert campaign. With news of more German tanks reaching Tripoli in late April, Churchill had rushed the 'Tiger' convoy through the Mediterranean, a total of 238 new tanks for Wavell reaching Alexandria on 12 May. Churchill expected his 'Cubs' to be used immediately, especially as Ultra had revealed the parlous state of Rommel's logistics. Wavell intended to go on to the offensive and launched Operation Brevity on 15 May in anticipation of making good losses from the newly arrived tanks. Unfortunately, Brevity failed as did a second operation – Battleaxe – launched with the new tanks on 15 June. There were severe mechanical defects in many of the new tanks and Ultra could not reveal either the qualitative superiority of the Germans nor how Rommel would deploy 88mm anti-aircraft guns in an anti-tank role to blunt the offensives. Churchill showed no sympathy for Wavell's problems and was critical of the choice of Lieutenant-General Beresford-Peirse to command Battleaxe. Wavell himself was much distressed by the débâcle, this being one of only two occasions during the war when he lost his formidable self-control. Having reported failure to London, Wavell received his telegram of dismissal on 22 June 1941.

Dill had wanted to bring Wavell back to England to rest but Churchill apparently feared the possible consequences of having Wavell in London and he was ordered to India direct to exchange places with Auchinleck. Churchill had remarked on 19 May that Wavell would enjoy 'sitting under a pagoda tree' but circumstances conspired to ensure that India provided no respite once Wavell reach Delhi on 11 July. In September he returned to London with much the same mission as that in August 1940, pleading for more resources and for the inclusion of Burma within his sphere of command. He reiterated the latter request in November but Burma only passed under his control after the Japanese attack on Pearl Harbor. Wavell had gone on from London to Tiflis – he covered almost 8,000 miles with 53 hours in the air in only ten days – to consult with the Russians on the operation to expel German influence from Iran. This well reflected the way in which the Middle East and Central Asia were more traditional concerns of the Indian Command than the eastern frontier. Thus, when the Japanese did attack in December, neither Burma nor Malaya were well prepared for defence.

Almost at once Wavell found his responsibilities widened, for the Anglo-American Arcadia Conference in Washington followed up a suggestion by Chiang Kai-shek to appoint a Supreme Allied Commander for the South West Pacific theatre. The American Chief of Staff, Marshall, suggested Wavell and this was agreed despite some British reservations. Wavell learned of his appointment on 30 December although his new command, ABDA (American, British, Dutch and Australian) Command did not formally come into existence until 3 January 1942. Supposedly embracing all Allied forces in Burma, Singapore, Malaya, the Dutch East Indies, the Philippines and (from 24 January) North-West Australia, ABDA was a nonsense from the start. There could be little effective co-ordination with American forces in the Philippines even from a headquarters established at Lembang on Java and Wavell did not attempt to exercise operational control over the Philippines. Nor, indeed, were there any disposable reserves and neither Wavell nor the Chiefs of Staff had any clear idea of what forces were actually available.

In the circumstances Wavell deserves some credit for managing to create an Allied Command at all but, in reality, he was not the man best suited to exercise such responsibilities. He knew little of the Far East and consistently underestimated the Japanese even though he did prepare a summary of their tactical methods in Malaya for the guidance of his commanders in Burma. More important, his personality was not conducive to working with difficult allies. Chiang Kai-shek, for example, offered his Fifth and Sixth Armies for the defence of Burma but, as Chiang unrealistically demanded a separate line of communications for them, Wavell initially declined more than one Chinese division. Wavell also had it in mind that only Imperial troops should be seen to defend British territory but he failed to appreciate the need to save Chiang's 'face' when refusing the offer. His relationship with the Chinese remained poor and he was also to fail in his relationship with the admittedly difficult American Chief of Staff to Chiang, Stilwell.

ABDA was disbanded on 22 February 1942 with the Japanese forces threatening to overrun the Dutch East Indies. Malaya and Singapore, of course, had already been lost despite Wavell's efforts to put heart into the defence. It is arguable whether Wavell should have replaced the GOC, Percival, and the Governor, Shenton Thomas, but it seems unlikely this would have made any appreciable difference. What was achieved, however, was in large measure due to Wavell's prompting, notably compelling Percival to make proper plans for withdrawal into Singapore island, for the island's defence and for demolition of installations. Wavell could not have saved Singapore but was correct in endeavouring to do so even when this meant concurring with the Chiefs of Staff decision to commit the 18th Division to Singapore in January 1942. Wavell himself visited Singapore for the last time on 9 February and was apparently tempted to stay and direct the defence himself in what would have been a futile gesture. Unfortunately, while waiting to be taken out to his flying boat on the night of 10 February Wavell stepped off the seawall and fell heavily on rocks below. Flown back to Java he insisted on returning to his desk despite the considerable pain and the advice of his doctors. It is possible that this contributed to his sometimes baneful influence on the campaign developing in Burma.

In December Wavell had decided to put his Chief of Staff in Delhi, Lieutenant-General Thomas Hutton, in command in Burma in the hopes of instilling some organization in its defence. As in the case of the Balkans, Wavell favoured forward defence. Still not fully appreciative either of Japanese capabilities or of the poor quality of some Burmese and Indian units in Burma, Wavell could not understand why Moulmein was abandoned on 31 December or how the Sittang River line was lost on 23 January 1942.

The possibility that Rangoon might also be abandoned appalled Wavell since it was the only port through which the forces in Burma could be adequately supplied and from which other supplies could be sent on to China. Wavell, who had returned to Delhi from Lembang, hastened to Magwe in Burma on 28 February to meet Hutton and the Governor, Sir Reginald Dorman-Smith. Wavell lost his self-control for the second time in the war and raged at Hutton in front of Dorman-Smith and others. Wavell then went further south to meet John Smyth, commanding 17th Indian Division, on 1 March. Smyth was a sick man and Wavell replaced him but there was unnecessary vindictiveness in having Smyth stripped of his rank of Major-General and accused of concealing his ill health when Wavell had previously ignored the latter factor. Wavell also decided to accept the offer of the Chiefs of Staff to send Lieutenant-General Harold Alexander to supersede Hutton. Yet, despite Wavell sending the 63 Indian Infantry Brigade to Rangoon and urging a counter-attack towards Pegu, Alexander was compelled to abandon Rangoon after all within two days of his arrival on 5 March. Indeed, Alexander was fortunate to avoid being captured.

The Burma campaign did not show Wavell at his best but while British forces were still retreating towards Assam he directed his staff on 16 April to begin planning for a return to Burma. It belied Stilwell's impression that Wavell was a tired defeatist. It was, indeed, courageous since it was hardly auspicious to contemplate a return when the enormous logistic and administrative difficulties had to be surmounted. Moreover, considerable internal unrest erupted in India itself after the leaders of the All-India Congress were arrested in July, and 57 battalions had to be deployed to internal security at a time when the Japanese appeared to threaten a seaborne invasion of eastern India. Churchill, too, favoured an offensive at an early stage and in mid-July the Chiefs of Staff approved a plan put forward by Wavell for seizing Japanese airfields at Akyab in the Arakan, which could be used for further operations aimed at Rangoon. It was also intended to mount operations in northern Burma for which the Chinese or, more specifically, Stilwell, also had ambitious plans.

Both the British scheme – 'Anakim' – and Stilwell's ideas of re-opening land communications between India and China were premature given the resources available. Returning from meeting Churchill in Cairo and accompanying the prime minister to Moscow in August, Wavell referred to more limited plans in September as 'Operation Fantastical'. In the event, even these – for a combined land and amphibious assault on Akyab – were severely modified when amphibious resources were diverted to Madagascar. There remained just a land advance into the Arakan by 14th Indian Division reinforced subsequently to a strength of nine brigades. However, between December 1942 and May 1943 the Arakan offensive floundered against new Japanese defensive bunkers. Wavell allowed a complicated command structure to evolve in the Arakan and he failed to stop increasingly costly frontal assaults on the bunkers. He also permitted Lieutenant-General Noel Irwin of Eastern Army to feed in brigades piecemeal. Again, he seems to have failed to perceive Japanese capabilities.

In retrospect Wavell considered that it had been right to launch the offensive because it yielded valuable lessons. The same might well be said for his support of the Chindits and in Burma Wavell once more revealed his liking for the unorthodox. In April 1942 he formed V Force as a unit capable of providing intelligence from behind Japanese lines and in May he attempted to deceive the Japanese, through the agency of Peter Fleming, by planting false documents in an abandoned car suggesting that large reinforcements were reaching India. He also encouraged Ian Lyon's ideas for raiding Japanese shipping in Singapore, a concept carried out in 1943. And, of course, he had summoned Wingate. Despite the abandonment of a Chinese offensive with which it was designed to coincide, Wavell personally authorized the first Chindit expedition on 5 February 1943. The value of long-range penetration remains controversial, but the first Chindit expedition did prove that troops could be supplied in the jungle by aircraft and the propaganda value derived from Wingate helped offset the damage done by the Arakan failure.

Churchill was certainly cheered by Wingate's operations and Wingate was directed to accompany the prime minister to the Quebec Quadrant Conference in August 1943. On the voyage as well as in London it became clear that the Arakan failure rankled with the prime minister. In Washington it was proposed that a new Allied Supreme Command be established for South East Asia. Wavell endorsed this and apparently expected to be appointed without realizing either that Churchill was looking actively for ways of removing him or that he had lost the confidence of the Americans. Back in England on 14 June Wavell was offered the Viceroyalty of India in succession to Lord Linlithgow. There had been other candidates but it was a neat way of replacing a man whom Churchill now regarded as a 'busted flush'. Wavell's final despatch as C-in-C showed some understandable irritation and resentment against what he claimed as lack of support for both the Arakan and Chindit operations. Once more his successor was Auchinleck, who resumed his former appointment as C-in-C India.

Wavell was described by Eden's private secretary as a 'funny choice' for Viceroy and the whole affair reeked of Churchillian expediency. Certainly, Wavell was no better suited to dealing with Indian nationalist politicians than with British politicians. Nor did Wavell share Churchill's views on India's political future. As a member of the Viceroy's Council since July 1942 Wavell was conversant with Indian political affairs and his outlook was decidedly more liberal than that of Churchill.

Indeed, Churchill was apparently horrified by Wavell's sympathetic treatment of Allenby's liberalism as High Commissioner in Egypt when a manuscript of his second volume of Allenby's biography was circulated in London in September 1943. Wavell favoured an early promise of independence but Churchill was not seriously interested in pursuing such a course.

Wavell found himself equally adrift when the Labour Party won the 1945 General Election. Wavell recognized the strength of the Muslim League and of muslim opinion but Attlee's Cabinet appeared to be under the spell of the Congress Party. His attempt to create a genuine coalition administration in India failed at the Simla Conference in July 1945 and the Cabinet would not endorse his 'Breakdown Plan' of 1946 for a progressive evacuation and handover of power. On 4 February 1947 Wavell was summarily dismissed by Attlee, with only one month's notice rather than the customary six. His successor, Mountbatten, possessed more natural charm with which to woo Indian politicians but he also enjoyed wide powers and discretion denied Wavell. Ironically, Mountbatten endorsed Wavell's belief that only a definitive timetable for withdrawal and partition could solve the impasse. Wavell had worked hard and sincerely in India, notably in tackling the Bengal Famine and in laying plans for future economic development. Not for the first time, the manner of his dismissal from an appointment was unworthy.

In the New Year's Honours List of 1943 Wavell had been promoted to Field-Marshal. He had actually requested this himself in August 1942 on the grounds of his responsibilities and, while acknowledging that he would enjoy the prestige, indicated that he felt it would help with the Americans and Chinese. In his letter to Churchill, Wavell listed those campaigns which he had directed since 1939. There were no less than fourteen – Libya, British Somaliland, Eritrea, Italian Somaliland, Abyssinia, Greece, Crete, Iraq, Syria, Iran, Malaya and Singapore, the Dutch East Indies, Burma and the Arakan. Of these, the first nine had occurred within a period of seven months and five of them simultaneously. As Wavell was the first to admit, not all had been successes. Armies under his command had triumphed only over Italians and Vichy French, Iraqis and Iranians; against German and Japanese forces he had known only defeat. Nevertheless, his achievements had still been significant. Wavell had his qualities as well as his defects and, in the last analysis, it was not his fault that he was seemingly always waging what Ronald Lewin has described as 'a poor man's war'.

BIBLIOGRAPHY

Books about Wavell

Collins, Major-General R. J., *Lord Wavell* (Hodder & Stoughton, London, 1948).

Connell, John, *Wavell: Scholar and Soldier* (Collins, London, 1964).

Connell, John (edited by Roberts, M.), *Wavell: Supreme Commander* (Collins, London, 1969).

Fergusson, Bernard, *Wavell: Portrait of a Soldier* (Collins, London, 1961).

Kiernan, R. H., *Wavell* (Harrap & Co., London, 1945).

Lewin, Ronald, *The Chief* (Hutchinson, London, 1980).

Moon, Penderel (ed.), *Wavell: The Viceroy's Journal* (Oxford University Press, Oxford, 1973).

Books by Wavell

The Palestine Campaigns (Constable, London, 1931).

Generals and Generalship (The Times, London, 1941).

Allenby: A Study in Greatness (Harrap & Co., London, 1940).

Allenby in Egypt (Harrap & Co., London, 1943).

Other Men's Flowers (Cape, London, 1944).

Allenby: Soldier and Statesman (Harrap & Co., London, 1946).

Speaking Generally (Macmillan, London, 1946).

The Good Soldier (Macmillan, London, 1948).

Soldiers and Soldiering (Cape, London, 1953).

CHRONOLOGY: ARCHIBALD WAVELL

1883, May 5	Born in Colchester
1893	Begins education at Summer Fields, Oxford
1896	Begins education at Winchester College
1900	Enters Royal Military College, Sandhurst
1901, May 8	Commissioned 2nd Lieutenant, The Black Watch
1901, September	Serves in South Africa with 2nd Battalion, Black Watch
1903–8	Serves in India with 2nd Battalion, Black Watch
1904, April 13	Promoted Lieutenant
1909, January	Enters Staff College, Camberley
1910, December	Graduates from Staff College
1911, February	Goes to Russia to learn language
1912, March	Appointed GSO3 in Russian Section of Directorate of Military Operations, War Office
1913, March 20	Promoted Captain
1914, November	Appointed Brigade-Major, 9 Infantry Brigade, France
1915, April	Marries Miss Eugénie Quick
1915, June 16	Loses left eye to shell splinter

1915, December	Appointed GSO2 at GHQ, France and Flanders
1916, May 8	Promoted Major
1916, October	Appointed British Military Representative at the headquarters of Grand Duke Nicholas of Russia in the Caucasus
1917, April	Leaves Russia
1917, June 3	Promoted to brevet Lieutenant-Colonel
1917, July	Appointed liaison officer between Chief of the Imperial General Staff and C-in-C Middle East
1918, January	Appointed to staff of Allied Supreme War Council
1918, April	Appointed Brigadier-General, General Staff to XX Corps, Palestine
1919	Awarded CMG
1920, March	Leaves Palestine and rejoins Black Watch in Germany
1921, June 3	Promoted Colonel
1921, December	Appointed AAG in the Adjutant-General's Department, War Office
1923, July	Appointed GSO1 in MO1 at War Office
1926, January 12	Goes on half-pay
1926, November 2	Appointed GSO1 to 3rd Division
1930, July 1	Promoted to temporary Brigadier and appointed GOC, 6 Infantry Brigade
1933, October 16	Promoted Major-General
1934, April 9	Goes on half-pay
1935, March 11	Appointed GOC, 2nd Division; awarded CB
1937, August 19	Appointed GOC in Palestine
1938, January 29	Promoted Lieutenant-General
1938, April 26	Appointed GOC Southern Command
1939, February	Delivers Lees Knowles Lectures at University of Cambridge
1939, July 28	Appointed GOC Middle East and promoted to General Awarded KCB
1940, February 15	Appointment designated C-in-C Middle East
1941, June 22	Dismissed as C-in-C Middle East and appointed C-in-C India Awarded GCB
1942, January 3	Appointed Supreme Allied Commander, South West Pacific (ABDA Command) and hands over as C-in-C India
1942, February 22	ABDA Command dissolved and reverts to C-in-C India
1943, January 1	Promoted Field-Marshal
1943, June 14	Offered Viceroyalty of India

1943, October 20	Sworn in as Viceroy
	Awarded GCSI, GCIE and appointed PC
	Raised to peerage as Viscount Wavell
1945	Becomes Chancellor of Aberdeen University
1946	Becomes Honorary Colonel of Black Watch
1947, February 4	Dismissed as Viceroy
	Becomes Earl Wavell
1948	Becomes Constable of the Tower of London
1949	Becomes Lord Lieutenant of London
1950, May 24	Dies
1950, June 7	Buried at Winchester College

5

ALANBROOKE

Field-Marshal Viscount Alanbrooke

DAVID FRASER

General Sir Alan Brooke – later to be Field-Marshal Viscount Alan-brooke – an artilleryman who had commanded with distinction II Corps in the British Expeditionary Force in 1940, was appointed Commander-in-Chief Home Forces soon after the Army's evacuation from Dunkirk, at a time when invasion of the United Kingdom seemed to threaten daily. In December 1941 he became Chief of the Imperial General Staff, professional head of the British Army; and shortly after taking office he also became Chairman of the Chiefs of Staff Committee, in effect the principal strategic adviser to the Government. He thus and without question was the doyen of Churchill's generals.

Brooke was an Ulsterman, one of the Brookes of Colebrooke in Fer-managh, member of a family of Irish Protestant soldiers and landowners; twenty-six Brookes had served in the First World War, twenty-seven served in the Second. He was brought up and educated in France, bilingual, artistic and sensitive; and his quickness of wit and speech often struck his contemporaries as having a spice of Gallic as well as Irish in its flavour. His relationship with Churchill was uneven.

At one level the two men had a good deal in common. They shared recollections of an earlier, close-knit professional Army in the Imperial heyday. Both had served in and greatly enjoyed the India of the Raj as it once had been. Churchill treasured the memory of friendship in youth with Brooke's brothers, in particular his adored elder, Victor Brooke. They shared backgrounds of social confidence, even distinction, with Churchill the grandson of a ducal house and Brooke the youngest of one of the greatest landowning dynasties of Ulster. They shared courage, self-confidence, sharp wits – and a good deal of intolerance of dimmer minds. Yet at another level they looked at each other with mixed feelings, right from the start of their supremely fruitful association; and in each man admiration – at good moments affection – alternated with exasperation and impatience. Brooke's private thoughts on Churchill – modified but by no means extinguished by subsequent reflection – held a good deal of continuing disapproval, while Churchill by contrast seldom let the sun go down on his wrath; but when the battle between them was on, it was often fierce.

Churchill had known what he was in for and had tried to evade appointing Brooke CIGS. 'I know these Brookes', he said beforehand vigorously, 'stiff-necked Ulstermen, and there's no one worse to deal with than that!' Did the long-ago Ulster crisis of '14 and Churchill's controversial part in it haunt him at such moments? Perhaps. But once their professional relationship was under way Churchill's periodic anger would be quickly succeeded by affectionate sentiment, as when he told General Ismay, his principal staff officer and confidant, 'Brooke hates me! I can see it in his eyes!', to be contradicted by Ismay – who had run to Brooke and had his answer:

'The CIGS doesn't hate you! He loves you! But he will never tell you he agrees when he doesn't!'

'Dear Brooke!' Churchill's eyes filled with tears.

There were many such occasions. And although the sparks flew right to the end, Churchill said and assuredly meant of Brooke, 'I love that man!'

Brooke, for his part, never wavered in his appreciation of what Churchill meant to Britain in terms of leadership, rhetoric, imagination. 'That man!' he used to murmur, tired and exasperated after some gruelling encounter, 'That man!' and then, with a sigh, 'Yet *what* would we do without him?' But his resentment – kept almost invariably under stern, courteous control – was aroused by three facets in particular of Churchill's conduct of affairs.

First, he was provoked and exhausted by the Prime Minister's way of doing business; by his endless meetings at intolerable hours, his seemingly total lack of consideration for others, his frequent late-night garrulity. This was understandable – but in the ultimate trivial, although it did not seem so to tired and responsible men directing a world war. The fact is that Churchill's was an indisciplined genius and he needed a certain disorder and spontaneity in his personal dealings, a certain self-indulgence in small things, if his imagination and energy were to flourish.

Second, Brooke (and his colleagues on the Chiefs of Staff Committee) were often angered by what they wrongly thought was Churchill's personal hostility in argument, the way he cross-examined and criticized and cavilled and condemned what they put to him – and did so, often, with peremptory brutality – only to adopt their advice, exactly, next day and advance their propositions as his own. In this Brooke failed to recognize an essential, a natural difference. Churchill was a politician, a parliamentarian. That was his strength – he may have loved to play the commander, the generalissimo (and that was at times his weakness) but his genius was for the political battle and in that battle loud argument, hard verbal knocks, the challenge of opponents' motives, the use of sarcasm and invective are the ordinary tools of the trade. Churchill would have found it astonishing that such attitudes, transported to the Chiefs of Staff Committee, could cause indignation or wounds. They were his way of arriving at the truth, the solution. He had to test other men's ideas by direct attack. Brooke seldom accepted this, but it could not be otherwise. Yet this, too, was ultimately trivial, a matter of words and manners, with the Prime Minister entirely within his rights to do things in his own idiosyncratic way.

But the third cause of Brooke's resentment of Churchill was substantive. Churchill's most provoking weakness in his direction of the war was his passion for detail. This absorption in matters operational or tactical – which he loved – led to a neglect of priorities and, often, to a temporarily hazy view of strategy. It led, furthermore, to frequent attempts at interference in the operational matters themselves, sometimes with startling and deplorable consequences. If a battle was conceived Churchill wanted to feel he had control of its every detail – and most certainly of its starting date. If a new weapon was brought into service Churchill was intrigued by it and would discharge periodic enquiries and proposals about its use, by no means always helpfully. If statistics were paraded Churchill would challenge them, even advance his own. Brooke fumed at all this. He found Churchill's interventions sometimes harassing (especially of commanders in the field), inappropriate to the head of the Government, and more often than not inept and uncomprehending in themselves. The root of dissension between Brooke and Churchill was the former's sense that the latter, instead of judiciously adopting and holding to a line on grand strategy, at his worst jumped with periodic inconstancy after novelties and fanciful ideas, making work, confusing issues and wasting time.

'At his worst' – but not typically. Both men grew more and more exhausted as the years passed, and with exhaustion irritation increased. But in fact the partnership was admirable, perhaps more admirable than either appreciated. Their personalities clashed at times, but their qualities were complementary. Brooke was, like Churchill (although it was concealed) emotional, but he was a realist, a pragmatist, a calculator. His will was very strong. He was never prepared to accede to an idea – or a campaign – unless he was personally convinced that it was the best way, that it had at least a decent chance of success, and that the fighting men attempting it were being committed to battle in as good order as could be managed. That, he said and felt – more strongly than he felt anything – was *his* responsibility as the professional head of the Army. Although in fact very often acting as what later generations would call a Chief of Defence Staff he, like his colleagues, utterly opposed a suggestion that such should formally exist. He believed – in this, a man of his time – that it was his position as head of the Army and that alone which gave him the right and the duty to reason thus. Brooke understood the political imperatives of grand strategy as clearly as any man, but to agree an unsound operation for a political motive however estimable would be to get soldiers killed unnecessarily; and that he would not do.

Nor would Churchill, once convinced, wish him to. On a professional issue of moment he never overruled the Chiefs of Staff. For Churchill's heart was in exactly the same place as Brooke's. Churchill loathed the casualties of war; like Brooke he was influenced, perhaps on occasions over-influenced, by memories of the Somme and Third Ypres. Like Brooke he preferred caution to risk. In one, fortunately fleeting, mood he even shrank at the eleventh hour from the invasion of France, the greatest Allied operation of the entire struggle. Churchill was a romantic, an enthusiast of history who envisaged battle in highly coloured and sometimes archaic pictures; but he was deeply sensitive to the human aspects of war and he was the last man to seek to drive his Chiefs of Staff towards recklessness or irresponsibility. Yet Churchill found the minds of the Chiefs at times pedestrian, their perspectives narrow, their vision disappointingly unimaginative – and on such occasions (and plenty of others) he would goad and challenge, and scoff at excessive logistic insurance, and enquire why some different and more unconventional or far-ranging scheme had not been considered. And in this Churchill was not always wrong, for his own conceptual reach, at best, far surpassed that of his professional advisers; including Brooke. In the terms of the artist he was, Churchill could compose a picture and convey the sense of distance and space and contrast which a great landscape presents; while, unfortunately, losing his way somewhat among the figures in the foreground where his touch was often unsure. Brooke, on the other hand, (also an artist) drew most exactly and precisely, setting each part of the composition in very proper relationship to the rest; but did not display superior (to Churchill) creative or innovative instinct, that with which the greatest masters are credited. The talent of each was indispensable.

An example of this can be adduced very early in their relationship. Within days of Brooke's assumption of office Churchill (leaving Brooke, the apprentice, behind) sailed on HMS *Duke of York* to meet Roosevelt in America. Churchill produced during that voyage a series of papers for the comments of the Chiefs of Staff – papers on grand strategy in the new situation created by Japanese aggression (Japan had attacked the American fleet at Pearl Harbor on 7 December 1941) and by the near-simultaneous declaration of war by Germany and Italy on the United States.

Churchill's papers on that occasion must rank as some of the most influential and prescient state papers of the war. In the European theatre he concentrated attention on the Mediterranean, arguing the merits of an ambitious 1942 campaign to win for the Allies the whole of North Africa, and thus free passage of the Mediterranean. He realized that any campaign in Europe, whether western or southern, must critically depend on the security of the United Kingdom and of the Atlantic sealanes. He appreciated that, for Germany, the crisis of the war was bound to come in Russia; German initial successes there had been dramatic but had stopped short of strategic decision and losses were huge, the front enormous and demanding. While in the Pacific, against the Japanese, Churchill envisaged a struggle for maritime supremacy, the winning of which could lead to an Allied progress from island to island, bringing air bombardment and the threat of invasion ever nearer Japan; one day decisively so. As for ultimate victory over Germany, Churchill was clear in his papers that the German armies must be defeated in Europe (unless inner convulsions brought the Reich to its knees) and that this must be the aim of a return to the Continent – probably after Italy had, somehow, been knocked out of the war. The strategic situation was looking black for the Allies, but Churchill's eyes were on the dawn.

Brooke agreed with the thrust of all this, but at that stage of the war it needed the vision, the historical grasp of a Churchill to articulate it, and it was this grand conceptual sweep which the Prime Minister, in this superior to his professional advisers, was able to provide. Brooke's part was to reduce the general to the particular, to point to the realities in time, space and resources which set the limits of opportunity; and to restrain – an unpopular task – Churchill's zeal that action be as early as possible by adamant insistence that the Army could only undertake successful operations when it was ready, and when the capacity of the other two Services to support it was sure.

In their first year together the occasional clashes of view and will between Churchill and Brooke generally concerned the Mediterranean; and these took place against a background of difficulty in agreeing with the United States how the war was to be carried on, a difficulty which was Brooke's chief preoccupation. By a complex interaction of military and (largely American) political factors the Allies had determined on an expedition to French North Africa – Operation Torch. The Americans, or some of them, regarded this as a distraction from the main task, the invasion of Western Europe, but Brooke, at a series of conferences, played the lead part in demonstrating that such an invasion was beyond Anglo-American capacity, certainly in 1942 and (as later became very clear) probably in 1943 as well. If the Anglo-American Armies were to fight the Germans somewhere in the short term it had better be – it probably could only be – in North Africa, where a British Imperial Army was already engaged.

In this Churchill and Brooke were at one. But Churchill began to attack on points of detail. First, he pressed the claims of opening (simultaneously) a campaign in northern Norway, an idea to which he often reverted and which was, equally often, demonstrated as wholly impracticable by Brooke. Second, and more troublingly, he demanded ever earlier offensive moves by the British imperial forces in the Western Desert – the only British land theatre of operations against Germany. Thus Churchill harassed Auchinleck, the Commander-in-Chief Middle East, urging him to earlier action in the spring of 1942 than he thought right.

Brooke, as ever on such occasions, had to fight strongly for the man on the spot. Commanders in the field, he had to make clear to Churchill more than once, must be supported and encouraged; or dismissed. They must not be directed in their professional judgements from London. In the event Auchinleck's offensive of mid-1942 was pre-empted by Rommel; and in a series of brilliant moves the Germans drove the British from their positions at Gazala in May, took Tobruk and harried their opponents back to Egypt. Brooke, in the summer of 1942, had the tasks of consoling a prime minister under domestic criticism, of maintaining Anglo-American planning unity for the agreed North African landings in view of this disagreeable reverse at the other end of the Mediterranean; and of sorting out the British Army – for Brooke, although he had stoutly defended Auchinleck against the strictures of Churchill, was by no means sure that changes in the high command in the Middle East were not due.

In August 1942 these changes were made, and after a visit by both Prime Minister and CIGS to Egypt Auchinleck was replaced by Alexander and the Eighth Army was placed under the command of Montgomery (Auchinleck had, for a while, been doing both jobs). These appointments were not secured without a good deal of difficulty with Churchill, who had strong reservations about Montgomery; indeed Brooke, very much against his better judgement and most atypically, had reluctantly agreed to Gott, a very experienced but overtired Desert Corps commander, being given command of Eighth Army. When Gott was killed in an air encounter, however, Churchill conceded and Montgomery got the appointment which was to make him famous.

It was an appointment which greatly relieved Brooke. He had always much admired Montgomery's abilities and he felt at last confident that Eighth Army was in good hands; Eighth Army, or most of it, soon felt the same. Alexander's appointment as Commander-in-Chief – nominally to be Montgomery's superior – was, on the face of it, curious; he was younger and junior in service. But Brooke realized two things about Alexander. First, that he would never interfere with Montgomery, a master of battlefield detail in a way which Alexander had no aspirations to be; and, second, that Churchill greatly admired him and that Alexander, thus, would be the perfect insulation between the Prime Minister and the Army Commander who, at that time, was in direct charge of the British Army's only effort against the Germans. In the huge Middle East theatre it was Eighth Army that mattered.

The North African campaign ultimately followed the path envisaged by Churchill and charted by Brooke. The Allies landed in North Africa, and Tunisia was reinforced by large German forces; while, in the eastern Mediterranean, Montgomery fought and won the battle of Alamein and drove the German–Italian forces from Tripolitania, so that the united Allies came to face the enemy in a Tunisian redoubt by the Spring of 1943. But by that stage there had arisen between the Allies the question 'What next?' The British pressed for exploitation in the Mediterranean of Tunisian victory and, once again, many Americans thought the British sadly reluctant to face the task – and the casualties – of cross-Channel invasion.

The British, the Americans sometimes said and often thought, were obsessed with the Mediterranean. Some of this, they suspected, might be Imperial nostalgia about the 'route to India' and British concerns in the Near East. Some of it might be an unhealthy (in Washington's view) preoccupation with the Balkans, with dreams of a southern European front which would, almost by definition, eliminate the chances of a simultaneous major effort in the West. Some of it might even be induced by suspicion of the future intentions of the Soviet Union – a cardinal sin in American eyes, for this was the period when Roosevelt's enchantment with Stalin was approaching its peak. Some of it might derive from exaggerated respect for German ability after the nightmare of 1940, and from grim recollections of losses in France and Flanders between 1914 and 1918. For whatever reason the British – and this principally meant Brooke – were suspected of being lukewarm towards a major Western European campaign, and thus of urging an essentially peripheral effort in the Mediterranean. Even Churchill – although he periodically grumbled that Brooke's proposals to invade Sicily or Sardinia were insufficiently ambitious – was suspected by the Americans of having too little heart in the cross-Channel business.

This was unfair, and Brooke took the lead part throughout the ensuing months of 1943 in demonstrating its unfairness. He was in no doubt that the culminating campaign of the war must follow a cross-Channel invasion of Western Europe. But the conditions had to be right. The first of these – too often, in his view, ignored – was that the German Army must be so weakened before the campaign opened as to ensure that the *Wehrmacht* could not build up forces in overwhelming strength against a beachhead and lodgement. Brooke appreciated, as Churchill sometimes failed to do, that with interior land lines of communication and a good railway system the Germans could concentrate in East or

West disturbingly fast. To pre-empt that, two things were essential: continued German casualties and attrition in Russia, and continued strategic air attack on European communications and German war-making potential. Both demanded time; more time than existed between victory in Tunisia (May 1943) and the end of that year. Invasion, Brooke argued from that alone, could not come before 1944. The view was unpalatable, but unanswerable; and any who contend with hindsight that with the amphibious resources then available the Allies *could* have invaded France from Britain in 1943 should consider the actual Normandy fighting in the summer of 1944 and ask themselves how it might have gone had a much stronger German Army (1943/44 was a terrible year for the *Wehrmacht* in Russia) been able to reinforce the western from the eastern front far more powerfully than in fact occurred. That, in 1943, could have been the situation; and Brooke would have none of it.

But there were other factors. The American Army in Britain in 1943 had not and could not have achieved anything of the strength or skill it was able to acquire during the additional months actually provided before a 1944 D-Day. The Battle of the Atlantic was only won in mid-1943 – indeed the March sinkings were the highest of the war, and the idea of cross-Channel invasion with a vulnerable Atlantic lifeline behind it was not one Brooke or his colleagues could contemplate. Perhaps most dramatic of all, the Mediterranean campaign offered the chance of eliminating Italy from the war – a development envisaged by both Churchill and Brooke from the earliest days and which actually happened in September 1943. The consequence was massive reinforcement of Italy by German forces, committing the *Wehrmacht* to a southern front; and the replacement of Italian by German divisions throughout the Balkans. To exploit Allied Mediterranean successes in 1943 was not only necessary, in that no respectable alternative existed; it was also highly beneficial to the Allies. It involved the invasion first of Sicily and then of Italy. And it led to the Italian campaign.

Anglo-American differences continued to dog the Italian campaign; and, in retrospect, some on the Allied side have argued that the diversion to Italy of resources from other fronts told more against the Allies than against the Germans. Brooke's view was clear. He regarded the Italian struggle as definitely subsidiary to a Western European campaign, but as playing a helpful part provided that it was conducted with sufficient vigour, so that the Germans would always devote troops to it, feel threatened by it (not least by Allied airfields opened increasingly northward towards a vulnerable Reich) and suffer casualties in it. This happened, and Brooke (like Churchill) opposed the American plan – Operation Dragoon – to remove divisions from Italy and land them in the south of France in 1944 to assist Eisenhower in north-west Europe. He reckoned that this was to give the Germans too easy a defensive battle in Italy, to 'let up' on the pressure there – while making no significant difference to a campaign in France by then, in the event, already won. Eventually, however, Brooke counselled graceful acceptance of Dragoon, when it was clear the Americans were set on it; and Roosevelt argued that he had promised it to Stalin. Churchill disagreed, and fought with greater ferocity to keep Alexander's forces undiminished. But Churchill's motive was at once stronger and different in kind from Brooke's.

For Churchill believed in a project which Alexander had now advanced, whereby the Allied Armies in Italy would defeat the Germans and advance by Ljubljana and the Julian Alps to the Danube, and then march on Vienna. It was this dream, among others, which Dragoon frustrated. This 'Vienna alternative' has acquired a good deal of retrospective merit, because it might have brought the Anglo-Americans to central Europe before the Red Army – an idea only tentatively argued at the time although undoubtedly in Churchill's mind, prescient as he often though intermittently was on that subject. Brooke, however, opposed the concept flatly. Militarily he regarded it as fantasy; the terrain, the season of the year, and an unbeaten *Wehrmacht* in his view made it so. And – in this, more politically sensitive than his political master – Brooke knew that to moot it to the Americans would provide yet another piece of evidence that the British still had no stomach for fighting the war in the West, were obsessed with southern and Danubian Europe, had their priorities wrong. The concept was, in Brooke's mind, militarily unsound and impossible of Allied acceptance. It would have required a completely different and agreed Anglo-American assessment of the strategic and political objects of the war. To Churchill's anger it died.

Before this, however, a mighty dispute had divided the two men on a wholly different subject, with Brooke voicing the hostility of a united Chiefs of Staff Committee to the Prime Minister's views. Early in 1944, as the war in Europe moved towards its consummation, eyes were inevitably turned more and more towards the Far East and to the question of how finally to defeat Japan. That theatre had been one of American primacy. The tide of Japanese aggressive expansion had been turned by the American maritime victories of the Coral Sea and Midway. The

British part had been to defend India – which had involved the loss and would subsequently imply the reconquest of Burma. There were, however, many other British possessions or associated territories in Japanese hands. There were French and Dutch Colonial Empires, all occupied by Japanese forces. There was an unbeaten Japan.

Brooke and his colleagues argued that when the war in Europe was over, the British contribution should be to deploy the maximum land, sea and air forces, massed together with the huge American amphibious and battle fleets, advancing towards Japan by a series of stages – via the Philippines, the Marianas, Formosa. The British Fleet and Armies would be based in and sustained from Australia. This, they believed, would be the great and final anti-Japanese effort. It could and should be joined by the British Empire. Anything else would be peripheral.

Churchill disagreed fundamentally. In his view the British Imperial effort should be based on India; should undertake and then exploit the reconquest of Burma; should liberate, with British forces, Malaya and other such dependencies; should, with a demonstrably British endeavour, avenge the loss of Singapore; and should be and be seen to be distinct and independent of the Pacific campaigns of the United States. This quarrel between Brooke (and his unanimous colleagues) and Churchill was the sharpest they fought, the only one which brought them to the brink of resignation. It was solved by a certain compromise. It did not adversely affect the brilliant campaign which drove the Japanese from Burma. And it was ultimately made irrelevant by the collapse of Japan, a collapse sealed but not solely procured by the atomic destruction of Hiroshima, and which took place within months of victory in Europe. It is easier to sympathize with Churchill than Brooke in the matter. Churchill's eyes were on the reactions of the peoples of South East Asia in the aftermath of war. Who should be perceived as victors?

In June 1944 Operation Overlord, the invasion by the Allies of north-west Europe, at last took place. Brooke accompanied Churchill to visit the beachhead six days after D-Day. He shared the Prime Minister's anxieties at what seemed the periodic slow progress, the threat of stagnation. He kept Churchill firm in support of Montgomery when the Americans (and some dissident British voices) criticized his conduct of operations. His heart lifted, with Churchill's, when the great moment of Allied breakout ultimately came.

In the north-west European campaign itself, as 1944 was followed by 1945, and as the Allies erupted from Normandy, closed in on the Reich, crossed the Rhine and advanced to final victory Brooke had little conflict with Churchill. They shared anxiety at Eisenhower's strategy, fearing loss of opportunity, inadequate concentration and prolongation of war. Both were influenced in this by Montgomery's impatient contempt of Eisenhower's generalship; and both, on occasion, did less than justice to Eisenhower. Brooke recognized and periodically rebuked Montgomery's egotism, his disservices to the cause of Anglo-American understanding, but he accepted, on the whole, his military judgement (although sceptical of the concept of Operation Market Garden, the attempt to cross the Waal and the Nederrijn, taking Arnhem by airborne assault and debouching towards the Ruhr; Brooke believed such ambitions were premature with the port of Antwerp still closed to the Allies). Brooke and Churchill visited the front together to watch the Rhine crossing in March 1945 and spent some days at Montgomery's headquarters. The end was very near. Prime Minister and CIGS felt very close.

We walked up and down in the moonlight [Brooke recorded]. It was a glorious night and we discussed the situation. ... He was in one of his very nicest moods and showed appreciation for what I had done for him in a way which he has never done before.

They spoke of the early days, when victory seemed so remote as to be unimaginable. Within months of that evening Germany had surrendered unconditionally; and within a few months more Japan had done the same. By then the partnership had been dissolved by a general election and Churchill was out of office.

As head of the British Army Brooke commanded the admiration – and often induced the fear – of all. He was quick in mind, speech and temper, master of his profession, uncompromising in upholding what he believed right and intolerant of pettiness, procrastination or incompetence. But, although formidable, Brooke was at heart a kind and sensitive human being, one loved by his few intimates, one for the gentle and understanding gesture where it was appropriate, one who took infinite trouble with ostensibly unimportant people, one who could talk directly and as one man to another with anybody of whatever degree, one totally without pomposity. His integrity shone. Robert Casey, later, as Lord Casey, Governor-General of Australia and a strict judge, wrote of Brooke:

I know of no Service Leader who contributed more to the winning of the Second World War than he did, by his military capacity, by his judgement, and by his complete honesty of thought and expression.

Brooke was a selfless man. On one occasion, however, he felt keenly what seemed to him Churchill's lack of understanding and magnanimity. Churchill had given Brooke clearly to understand that he was to have the supreme command of the Allied Forces for the invasion of Europe in 1944, Operation Overlord. Almost casually and certainly without expression of regret Churchill told him, late in 1943, that he had agreed with Roosevelt the command should be Eisenhower's. It was, by that stage of the war, inevitable that an American would be appointed and the character of Eisenhower in fact fitted the peculiar and primarily diplomatic requirements of Supreme Allied Command particularly well. Brooke's military judgement and generalship would have been superior but his handling of Allies almost certainly would have not; although they admired him the Americans were always wary of Brooke, feeling uneasy that his speed and incisiveness were putting them at a disadvantage, stealing a march. But Brooke felt the blow keenly; not least because it would have meant escape from Churchill and Whitehall. He stayed at his post, uncomplaining except in his diary. And he was at Churchill's side until the last day.

Brooke – Field-Marshal Viscount Alanbrooke in the aftermath of War – was the greatest Chief of the Imperial General Staff ever produced by the British Army. It was his destiny to come to authority at exactly the right hour; an hour when the country was in fearful peril, and was being certainly sustained but sometimes endangered by the mercurial genius of Churchill. Alanbrooke was the perfect complement to that genius. He and Churchill formed an incomparable partnership in the higher direction of the Second World War.

BIBLIOGRAPHY

Butler, J. R. M., *Grand Strategy* (HMSO, 1954–64).
Churchill, W. S., *The Second World War* (Cassell, 1948–54).
Ehrmann, J., *Grand Strategy* (HMSO, 1956).
Fraser, D., *Alanbrooke* (Collins, 1982).
Gwyer, J. M. A., *Grand Strategy* (HMSO, 1964).
Horne, A., *To Lose a Battle* (Macmillan, 1969).
Howard, M., *Grand Strategy* (HMSO, 1972).
Ismay, Lord, *Memoirs* (Heinemann, 1960).

Kennedy, J., *The Business of War* (Hutchinson, 1957).
Liddell Hart, B., *Memoirs* (Cassell, 1965).
Liddell Hart, B., *History of the Second World War* (Cassell, 1970).
Slessor, J., *The Central Blue* (Cassell, 1956).
Wilmot, C., *The Struggle for Europe* (Collins, 1952).

CHRONOLOGY: ALANBROOKE

1883, July 23	Born, Bagnères de Bigorre, youngest child of Sir Victor Brooke, Baronet, of Colebrooke in Fermanagh and Alice Bellingham, Lady Brooke
1902, December 24	Commissioned, Royal Artillery
1902–14	Service with Royal Artillery in Ireland and India
1909	Appointed to Royal Horse Artillery – Eagle Troop
1914, July 28	Marries Jane Richardson of Rossfad, Fermanagh
1914, September	To France with Eagle Troop
1915, January	Staff Captain RA, 2nd (Indian) Cavalry Division
1915, November	Brigade Major RA, 18th Infantry Division
1917, February	Staff Officer, Royal Artillery, Canadian Corps
1918, June	GSO1, RA (Lieutenant-Colonel), First Army
1919	Student at Staff College, Camberley
1920–22	General Staff, 50th (Northumbrian) Territorial Division
1923–6	Instructor, Staff College
1925, April	Mrs Brooke killed in car accident
1927	Student, Imperial Defence College, London
1929, February–1932	Commandant, School of Artillery, Larkhill (Brigadier)
1929, December 7	Marries Benita Lees (née Pelly)
1932	Instructor, Imperial Defence College
1934–5	Commander, 8 Infantry Brigade (Plymouth)
1935, November	Inspector of Artillery (Major-General)
1936, August	Director of Military Training
1937	Commander, Mobile Division (Salisbury Plain)
1938	Commander, Anti-Aircraft Corps (Stanmore) (Lieutenant-General)
1939, August	Commander-in-Chief, Southern Command (Salisbury)
1939, August 31	Commander II Corps, British Expeditionary Force
1939, September–1940, May 30	France and Flanders
1940, June 11	Knight Commander, Order of the Bath
1940, June 12–18	Returns to France, Commander-in-Chief (designate) British Expeditionary Force (reconstituted)

1940, July 19– 1941, December	Commander-in-Chief, Home Forces (General)
1941, December 25– 1946, January 25	Chief of Imperial General Staff
1945	Knight Grand Cross, Order of the Bath
1945, September 18	Created Baron Alanbrooke
1946, January 29	Created Viscount Alanbrooke
1946	Knight of the Garter
1963, June 17	Dies at Ferney Close, Hampshire

6

ALEXANDER

Field-Marshal Earl Alexander

BRIAN HOLDEN REID

In 1943 a young subaltern returning from the front line had an unexpected meeting with his Army Group Commander. Stricken with toothache he was making his way wearily to the rear when a jeep pulled up. Sitting at the steering wheel was a handsome, immaculate senior officer, who could have been a film star at dress rehearsal inspecting the set. 'Hallo, how are you?' he asked. It was Alexander, then commander 15th Army Group. When the subaltern informed him that he had toothache, Alexander was most concerned; the subaltern also became concerned, for the enemy were getting their range and artillery fire encroached on their conversation. Alexander continued to chat nonchalantly. 'Sir', the subaltern insisted, 'I really do think you should move out of range.' 'Yes, I suppose I'd better', Alexander replied without enthusiasm. He climbed back into the jeep and drove on – nearer to the front line and the enemy's artillery.

Every great soldier has an individual style of command – a unique footprint that he makes upon the battlefield – which identifies him and his methods at once. Alexander's style of command was singularly British. The immaculate clothes, fastidiousness of person, coolness under fire and imperturbability were reminiscent of Wellington without the wit. The effortless superiority, languid manner and polished manners signalled that he was a perfect Anglo-Irish gentleman of a type that had officered the British Army for centuries. In his zeal for the front line he demonstrated not only a disdain for the 'château generalship' of the First World War, but upheld the very best traditions of British generalship. He was the spiritual heir of Marlborough and Wellington. He was a general who kept his head while all others were losing theirs, and like these ducal forebears, he too was a scion of the aristocracy.

Alexander's formative years were happy and comfortable. He cruised confidently and smoothly through childhood and adolescence as he was to do through adulthood. Born in 1891, the third son of the 4th Lord Caledon, The Hon. Harold Rupert Leofric George Alexander had the conventional upbringing of a young upper-class Edwardian gentleman. Sent to St Michael's preparatory school (Hawtrey's) and then in 1906 to Harrow, he proved an exemplary product of that illustrious school: well-liked, even admired; not for the last time in his life, Alexander fitted the bill. He was a good all-round athlete, showed some talent at cricket, and a touch of distinction as a miler. But he was not over-blessed with intellect – though Alexander took away from Harrow a taste for painting and Classical history and culture which he was never to lose. In his penetrating discussion of the English national character, 'The English Sense of Humour', Sir Harold Nicolson observed that 'one of the most common defects of the English temperament is intellectual indolence. The average Englishman does not take pleasure in cerebral effort as an end in itself.' Neither did Alexander. He entered the Army Class and regarded himself as a man of action, not reflection, of decision, not indecision, and he never had the slightest doubt that he wanted to be anything else other than a soldier. In 1910 he entered Sandhurst, and the following year was commissioned into the Irish Guards, the newest of the Guards regiments raised in 1900.[1]

One of the most striking facets of Alexander's character was his lack of inner conflict and self-doubt. He was to develop into the archetypal Edwardian hero. He did not need to indulge himself in introspection for the simple reason that it had never occurred to him that he needed it. He fitted the pattern of regimental life as a hand fits a glove. 'Alex' loved the regiment and the regiment loved him. Not overburdened with duties he developed his taste for art and his considerable talent as an artist. He contemplated retiring and making a career as a painter. All the photographs of the young 'Alex' taken immediately before the outbreak of the First World War in 1914, reveal a shy, immaculately dressed and exceedingly handsome young subaltern, not greatly troubled by the strife inflicted on the world. Indeed, the best of these, in which he leans languidly against a gun carriage with his fellow subalterns at Wellington Barracks in August 1914, only reveals an impatience to get to the front before the war ended. For every soldier war is the acid test, not only of his professional skill, but of his character. The British Army has traditionally placed the attributes of character above those of the intellect. An officer could be a good soldier without being clever, but a clever officer was rarely a good soldier. Alexander in his diffident and unselfconscious way had developed an abundance of character – of a type cherished and praised by his fellow Englishmen.[2]

In discussing the English national character, Nicolson delineated a number of important features which described accurately Alexander's own character. His good humour, tolerance and kindness, his deep fund of common sense, were matched by a typical Englishman's dislike of extremes, over-emphasis, and all forms of boastfulness. Alexander also exhibited what Nicolson called 'A preference for compromise and understatement. ... A dislike of appearing conspicuous or inviting ridicule' and had a pronounced 'respect for individual character rather than individual intelligence' which manifested itself in the display of an 'instinctive sense of human values which reacts unfavourably against any deformation of those values'. Alexander had inherited or consciously nurtured all of these characteristics. In 1914–18 his values were put to the test and triumphantly vindicated. The test of war did not result in trauma and crisis for him; quite simply 'they were the happiest years of my life'.[3]

All of Alexander's soldiering in the First World War was spent on the Western Front. He was to prove himself a regimental soldier of great distinction. His wartime career began inauspiciously with a wound in the thigh and hand at the First Battle of Ypres in November 1914. On returning to active duty he was posted to the 2nd Battalion Irish Guards which had been recruited since the outbreak of war. The battalion's baptism of fire was the Battle of Loos in September 1915. Its objective was the Chalk Pit Wood, which was taken by Alexander's company. The most controversial aspect of the battle was the failure to commit the reserves rapidly enough. Alexander sent back to the rear a characteristically worded request, 'he would be greatly obliged if they would kindly send some more men up, and with speed'. 'The actual language was somewhat crisper', noted the regimental historian, Rudyard Kipling, but no less polite. The reserves were not forthcoming, but recognition of Alexander's initiative and dispatch was, for he was awarded the Military Cross.[4]

In the months preceding the Battle of the Somme in 1916, Alexander was switched back and forth in temporary command of both the 1st and 2nd Battalions, before returning finally to the 2nd as second in command. In September 1916 he took part in the third phase of the Somme Offensive and the battalion seized its objective, Lesboeuf. Once more he called for reinforcements that were not there to be had; but once more also, his drive was rewarded, this time with the DSO. In March 1917 he was given permanent command of the 2nd Battalion: he was only 26, but already an experienced veteran.

Alexander's tactical skills were revealed later that summer at Third Ypres (Passchendaele) when after careful preparation and rehearsal, the battalion seized its objective, the Broembeke, at the first attempt. All of Alexander's talents were needed the following year even to keep the battalion in being after the storm of Ludendorff's Spring Offensive fell on the British Armies. Lord Ardee, commander 4 (Guards) Brigade was gassed, and Alexander, at 27, assumed command. So great were the brigade's casualties that by May 1918 companies were down to 40 men each; but a worse fate was to befall the battalion; Alexander was to be taken from them, posted to command X Corps School. The battalion said farewell, Kipling recorded, 'with an affection few Commanding Officers have ever awakened'. Alexander took responsibility without blinking, always remained 'both inventive and cordial' and 'would sometimes continue to dress the affair as high comedy'. The Great War had bolstered Alexander's confidence, and with good reason; he waxed his moustaches and walked with a jaunty air.[5]

This histrionic side was fortified by a sojourn for two years in Latvia. George Washington once remarked that bullets had a charming sound; for Alexander their sound was no less charming. He was bored without the exhilaration of battle and through regimental connections volunteered to serve in Latvia against the Bolsheviks. He was to receive the title of 'Relief Adviser' but took command of the Baltic Landeswehr, consisting of German and Baltic soldiers, with a German chief of staff, Baron Rahden. Such a command speaks volumes for his open-mindedness. He was wounded again, but not seriously, and drove the Bolsheviks back into Russian territory. The *New York Times* correspondent, Walter Duranty, wrote that 'Alex ... is the most charming and picturesque person I have ever met, and one of the two soldiers I have known who derived a strong, positive and permanent exhilaration from the worst of danger'. As for Alexander himself, he had enjoyed himself, indulging his taste for exotic headgear. On handing over command of the Baltic Landeswehr in March 1920 he declared, 'You are gentlemen and sportsmen. I am proud to have commanded an Army composed entirely of gentlemen.' He retained an interest in these men, and after 1945 succeeded in getting a number of them entry into the United States, safe from the avenging hands of the Soviet Union.[6]

In May 1922 Alexander was gazetted Lieutenant-Colonel at the age of 31 (the average age to attain this rank in peacetime was usually 40–42). His experience thus far had been exclusively of field commands. In 1926 he passed into the Staff College. He did not excel there, and two of the Directing Staff instructors, Brooke and Montgomery, formed the opinion that he was an 'empty vessel'. Indeed Montgomery, desirous to denigrate anybody associated with his wartime triumphs, later claimed that the DS 'came to the conclusion then that he had no brains – and we were right'. Such accusations were to surface in the following years with increasing frequency; actually they are distorted, if not untrue. Alexander's intellect was not his most conspicuous asset, but his attainments as a practical soldier were, and so was his 'mass of common sense', to quote another former Staff College instructor, General Sir Robert Gordon-Finlayson. If Alexander never acquired a taste for staff work, a stint at the Imperial Defence College and a posting as GSO1, Northern Command, taught him the supreme value of making the best use of able, staff-trained subordinates.

The last contributory factor in Alexander's pre-war development as a commander sprang from his appointment as commander of the Nowshera Brigade on the North West Frontier. Alexander's career before 1939 was unrivalled in its diversity. Command of a brigade underscored publicly a recognition that Alexander was one of the Army's future commanders. Imperial policing was the traditional function of the Army, and was the main school of its generals: all the principal commanders of the First World War had been nursed on 'small wars'. Imperial policing with its stress on improvisation, minor tactics and highly mobile (horsed) operations suited Alexander's own, fairly unsophisticated military outlook. He distinguished himself in two frontier campaigns in 1935, the Loe Agra and the Mohmand. When in 1938 the new CIGS, Lord Gort, was cutting away the 'dead wood' and looking for new, vigorous general officers with established fighting records, the name of Alexander could hardly be overlooked, and he was posted to command 1st Division. High command in the next war seemed certain.[7]

A variety of reasons may be advanced for the promotion of a particular officer while another of equal or even better attainments is held back. Sometimes an officer's 'background' is crucial; the British Army before 1945 was acutely class conscious, as to a lesser degree it still is; here Alexander, as an aristocrat and a Guardsman, scored highly. But his social graces would not have seemed so alluring without the added lustre of his impeccable wartime record. Nothing succeeds like success, and every command that Alexander had held redounded to his credit. He had shown not only superlative abilities as a regimental soldier but as a tactician. He was the aristocratic apotheosis of the 'real soldier'. Unlike Montgomery, he was not greatly affected by a disgust with the style of command adopted by First World War generals. It had never occurred to him not to apply his regimental skills to any level of command that might be thrust upon him. Though he had not disclosed to his teachers at the Staff College a penetrating intellect or quick-silver intelligence, and later they (and their biographers) were to point this out to his detriment, he nevertheless had a receptive brain. His common sense was a formidable tool. Alexander absorbed *impressions* rather than detailed formulae. Once absorbed he clung to them tenaciously. An idea might come to him slowly, but once grasped, he would develop it remorselessly. Others would attend to the details. Alexander would *command*. In the conduct of great campaigns this attitude would be a source of both strength and weakness.

In the early years of the Second World War Alexander was the available man: the safe pair of hands, the cool Guardsman always in control. 'Alex' would sort it out. He perfected a style of operations for the conduct of which British generals have always shown a special aptitude – the art of retreat and evacuation. Yet the stigma of failure never hung about him – the mud never stuck to his immaculate uniform. The 1st Division took its place in France in the centre of the BEF's line in I Corps, commanded by Lieutenant-General Michael 'Bubbles' Barker. During the ill-fated advance to the Dyle in May 1940, and the subsequent retreat, Alexander's tactics and dispositions were faultless. On reaching the Dunkirk perimeter, he had his personal possessions destroyed. 'Thus my sole surviving possessions for the remainder of the battle were my revolver, my field glasses, and my briefcase.' In an unexpected move, Montgomery then prevailed on Gort, the Commander-in-Chief, to transfer command of I Corps, which was responsible for the perimeter's defence, to Alexander. This move is surrounded by mystery and was probably less neat than the transition described in Montgomery's *Memoirs*. The Prime Minister, Winston Churchill, had given permission to surrender, but Alexander on assuming command of I Corps stated his intention 'at all costs to extricate his command and not surrender any part of it'.

Although Alexander was to share many greater triumphs, his behaviour in sitting out the final hours of daylight covering the concluding phase of the Dunkirk evacuation was his 'finest hour'. He immediately displayed 'grip' – that most cherished of all a British general's attributes. He appraised that the perimeter could not be defended beyond 1–2 June. 'Consequently', he reported to his French colleagues, 'I have decided to re-embark without delay.' Perhaps Alexander underestimated the fighting power of the remaining French troops; at any rate, the French considered his action entirely self-interested. Alexander took a small boat along the beach. 'Is there anyone there?' he shouted. Repeating the question in French, he received no reply.[8]

Alexander's conduct at Dunkirk made his reputation as a field commander. Confirmed in command of I Corps, he threw himself into preparations to resist a German invasion. In the event, he was not to face the Germans in the field again for another two years. The most formidable foe he had to face before his next field command, in Burma against the Japanese, was Alan Brooke. In October 1941 during Operation Bumper, a large anti-invasion exercise in which Alexander commanded the defending forces, Brooke gave public vent to doubts about Alexander which he had long nursed in secret. He criticized him for 'sadly mishandling' the armoured forces. Alexander did not respond to this unfair comment, for the same reason that he accepted a command in Burma which no less an authority than Slim regarded as an impossible mission: 'I will do my duty.' Alexander's mission was to salvage something from disaster. He almost became its greatest victim. He underestimated the speed of the Japanese outflanking advance (as he had overestimated the German advance at Dunkirk). Alexander and his headquarters escaped only thanks to the rigid adherence of the Japanese commander in advancing on the city from the west; had he continued to block the roads to the east, Alexander's career would have come to a premature and inglorious end.[9]

Conducting yet another long retreat brought out all that was phlegmatic and noble – and foolhardy – in Alexander. En route to a divisional headquarters, Slim recalled that their car was machine-gunned by Japanese aircraft. 'General Alexander, as usual, was quite unperturbed', recalled Slim, 'and refused to take shelter in a trench, as I did very briskly, preferring to stand upright behind a tree. I was very annoyed with him for this ... because we had been trying to stop the men doing it.' In dealing with his allies Alexander would need all his coolness and patience. In this delaying action the suspicious and surly French were replaced by the no less touchy Americans in the person of General Joseph W. Stilwell, a cantankerous braggart, whose not inconsiderable intellect was perverted by numerous phobias, not least that directed against the egregious British. Alexander, who was instinctively repelled by neurosis of any kind, dealt patiently with Stilwell, but formed a low opinion of American soldiers and their generals. Once formed, Alexander did not shed such impressions easily.[10]

Defeat in his first independent command did not damage Alexander's reputation, and nor did it draw prodigiously on the stock of admiration that he had built up with Churchill since Dunkirk. Alexander had shown too much obstinacy at Rangoon and not enough constancy during the retreat. The objectives of the campaign kept changing, though these had been handed down by his Commander-in-Chief, Wavell. The enemy retained the initiative and maintained air superiority. A determined counter-attack with the demoralized and ill-trained soldiers available was not a feasible proposition. Alexander had made the best of a bad, probably impossible job.[11]

Up to this point Alexander had to wage war always at a disadvantage, whether material or moral. He had to help shoulder the baleful burden of unpreparedness. He was now to enter a new world of material plenty. On returning to England in the summer of 1942 he was appointed British Task Force Commander for the forthcoming invasion of French North Africa, Operation Torch. But within weeks an even greater challenge was presented to him. Affairs were reaching a pitch of crisis in the Western Desert. Auchinleck's victory in the confused action known as First Alamein was little compensation for the defeats and humiliating retreats forced upon Eighth Army earlier that summer. Both Churchill and Brooke agreed that something was 'wrong' with the command in North Africa. Auchinleck, still doubling as Commander-in-Chief and GOC Eighth Army, was held accountable for this and in a reshuffle of generals returned from whence he came as Commander-in-Chief India. Alexander was posted to succeed him. Churchill had originally canvassed Brooke himself as Commander-in-Chief; though tempted, Brooke felt that he could not leave his present post as CIGS. He then suggested Alexander to Churchill. The Prime Minister was increasingly enamoured of Alexander, whom he regarded as his aristocratic beau ideal of a general – a twentieth-century Marlborough with scruples.

Brooke's ambivalence towards Alexander had hardly diminished since Bumper. Though recognizing that Alexander had a gift for making divergent personalities work together harmoniously, when he had earlier considered Alexander for the post of C-in-C, he dismissed the idea because he 'has not got the brains'. Yet after the propitious death of the original Eighth Army Commander designate, 'Strafer' Gott, in an air crash, and Montgomery was sent out to take command, Brooke was satisfied that Alexander would give Montgomery his head, carry trust and smooth troubled waters. Always inclined to criticize Alexander whatever he did, within a year Brooke was complaining that he was not 'gripping' Montgomery sufficiently.[12]

Alexander's appointment as C-in-C Middle East was the first stage in a reordering of the command relationships in North Africa, which had become blurred and confused under Auchinleck's tenure. Alexander administered to the sprawling bureaucratic jungle of GHQ Cairo a revitalization equal to that given to Eighth Army by Montgomery, making it more responsive to the needs of the army in the field. He oversaw a vast area stretching from the frontiers of Kenya to Afghanistan. He was the ultimate authority. Montgomery should concern himself with the defeat of Rommel's army. The policy would be *agreed*, and Montgomery would be its executive instrument, responsible for battlefield planning; Alexander was responsible for the overall strategy. His main priority at the beginning of the campaign was protecting Montgomery from excessive political interference, which he did skilfully. The transfer of Auchinleck was largely prompted by political reasons and Churchill's exasperation that Auchinleck refused to mount a counteroffensive before September. Ironically the new men, free from the stigma of defeat, claimed that an offensive could not be mounted until October. Alexander diverted the stream of Churchillian thunderbolts onto himself and away from Montgomery. The Second Battle of El Alamein did not open until 23/24 October 1942, and victory was not clear until 4 November. Montgomery's behaviour during this period was self-confident and high-handed, and such a showman inevitably overshadowed his C-in-C, who was a diffident and poor speaker and disliked self-advertisement. But a study of Alexander's correspondence reveals that Alexander was not reluctant to exert his authority as C-in-C; as far as he was concerned, Montgomery could be as bombastic as he liked, so long as he was successful. Alexander carried the primary responsibility.[13]

Alexander and Montgomery were complementary: the one charming, calm and phlegmatic; the other dynamic, arrogant and abrasive. Alexander was not merely Montgomery's rubber stamp. Nowhere is this more clearly seen than in his dealings with Major-General A.H. Gatehouse and Lieutenant-General H. Lumsden, both dismissed by Montgomery during Alamein. Of the former, Alexander wrote to Brooke that 'I think he is a borderline case. There is no doubt that he is slow and stupid.' Alexander went on:

Against this he has had more experience of actually fighting armour than anyone else. He has the confidence of his subordinates. He handles artillery well. His battle technique is to manoeuvre and win his battles by standing back and knocking out the enemy by his gunfire. He is not a thruster.

This was a fairer assessment of Gatehouse's ability than Montgomery's brusque 'useless'.[14]

Alexander's natural diplomatic flair had served all well during the Alamein campaign, not least himself. He had resisted the strong temptation to interfere in the conduct of the battle. Montgomery had been given his head and advanced prudently towards Tripoli. The 'tide' of the Desert War had finally turned. In January 1943 Roosevelt, Churchill and the Combined Chiefs of Staff (CCS) met at the Casablanca Conference. Alexander was appointed Ground Forces Commander in North Africa, and in February, Commander 18th Army Group and Deputy to the Supreme Commander, Eisenhower. While Montgomery advanced to Tunisia, the forces which had been landed in Algeria, the First Army, commanded by Lieutenant-General Sir Kenneth Anderson, had advanced from the west, and run into difficulties. 'I am afraid you have taken over a parcel of troubles!' wrote Brooke. 'I am very glad to feel that you are there to take a grip of things.' The CIGS did not exaggerate. The mountains of Tunisia presented a tactical problem quite different from the Western Desert – of a type that Alexander had not encountered since his days on the North West Frontier. The problem was complicated because the Americans disliked the aloof, dour Anderson. Of affairs in Tunisia, Alexander wrote to Brooke:

I am frankly shocked at what I have found here – no plan, no policy, no proper direction but complete disorganization. I cannot blame Anderson entirely for this ... but I do think he has been slow in getting things going ... such a job is beyond his ceiling ... I only ask for a little time and average luck, and they will soon get things ship shape here.

Alexander added: 'Eisenhower is such a nice chap and could not be more frank, friendly and helpful.' The two men had first met the previous summer and had immediately struck a sympathetic chord. To be acceptable to the Americans and show a willingness to understand their problems was an enormous asset to Alexander: but were the Americans acceptable to him?[15]

On 14 February Rommel routed the American II Corps in Kasserine Pass. Inspecting the front, Alexander was shocked by what he found. His worst suspicions were confirmed. The American troops, he wrote, were 'very shell and bomb conscious ... [their] training too defensive'; in the attack 'There is a great lack of urgency amongst all ranks and ... the value of surprise has been thrown away. It is NOT appreciated that if the first attack fails the next attempt will be more difficult. . . .' In a very long letter to Brooke, he confided that 'Unless we can do something about it, the American Army in the European theatre of operations will be quite useless and play no useful part whatsoever.' According to Alexander, the US II Corps was bereft of basic tactical skills: 'In fact, they are soft, green and quite untrained. It is surprising them that they lack the will to fight and I am afraid as a generalisation this is true.' After Rommel withdrew from Kasserine, Alexander averred, 'I took infinite pains to lay on for them what should have been a first class show in the Gafsa-Maknassy area ... I handed them a victory on a plate, but their hands were too weak to take it.' As for the American generals, Eisenhower, his chief of staff, Bedell Smith, and Patton, the new commander of II Corps, 'they are not professional soldiers, not as we understand that term'. But Alexander was too much of a gentleman to descend into crude anti-Americanism, and his political sense reasserted itself:

We must tread very warily – if they think we are sneering at them – and God forbid that – or that we are being superior, they will take it very badly, as they are a proud people. We must take the line that we are comrades and brothers in arms, and our only wish is for them to share the horrors of war (and the handicaps) and reap the fruits of victory together.

This basic insight was to fertilize Alexander's career and harvest great triumphs; but for the moment, the earlier doubts remained.[16]

Whereas Montgomery and Anderson were given a wide latitude in developing operational plans, Patton was required to submit all tactical decisions to 18th Army Group HQ for consideration. Alexander's main concern was to get Eighth Army north of the Gabes Gap and through the Mareth Line. This would bring the two armies together and give the opportunity of mounting a two-fisted offensive. Alexander had for some time been attracted by an analogy popularized by Major-General J.F.C. Fuller in the interwar years, of the boxer, feinting with one fist, striking with another. This permitted a more flexible mode of operations to develop than was permissible with Montgomery's 'master plan' which emphasized a single punch.

> In this region we must seize the various dominating ridges and gateways in the mountains which give on to the plains before our armour can be usefully employed for the decisive stage. ... We now hold the initiative and I intend to keep it – punching here and there. ... [the enemy] is now ... hurrying reserves from this place to that plugging holes.

The enemy was to be worn down, distracted and then annihilated. This was to be the object of Operation Vulcan – the drive to Tunis. Montgomery attacked at Enfidaville, and though supposed to feint, vanity and conceit persuaded him to transform his attack into a breakthrough attempt; this was repulsed. Alexander drove to Montgomery's HQ and decided that elements of Eighth Army should be used to reinforce the centre of First Army. On 6 May Operation Strike was launched by a massive artillery bombardment down the Medjerda Valley, and within twenty-four hours Tunis and Bizerta had fallen. The victory was entirely Alexander's, yet he remained as modest and as unaffected as ever. The sense of triumph only surfaced in his noble signal to the Prime Minister: 'Sir, it is my duty to report that the Tunisian campaign is over. All enemy resistance has ceased. We are masters of the North African shores.'[17]

Amid the drama of the final stages of the North African campaign, Alexander's attention was already distracted by the initial planning for Operation Husky – the invasion of Sicily called for by the CCS at Casablanca. His conduct of this campaign has recently been criticized for a lack of 'grip'. As Alexander had exercised 'grip' in his earlier campaigns, this accusation requires careful analysis, as it also reflects on Alexander's methods and his conduct of greater operations in Italy. Alexander complained even before the Sicilian campaign was over that 'It was quite impossible for me to give the necessary attention to Husky planning – I was hundreds of miles away at the front and far too busy to come back to Algiers or to really give the required thought to such a complicated affair.' Nonetheless, Alexander was optimistic. 'We have two grand armies and lots of good young commanders.' Perhaps it was Alexander's own methods that were at fault. In his diary, the British Resident Minister in North Africa, Harold Macmillan, gave a vivid description of Alexander's HQ. 'The whole atmosphere of the camp', he wrote, 'is dominated by his personality – modest, calm, confident.' 'Shop' was largely ignored.

The conversation is the usual tone of educated ... Englishman ... – a little history, a little politics, a little banter, a little philosophy – all very lightly touched and very agreeable. ... Very occasionally an officer comes in with a message. ... After pausing sufficiently for politeness the conversation ... – the campaign of Belisarius, or the advantages of classical over Gothic architecture, or the right way to drive pheasants in flat country ... [continues] – General Alex will ask permission to open his message – read it – put into his pocket – continue the original discussion for a few more minutes and then ... unobtrusively retire, as a man may leave his smoking room or library after the ladies have gone to bed, to say a word to his butler, fetch a pipe, or the like.

'I have never enjoyed so much', Macmillan added, 'the English capacity for restraint and understatement.' Nothing could be further from the atmosphere of Montgomery's forward HQ with its intense air of monastic dedication. Alexander was perhaps the last of the great British amateur generals: though a resourceful commander, able to tackle any problems sent his way – the true 'all-rounder' – warfare was for Alexander a tiresome distraction from better things. As Macmillan observed on a later drive with him, 'he likes to talk of other things – politics, ancient art (especially Roman antiquities), country life. He hates war.' As a gentleman rather reminiscent of Robert E. Lee in his command methods, Alexander preferred to make suggestions rather than give orders. Macmillan thought them 'most effective. These are put forward with modesty and simplicity. But they are always so clear and lucid that they carry conviction.'[18]

Alexander's style could be misinterpreted. 'He agrees, as he always does when I suggest something to him', Montgomery observed in 1943. A strong-minded, almost dictatorial commander like Montgomery could misunderstand Alexander's self-effacing methods as evidence that he lacked ideas of his own. Indeed for Brooke and Montgomery it was not so much economy of force that characterized Alexander's campaigns, as economy of mental effort. The Sicilian campaign does not show Alexander's methods at their best. It reveals irresolution compounded by prejudice. After his eclipse in Tunisia, Montgomery felt impelled to assert himself, and rejected the original Husky plan which had projected twin landings by US Seventh Army at Palermo and by the Eighth Army at Catania. This operation, Montgomery wrote, 'breaks every common-sense rule of practical battle fighting and is completely theoretical'.

He also took the view that Alexander 'Must use experienced troops to [the] utmost extent'. Here Montgomery played on Alexander's doubts about the Americans. Distracted by other concerns, he agreed with Montgomery that the two armies should land in a mutually supporting operation, with Seventh US Army restricted to supporting the flank of the Eighth Army. The main thrust, advancing north to Messina, was reserved for the British.

Alexander's position was anomalous. The Supreme Commander, Eisenhower, had not stamped his authority on the planning process, and as his Deputy and Commander 15th Army Group, Alexander lacked authority over the naval and air C-in-Cs, Cunningham and Tedder, with whom he had to 'coordinate' plans. The landings were successful, but Montgomery was held up in the mountains above Catania. Patton, determined to demonstrate the fighting qualities of his troops, secured Alexander's permission to advance on Palermo, and then drove on Messina, arriving a few hours before Montgomery. As Nigel Hamilton has pointed out, Patton's advance in pursuit of geographical objectives was a distraction from the decisive point, and permitting such a divergence was typical of Alexander's indolent methods. This campaign 'now ushered into Allied operations a political principle that committed the Allies to failure upon failure', as no commander had either the tact or military genius to command the coalition armies in the field and reconcile their national rivalries. The conquest of Sicily had been incomplete. The Germans had escaped; Alexander could have prevented this had he stopped Patton from moving on Palermo. Yet Alexander had to respond to political requirements and the overall demands of Allied unity, as he was to do again. This required above all that the assuaging of public (especially American) opinion, the reassurance of political leaders, and the soothing of commanders' egos, should take precedence over the technical demands of the military art. Hamilton's comment seems to imply that the Allies were defeated rather than victorious. The Anglo-American alliance demanded a series of modest and uninterrupted successes rather than spectacular victories pregnant with disruption. These Alexander, a modest general, in both character and attainments, was well equipped to provide.[19]

Sicily was succeeded rapidly by the invasion of mainland Italy. Two amphibious operations were mounted, Baytown by Eighth Army, which was virtually unopposed, and Avalanche, which hurled Alexander into another crisis. Modern critics condemn the Avalanche plan as thoroughly unsatisfactory, as indeed it was. Alexander accepted the plan because the time factor forced him to accept a bad plan rather than have no plan at all. Italy had to be invaded at the earliest possible moment before the Germans could overrun the country. That the Allies failed to gain this objective was through no fault of Alexander. As ever, he willingly subjected himself to the tyranny of political requirements. Nevertheless, he could not do the impossible. Amphibious landings are the most complex in the military canon. Yet in the Mediterranean theatre they had to be improvised hastily to seize unexpected opportunities. Alexander could not resolve this contradiction.

The landings at Salerno by Lieutenant-General Mark Clark's Fifth Army were hardly models of the planner's art: secrecy had been compromised, there had been no preliminary bombardment, the Allied forces were unnecessarily dispersed and in his corps commander, Ernest J. Dawley, Clark hardly had an inspiring figure. The Allies were almost driven back into the sea. Alexander, who had weathered the typhoons of Dunkirk and Rangoon, rose to the occasion; he was always at his best in a crisis. Visiting the beachhead he was impressed by Clark but appalled by Dawley. Turning to the inexperienced Clark, he said quietly, 'I do not want to interfere with your business, but I have some ten years' experience in this game of sizing up commanders. I can tell you definitely that you have a broken reed on your hands and I suggest you replace him immediately.' Alexander elevated suggestion to a high military art, but some of his commanders, not least Clark, sometimes failed to respond in the spirit in which they were offered. To Churchill, he reported some of the common-sense suggestions which he had proffered Clark: 'Hold what we have gained at all costs consolidating key positions by digging-in. ... Reorganize scattered and mixed units. Form local reserves and a strong mobile reserve as possible.' With such a firm rock to lean on, the Allies could stick it out, and shortly Clark would not only consolidate but by October occupy Naples.[20]

Later that month Churchill telegraphed to Alexander: 'I have studied the plan you have sent home and note that you have already accomplished the first and second phase of it. I hope the third phase will be accomplished by the end of the month ... and that we shall meet in Rome.' The accomplishment of this phase was to be greatly troubled. Field-Marshal Albert Kesselring, following Hitler's orders, constructed a defensive line from Gaeta to Ortona – the Gustav Line – in order to hold the Allies south of Rome. On the Allied side, the operation was transformed from a lightning campaign to seize opportunities into a protracted campaign designed to distract the greatest number of German divisions before Overlord. In such difficult mountainous terrain, dissected by lateral river lines – as Graham and Bidwell point out, surely the worst the British Army had fought over since Wellington crossed the *Tras os Montes* in 1813 and Roberts set off from Kabul to Kandahar – the war in Italy inevitably became a battle of attrition. Alexander's problem was compounded by a numerical deficiency: 18 Allied divisions to 23 German. Furthermore, at Tehran the Allies agreed that Operation Anvil, the invasion of southern France, should be nourished by forces already based in the Mediterranean. By Overlord it was hoped that Rome would have fallen, with Alexander's armies advancing as far as the line Pisa–Rimini. The Italian campaign, however, could not be fought according to timetable.[21]

On returning from Tehran in December 1943, Brooke visited the Italian front, and was depressed by what he saw. 'Alex fails to grip the show', he wrote, but as the strategic aim of the campaign was continually being altered there was little of substance that could be gripped. A more serious source of weakness was that Alexander lacked a properly organized HQ; his improvised tactical HQ was not sufficient to control two international armies. At the end of the year General Sir Henry Maitland Wilson was appointed Supreme Commander Mediterranean, Alexander was relieved of the post of Deputy and given the title of Commander of the Allied Group of Armies in Italy (AAI). On New Year's Day 1944 John Harding arrived as his new Chief of Staff. Harding had the kind of cool and penetrating intellect that Alexander lacked; the two were complementary and formed a potent partnership. But his insistence on 'gripping' problems rather than letting sleeping dogs lie, as was Alexander's inclination, was apt to stir up more problems than it resolved.[22]

On Christmas Day 1943 Alexander accepted somewhat reluctantly yet another scheme for an opportunistic amphibious landing – Operation Shingle, a landing of two divisions at Anzio. They could turn Kesselring's long and vulnerable flank up the 'thigh' of Italy. Alexander, the metaphorical boxer, was preparing to knock his opponent off balance. 'The only method of progress is to concentrate on each dominating position in turn and so the advance will go slowly step by step', he assured the CIGS. Alexander was convinced that the longer the Germans remained south of Rome, the greater ultimately would be the defeat that could be inflicted upon them. He would batter his way through the Gustav Line, drawing in as many German divisions as possible, so that a complete collapse could only be avoided by transferring yet more divisions from France. If the US VI Corps advanced audaciously from Anzio into the German rear, Kesselring's entire army could be destroyed. But the risk was great. US VI Corps only fielded two divisions. Churchill was also concerned to ensure 'equality of hazard and sacrifice between British and American troops' under the new British-dominated command system. 'I do not like the idea that the first and most risky operation in the Mediterranean under British Command should fall exclusively on American troops.' Though Alexander was content that 'This is pretty well fifty fifty', he failed to make his intentions clear to his American subordinates. Clark virtually undercut his design by telling Lucas, VI Corps commander, to act cautiously on landing at Anzio.[23]

The assault on the Gustav Line resulted in the Three Battles of Cassino, astride the Liri Valley, which were an ordeal for the troops, as they resembled the battles of attrition of the First World War. The monastery at Monte Cassino came to assume symbolic importance – of German resolve and defensive skill. The 'maximum use of artillery to cover every small attack has avoided exceptionally heavy casualties', Alexander informed the CIGS. By Third Cassino 1,060 guns were supplemented by medium and heavy bombers. This emphasis on firepower was to a large degree self-defeating. The greater the firepower deployed, the greater was the destruction of the terrain, and thus the more mobility was impaired. The operational design was turned on its head. Instead of US VI Corps seizing the Alban Hills, forcing Kesselring to loosen his grip on the Gustav Line, and trapping them in an envelopment as Fifth Army advanced up the Liri Valley towards Rome, Alexander now had to mount a costly offensive to ease pressure on the beleaguered Anzio beachhead. The Third Battle of Cassino ended with the destruction of the monastery and the neighbouring communications, but failed to capture the high ground. Despite 4,000 casualties for little gain, Maitland Wilson urged that the offensive continue. Alexander, remembering the ghastly winters of 1916 and 1917, ordered a cessation; he would wait for better weather.[24]

These battles form the prelude to Alexander's greatest triumph – Operation Diadem, culminating in the fall of Rome. This campaign was the most mature example of Alexander's two-handed punch. It aimed at nothing less than the complete destruction of the German Tenth Army south of Rome. After Third Cassino Alexander and Harding took stock. 'We have had a hard and trying time since I last saw you', Alexander informed Brooke, 'we were a bit rushed into the Anzio landing

– it was put on in 3 weeks, no time to get out a good Corps Commander and Staff, like Dick McCreery. I had to be content with Lucas ... – he proved to be an old woman.' Amphibious operations, he argued, had to be tailored to the strategic aim. His experience had been the opposite: 'here is so much craft – now make the best of it'. The entire strategic concept had to be revitalized.

I am regrouping the whole of our forces. The main reason is I want Oliver [Leese] to lay on, stage, mount and run the break into and I hope – through Minouri in the Liri Valley. Between ourselves, Clark and his Army HQ are not up to it, it's too big for them.

Alexander's suspicion of American military capacities had resurfaced after Shingle, though he gave no hint of it during his dealings with Clark. 'Have been all round the front with Alex', Clark wrote, 'and he seemed greatly pleased and very flattering in his remarks on the Fifth Army.' Alexander, it seems, was not incapable of dissimulation.[25]

Diadem opened on 11 May 1944. A greatly strengthened Eighth Army smashed through the centre of the Gustav Line and in an 'end-run' overran the Hitler Line that lay behind it. The pivot, or 'left hook', was to be US II Corps, which was to envelop the enemy's left flank, advance on the town of Valmontone, south-east of Rome in the enemy's rear, and block his retreat. This seemed certain once the US VI Corps had broken out of the Anzio bridgehead and advanced towards the Alban Hills on 23–26 May. Alexander always assumed that if a plan could go wrong, then it would; this expectation was to be confirmed during Diadem. The root of the matter was quite simply that the Allied Armies in Italy were structurally incapable of fulfilling a strategic design as ambitious as that set down by Alexander. His international force was riddled by jealousy, suspicion and intrigue. The two-handed-punch concept demanded the intimate co-operation of his two Army commanders, Clark and Leese, both vain prima donnas. Alexander's combination of tact and diplomacy eased these tensions under circumstances in which Montgomery's firmer methods might have been a recipe for disaster. But he still tended to give Leese the benefit of the doubt. Clark's jealousy, therefore, was not completely without justification.

Clark was obsessed by two things: seizing Rome before Eighth Army and before Overlord. Behind his charming, facile and superficially accommodating exterior lurked a rampant Anglophobia. 'I feel there is some inclination on the part of Alexander to commence alibiing for his Eighth Army', Clark confided to his diary. 'Alexander is worried that I have sabotaged his directive to attack Valmontone. I have not done so.' In fact Clark had: his sabotage lay not so much in his later claims that there were too many roads in the Valmontone area, or that US II Corps was too weak to carry out a large-scale envelopment, and hence that his concentration towards Rome was justified, for these claims are not without foundation; his error lay in a fundamental misunderstanding. Clark supposed that the object of battle was not the destruction of the enemy's army but the seizure of geographical objectives. This appears to be a major weakness of several American commanders in the Second World War. All Clark's thoughts were concentrated on the glory of seizing Rome, and no doubt the greater glory of Mark Clark. Valmontone was not occupied until after rather than before the fall of Rome. Diadem may be added to the ignoble catalogue of Allied victories which failed to bring the battle of annihilation to a final climax with a crushing and decisive encirclement, followed by a devastating pursuit. If the tables had been turned it is difficult to imagine the *Wehrmacht* (or the Red Army) permitting the enemy to escape.[26]

The failure of Diadem to annihilate the German Tenth Army could be put down to weaknesses inherent in Alexander's consultative style of command, in which major differences were tacitly swept under the carpet. It might have been better for all concerned if Mark Clark had publicly declared his hand so that Alexander knew where he stood, rather than merely confided his frustrations to a diary; Alexander's habitual courtesy made such confrontations virtually impossible In his *Cyropaedia*, Xenophon described Proxenus the Boeotian, 'a good commander for people of a gentlemanly type', who 'imagined that to be a good general ... it was enough to give praise to those who did well and to withhold it from those who did badly'. Alexander fitted this pattern exactly. But those who demanded more 'grip', like Brooke, tended to underestimate his difficulties, and the impossibility of commanding an international force like an extension of the British Territorial Army. As always, Alexander had to make the best of a bad job. As General Jackson observes, 'He was too experienced to be ruffled by misfortune.' A photograph was taken of Alexander on 7 June, three days after the fall of Rome. He stands by the roadside, determined, hands on hips, elegant, poised, his eyes focused on the distant horizon, thoughts revolving with some exasperation, like a latter-day Robert E. Lee, around the problem of how to bring the enemy to battle once more; for though he won victories, the destruction of the enemy eluded him.[27]

Concentrating his thoughts on how to defeat the enemy north of Rome, Alexander faced an additional problem. The ghost of Anvil, now rechristened Dragoon, returned to haunt him. Earlier efforts to exorcise the ghost – such as Harding's recommendation that it be abolished – had only stirred up the murky demons of Anglo-American suspicion. As an alternative to Anvil/Dragoon Alexander, in a paper drafted by Harding, argued that the Germans would be forced to reinforce their armies in Italy if AAI bounced through the Gothic Line, Kesselring's new defensive position, seized Bologna and drove towards Vienna through the Ljubljana Gap. The CCS were not persuaded; instead he lost a US Corps and the Free French Corps. 'It seems to me that it would be criminal to throw away such a wonderful opportunity of bringing off a really great coup', Alexander wrote. As for his armies, 'the whole forms one closely articulated machine capable of carrying out assault and rapid exploitation in the most difficult terrain. Neither the Apennines nor even the Alps should prove a serious obstacle to their enthusiasm and their skill.' Here Alexander could be forgiven some pardonable exaggeration, but he rather glossed over the formidable topographical problems facing AAI, which would worsen as it advanced northwards. The plan was too ambitious and could the more easily be dismissed by the Americans as impracticable. As Alexander wrote to Brooke, his armies had been 'torn to pieces by the demands for Dragoon. ... Everyone was sympathetic and helpful and I returned to Italy with hopes – I won't say with high hopes.' These hopes were not to be fulfilled in his next major offensive.[28]

In September 1944 Alexander launched Operation Olive. He did not outnumber the enemy, still fielding 18 divisions against 23 German. Leese planned a concentrated blow without the co-operation of Clark, whom he disliked. Clark complained that Alexander was deliberately letting German reserves build up on the Fifth Army front, to smooth the path for Eighth Army's advance. The contrary was true. Alexander saw one more opportunity for a double envelopment before winter closed in. By drawing the German reserves against the Eighth Army, Fifth Army would be permitted to strike against Bologna from the west. By the end of September, Leese had broken through the Gothic Line, but the rain-drenched valleys were as unsuitable for armoured warfare as the mountains, and both armies plunged into a muddy quagmire, exhausted before they could reach Bologna. Once more Alexander would wait for the spring

The autumn of 1944 brought Alexander a field-marshal's baton for his victories in Diadem, and in November he was promoted Supreme Commander Mediterranean, to replace Maitland Wilson who was sent to Washington to head the British Military Mission. Clark succeeded Alexander in the now restored 15th Army Group. Within a month Alexander dispatched a long 'Memorandum on the Command and Staff Organization in the Mediterranean Theatre of Operations', arguing that to bring the enemy to battle on ground on which he must stand and fight, was dependent on mobility and economy of force. To achieve this, the Mediterranean theatre must be expanded beyond Italy to embrace Austria and Yugoslavia. To continue to engage the enemy along a series of short river lines would be to fight him at a disadvantage.

If we provide ourselves with the means to engage the enemy anywhere on a front extended from the Dravina through Istria to the Adige line and thence across the Alps to the Swiss frontier, the economy of force which the enemy can effect by withdrawing to the Adige will be counteracted and our mobility will again have full scope.

Alexander, distant from London, had miscalculated the prevailing mood in the Anglo-American alliance, and failed to grasp what Brooke had already appreciated, namely that Churchill's support for such a grand design was almost a *sine qua non* of a plan's rejection. Moreover, Brooke resented this unwelcome intrusion into the planning process; he regarded it as a red rag to the American bull which would render all efforts at changing Eisenhower's 'broad front' advance into Germany the more difficult.[29]

The finale of Alexander's military career was prefaced by a short prelude in Athens. The crisis in Greece at the end of 1944 was relished by Alexander, jumping in and out of tanks, snipers' bullets flying in the streets, urgent decisions required on the spot – he was in his element. Tightening the British grip in Athens ensured that whatever happened in Eastern Europe in lieu of an advance on Vienna, Greece would not be counted in the Communist camp.

The most acute student of Alexander's campaigns, General Jackson, considers the spring offensive of 1945 a 'masterpiece'. When Brooke visited Italy en route to Moscow in December 1944 he was pessimistic. 'Alex is getting stuck in the Apennines with tired forces and cannot spare any for amphibious operations. ... It is therefore hard to estimate what the situation will be when Alex can find forces, namely in February.' After the Yalta Conference he was instructed to exert pressure but seize any opportunities that presented themselves. Alexander responded, despite these difficulties, with the complete military victory that had eluded him the year before. The plan was initiated by a deception scheme that persuaded von Vietinghoff, who had succeeded Kesselring, to move his reserves to the Adriatic coast to throw back into the sea an amphibious landing which Alexander lacked the forces to launch. By thinning the westerly end of the line, Fifth Army would strike west of Bologna, while Eighth Army would smash through the Argenta Gap. The victory was completed south of the Po – the Fifth and Eighth Armies joining hands at a town called Finale. An armistice was agreed with the defeated German forces commencing 2 May 1945.[30]

Though the Second World War was over, Alexander's career was not. Asked by Churchill to assume the responsibilities of Governor-General of Canada, he later entered the political arena in 1952 as Minister of Defence, finally retiring to his brushes and easel in 1954. Though the most noble in character of Churchill's generals – selfless, diffident, he cared nothing for praise – he was also the most enigmatic. He had none of Montgomery's iron dedication to the profession of arms, Slim's intellect, or Auchinleck's instinctive grasp of the ebb and flow of battle. Yet he rose to the pinnacle of his profession, and would have been CIGS, if Churchill had not persuaded him to go to Ottawa instead. Liddell Hart once wrote perceptively that 'Alexander was a born leader, not a made one. He won men's confidence at first sight. He was "good looking" in every sense, yet self-effacing to the point of handicapping his own powers.' Not subscribing to the view that Alexander lacked brains, Liddell Hart believed that Alexander, though highly intelligent with an open mind, was fundamentally a lazy general: 'success came so quickly and continuously that there was no compelling pressure to set him to the grindstone of hard application'; despite his eminence 'he might have been a greater commander if he had not been so nice a man, and so deeply a gentleman'.[31]

The final verdict on Alexander's generalship was that he was not a great soldier, though he was a strategist of some insight. Alexander was not a great diplomat, though he had a remarkable facility for making divergent and powerful personalities work together. Alexander was not a great battlefield commander, though he never lost a battle. Alexander could never be said to be a master of detail, nor a managerial wizard, though his armies operated over the most difficult terrain encountered in the European theatre of operations, and yet they were universally regarded as well administered. Like another successful commander considered unintelligent by several critics, George Washington, the whole of Alexander's talents were greater than the sum of their parts. Judged by the demanding standards of his Edwardian ideals, the career of Alexander was a very great success.

NOTES

The author is grateful to the Trustees of the Liddell Hart Centre for Military Archives, King's College, London, for permission to quote from copyright material in their possession.

1 Harold Nicolson, *The English Sense of Humour and Other Essays* (London: Constable, 1956), p. 44.

2 Nigel Nicolson, *Alex: The Life of Field Marshal Earl Alexander of Tunis* (London: Weidenfeld and Nicolson, 1973), pp. 15–22; Norman Hillson, *Alexander of Tunis* (London: W.H. Allen, 1952), pp. 10–14.

3 On the British Army's attitude to the intellect, see Brian Holden Reid, *J.F.C. Fuller: Military Thinker* (London: Macmillan, 1987), p. 82; H. Nicolson, *The English Sense of Humour*, p. 33.

4 Rudyard Kipling, *Irish Guards in the Great War* (London: Macmillan, 1923), II, p. 13.

5 Ibid., II, p. 215.

6 Ibid., II, p. 117n1: W.G.F. Jackson, *Alexander of Tunis as Military Commander* (London: Batsford, 1971), pp. 59, 64; Alexander to Liddell Hart, 2 July 1957, Liddell Hart Papers 1/7/30.

7 David Fraser, *Alanbrooke* (London: Collins, 1982), p. 162; Nigel Hamilton, *Monty*, I, *The Making of a General, 1887–1942* (London: Hamish Hamilton, 1981), p. 583 (this quotation is reported in an interview with Lieutenant-General Sir Ian Jacob); Jackson, *Alexander of Tunis as Military Commander*, pp. 71, 72, 88. If Montgomery had such a low opinion of Alexander, it was rather odd that he found it most valuable to take a number of students from the Staff College, Quetta, to study his methods in this campaign on the ground.

8 N. Nicolson, *Alex*, pp. 104–14; Jackson, *Alexander of Tunis as Military Commander*, pp. 103, 105–9; Hamilton, *Monty*, I, pp. 389–90; Montgomery of Alamein, *Memoirs* (London: Collins, 1958), p. 64.

9 John North (ed.), *The Alexander Memoirs 1940–45* (London: Cassell, 1962), pp. 75–81; N. Nicolson, *Alex*, p. 23; Jackson, *Alexander of Tunis as Military Commander*, pp. 113, 118–19; Arthur Bryant, *The Turn of the Tide* (London: Collins, 1957), p. 257; Field-Marshal Viscount Slim, *Defeat into Victory* (London: Papermac, 1986 edn), pp. 14–15.

10 Ibid., p. 55; Jackson, *Alexander of Tunis as Military Commander*, p. 123.

11 Ibid., pp. 137–40.

12 Fraser, *Alanbrooke*, pp. 271–2, 285–6, 347.

13 N. Nicolson, *Alex*, pp. 153, 155, 157, 160–6.

14 Alexander to CIGS, 10 Dec. 1942, Alanbrooke Papers 14/63.

15 CIGS to Alexander, 20 Feb. 1943; Alexander to CIGS, 27 Feb. 1943, ibid., 14/63.

16 Notes on Recent Operations of US II Corps, 3 Apr. 1943; Alexander to CIGS, 3 Apr. 1943, ibid., 14/63; Fraser, *Alanbrooke*, p. 315.

17 Brian Holden Reid, 'J.F.C. Fuller's Theory of Mechanized Warfare', *The Journal of Strategic Studies*, I (1978), p. 296; Jackson, *Alexander of Tunis as Military Commander*, pp. 95, 204; Alexander to CIGS, 20 Mar. 1943, Alanbrooke Papers 14/63; Hamilton, *Monty*, II, *Master of the Battlefield* (London: Hamish Hamilton, 1983), pp. 237–41.

18 Alexander to CIGS, 19 May 1943, Alanbrooke Papers 14/63; Harold Macmillan, *War Diaries: The Mediterranean, 1943–1945* (London: Macmillan, 1984), pp. 47, 154, 374 (entries for 21 Mar., 18 July 1943, 29 Jan. 1944).

19 Montgomery to Alexander, 13 Mar., 7 Apr. 1943, Alexander Papers PRO WO214/20; N. Nicolson, *Alex*, pp. 195–8; Jackson, *Alexander of Tunis as Military Commander*, pp. 211–18; Hamilton, *Master of the Battlefield*, p. 270.

20 Dominick Graham and Shelford Bidwell, *Tug of War: The Battle for Italy, 1943–45* (London: Jonathan Cape, 1986), p. 139; Alexander to Prime Minister, 16 Sept. 1943, Alexander Papers PRO WO214/20.

21 Prime Minister to Alexander, 2 Oct. 1943, ibid., PRO WO214/13; Graham and Bidwell, *Tug of War*, p. 109.

22 Fraser, *Alanbrooke*, p. 394; Michael Carver, *Harding of Petherton* (London: Weidenfeld and Nicolson, 1978), pp. 121, 123; N. Nicolson, *Alex*, p. 242.

23 Jackson, *Alexander of Tunis as Military Commander*, pp. 259–60; Alexander to CIGS, 23 Oct. 1943, Alexander Papers PRO WO214/13; Carver, *Harding*, p. 125.

24 Alexander to CIGS, 25 Sept. 1943, Alexander Papers, PRO WO214/13; Carver, *Harding*, p. 133.

25 Alexander to CIGS, 22 Mar. 1944, Alanbrooke Papers 14/65; Martin Blumenson, *Mark Clark* (London: Cape, 1985), p. 210.

26 Jackson, *Alexander of Tunis as Military Commander*, pp. 287–92; Graham and Bidwell, *Tug of War*, pp. 335–40, who emphasize other opportunities for encirclement; Blumenson, *Clark*, p. 211; N. Nicolson, *Alex*, pp. 248–54, based on interviews with Clark, tends to give him the benefit of the doubt.

27 Xenophon, *The Persian Expedition* (Harmondsworth: Penguin, 1949), II, 6, pp. 91–2; Jackson, *Alexander of Tunis as Military Commander*, p. 282.

28 Alexander to CIGS, 8 June 1944; Alexander to Maitland Wilson, 13 June 1944, Alexander Papers PRO WO214/15; Alexander to CIGS, 21 Sept. 1944, Alanbrooke Papers 14/65.

29 Memorandum on the Command and Staff Organization in the Mediterranean Theatre of Operations, 1 Dec. 1944, Alanbrooke Papers 14/66; Jackson, *Alexander of Tunis as Military Commander*, pp. 305–9.

30 Fraser, *Alanbrooke*, pp. 469, 480.

31 Extracts from an article written by BHLH in June 1946, Liddell Hart Papers 1/7/54A.

CHRONOLOGY: HAROLD ALEXANDER

1891, December 10	Born in Chesterfield Gardens, Mayfair, London
1902	Sent to St Michael's, Westgate-on-Sea, preparatory school (Hawtrey's)
1906	Harrow
1910	Sandhurst
1911, September 23	Commissioned as Second Lieutenant, 1st Battalion Irish Guards
1914	Lieutenant
1914, September	Legion of Honour
1915, February	Captain
1915, August	Transferred 2nd Battalion Irish Guards
1915, September	Awarded Military Cross (MC)
1915, October	Temporary Command 1st Battalion Irish Guards
1916, September	Awarded Distinguished Service Order (DSO)
1917, October	Commander 2nd Battalion Irish Guards
1918, March	Temporary Command 4 Guards Brigade
1918, October	Command X Corps School
1919, March	Allied Relief Commission, Poland
1919, July	Commander Baltic Landeswehr
1922, May	Lieutenant-Colonel, commander 1st Battalion Irish Guards
1926	Staff College (Colonel; temporarily reduced to Major while student)
1927	Commander Regimental District Irish Guards
1930	Imperial Defence College
1931	Marries Lady Margaret Bingham, younger daughter of Earl of Lucan
1932	GSO1 Northern Command
1934, April	Brigadier Commanding Nowshera Brigade
1935	Loe Agra and Mohmand Campaigns
1938	Major-General Commanding 1st Division; ADC to King George VI
1939, May	1st Division sent to France
1940, May	Advance to Dyle; retreat to Dunkirk
1940, May 31	Commander I Corps and Dunkirk perimeter
1940, June 2	Final evacuation at Dunkirk
1940, December	Lieutenant-General; GOC-in-C Southern Command
1942, New Year	Knight Commander of the Order of the Bath (KCB)

1942, February	Commander, Army in Burma
1942, March	Evacuation of Burma
1942, May	Burma Army arrives in India
1942, July	GOC First Army
1942, August	Commander-in-Chief Middle East
1943, February	General; C-in-C 18th Army Group; Deputy Supreme Commander
1943, May	Fall of Tunis
1943, June	C-in-C 15th Army Group
1943, July	Invasion of Sicily; Governor of Sicily
1943, September	Operation Avalanche – Salerno
1944, January	Operation Shingle – Anzio
1944, January–March	Three Battles of Cassino
1944, May	Operation Diadem
1944, June	Fall of Rome; opposes Operation Anvil
1944, September	Operation Olive
1944, November	Field-Marshal; Supreme Allied Commander Mediterranean
1944, December	Visits Athens during Greek crisis
1945, April	Final offensive in Italy
1945, May	Unconditional surrender of German forces in Italy
1945, October	Hands over command in Italy
1946, New Year	Created Viscount Alexander of Tunis; Knight of the Garter
1946, April	Governor-General of Canada
1946, August	Colonel of the Irish Guards
1952, January	Created Earl Alexander of Tunis
1952, February	Minister of Defence
1954, October	Resigns from Cabinet
1957–65	Lieutenant of the County of London
1958	Order of Merit
1969, June	Dies

7

AUCHINLECK

Field-Marshal Sir Claude Auchinleck

PHILIP WARNER

Field-Marshal Sir Claude Auchinleck was one of the most capable generals of the Second World War but through a combination of misfortunes was unable to stay to the end at the operational centres where the ultimate accolades were to be won. Like his contemporary Wavell, he was faced with virtually impossible tasks and then, having failed to complete them to Churchill's satisfaction, he was moved out to what appeared to be a backwater appointment, that of Commander-in-Chief India. In the event, his presence in this post had a greater effect on the outcome of the war than is generally realized, for he mobilized the resources of the subcontinent with great skill, thus enabling India to send invaluable troops and supplies to several fronts. The final irony of his career was that he was required to preside over the partition of the country which he loved and was unable to slow down government policy sufficiently to prevent widespread bloodshed.

Surprisingly he never became embittered, even though his wife left him for a friend and colleague, he was childless, and he watched others receive the credit he had earned. A lesser man might have been consumed with envy or self-pity, the Auk, on the other hand, could have been the subject of Kipling's poem 'If', able to '... meet triumph and disaster/ And treat those two impostors just the same.'

Claude John Eyre Auchinleck was born in Aldershot on 21 June 1884, the eldest son of Colonel John Auchinleck R.A. His father died of pernicious anaemia when the boy was eight, and his mother was left to bring up four children with no other resources than an army pension of £90 per annum. However, army wives were used to coping with unexpected disasters in the course of their husbands' careers, and Mary Auchinleck faced her problems cheerfully and was soon supplementing her slender means by doing a little part-time nursing when the children were at school. The Auchinlecks were a closely knit family and these early struggles undoubtedly helped to create the stoic attitude which characterized Auchinleck in the future. He was devoted to his mother. Ironically, it was his fervent wish to give her a memorable holiday that caused him to take her to Hyères in the south of France for the first visit abroad he had been able to afford for her (although he was then in his mid-thirties), and this produced a meeting with his future wife and a marriage that was to end in disaster twenty-five years later.

As the son of a deceased officer, Auchinleck was eligible for a Foundation place at Wellington College, Berkshire, which he entered at the age of twelve. Foundationers had their fees reduced to £10 a year, but even that sum was a struggle for his mother to find. Conditions at home and at school were spartan and were even more so when he went to stay with his mother's relations in Ireland. This upbringing seems to have instilled in Auchinleck an indifference to personal comfort which was useful in his military career, but which irritated Churchill when he came to visit Auchinleck in Egypt many years later. Although not distinguished academically, Auchinleck did well at Wellington and was awarded the Derby Gift, a prize for industry and good conduct. The sum was approximately £50, a marvellous bounty for a boy who had never seen so much money. It proved very useful in the next stage of his career, for he had now passed into Sandhurst. By a further stroke of luck he had reached a high enough position in the entrance examination to be accepted for the Indian Army. Forty-five places had been allocated and Auchinleck took the forty-fifth. The number of places in the Indian Army fluctuated from year to year. When, a few years later, Montgomery tried for the Indian Army, there were only thirty-five places and his position in the order was thirty-sixth.

In India Auchinleck joined the 62nd Punjabis and soon showed a marked aptitude for learning local languages. His ability to converse fluently with his soldiers, and his understanding of their dialects, customs and religions helped to create a mutual respect. There were, of

course, many other Indian Army officers who acquired a close understanding of the customs and language of the soldiers under their command, but few made as great an impression as the charismatic
Auchinleck. It was said that he was never happier than when in a frontier
village talking and reminiscing with former soldiers of the Indian Army.
His early days on the frontier, where constant alertness and keen obser-
vation were essential for survival, also helped to develop an instinct
for sensing impending trouble. Up on the frontier, warfare large or
small was regarded as a way of life and a tribesman would take a shot
at someone he did not know, or even someone he did, without giving
much thought to the matter. The price of life, rather than the price
of peace, was eternal vigilance.

On the outbreak of the First World War in 1914, the Indian government
offered four divisions to Britain for service overseas. The first three
went to France, but the fourth, which contained Auchinleck's regiment,
was a reserve division which was not mobilized till 28 October. Although
it too was earmarked for France, it was diverted en route to be deployed
along the Suez Canal, ready for a possible Turkish invasion. The Turks,
who had entered the war on the side of Germany, were under the impression that if they entered Egypt the entire country would rise and over-
throw the British government. This ambition gave Auchinleck his first
experience of battle; it was in February 1915. He was now a captain
and, after his regiment had checked the Turkish attempt at crossing
the Canal, he led a counter-attack which captured the forward Turkish
trenches. The Turks surrendered and the battle was over. After some
further skirmishes in the region, the 62nd Punjabis were sent to Basra
as part of the 6th Indian Division. From Basra they were sent upstream
(the Tigris) and were soon involved in heavy fighting in appalling conditions. Continuous rain had turned the entire area into a sticky swamp
and the bitterly cold wind seemed as dangerous an enemy as the Turkish
machine-gunners. Nearly half the regiment became casualties. Auchinleck had now fought in mountains, on torrid plains, and in liquid mud.
In the future he would experience snow and desert sand. Subsequently,
when he became a general, he would know from first-hand experience
all the conditions in which his soldiers might have to fight, except jungle,
and he demonstrated later that he understood that also.

The Mesopotamia (Iraq) campaign has tended to be dismissed by
historians as a 'sideshow', not comparable with the great battles in
France. In terms of numbers this is true but for the individual soldier
with a bullet coming in his direction it makes no difference whether

he is part of a patrol or a D-Day size army. After a fierce battle in 1916, the 62nd Punjabis were down to 247 men and, as the commanding officer had been wounded, Auchinleck took his place. In the later stages of this campaign the 62nd saw plenty more fighting and was also tormented by the diseases and pests which affect armies in the field. Lice, bugs and fleas not only produce disease but they also disturb sleep and thus impair efficiency and judgement. Auchinleck had ample opportunity of observing the importance of rest, hygiene, medical supplies and good food for troops in the field, even though most of his deductions would be made from their absence, rather than their presence. He also learnt much about faulty tactics and the stupidity of sending infantry to charge machine-guns sited in well-positioned trenches. He resolved that if he reached high command himself he would avoid all pointless bravado attacks, knowing only too well that these are often ordered because a general can think of nothing better and is afraid that if he waits until a more promising opportunity occurs, he will be considered to be lacking in offensive spirit. Later, in the Western Desert, he showed moral courage in holding to his convictions even though urged by Churchill and others to take the offensive without adequate training, preparation and material. Unfortunately it cost him his command.

In the 1920s Auchinleck was a student at the Staff College at Quetta, held various staff appointments, attended the Imperial Defence College (now called the Royal College of Defence Studies), and commanded his battalion when it was stationed at Jhelum. In the early 1930s he was back at the Staff College at Quetta, now as an instructor and a full colonel. In 1933 he was given command of the Peshawar Brigade, which was engaged in quelling disturbances originating in Afghanistan. Subsequently the frontier was enlivened by the Mohmand operation of 1935, when tanks were used for the first time in India. Auchinleck received both the CSI and another mention in despatches for his skill in handling the Mohmand campaign.

After a period of leave, he was once again promoted, this time to become Deputy Chief of the General Staff, India. His new post took him away from the area where he could make his own simple, clear-cut decisions; in the future he would be dealing with committees and policy-makers, many of them having ideas widely differing from his own. Among this tasks were the modernization of the Indian Army and at the same time supervising its 'Indianization'. The latter meant replacing British officers by Indians; it was easy enough to get rid of the former but finding replacements for them of equal standards of training and experience was far more of a problem.

On the outbreak of war in 1939 Auchinleck was given command of 3rd Indian Division with the brief of preparing it for war. At that time few people in India regarded the war as a serious threat to their existence; even if it continued it would be confined to Europe, they believed. From this complacent atmosphere Auchinleck was relieved to be posted to England in January 1940; it was to take command of IV Corps and prepare it for taking up position in France around Lille in six months' time. In the event, six months later, the only British troops in France were prisoners of war.

IV Corps was a mixture of Regular and Territorial Army units, mostly untrained. Its component parts were scattered over Britain from Peebles-shire to Dorset. Travelling to visit the various parts of his command was made doubly difficult by weather which many described as 'the worst in living memory'. Nevertheless the Corps began to take shape and there were hopes that, by the time it reached France, it would be reasonably efficient. But on 9 April the Germans, who had a non-aggression treaty with Denmark, invaded that country, which capitulated within hours. On the same day, German forces seized Oslo, Stavanger, Bergen, Trondheim and Narvik. The war which had been nicknamed by American journalists 'the phoney war', had now become real. The Norwegians, who had also been neutrals, were able to put up a stronger resistance than the unfortunate Danes. Their country is three times as large as Britain but at that time had a population of only three million. Half the land is over three thousand feet above sea level and only thirty per cent of the total area is cultivated. Bodo and Narvik are both within the Arctic circle.

Although the Germans had prepared the way for their Norwegian venture by training and equipping suitable troops and establishing a network of fifth columnists, they did not complete this campaign without loss, particularly in naval forces. After the initial surprise, the Allies decided that their best policy would be a counter-attack and the most suitable objective would be Narvik. Other ports would be captured later if matters went well.

This somewhat optimistic plan proceeded more slowly than expected, so after two weeks the Chief of Staff decided that Mackesy, the local commander, should be replaced by Auchinleck. The basis of this decision seems to have been that because Auchinleck was accustomed to mountainous terrain on the North West Frontier he would find himself equally at home among the snow-covered peaks and valleys of Norway.

Auchinleck thereupon drew up a minimum shopping list of military requirements. He assumed that air cover would be available, though of course it was not, but the 'minimum requirements' he listed were so obviously impossible that they indicated that to attempt the campaign with anything less would be a waste of time, material and lives. In the event, it proved to be all three of them. Auchinleck's calm, deliberate attitude annoyed Churchill, at that time First Lord of the Admiralty, who had high hopes of a successful Norwegian campaign. Churchill's attitude to Auchinleck was ambivalent: he admired him as a soldier and as a man, but he found that Auchinleck's determination not to make a bad situation worse – as he saw it – was infuriating.

In fact the campaign developed much as Auchinleck had envisaged. The expedition set off with inadequate equipment. Auchinleck had insisted it must take 3.7 anti-aircraft guns. These were loaded on to one ship and their ammunition on another. When the latter was sunk, the guns were useless: no one had thought of dividing guns and ammunition equally between the two ships. They did not set off for Norway until 7 May. On the third day of the four-day journey, a message was received to say that the Nazis had now launched an attack through the Low Countries towards France. Nevertheless, when Auchinleck landed on the 11th he had no orders to cancel his instruction to capture Narvik; in any event, he did not become the official commander until the 13th.

On 18 May Admiral of the Fleet Lord Cork and Orrery, who was the overall commander of the expedition, received a message from London that a total evacuation of Norway might be a possibility. Meanwhile, in France Lord Gort, the British Commander-in-Chief, was on the point of telling London that a retreat to Dunkirk might now be essential if any part of his force was to be saved. Cork then sent a message to London saying Narvik had still not been captured and, even if it were, it would be of no use in the immediate future. This was followed by a telegram from Auchinleck specifying minimum requirements for this stage in the battle but saying that he would do his best with the inadequate material and forces he possessed. On 24 May, Lord Cork received a telegram from the War Cabinet saying that the Norwegian force must be evacuated, as it was now urgently required for the defence of the United Kingdom. By 7 June the evacuation was complete.

The Norwegian campaign had done nothing for Auchinleck's reputation either way. The few tactical moves he had been able to make had been effective enough, but he realized that – short of a miracle – the enterprise was doomed from the start. The only positive gain was that it had enabled him to observe British and French troops on active service. Many of these were inexperienced and, though the potential was there, it would require long and hard training. Of the two forces, the French had impressed him most. The report to the War Cabinet, in which he conveyed this information, was not well received, and it was suggested that the long period he had spent in India had given him a false perspective. Nevertheless he was immediately instructed to form V Corps, for the defence of Southern England. Although a Corps normally contains three divisions, this one was composed of two only, the maximum number which could be equipped with material in England: the equipment for the remaining twenty-two potential divisions had been left behind in France. The defence of Britain therefore rested on some forty thousand men; the area they had to cover was not less than one hundred miles.

On 19 July, Auchinleck was again promoted, this time to GOC Southern Command. His former command was given to Major-General (now Lt-General) B.L. Montgomery, and from then on clashes between the two were continuous. Auchinleck was aware that Montgomery's defiance and insubordination were deliberate, rather than accidental, but he hesitated to dismiss him and create a crisis at such a dangerous time. He decided to exercise great patience with Montgomery, although he had to reprimand him for various unorthodox practices, such as arranging the transfer of officers from other formations (whose commanders were extremely annoyed) by making direct approaches to the Adjutant-General. Auchinleck's anti-invasion policy was to meet the Germans on the beaches and destroy them there and then; Montgomery disagreed and wished to keep his main strength in reserve until the Germans had landed a substantial force, which he would then, theoretically, destroy; he accepted Auchinleck's orders under protest. Four years later, when the Allies invaded France, Rommel wished to attack them as they landed, but von Rundstedt believed it would be better to destroy them when they were ashore. Fortunately for the Allies, von Rundstedt's views prevailed and were obviously wrong.

Not least of Auchinleck's achievements at this time was the manner in which he organized and inspired the Home Guard. With his encouragement it became a strong military asset, very different from the traditional 'Dad's Army' concept.

By November 1940 the immediate threat of invasion seemed to have passed. The Middle East, which contained most of the Allies' oil suppliers, now seemed more vulnerable than the United Kingdom. Surprisingly, Churchill authorized the despatch of tanks and arms to the Mediterranean area, even though the defences of Britain were far from adequate. In November Auchinleck was appointed Commander-in-Chief India and promoted to full general; his post of GOC Southern Command went to Lieutenant-General Alexander.

Auchinleck's transfer to India indicated the importance which the War Cabinet now attached to that country. It could clearly be a source of many divisions of trained troops, all equipped from local manufacturing resources. It could also act as a deterrent to the Japanese, who were becoming increasingly belligerent, now that their European allies, Germany and Italy, appeared to be so consistently successful. But India could also be an area of much trouble. The country was known to be full of agitators and demagogues, who might choose this awkward moment to create the maximum problems for the British government in India. If they should manage to subvert portions of the army, a highly dangerous situation would be created. To avert this, a man who was honoured and liked was needed to command the Indian Army. There was no more suitable person than Auchinleck, even though his removal from the front line to the support area seemed surprising.

One of Auchinleck's first moves in his new post was to despatch a force to Iraq, where it placed a vital part in crushing the Rashid Ali rebellion. This prompt action pleased Churchill, who was deeply concerned about the possibility of German forces obtaining a foothold in such a vital strategic area. Churchill had felt that Auchinleck's 'minimum requirements' for the Norway campaign indicated a cautious outlook: now he saw that he had a clear, realistic mind and could act quickly when he thought it necessary. In his history of the Second World War, Churchill wrote:

When after Narvik he had taken over Southern Command I received from many quarters, official and private, testimony to the vigour and structure he had given to that important region. His appointment as Commander-in-Chief in India had been generally acclaimed. We had seen how forthcoming he had been in sending troops to Basra and the ardour with which he had addressed himself to the suppression of the revolt in Iraq.

This revised opinion now made Churchill decide that Auchinleck should replace Wavell as C-in-C Middle East as soon as possible, even though he had been in India for only a short time. On 21 June telegrams were sent to Wavell and Auchinleck informing them of his decision to change them over. One can understand Churchill: favourable results were badly needed and he felt that Wavell was now too exhausted to achieve them. Churchill was, of course, under great pressure himself, both from his own Parliament and from German air raids which had been killing about a thousand people a night.

Sir John Dill, the CIGS, wrote to Auchinleck, warning him that Churchill would expect good results early and if he could not provide them he must explain why very diplomatically. Unfortunately Auchinleck was a soldier, not a diplomat, and his insistence on making decisions for military, rather than political, reasons would soon begin to alienate Churchill's sympathies.

From then on, Auchinleck's military fortunes began to decline. The area in which he was expected to campaign was new to him; it was also vast, being approximately the size of India. His opponent was one of the most talented German generals, Erwin Rommel. Nevertheless he was fully capable of winning victories. He began by once more stating his minimum requirements. Although these were met in numbers of men, tanks and guns, none were of the calibre necessary to defeat Rommel's forces. The troops he received from England were inexperienced in war and would require training and acclimatization before they could be of any use in the desert; the army he had inherited from Wavell was tired, and inclined to be dispirited. The guns he possessed were totally inadequate for destroying German tanks. His own tanks were far inferior to the German panzers. His experienced eye told him this, and it was confirmed by reports from units in the field.

Unfortunately for Auchinleck, Churchill was receiving information from the most closely guarded secret source in the war – Ultra, of which the story has now been told elsewhere. Ultra intercepted Rommel's pathetic laments to his higher command, his sad reports of the inadequacy of his numbers of tanks, troops, guns and aircraft. The War Cabinet, one of the few bodies entitled to receive this information, believed every word of Rommel's hard-luck story, apparently unaware that no field commander *ever* had enough troops or material. The German High Command was not deceived: it knew that Rommel had the efficient PzIII and PzIV tanks and 88 mm guns, all of which were far superior to anything the British army possessed. The most iniquitous aspect of this situation was that, during Wavell's last, unsuccessful campaign, one of Rommel's tanks had been captured intact and shipped back to England for detailed examination Although the armour of the tank was case-hardened and therefore capable of resisting everything which British anti-tank guns could launch against it, this fact was not appreciated until nine months later. In the interval Auchinleck had been prevailed upon to launch an offensive which after initial success had achieved little. Auchinleck was fully aware that unless he had superiority in quantity to overcome his army's deficiencies in quality, any further offensive action was doomed.

This eminently sensible policy infuriated Churchill, who was unaware of the facts behind the situation – facts which should have been made clear to the War Cabinet by technical intelligence. He began to feel that he had made a mistake in appointing Auchinleck, who was not going to be the forceful, adventurous commander he required. Even Auchinleck did not know why his tanks and guns were so inferior to the Germans', but he did know that if he went into battle as Churchill was constantly urging him to do, the result would be catastrophe. Methodically he began to build up an army which would bring victory and satisfy Churchill.

The jackals were now beginning to snap around Auchinleck's feet. The disgust with which he had viewed the idlers of Cairo in their huge, unnecessary and cumbersome bureaucracy had caused him to make sweeping changes. He had left his wife in India, so that he would not be distracted in any way from his demanding task, and even this was seen as a character fault. A fact which was overlooked was that he had authorized the formation of the SAS (Special Air Service), which had taken a dramatic toll of German aircraft while they were still on the ground. Surprisingly, the man criticized by Churchill for being unenterprising was considered by many to be too favourable to unorthodox and venturesome units. But with the hindsight of history we can see that his policy of giving opportunity to new ideas, while refusing to throw away lives by reckless moves urged upon him by the government at home, saved many lives in the Western Desert.

An offensive (Crusader) had been launched by the Eighth Army in November 1941 but after initial success, which included the relief of Tobruk, was forced back to the Gazala line. During the next four months Churchill constantly urged Auchinleck to take the offensive once more, even though three divisions and a substantial part of the Desert Air Force had been sent to other theatres, and promised equipment was still lacking.

Eventually, when Auchinleck, still with misgivings, was ready to begin his own offensive in May, Rommel struck first. His skill, his equipment and his generalship proved too much for the Eighth Army, which through June 1942 was gradually torn to pieces. By the 25th of that month Auchinleck had decided to take over command in the field himself. At this moment he showed what a skilful fighting general he was. On 1 July, Rommel was stopped at El Alamein.

A few weeks later, Auchinleck was accused, mainly by Montgomery, of having a defensive, defeatist attitude to the war. The injustice of this slander was almost ludicrous. Rommel's advance to Cairo had been stopped by Auchinleck by lively, aggressive tactics; his efforts to break through were frustrated at every point. At the end of July Rommel admitted in his despatches that he had been outfought. 'I could weep', he said.

But Auchinleck's magnificent performance was not enough to satisfy Churchill, who felt that as Rommel had been checked now was the time to put in a counter-attack and drive him right back to beyond Benghazi. Auchinleck was too wise to make such a foolish move. Experience had shown him that once the Eighth Army left its tight position, Rommel's superior armour and guns would slice it to pieces. Then Rommel would come back once more and there would be nothing to hold him at Alamein this time.

Auchinleck did not rule out an offensive in the near future, but before he could launch it he would need to rebuild his battered army with more troops, tanks and guns. This would take time. When, in August, Churchill flew out to visit Auchinleck in the field, he asked him point-blank how long it would take to prepare for a new offensive. Auchinleck replied, 'Six weeks.' Churchill, already annoyed at having to come out to see Auchinleck, who had steadfastly refused to leave his command and come home, was far from pleased. The spartan conditions in Auchinleck's field headquarters did not please him either. He decided that Auchinleck must be replaced by a more forceful, more amenable commander. He proposed therefore to appoint Auchinleck to a new Middle East Command made up of Palestine, Syria, Iraq and Persia. Alexander should replace him as Commander-in-Chief Middle East and Major-General 'Strafer' Gott should take over the Eighth Army, which Auchinleck had been commanding personally for the critical July battles. Unfortunately for this plan, Gott was then killed in an air crash. Asked whom he would now recommend to command Eighth Army, Auchinleck suggested Montgomery. At the same time he himself was not prepared to accept the ramshackle command in the Middle East which he had been offered.

Undoubtedly Auchinleck was too high-minded for his own good. He should have been more sympathetic to Churchill's predicament and given him forecasts which, even if he could not fulfil them, would be useful for Churchill to brandish in the faces of his critics in Parliament. They would also be useful to impress Stalin, whom Churchill was to see in mid-August. The Americans would welcome assurances too. But Auchinleck was too honest to promise pie-in-the-sky. He had already made plans to destroy Rommel's next attack, which he guessed would come in the south of the Alamein position, at Alam-el-Halfa. By the time that attack came on 30 August, Auchinleck had departed, but his plan was used by Montgomery. It proved a resounding success, although it too was criticized by Churchill for not being sufficiently offensive. Subsequently, on 23 October, Montgomery would use yet another of Auchinleck's plans to obtain a final victory at El Alamein. By that time he would have collected forces far in excess of Auchinleck's 'minimum requirement'; twice as many men, twice as many aircraft, twice as many tanks and twice as many guns as the Germans had. Even more to the point, three hundred of those tanks would be Shermans, more than a match for Rommel's Panzers. Even so, the victory was held long in the balance.

An unsavoury feature of Auchinleck's last days in the Middle East was that Montgomery produced a mendacious account of the final interviews between the two men. Auchinleck, he claimed, had plans to retreat up into the Nile valley, regarding Alexandria and Cairo as virtually lost. This confirmed Churchill's view that he had been right to replace Auchinleck, but was a wild distortion, as Montgomery was forced to admit later. There were, of course, 'worst possible case' contingency plans for the Eighth Army if Rommel had been able to break through the Alamein position in July 1942, but they had been made *before* the battle, not after it. July was the turning point of the desert campaign. With Germany now running deeply into trouble in Russia, it was unlikely that Rommel would ever receive the arms and men he was begging for: the Russian front had priority.

Churchill's decision to replace Auchinleck in favour of Alexander, and to bring in Montgomery to command the Eighth Army, had certain points in its favour, brutally unfair though it was to Auchinleck. At that time British troops in the Middle East were so accustomed to moving back and forth across the desert that they had come to accept it as inevitable. Wavell's offensive had failed and Auchinleck, though he had eventually held Rommel at Alamein, still had to live down the fact that his own last offensive had ended in stalemate. Enormously impressive though Auchinleck's bearing and personality were to those who came in contact with him, the Eighth Army at this time probably needed a new, flamboyant, public relations expert at its head. Montgomery had no inhibitions about building on another man's success and claiming it all as his own, but he was also capable of inspiring the army while at the same time impressing Churchill. Montgomery never had to fight a desperate defensive battle and probably could not have done so; on the other hand, when it came to politics and public relations, Montgomery was in the highest class. Unfortunately he became so besotted with his own grandeur that he was unable to see any general, British or American, as his equal, or to reflect that on his climb to eminence he had behaved with contemptible unscrupulousness to a fellow soldier.

After handing over, Auchinleck returned to India to work on the dispatches which he had been unable to complete during the last campaign. He assumed that his military career was now over and that he would be retired as painlessly as possible. Had this occurred, and he and his wife returned to England or some other place of retirement abroad, he might not have lost her to a colleague, as happened three years later.

Churchill had not lost faith in Auchinleck completely. In February 1943, he suggested that Auchinleck should be offered the Persian command he had refused earlier. But neither this nor another plan to give Auchinleck a command in Burma took shape. Unfortunately for Auchinleck Churchill and Brooke discussed both proposals with Montgomery, and that was the end of the matter. Monty gave a suitably damning account of the state of the Eighth Army when he had taken it over. It was an awkward moment for Montgomery, but he was equal to it. If Auchinleck once more had an active command, he would still be in contention for the post of Supreme Commander Land Forces Europe, on which Monty had his eye firmly fixed. As a result, Auchinleck was offered the post of Commander-in-Chief India, which he had held before; this time it would be without responsibility for the Burma theatre, which would now come under the newly-created South East Asia Command.

But even without an active command in SEAC, Auchinleck's responsibilities were enormous. The task of arranging the supplies for SEAC fell to him, as also did that of those for the Chinese in Burma. His new job soon brought him into contact with Orde Wingate, whose Chindit expedition into Burma seemed to Auchinleck badly conceived and organized. Events, of course, proved him right, but his efforts to instil a little basic common sense into Wingate's higher flights of fancy made him once again unpopular with Churchill. However, his achievements in mobilizing the resources of India to support the war effort, and his organization of the training of armies probably contributed more to final victory than he could have produced from an active command.

Sadly, the worst was still to come. On 1 June 1946, he was promoted Field-Marshal, a rank he could well have reached two years earlier, but his pleasure in this was clouded by the fact that his divorce came through at the same time. He never married again and, as his wife soon found life with her new consort impossible, both lived to the end of their days – some thirty years later – less happily than if they had stayed together.

With the war over, and the Japanese threat removed, India looked forward to her long-promised independence. The new Labour government in Britain, under the premiership of Clement Attlee, held the view that the transfer of power should take place as soon as possible. However, there were problems in India which well-meaning but uniformed politicians at home could not easily understand. There were over 350 million Hindus in India and 76 million Muslims. So far no constitution had been devised which was acceptable to both parties. Auchinleck sincerely hoped that the Indian Army, which represented stability and impartiality (Hindus and Muslims had served alongside each other during the war in perfect amity), would remain intact. It was not to be. Jinnah, the Muslim leader, and Nehru, for the Hindus, were in no mood for compromise. Partition was envisaged as the only practical solution. Auchinleck viewed the prospect gloomily: it seemed a recipe for disaster. However, as sporadic rioting continued and the whole country seemed likely to erupt in scenes of violence, a date was fixed for the independence; it was to be not later than June 1948. The announcement was made on 20 February 1947; on the same day Attlee announced that Admiral Lord Mountbatten of Burma would take over from Wavell as Viceroy, and be responsible for a smooth transfer of power.

Talks with Jinnah and Nehru immediately convinced Mountbatten that an independent united India was impossible: it must be partition or anarchy. He advised Attlee that the transfer could not be delayed till 1948 but must be brought forward to December 1947. As unrest grew, he decided that even that date was too far ahead. It must come forward to mid-August 1947; the 14th was eventually the chosen date. Auchinleck's last service to India was to try to warn Mountbatten and the Cabinet that partition and the splitting of the army would lead to civil war. But even he did not visualize a figure as high as four million for the casualties which eventually resulted.

Attlee now told Auchinleck that the King had already agreed to offer him a peerage, if he would accept it. Auchinleck refused, feeling that to be honoured for presiding over the dissolution of the army to which he had devoted his life was absurd. In any event he had scant regard for titles. He knew he had earned his rank by merit, but had no wish to become a peer – 'There are too many of them, at least that sort of peer.'

He died in 1981 at the age of ninety-six, never expressing bitterness over the blows life had dealt him. He had received a DSO, and six mentions in despatches 'for gallant and distinguished service', but he placed no value on the certificates for these honours, most of which he burnt when he left England to settle abroad. No doubt he would have accepted a peerage if it had been offered directly by King George VI or Queen Elizabeth II, but to receive the offer from a go-between such as Attlee or Mountbatten made it unacceptable; it was a reminder of events he felt represented a betrayal of trust. This was regrettable, because his presence in the House of Lords, and in other places where he could have expressed opinions based on experience, would have been invaluable.

The verdict? As a soldier he was a complete professional and highly talented. He had a distrust of politicians which is shared by many soldiers, and he would not compromise his principles or adopt methods which appeared to him to be dishonest. He could not accept the thesis that the end justifies the means; from his background, upbringing and training, honesty was not merely the best policy, but the only policy. In later life, inevitably, he took a sympathetic view of Churchill's reasons for dismissing him from his post in the Middle East. He also commented politely that Montgomery was an excellent general, but that they had 'a different way of doing things'. Montgomery remained convinced of his own rightness and infallibility to the end. Auchinleck could never have wished to resemble Montgomery or envied him his achievements. He lived and died according to his own code of honour.

It has been suggested that Churchill's failure to use Auchinleck's abilities to their best advantage was his greatest mistake. The proponents of this view claim that Auchinleck would have handled the Italian campaign better, would not have taken so long to reach Caen after the D-Day landings, and would never have made the supreme blunder of Arnhem. As a counter-argument, it has been suggested that Montgomery's less than distinguished performance in the Normandy battles was due to inferior equipment, rather than incorrect tactics. And Auchinleck, it has been suggested, would have lost the political battle of wits to the Americans.

The facts are that Auchinleck would not have lost any battle of wits with the Americans because there would not have been one. Montgomery's waspish attitude to his allies infuriated them and made them stubborn. Largely for this reason, Eisenhower refused to be diverted from his disastrous broad-front advance which enabled the Russians to reach Berlin, Prague and Vienna before the Allies. Montgomery had a record of upsetting Americans, whether Mark Clark, Patton or Collins; Auchinleck, by contrast, could even get along with 'Vinegar Joe' Stilwell, something which even Americans found near-impossible. The British generals who got along best with the Americans were men like Auchinleck, Slim and Alexander, men recognizable for their integrity and modesty. The American Army had its own share of prima donnas and knew how to identify them when they saw them. Montgomery's firmness and flamboyance were no doubt excellent assets for winning the war, but they were counter-productive with his American allies. With Auchinleck in command of 21st Army Group, SHAEF (Supreme Headquarters Allied Expeditionary Forces) could well have worked more harmoniously. But he was not, and we shall never know what might have been.

BIBLIOGRAPHY

Very little has been written specifically on Auchinleck although there are many references to him in more general books. Apart from *Auchinleck: The Lonely Soldier* (London, 1981) by Philip Warner, there are *Auchinleck: A Critical Biography* (London, 1959) by John Connell and *The Auk: Auchinleck, Victor of Alamein* (London, 1977) by Roger Parkinson. Recommended reading are Sir David Hunt, *A Don at War* (London, 1966) and Major-General Sir Francis de Guingand, *Generals at War* (London, 1964).

CHRONOLOGY: CLAUDE AUCHINLECK

1884, June 21	Born at Aldershot
1896–1901	Wellington College
1902, January–December	RMC, Sandhurst
1904, April	Joins 62nd Punjab Regiment
1906–7	Frontier duties at Gyantse, Tibet

1912	Assistant Recruiting Officer, North Punjab
1914, October 28	62nd Punjabis sail for France, but diverted to defend Suez Canal
1915, December 31	62nd land at Basra for Mesopotamian campaign
1916, March 8	Attack on Dujaila Redoubt. After heavy casualties and death of Lt.-Col. Commanding, Auchinleck takes command
1916, April 29	Townshend surrenders Kut
1916, August– 1917, March	62nd in operations to recapture Kut. Auchinleck temporary Regimental Commander 8 February 1917. Operations north of Baghdad
1919, August	GSO1, operations in Kurdistan
1921	Marries Jessie Stewart of Kinloch Rannoch, Scotland
1929–30	Commanding Officer 1/1st Punjabis. Promoted full Colonel
1938	Commander, Meerut District. Member, Expert Committee on the Defence of India (Chatfield Committee)
1940, January	Returns to England to take command of IV Corps. Promoted Lieutenant-General
1940, April	Appointed GOC-in-C Northern Norway
1940, May 27–8	Allies capture Narvik
1940, June 3–7	Allied evacuation of Norway
1940, June 14	Takes command of V Corps, Southern Command
1940, July 19– November 21	GOC-in-C Southern Command
1941, June 30	Arrives in Cairo to take over from Wavell as C-in-C Middle Eastern Command
1941, November 18– 1942, January 6	'Crusader' (Sidi Resegh offensive). Rommel pushed back to El Agheila. Tobruk relieved, Benghazi, Bardia and Halfaya retaken, Cyrenaica cleared of Germans
1942, January 29	Rommel retakes Benghazi. Ritchie falls back on Gazala line
1942, March 7	Auchinleck ordered to London – refuses and continues to refuse early offensive
1942, March 20	Cripps and General Nye visit Auchinleck in Cairo on Churchill's orders. They confirm sense of Auchinleck's plans
1942, May 26	Rommel attacks Gazala Line
1942, May 29– June 14	'Cauldron' and 'Knightsbridge' box battles. Ritchie orders withdrawal from Gazala line
1942, June 14	Auchinleck orders line west of Tobruk to be held

1942, June 20	Ritchie decides to fall back beyond frontier to Mersa Matruh
1942, June 21	Tobruk captured with loss of 33,000 Allied prisoners
1942, June 25	Auchinleck dismisses Ritchie and personally takes command of Eighth Army
1942, July 1–27	First Alamein checks Rommel, then counter-attacks, causing havoc, notably among Italians. British positions strengthened
1942, August 5	Churchill decides to replace Auchinleck with General Alexander as C-in-C, with Gott in command of Eighth Army
1942, August 7	Gott killed, Montgomery chosen as Eighth Army commander
1942, August 8	Auchinleck notified, by letter, of his dismissal
1942, August 12	Montgomery arrives in Cairo. Takes over command of Eighth Army on next day, though official handover date fixed for 15th
1942, August–1943, June	Auchinleck in India without formal position, having refused Iraq–Persia command
1943, June 18	Appointed C-in-C India for the second time, with effect from the 20th, with Wavell as Viceroy
1946, June 1	Promoted Field-Marshal. Divorce from wife announced
1947, February 20	Announcement by British government for date of transfer of power – not later than June 1948. Mountbatten succeeds Wavell as Viceroy
1947, June 4	Mountbatten advances date again to 14 August 1947
1947, August 14–15	Last Indian Army order. Indian Independence and Partition
1947, September 27	Auchinleck offered peerage, which he refuses
1947, October	Auchinleck prevents Jinnah's attempted takeover of Kashmir, which accedes to India
1947, December 1	Leaves India
1948–67	In Italy, London and Beccles. Moves to Marrakech in 1967
1981, March 23	Dies at his home in Marrakech

8

MONTGOMERY

Field-Marshal Viscount Montgomery

MICHAEL CARVER

Winston Churchill was no great admirer of generals, at least not those of his generation. His experience in the First World War, and in the second up to the Battle of El Alamein, gave him good reason for that. He thought them too cautious, always demanding more and more resources, human and material, before they were prepared to put matters to the test of battle, with the result that, by that time, the enemy had built up his resources too. In recounting his arguments with Auchinleck on this score, in his history of the Second World War, he quoted the tale of the man who prepared powder to blow down the throat of a bear 'But the bear blew first'. He took a romantic view of war and preferred generals of a heroic hue like Alexander. In his life of his great ancestor Marlborough, he wrote that war's 'highest solution must be evolved from the eye and brain and soul of a single man', and, dismissing the efforts of 'almost any intelligent scribe [who] can draw up a lucid and logical treatise full of laboriously ascertained facts and technical phrases on a particular war situation', he asserted that 'Nothing but genius, the daemon in man, can answer the riddles of war, and genius, though it may be armed, cannot be acquired, either by reading or by experience.'

It was ironic therefore that the general who gave him, at last, the victories that he, and the nation of which he was Prime Minister, so sorely needed, made caution and calculation the bedrock of his military art. The essence of it was that one should not commit oneself to a battle until one has assembled the forces, land and air, and the logistic resources to support them, which will make it possible to penetrate a vital point of the enemy's defence, and then to keep up the pressure by feeding in more forces, so that one retains the initiative and forces the enemy to 'dance to one's tune'. Before starting that process, one must do one's best to deceive one's opponent as to where the blow will fall, so that he dissipates his defence. But one must not allow that to lead one into a dissipation of one's own forces, so that the main thrust is so weakened that either it fails to penetrate, or having done so, cannot be developed.

Montgomery was fortunate in that, except for the brief interlude of his command of the 3rd Division in the British Expeditionary Force in France and Belgium in 1940, circumstances favoured the application of his principles. From the time that he assumed command of Eighth Army in Egypt in August 1942 until the end of the war, he enjoyed an overwhelming superiority of resources over the enemy, and was hardly ever liable to have his plans or operations seriously disturbed by a counter-thrust. Nevertheless he was not always able to put his principles into practice: what Clausewitz called 'the friction of war' interfered with that; and Montgomery's conduct of battles did not always, or even often, coincide with the principles he espoused. Indeed, he was not consistent in his exposition of them.

How did this most professional of British soldiers come to reach the pinnacle of his profession? Bernard Law Montgomery was born on 17 November 1887 in St Mark's Vicarage at Kennington in South London, the fourth child of the Reverend Henry Montgomery and his wife Maud, who was still only twenty-two. She was the daughter of Dean Farrar, best known for his sickly sentimental children's story, *Eric or Little by Little*. Henry Montgomery had been his curate and became engaged to Maud when she was fourteen, marrying her as soon as he could legally do so two years later.

When Bernard was two, his father was sent to Tasmania as Bishop and remained there for eleven years. It was a formative period in the future field-marshal's life. His father spent much of his time away from home, travelling round his huge diocese, leaving Maud to run the house and family, which she ruled with a rod of iron. Her youngest child, Brian, born after their return to England, wrote that 'She longed to·

organize and control both people and events.... She developed a passion for order and method, all governed by a strict routine and subject to the absolute priority of religious practice and a strict morality', characteristics which her son Bernard inherited and was to develop to the full in later life. Meanwhile their strong wills clashed, Bernard rebelling against her authority, while the trouble he caused her, on top of her struggle to make ends meet and cope with all her domestic problems, meant that she displayed less affection towards him than she did to the rest of her large brood. He became a loner and his feeling of rejection was to affect his ability in later life to establish harmonious relationships with others.

There is no certainty about what motive lay behind Bernard's decision, on entering St Paul's School in London as a day boy aged fourteen in January 1902, to join the Army Class, and, in spite of opposition from his parents, to persist in his choice. Defiance of his mother may have influenced him; but it may just have been that, uninterested in any form of intellectual activity and keen on sports and an outdoor life, the army seemed to offer an attractive alternative to the church. Faced with the possibility that he might fail the entrance examination for the Royal Military College at Sandhurst, he belatedly applied himself to serious work and entered the college on 30 January 1907, having passed in 72nd out of 177 cadets. His performance there was not remarkable, except for a serious misdemeanour. He set fire to the shirt-tails of a cadet, who suffered severe burns as a result, for which Montgomery was reduced in rank and held back for a term, before being commissioned into the Royal Warwickshire Regiment on 19 September 1908, joining the 1st Battalion on the North-West Frontier of India in December. There he took his profession seriously, while maintaining his enthusiasm for ball games, and, when his battalion returned to England at the end of 1912, he was appointed Assistant-Adjutant at the age of twenty-five.

When the First World War broke out in August 1914, the battalion was sent to France, Montgomery commanding a platoon. In the First Battle of Ypres in October, he was severely wounded after he had led his platoon in a gallant attack on the village of Meteren, for which he was promoted captain and awarded the Distinguished Service Order, a rarity for a platoon commander of twenty-six. He was lucky not only to survive at the time, but because a severe wound at that early stage of the war led to his service on the staff for the rest of it. Had he returned to a battalion in the front line, his chances of survival would have been small, and his experience in succession as a brigade-major, GSO2, first at a divisional then at a corps headquarters, and finally, in 1918, as GSO1, virtually chief of staff, of a division, provided him with an experience at different levels of command of planning and executing operations involving all arms, which was the foundation of his military expertise. The 1918 experience was especially formative. In a series of successful offensive operations, from August until the armistice, he proved what meticulous planning and carefully controlled execution could achieve, in contrast to his experience on the Somme and at Passchendaele. Ingrained in his attitude to war, henceforward, was that soldiers' lives must not be squandered in ill-planned, sloppily executed operations, based on failure to take all relevant factors into account; but that results could not be achieved without casualties, from which he would not flinch if they promised results. To send men to their death for no gain, or through failure to think the problem through, or as a result of inefficiency in execution, was unforgivable.

That experience was to be distilled after the war in a succession of appointments, in which training played a prominent part, notably as an instructor at the Camberley Staff College from 1926 to 1929, having been a student there himself in 1920, and as a senior instructor at the Quetta Staff College from 1934 to 1937. He excelled as an instructor, analysing the problem with remorseless logic, simplifying and explaining it with terse clarity and mastery of detail; and, while encouraging his students, accepting no excuse for idleness or loose thinking. In between these posts, he commanded the 1st Battalion of his regiment in Palestine and Egypt. Soon after return from Quetta to command a brigade at Portsmouth, he suffered a shattering blow in the sudden death of his wife, whom he had married ten years before. She had transformed his life, introducing him to a cultural circle as strange to him as he must have appeared to them. With her death, leaving him with a nine-year-old son and two stepsons in their twenties, both in the army, he shut himself up again behind the mask he had worn before his marriage.

Nineteen thirty-nine found him in Palestine again, this time as a major-general, commanding the 8th Division, faced with enforcing order on the Arabs who were rebelling against Jewish immigration and the British 'mandatory' authority which reluctantly permitted it. He had not been there long before he fell ill, possibly the result of his war wound. In July he was sent home by sea, which effected a miraculous cure. He had already been selected to command the 3rd Division in October, and, when war clouds gathered in August, the influence of the corps commander, Alan Brooke, who had been a fellow instructor at Camberley, was brought to bear to ensure that he should immediately assume command of the division, which he took to France with the rest of Gort's British Expeditionary Force.

Alan Brooke's confidence in Montgomery was fully rewarded when the crisis came in May 1940. He had not wasted the 'phoney war', but had trained his division to a high pitch, so that its move up to the River Dyle was a textbook example of good planning and march discipline. It was in this period that he developed his strict routine, including his insistence on an early bed and not being disturbed. He exuded an aura of self-confidence and calm, however depressing the news. The division saw little active fighting before the BEF began its withdrawal, in the course of which Montgomery executed a remarkable move at short notice from one flank to the other. After his division had been withdrawn into the Dunkirk perimeter, Alan Brooke was ordered back to England and Montgomery took over command of II Corps, before he himself was evacuated on 1 June, reverting to command of the 3rd Division on his return.

Montgomery's experience in France convinced him that a purely defensive attitude was fatal, and he resisted orders to commit his division to manning coastal defences or 'stop-lines' behind them. He sought a mobile counter-attack role, enlisting the support of Churchill himself, bypassing his superiors to their annoyance. When he took over V Corps from Auchinleck in July 1940, becoming a subordinate of the latter who had succeeded Alan Brooke at Southern Command, he took the same line, which brought him into a head-on clash with Auchinleck. At that stage Montgomery was being unrealistic in thinking that an infantry division with hardly any tanks could conduct anything other than a very local counter-attack. However he must be given credit for recognizing, when he was transferred to command XII Corps in May 1941, that the threat of invasion had passed and that it was more important to instil an offensive spirit into the army and to organize and train it to attack. In order to succeed in that, he realized that he had to pay great attention to morale and to convince soldiers that they could defeat the Germans.

Once more he showed his excellence and energy as a trainer, ruthlessly weeding out the inefficient or unfit. His unorthodox methods and penchant for self-advertisement incurred criticism in many quarters. But the reputation he had established, and the confidence which Alan Brooke, promoted from Commander-in-Chief Home Forces to Chief of the Imperial General Staff on Christmas Day 1941, reposed in him meant that, when Alexander was chosen to succeed Auchinleck as C-in-C Middle East, after the withdrawal of Eighth Army to the Alamein Line, Montgomery was selected to replace him in command of First Army, earmarked to take part, under Eisenhower's command, in Operation Torch, the Anglo-American invasion of French North Africa. No sooner had that decision been made than Gott, chosen to command Eighth Army, was killed, and Montgomery, on Alan Brooke's insistence, was flown to Cairo to take his place.

Fortune, which had been kind in some ways but cruel in others, now favoured him. He took over the army's most important command when everything was turning in its favour and in circumstances which related fairly closely to his previous experience and expertise. The front was limited and, not having a wide open flank, less likely to be subjected to the bewildering uncertainties of desert warfare than at any time since the war there had started against the Italians in 1940. The strength of both the army and the air force, in quality and quantity, had been substantially improved. It was much easier for him than it had been for his predecessors to be 'well-balanced', one of the criteria on which he laid great emphasis. He arrived brimming with confidence that he knew all the answers, treating Auchinleck, his old sparring partner, and almost every old desert hand with contempt. He was fortunate to find, ready to hand and keenly attuned to all the nuances of the situation, an old acquaintance in Freddie de Guingand, whom he could appoint as a stop-gap chief of staff until his favourite nominee, Frank Simpson, could be summoned. Luckily for him Alan Brooke would not release Simpson and de Guingand was to prove invaluable to Montgomery until the end of the war.

One of the answers he thought he knew was that he should have a *corps de chasse*, equivalent, as he wrongly imagined, to Rommel's Afrika Korps. The latter was in fact Rommel's spearhead for all purposes, not just a formation to be let loose when the infantry, in his case mostly Italian, had broken the enemy's line. One of Montgomery's first acts was to get GHQ, presided over by Alexander, to organize X Corps for that purpose, reluctantly having to accept that Lumsden, the cavalry commander of 1st Armoured Division, who had been in the desert since January 1942, should command it instead of one of his nominees, brought out from England, as Leese and Horrocks were, forty-eight and forty-seven years old respectively. Montgomery was nearly fifty-five, old by Second World War standards.

His first impact was on the staff of Eighth Army Headquarters, and it was electric. Having taken over command before he had been authorized to do so, he cancelled all existing plans without bothering to look at them. He told Churchill a few days later that he had found that 'It was intended in face of heavy attack to retire eastwards to the Delta. Many were looking over their shoulders to make sure of their seat in the lorry, and no plain plan of battle or dominating will-power had reached the units.' He was forced to retract that accusation when he published it in his memoirs, but it was not far off the mark. His decisive contribution was to realize that, if the recently arrived 44th Division, which was being held back as an insurance for the defence of the Delta, were sent up to reinforce Eighth Army, he would have enough troops to hold a continuous line of defence as far south as the ridge of Alam Halfa. He could then safely discard Auchinleck's plan for a series of 'boxes', based largely on artillery, scattered about the desert, between which the armoured brigades would fight a mobile battle. He had no intention of fighting a mobile battle, at which Rommel was an expert and he was not. Alexander agreed, and Montgomery's decision bore fruit in the successful Battle of Alam Halfa at the end of September, which halted Rommel's attempt to reach the Nile and proved to be the final turn of the tide in the desert war.

But it was not as immediately decisive as Montgomery hoped. He had planned to cut off Rommel's thrust with a counter-attack by Freyberg's New Zealanders, reinforced by brigades of the 44th, and then launch Lumsden's *corps de chasse* in a wide sweep round Rommel's rear; but the New Zealand attack petered out ineffectively and Montgomery, the realist, saw that his army needed more thorough training before it would be able to respond to his demands. Pretending that he was satisfied with the outcome, he turned his attention to the major set-piece battle he would have to wage to penetrate Rommel's defences, the minefields covering which would have become more intricate by the time that Eighth Army would be ready to assault them in the next full-moon period. Daylight attack by infantry in the desert was near suicidal.

His first plan, explained to his corps commanders on 14 September, envisaged that Leese's XXX Corps would force gaps through the minefields in the northern half of the front in one night, through which the two armoured divisions of Lumsden's X Corps would pass. The latter corps would then 'position itself on ground of its own choosing' astride the enemy's supply routes, forcing Rommel's tanks to attack and be destroyed in the process. Horrocks's XIII Corps would force a gap in the south and pass his one armoured division, the 7th, doyen of desert rats, through to draw off some of Rommel's tanks from Lumsden. Montgomery stressed that X Corps must be through the minefields by dawn of the first day and must not become embroiled in fighting in the early hours before getting there.

He immediately instituted a thorough training programme for all the troops involved, particularly in the complicated operation of making gaps through the minefields. As the weeks passed and the enemy thickened and developed them, Leese's infantry division commanders expressed doubts as to whether they would be able to ensure free passage to Lumsden's tanks before dawn on the first day, unless the latter participated in the fighting to clear the gaps, while Lumsden made it clear that he had no intention of doing so. Reacting to this, Montgomery changed his plan on 6 October, giving Lumsden the less ambitious task of holding off the enemy armour, while the infantry 'crumbled' his infantry. He did not, however, clarify the issue as to whether Lumsden's armoured divisions were to expect that the infantry divisions would have cleared a passage for their tanks to the far side of the minefields or should be prepared to fight their way out, if the infantry had not done so. If he expected the latter, it was unfortunate that he did not change the command arrangements. The superimposition of one corps on another, both commanding troops fighting in the same area, was undoubtedly one of the principal causes of the problems that were to arise in the battle. However Montgomery was clearly right to insist that the attempt to break through should be made in one night. When it had not succeeded even by the end of the second night, Montgomery was quick to change to a different method: that of making a succession of thrusts in different sectors, each drawing counter-attacks by Rommel, which wore down the latter's forces until he had almost nothing left with which to prevent the final breakthrough in the centre of the northern sector. The battle had not followed Montgomery's 'master-plan'; but he had won it by his thorough preparation, his determination, his clear-headed realism and the flexibility with which he applied it, as well as by his considerable superiority in resources of all kinds, including in the air.

Elation at victory after so many disappointments obscured criticism of deficiencies in his exercise of command in the subsequent six months. Over-insurance and caution contributed to his failure to prevent Rommel from withdrawing the remnants of his German forces not only from El Alamein, but also from a series of delaying positions all the way back to the Tunisian border. Beyond it, a model defensive victory at Medenine on 6 March 1943, to which Montgomery's contribution was to act promptly on Ultra information to reinforce Leese, who commanded the battle, was followed by the attack on the Mareth Line, which was not a battle of which Montgomery could be proud. Neither in concept nor, initially, in execution did it follow any of the principles by which he maintained that battles should be fought. He himself was not consistent on that issue. The recipe he had given at a study period which he conducted at Tripoli in February 1943 was

Careful planning of the break-in battle. You must be so positioned at the close of this phase that you have the tactical advantage. Rapid switching of the thrust line as opposition grows too stiff on any one axis. Axes of operations must be so thought out that the enemy is led gradually to believe that your main subsequent effort is going to be in a definite area. Having thus deceived him, you put in a really hard blow at some other point, which is so selected that he will be thrown off balance.

That is what happened at El Alamein, although his original intention had been more like what he wrote in a letter to Alanbrooke, criticizing the way Anderson's First Army was being handled on the approach to Tunis. 'The attack plan for the major effort on First Army's Front is NOT the way that I fight the Germans', he wrote. 'My experience is that the way to beat him is to concentrate all your strength and hit him an almighty crack; then, through that place, while the enemy is reeling under your blow, you burst through with armoured and mobile forces; the armoured forces have got to be prepared to fight their way out, dealing with any jagged edges that remain.' Mareth was not fought according to either of those recipes. He underestimated both the enemy and the difficulty of attacking across a wet watercourse, and did not allot sufficient strength to either of the widely separated attacking forces. He must be given credit for reacting quickly to the initial failure; but the fact that his first plan failed meant that he had to stage another set-piece attack at Wadi Akarit. The only excuse for his lapse in committing first the New Zealand Division and then the completely green 56th to a hopeless front assault at Enfidaville in the final stage of the campaign is that he was by then preoccupied with revising the plan for the landings in Sicily.

There is no doubt that he was right to raise serious objections to the plan which Eisenhower inherited from the planners in London.

Emphasis on the early capture of ports and airfields led to a dispersion which would have prejudiced the success of operations once the troops were ashore, particularly if the Germans reinforced the island, as they were likely to do once Tunis had fallen. But the tactless way in which Montgomery raised his objections added to the foundation he had already laid in antagonizing the Americans. Although it was right to demand a greater concentration, it is less certain that his insistence that the whole force, his own Eighth Army and Patton's Seventh (with only one corps), should land in the southeast corner was the best choice. If the latter had been landed concentrated near Palermo, the Germans might not have been able to withdraw all their forces to the mainland, although it could have led to their concentration against Patton before Montgomery could help him. Montgomery's attempt to take over some of the routes assigned to Patton was bound to ensure that the latter did nothing to help Montgomery and to go off on his own towards Palermo. The campaign in Sicily served one valuable purpose for Montgomery personally. The fact that his army was concentrated in a restricted area and moved slowly in fair weather gave him the opportunity to see and be seen by soldiers of all ranks. That had not been possible since the training period before El Alamein. It fostered the image of a commander who was close to his troops.

The failure of Alexander, under Eisenhower, to exercise a firm command over either Montgomery or Patton encouraged the former, after another over-insured operation to cross to the mainland, to complain about the lack of direction from above. He was not at his best in Italy, fundamentally perhaps because he did not believe in the campaign at all. He thought it a blind alley. Ever since El Alamein, his thoughts had returned to the English Channel. Soon after the battle, he had suggested to Alanbrooke that it was illogical for Eighth Army, supplied by a long line of communication round the Cape to Egypt, to advance westward through North Africa, when Eisenhower's forces could be supplied and reinforced by a much shorter one. That had earned him a sharp rebuff. Italy seemed to Montgomery to lead nowhere. He was constantly demanding a clear aim and plan, which the campaign never could provide. Its justification was that it drew off German forces that might otherwise be used to reinforce France. To do that, they had to be attacked, and, paradoxically, the further south in Italy they were, the more effective was the containment policy. It was an attrition campaign like that on the Western Front in the First World War. At times Montgomery took the over-optimistic view that, if McCreery's X British

Corps and the bulk of the logistic support then being supplied to Mark Clark's Fifth US Army, in which it served, were transferred to him, he could outflank the Germans holding up Clark and reach Rome before midwinter. At others, he took the pessimistic line that nothing much was likely to be achieved, given the strength of the German resistance, the terrain and the weather. It was therefore with no real regret that he handed Eighth Army over to Oliver Leese on the last day of 1943, and flew to England to assume command of 21st Army Group.

Montgomery's claim to rank among the great commanders must rest on his victory at El Alamein and the success of the landings and subsequent operations in Normandy. In both, the effort he devoted to preparation was as important as his actual conduct of operations. It involved planning, from the general concept to intricate detail, training and inspiration. The last, on the second occasion, extended beyond the soldiers he commanded to the people, of all kinds and at all levels, of the nation that supported them. As before Alam Halfa and El Alamein, he spread the supreme confidence he had in his own ability to choose the right solution, and impose it on both his own forces and on the enemy, on those he commanded and those who supported them or were only spectators. That confidence stemmed from his insistence on getting the 'master-plan' right. Although he was fond of emphasizing that morale was the most important single factor in war, he knew that morale could not be maintained unless everyone, from the top to the bottom, was confident that they could succeed. For that, the strategy, the 'master-plan', had to be sound, the tactics adapted to the circumstances and the soldiers thoroughly trained to implement them.

He started with the intermediate stage between strategy and tactics, operations at formation level. Before leaving Italy, he had flown to Algiers to see Eisenhower, who had told him that he would have command of all the land forces, British, Canadian and American, involved in the Normandy landings until Eisenhower himself could transfer his headquarters from England to France, at which stage Omar Bradley would be promoted from command of First US Army to that of 12th US Army Group alongside Montgomery's 21st, which would then be commanding the First Canadian and Second British Armies. It was a highly significant decision by Eisenhower, which, given the friction that Montgomery had already caused, did him great credit. The accounts of the participants at that meeting conflict as to the degree of knowledge both obtained of the draft plan prepared by the Anglo-American staff under the British General Morgan, and of their reactions to it. Each claims to have been the originator of dissatisfaction at the limited strength, and therefore of the width, of the planned initial assault, determined by the number of landing-craft which the Anglo-US Joint Chiefs of Staff had said could be available. Wherever the credit may lie, both were agreed on the issue and persuaded the Joint Chiefs that a combination of deferment of the target date from May to early June 1944, allowing for production of more craft, and postponement of the controversial Operation Anvil (later Dragoon) in southern France would make it possible to increase the initial assault force to five divisions, supplemented by the airdrop of three more. That, combined with a change in the command organization, so that each corps would retain responsibility for the same area, from the initial landing through to follow-up forces, undoubtedly laid sound foundations for the operation.

The danger in all amphibious operations, as Sicily had shown, was that so much attention needed to be paid to the very difficult problems of landing on a defended shore that what happened thereafter took second place. Montgomery did not make that mistake. As early as 7 January 1944, at a meeting with Bradley, Dempsey and their chiefs of staff, he declared that the task of Bradley's First US Army would be 'the capture of Cherbourg and the clearing of the Cherbourg peninsula; subsequently to develop operations to the south and west', and that of Dempsey's Second British Army 'to operate to the south to prevent any interference with the American army from the east'. At a later conference he said:

We must blast our way on shore and get a good lodgement before the enemy can bring up sufficient reserves to turn us out ... we must gain space rapidly and peg out claims well inland ... once we get control of the main enemy lateral Granville–Vire–Argentan–Falaise–Caen and have the area enclosed in it firmly in our possession, then we will have the area we want and can begin to expand.

The first step in expansion would be the break-out of Patton's Third US Army into Brittany, in order to secure its ports for American use, after which the Allied armies would sweep eastward, the left pivot being advanced from Caen to Cabourg. They should be lined up ready to cross the Seine by about the beginning of September. That lodgement area, particularly in the open terrain between Caen and Falaise, would provide sites for airfields for fighter-bombers, redeployed from England, to support the advance beyond the Seine. Montgomery hoped that Dempsey would capture Caen early on, preferably on D-Day, 6 June, and thrust rapidly south from there to Falaise, thus forming the left flank of the shield to hold the Germans off Bradley. At no time was it ever suggested, as his critics then and since have claimed, that Dempsey would attempt to break out towards the Seine while Bradley was still involved in clearing the Cotentin peninsula.

In the event the enemy's resistance proved tougher than some expected, and the slow progress in establishing the lodgement area forced Montgomery to use the methods he had outlined at his study period in Tripoli rather than the 'almighty crack' he had recommended in his letter to Alanbrooke. He made several attempts at such a 'crack', of which the most spectacular was Operation Goodwood on 18 July, designed to take Dempsey's armoured divisions from Caen to Falaise. Its failure to do so raised criticism to the level of hysteria, stemming largely from Eisenhower's frustrated staff and senior air force officers, stuck in England under bombardment from VI cruise-missiles. Montgomery must bear some of the blame for that in raising their expectations, partly in order to persuade the senior airmen, Tedder and Harris, to support it with the latter's heavy bombers, partly by making a falsely over-optimistic report of its initial success. In the event it did not matter, as Bradley's postponed attack further west led, at last, to the break-out and the unleashing of Patton.

Montgomery's strategy had worked, although it had taken longer and cost more than he had anticipated. He had certainly hoped to secure Caen and Falaise early on, but he was not going to be forced into expensive attempts to do so, if they were liable to prejudice his ability to follow the general pattern of his original strategy. For that, he had to conserve the resources of the Second British Army, which he had not reckoned on expending at the rate they had been in the initial stages. Because the close-in fighting in the Normandy bocage lasted longer than expected, Dempsey's resources of British infantry, a wasting asset, were dwindling; while, because there had been little in the way of mobile operations, he had a surplus of tanks at that stage. Regardless of pressure from the airmen, the Americans, Churchill and others, Montgomery had to keep up pressure in the east, if the German panzer divisions were not to be transferred to the west and frustrate his basic strategy.

The idea that a break-out southwards from the American sector was a concept dreamed up at this stage by Bradley and Patton, in frustration at the lack of progress in Dempsey's sector, is disproved by ample evidence. Montgomery was a realist. He did not shrink from accepting casualties; but he did not believe in inflicting them on his soldiers to no good purpose. He refused to press on with attacks, as Haig had done in the First World War, when they were clearly getting nowhere. Above all, he was sensitive to the morale of his soldiers. He knew there were limits, beyond which he could not push them without a serious risk that their performance would rapidly deteriorate. That applied as much to those formations new to battle as to the veterans from North Africa. The quality of his divisions, and of their commanders, was very varied, and he knew it. He never had any illusions about anyone. He also knew that, for all the fuss the airmen made about the need to acquire the area south of Caen for airfields, it would make little difference to the air situation. The air forces were able to dominate the skies from bases in England, and would not have been able to operate from airfields in that area until his forces had got well beyond it; until in fact the break-out occurred.

The Germans had been forced by Hitler to play into his hands. By forbidding any withdrawal and fighting the battle forward, including the fatal counter-attack towards Mortain, Hitler ensured that the Battle of Normandy decided the Battle of France. The French should be grateful. Although the Normandy battlefield area suffered terrible destruction, the rest of France was largely spared, operations between the closing of the Falaise–Argentan gap and France's eastern borders being limited to a virtually unopposed pursuit. The first controversial issue which arose concerned the closing of that gap. Montgomery had initially intended to close the pincers nearer to the Seine, but was persuaded by Bradley to agree to the shorter hook, from which the remnants of the German army, only 20,000 men, 24 tanks and 60 guns, escaped. Patton, having been refused permission to cross the inter-army group boundary north of Argentan, disobeyed Bradley and set off towards Paris. It was perhaps a pity that Montgomery, who was still in overall command, although Eisenhower was with Bradley, did not stick to his original intention; but at that stage he no doubt realized that there were limits to the extent to which he could impose his will on the Americans.

A more important issue was that of the strategy to be pursued beyond the Seine. From the end, in August 1944, of the Normandy campaign onwards, Montgomery urged that a force of at least forty divisions, most of which would have been American, should be concentrated in a thrust aimed north of the Ardennes to the north of the Ruhr. It should have priority, including that of logistic support, over all other operations; and the army groups involved should be under one commander, who he assumed (and the Americans suspected that he did) would be himself, although at one stage he offered to serve under Bradley, if Eisenhower accepted the principle of the strategy. Montgomery contended that, by failing to accept his proposal, Eisenhower forfeited the opportunity to exploit the victory in Normandy and to finish the war in 1944. Once Patton had started to head for Metz and Nancy from Paris, Eisenhower was unable and Bradley unwilling to restrain him and make the major American effort in the north. Eisenhower did give Montgomery's 21st Army Group, and Hodge's First US Army on his right, priority as far as Belgium; but thereafter Bradley's effort diverged and was dissipated between Hodges's thrust towards Aachen and Patton's towards Metz and Nancy, so that the momentum of the thrust in the north petered out.

It is by no means certain that Montgomery's claim was valid. The chances of success would have been greatest if, after the capture of Brussels, Eisenhower, accepting Montgomery's strategy, had allotted to 21st Army Group the task of clearing the Channel ports and the Scheldt estuary, while giving the task of thrusting north of the Ardennes, to cross the Rhine north of the Ruhr, to Bradley's 12th Army Group, headed by Patton's Third US Army and supported by the whole of the Allied Airborne Army. Neither Montgomery nor Churchill would have liked that relegation of all the British formations to such a subsidiary role, the one to which in fact Crerar's First Canadian Army was restricted.

Montgomery's decision to launch Operation Market Garden has rightly been criticized. The original concept was limited to protection of the left flank of a major thrust by Dempsey's Second Army; but when the switch of priorities and of US forces after Brussels made that impractical, Montgomery gave way to pressure from the frustrated Browning in an attempt to force Eisenhower's hand. Its failure gave a handle to his critics, who could deride his concept of bringing the war to an end by 'a pencil-like thrust towards Berlin'. Neither before nor after Arnhem had that been his concept. He consistently pressed for a single concentrated thrust of at least forty divisions. Back on his 'almighty crack' line, he claimed that such a strategy had always been successful. His claim cannot be upheld. In both world wars there were countless examples of single thrusts, however concentrated and strong, attracting the enemy's reserves and thus being brought to a halt. Given the forces that the Germans were able to assemble for their Ardennes offensive, it is at least arguable that, at any rate after the Allied pause in Belgium, they could have used sufficient strength to halt a single concentrated thrust, if not on the Rhine, at least into bridgeheads on the far side. The strategy which had been generally successful was one of alternating thrusts, delivering a blow in an unexpected area when the enemy's reserves had been attracted elsewhere and tied down there by a previous thrust. That was how the battles had been won at El Alamein, in Normandy, and at Mareth after the failure of a single thrust: in fact by the methods Montgomery had outlined at Tripoli. Montgomery's tactless and arrogant manner, seen at its worst over the Ardennes offensive, defeated his own purposes. Once over the Rhine, he might have achieved his desired strategy of heading straight for Berlin, if he had accepted that two army groups could operate side by side north of the Ruhr without a single overall commander.

Whether Stalin would have let Anglo-American forces reach Berlin before he had surrounded it, and, whether, given the Yalta agreement, it would really have transformed the political development of post-war Europe if they had got there first, as Montgomery and some of his admirers claimed, is very doubtful.

BIBLIOGRAPHY

Montgomery, Field Marshal The Viscount, *Memoirs* (Collins, London, 1958).

Hamilton, Nigel, *Monty: The Making of a General, 1887–1942* (Hamish Hamilton, London, 1981); *Monty: Master of the Battlefield, 1942–1944* (Hamish Hamilton, London, 1983); *Monty: The Field Marshal, 1944–1976* (Hamish Hamilton, London, 1986).

Lewin, Ronald, *Montgomery as a Military Commander* (Batsford, London, 1971).

Moorehead, Alan, *Montgomery* (Hamish Hamilton, London, 1946).

Chalfont, Alun, *Montgomery of Alamein* (Weidenfeld & Nicolson, London, 1976).

Montgomery, Brian, *A Field Marshal in the Family* (Constable, London, 1973).

de Guingand, Major-General Sir Francis, *Operation Victory* (Hodder & Stoughton, London, 1946).

Carver, Michael, *El Alamein* (Batsford, London, 1962).

Lamb, Richard, *Montgomery in Europe, 1943–45* (Buchan & Enright, London, 1983).

CHRONOLOGY: BERNARD MONTGOMERY

1887, November 17	Born at St Mark's Vicarage, Kennington
1907, January 30	Enters Royal Military College, Sandhurst

1908, September 19	Commissioned 2nd Lieutenant Royal Warwickshire Regiment
1914, October 13	Wounded in First Battle of Ypres. Promoted Captain and awarded the Distinguished Service Order
1915, February 12	Brigade-Major 112 Infantry Brigade (later 104)
1917, January 22	GSO2, Headquarters 33rd Division
1917, July 6	GSO2, Headquarters IX Corps
1918, March	Promoted Brevet-Major
1918, July 16	GSO1 Headquarters 47th Division. Temporary Lieutenant-Colonel
1918, September 5	Commanding Officer 17th Battalion Royal Fusiliers
1920, January 22	Student, Staff College, Camberley. Brevet-Major
1921, January 5	Brigade-Major 17 Infantry Brigade (Cork)
1922, May 24	Brigade-Major 8 Infantry Brigade (Plymouth)
1923, May	GSO2, Headquarters 49th Division (TA) (York)
1925, March	Commander A Company, 1st Battalion Royal Warwicks (Shornecliffe)
1926, January 23	Directing Staff, Staff College, Camberley. Lieutenant-Colonel
1927, July 27	Marries Betty Carver (née Hobart)
1928, August 18	Son, David, born
1931, January	Commanding Officer 1st Battalion Royal Warwicks (Palestine and Egypt)
1934, June 29	Senior Directing Staff, Staff College, Quetta. Colonel
1937, August 5	Commander 9 Infantry Brigade (Portsmouth). Brigadier.
1937, October 19	His wife dies
1938, December	GOC 8th Division (Palestine). Major-General
1939, August 28	GOC 3rd Division (England and BEF)
1940, July 22	GOC V Corps (England). Lieutenant-General
1941, April 27	GOC XII Corps (England)
1942, August 13	GOC Eighth Army (Egypt)
1942, November 11	Promoted General. Created Knight Commander of the Order of the Bath
1944, January 3	Commander-in-Chief 21st Army Group (England)
1944, September 1	Promoted Field-Marshal
1946, January 1	Created Viscount Montgomery of Alamein
1946, July	Chief of the Imperial General Staff
1946, November	Created Knight of the Garter
1948, October	Chairman of the Western Union Chiefs of Staff Committee

1951, April	Deputy Supreme Allied Commander Europe, NATO
1958, September 18	Retires. Publishes memoirs
1976, March 24	Dies at Isington Mill

9
WILSON

Field-Marshal Lord Wilson

MICHAEL DEWAR

The mourners who attended Field-Marshal Lord Wilson's memorial service in January 1965 at Westminster Abbey must have been conscious of the fact that Churchill was lying in state in Westminster Hall only yards away. Wilson died aged eighty-three, Churchill at ninety. Unlike most of Churchill's generals, Wilson was of the same generation as the Prime Minister. This, perhaps more than any other factor, accounted for the mutual understanding the one had for the other.

Henry Maitland Wilson was born in September 1881, educated at Eton and the Royal Military College Sandhurst and commissioned into the Rifle Brigade in March 1900. He served as a junior officer in the South African War and in a succession of staff appointments during the First World War. There followed a period as a company commander at Sandhurst in the early 1920s before Wilson commanded the 2nd Battalion of the Rifle Brigade in India. In 1930 his considerable experience as a Staff Officer was put to good effect when he was promoted full Colonel and appointed a senior instructor at the Staff College, a post he filled with great distinction. After commanding 6 Infantry Brigade he was promoted Major-General in April 1935 and then promptly put on half pay for two years until given command of the 2nd Division in Aldershot in August 1937. This must have been a frustrating time for Wilson, who was already a good deal older than his fellow divisional commanders. However, he put all this behind him when he went to Cairo in June 1939 as Commander-in-Chief of British Troops in Egypt in the rank of Lieutenant-General.

In appearance Wilson cut an impressive figure. At over six feet tall and no lightweight, it was probably inevitable that he should acquire the nickname 'Jumbo' early in his military career. He was a man who inspired confidence and who by 1939 had accrued a considerable wealth of military knowledge and experience, particularly as a staff officer and a trainer. In character he was steadfast, imperturbable, unflappable – very much a soldier's soldier. He had made a popular commanding officer of the Rifle Brigade, where his first concern had always been his Riflemen; he had always been good with people and was much loved by those who worked closely with him. His confidential report covering the period April 1929 to March 1930 whilst he was commanding officer of 1RB read in part: 'An exceptional officer in every way. I have never met a Commanding Officer who has, to a great extent, the respect and affection of both officers and men of his battalion. ... Possibly his most outstanding characteristic is his gift of getting the best out of everyone, both juniors and seniors.'[1] It was signed by Lieutenant-General Walter Leslie, Commander Lahore District. More than anything else, Jumbo Wilson got things done – nothing was too difficult – and he was not afraid to speak his mind.

So at the outbreak of war in September 1939 Wilson, at the age of fifty-eight, found himself in what, at the time, must have seemed to him something of a military backwater. His old command, the 2nd Division, departed for France with the British Expeditionary Force. But whether by luck or design, he was in many ways just the man for Egypt. During the first nine months of the war, until Italy joined the Axis in June 1940, Wilson was heavily involved in the minefield of Egyptian politics. The Egyptians, realizing that the Italians were playing a waiting game, decided to sit on the fence themselves. Whilst they were not prepared to commit themselves as an active ally, they maintained for the most part close and friendly relations with Wilson and his staff. A commander who was less of a diplomat than Wilson would surely have come to grief during this delicate period in Anglo-Egyptian relations.

At the same time Wilson prepared the Army of Egypt for operations against the Italians in the Western Desert. Despite the somewhat cumbersome system of command in the Middle East – Wavell was C-in-C

Middle East and O'Connor was in command of the Western Desert Force – Wilson played a leading role in the planning of the operations against the Italians. He decided to take the offensive from the outset. Thus when on 10 June Mussolini declared that he would be at war with Great Britain from midnight, at one minute past midnight British troops and aircraft crossed the frontier into Italian-occupied Cyrenaica. After initial British successes, the strategic picture was drastically altered by the collapse of France which allowed the Italians in Libya to release their forces on the Tunisian frontier to reinforce Cyrenaica. The resulting Italian offensive met with limited initial success, penetrating as far as Maktila about sixty miles into Egypt where it fizzled out. This was at great cost to the Italians and at remarkably little to the Western Desert Force – 150 casualties between 11 June and 16 September – whilst over 700 Italian prisoners were taken and the enemy admitted 3,500 casualties during the same period.

It was Wavell who, with Eden's backing, actually decided that the time was right for a counter-offensive. Enemy forces around Sidi Barrani were estimated to total six divisions, of which four were Italian and the remainder Libyan troops. The Western Desert Force consisted of the 7th Armoured Division and the 4th Indian Division. Odds were about 2.5 to 1 in favour of the enemy but the British had several crucial advantages, for many of which Wilson was in large part responsible. He had insisted on an intensive programme of all-arms training by the 4th Indian and 7th Armoured Divisions, debunking the fashionable but dangerous doctrine that tanks could win battles by themselves. He had given the 7th Armoured Division generous periods of time to overhaul and service their vehicles, immediately recognizing the importance of this one area in which the British had a numerical superiority of 275 to 120 tanks. Rightly he saw this capability as being crucial to the outcome of any future test of arms.

Wilson had also encouraged the formation of long-range patrols into the desert by a Major Bagnold of the Royal Tank Regiment, which brought back valuable information on Italian dispositions and intentions and which were the forerunners of the legendary Long Range Desert Group. But his greatest contribution to the success of the December offensive was his insistence on complete surprise. Wilson was arguably one of the first commanders during the Second World War to appreciate the importance of deception and surprise in warfare. He adopted elaborate measures to ensure that complete secrecy was maintained. Troops were moved into their assembly positions under the impression that they were about to take part in a major exercise. Wilson himself maintained as normal a routine as possible and did not leave Cairo until the afternoon of 9 December, the day the attack was launched. Two days later the Italian Army had been broken at Sidi Barrani, the British taking 38,000 prisoners, 400 guns and 50 tanks. Wilson capitalized on this early success, so that by 7 February all of Cyrenaica was under British control. A campaign which had started with a limited objective ended after an advance of 500 miles in two months. The tally was now 130,000 prisoners of war, 400 tanks and 1,290 guns whilst British casualties totalled 500 killed, 1,375 wounded and 55 missing.

Although executive command was always in the hands of O'Connor, Wilson had played a major part in the planning of the initial stages of this offensive and in the direction of operations during the first few weeks. After this great victory he was appointed the Military Governor and Commander in Cyrenaica.

His tenure, however, was short-lived. On 22 February Wilson was handed a letter from Wavell telling him that he would be commanding the British Imperial Force that was about to be sent to Greece. The letter ended: '... I am very sorry at having to push this on you at such short notice but you, with your tactical and strategical knowledge and the prestige of your recent successes are undoubtedly the man for the job, and it will greatly relieve my mind to know that you are there; both the CIGS and I agreed that it was the only solution.'[2]

In 1939, faced with growing German intrigue in the Balkan region, the Chamberlain government had, together with France, issued a guarantee of Greek independence. Although by 1941 the Greeks were more than holding their own against the Italians on the Albanian front, Whitehall – thanks to Ultra – was becoming aware of the movement of German ground and air forces into Bulgaria. Eden, backed by Wavell, signalled to Churchill that 'assistance to the Greeks, who are fighting and threatened, must have first call on our resources'.[3] British involvement would be a demonstration of good faith to both the United States and Turkish governments that Great Britain was honouring its undertakings to Greece and at the same time retaining a foothold on an increasingly Nazi-dominated European continent. But there were daunting military risks to this political gesture, which Wilson was amongst the first to recognize. The weakening of our forces in Libya, which were facing an Italian Army recently bolstered by the arrival of Rommel and a single German division, made little sense, whilst the force being sent to Greece promised not to be strong enough to defeat the likely German tank and air threat. Moreover success in Greece was only possible if the Greek Army honoured their undertaking to withdraw from Macedonia to the line of the River Aliakmon which the combined British and Greek Armies might have some chance of holding against the German threat. (In fact by 2 March both Wavell and Eden knew this withdrawal was not being made.) Nevertheless Churchill decided to back the judgement of the man on the spot. On 15 March the Prime Minister signalled Cairo, 'While being under no illusions we all send you the order "Full Steam Ahead".'⁴ Wilson did what he was told.

The Imperial Force consisted of 1 Armoured Brigade, the New Zealand Division, the headquarters of the Australian Corps and 6th Australian Division. It was hoped that reinforcements consisting of the Polish Independent Brigade Group and 7th Australian Division would arrive in due course. Whilst this force was in transit, Wilson flew to Athens in civilian clothes to discuss the deployment of Imperial forces with the Greek Government. He made it clear that in his view the Albanian front represented a serious distraction which tied down 300,000 Greek troops and deprived the Allies of any reserves for the eastern and central Macedonian sectors of operations. In fact only three Greek divisions were made available to Wilson. This combined force, under Wilson's command, became known as 'W' Force. He was also anxious about the state of Greek morale when battle was joined with the *Wehrmacht*. Nevertheless despite difficulties he accepted his orders as a soldier is bound to do. He realized that the outcome of the impending battle depended on three main factors: the reaching, occupation and fortification of the Aliakmon Line before the German onslaught; the willingness of the Greeks to abandon their forward positions and adopt a more realistic strategy; and the timing of the German attack – which could be delayed by bad weather. Undaunted, Wilson drew up his plans. By 2 April he had deployed most of the limited forces available to him along the Aliakmon Line in such a way that British and Greek formations were interleaved with each other. By so doing Wilson hoped to infect the Greek forces with some of the metal of Imperial forces.

On 6 April 1941 Germany declared war on Greece and Yugoslavia simultaneously. In the air this meant that the 320 aircraft of the Italian forces were supplemented by 400 Luftwaffe bombers and 380 fighters and reconnaissance planes. Air Vice Marshal D'Albiac commanding the RAF element in Greece could muster barely 80 aircraft by this time, approximately a third of which were committed to the Albanian front. On the ground, after the capitulation of the Greek Army of East

Macedonia in Thrace on 9 April, the five divisions of 'W' Force faced the full might of von Weich's Second Army, comprising three corps totalling eight infantry divisions, three motorized divisions and two panzer formations deploying over 200 tanks. Over the next few days as the fighting increased Wilson was told by Wavell that he could offer little hope of any further reinforcements from Egypt owing to the mounting pressure being exerted by Rommel in Cyrenaica. In view of the general situation Wilson decided to develop his plans for a withdrawal to a more defensible position. His first intention was to link up with Greek forces which would abandon Albania and Western Macedonia and, together with 'W' Force, establish a line across central Greece from Mount Olympus in the east through the Pindus mountains to the Adriatic.

But by now 'W' Force was sustaining serious losses, the state of morale of the Greek forces falling back – at last – from Albania was not reassuring, formal resistance in Yugoslavia was fast collapsing and the Germans had almost complete control of Macedonia. It now appeared doubtful if his latest planned fall-back position would be tenable. Wilson decided to withdraw to a line that could be held by 'W' Force alone. This he called the Thermopylae Line. It would involve a rapid retreat of 100 miles, with German air superiority making the operation extremely hazardous. On 13 April Churchill sent a signal to his commander in Greece: 'It is impossible for me to understand why the Greek Western Army does not make sure of its retreat into Greece. ... All good wishes to you in this memorable hour.'5 Wilson's decision to retreat to the isthmus at Thermopylae was approved. The successful completion of this operation was much to the credit of the staff officers and men concerned and not least to Wilson, who had the courage to follow his own instincts and judgement when he must have felt terribly isolated. Enemy air superiority had made the retreat a hellish manoeuvre to carry out.

Whilst 'W' Force reorganized in its new positions, Wilson was heavily involved in a number of crucial conferences that sealed the fate of the Imperial presence in a rapidly collapsing Greece. Some Greek troops had actually been demobilized, others sent on leave. On 18 April the Greek Prime Minister Korysis, unable to face the ruin of his country, killed himself. On the 19th Wavell, who had flown in from Cairo, after conferring with Wilson and the Greek Government, decided on the evacuation of Imperial forces.

It was at this stage that the relationship between Churchill and Wilson received a temporary setback. The Prime Minister had signalled Wavell in Cairo on the 15th: 'We have no news from you of what has happened on the Imperial front in Greece.' On the 19th he followed this up with another signal to Wavell copied to Wilson deploring the lack of any reports ' ... from General Wilson or from you. ... This is not the way the Government should be treated. It is also detrimental to the Service as many decisions have to be taken here and we are in constant relations with the Dominions and with foreign countries. ...' The signal went on to demand ' ... a short, daily report on what is happening on the front of the British and Imperial Army'.[6]

General Wilson was, understandably, put out by the implied criticism. Wavell lost no time in replying to London that, although he agreed that communications had been bad, this was not the fault of the force commander. Signal links had broken down; two of the three liaison officers had been wounded; the single flight of Lysander army co-operation aircraft had been out of action since 7 April and the critical situation inevitably resulted in Wilson giving priority to more immediate matters.

Despite fierce fighting involving 4 and 6 New Zealand Brigades in particular – and which resulted in considerable loss of life on both sides on the 24th and 27th – the bulk of the Imperial Forces had been evacuated by 29 April. An estimated 43,000 troops were brought safely out of Greece. The original strength of 'W' Force is normally put at 57,660; thus much more than the original estimate of about thirty per cent were rescued, but at a heavy price in equipment and shipping. The impact of Wilson's 'W' Force had not proved negligible. Britain had been seen to honour her undertakings and the lesson was not lost on America. Indeed it has been claimed that the German need to mount a campaign against Yugoslavia and Greece caused the invasion of Russia to be put back from May to June with critical results, as this delay cost Hitler his chance to occupy Moscow and possibly destroy the Stalin government. This is, of course, to argue with the benefit of hindsight; but Jumbo Wilson, to the end of his days a Rifleman first and foremost, liked to compare his campaign in Greece to that of Sir John Moore in 1808–9, which prevented Napoleon from completing the conquest of Spain, even if the cost was another desperate evacuation operation and ultimately the loss of the commanding general's life at Corunna. The entire Balkans expedition, including operations in Albania and Yugoslavia, absorbed twenty-seven German divisions including seven armoured, over a critical period. The Greek campaign also gained a valuable breathing space which allowed British and Imperial reinforcements to reach the Middle East from East Africa, India and Great Britain. For Wilson, the campaign ended in predictable but honourable defeat, though not through any fault of his own. The task had been an impossible one from the outset but he had tackled it with a brave heart and considerable military skill. He wrote to his wife Hester on 1 May 1941: 'So ended a military adventure which I hope I will not participate in again. The political considerations overrode the military ones and led us into a gamble based on the uncertain quality of Balkan allies.'[7]

As soon as General Wilson returned to Cairo from Greece, Wavell appointed him Commander of British Troops in Palestine and Trans-Jordan. He arrived in Jerusalem in early May to find that the Iraqi Army was laying siege to the RAF station at Habbaniya. Since early 1941 the political situation in Iraq had steadily worsened as the Prime Minister, Rashid Ali, began collaborating openly with the Germans, supported by a substantial part of the Iraqi Army. In March the Regent of Iraq had fled the country, and Rashid Ali had seized power. In the face of these events Wilson organized a small column which made its way by desert route from Palestine to the relief of Habbaniya and the occupation of Baghdad. This was accomplished in co-operation with the Habbaniya garrison and a brigade which had been sent from India. Wilson's force was in Baghdad by 31 May when an Armistice was signed. The assistance given by the Vichy French in Syria to German aeroplanes using Syria as a staging post on their way to support the Rashid Ali revolt in Iraq caused Churchill to instruct Wavell to occupy Vichy Syria and Lebanon. If either country were occupied by the Axis, they would clearly constitute a threat to British forces in the Middle East and result in the isolation of Turkey. Most of the 7th Australian Division, 5 Indian Infantry Brigade and the Free French Middle East contingent were available for operations. Wilson decided on a three-pronged advance northwards along the coast to Beirut. This was not, however, a straightforward military undertaking. De Gaulle had arrived in Jerusalem at the end of May and he had some very definite ideas not only about the role of the Free French but also as to how the Vichy French were to be treated.

Allied troops crossed the frontier into Lebanon on 9 June and very soon encountered stiff resistance from Vichy French forces; some bitter fighting took place between Free and Vichy French. Damascus was taken on 3 July and Beirut surrendered on 12 July after Wilson had threatened to bomb the city. It had been a most unpleasant and messy campaign. Badly handled, the affairs in both Syria and Iraq could have landed the British Government in a great deal of trouble. Faced with these events Wilson demonstrated his not inconsiderable abilities as a negotiator and diplomat. De Gaulle was, even at this stage, notoriously difficult to deal with; Wilson seems to have handled him with consummate skill. Despite his direct manner and bluff exterior those who had served with Wilson when he was an instructor at Staff College in the early 1930s knew him as a man who was capable of wise and balanced judgement and a degree of tact and sensitivity which was put to good use in negotiations with the Vichy French after their surrender in Syria and Lebanon and before their repatriation to France.

Early in July 1941 General Wavell was replaced by Auchinleck as Commander-in-Chief Middle East. Why did Auchinleck not choose Wilson for command of the Eighth Army? In a letter to Dill (then Chief of the Imperial General Staff) on 16 August 1941 he wrote: 'Cunningham ... ought to fit the bill very well at GOC-in-C Western Desert. The South Africans who will be under him know him well and think a lot of him, which cannot fail to help. ... In view of the PM's strong advocacy for Wilson for the Western Desert, I have sent him a private wire today telling him that my final choice is Cunningham. ... I am quite sure that Jumbo [Wilson] is best where he is.'[8] On 2 July Churchill had urged the new C-in-C to consider Wilson for command in the Western Desert. 'It is much to be regretted,' Churchill later wrote, 'that this advice, subsequently repeated, was not taken.'[9]

Wilson was in many ways the obvious choice for command of the Eighth Army. He had a high reputation as a tactician and he had gained valuable experience of tank warfare in the Western Desert during the successful winter campaign of 1940–41. Planning for the 'Crusader' campaign of November 1941 started in August, by which time Wilson had brought his operations against the Vichy French in Syria to a successful conclusion. He could have been moved. The precise reasons for passing Wilson by for this key appointment will never be known for certain. It may be that Auchinleck thought it preferable to appoint the victor of East Africa rather than the man who had been unlucky enough to be given the Greek command. It is more likely that he thought Wilson was too old at sixty for field command.

Meanwhile Wilson got on with the business of bringing Syria into the orbit of defence of the Middle East. The time that he had available to prepare for attack from the north depended upon the outcome of the battle being fought in south Russia where the right wing of the German armies were pressing on into the Donetz Basin; it was not outside the bounds of possibility that it might reach the Caucasus the following spring. By this time Wilson's command had been redesignated the Ninth Army. The entry of Japan into the war on 7 December meant that he was soon becoming aware of the diversion of men and resources to the Far East. This did not make life any easier when, after the fall of Tobruk in June 1942, he had to prepare contingency plans for the defence of Palestine against attack by Rommel across the Sinai.

During the first week in August 1942 Wilson met Churchill for the first time in Cairo. Out of their meeting, at which Smuts, Wavell and Alanbrooke were also present, came changes in the Middle East Command structure: Alexander took over as C-in-C Middle East, Montgomery the Eighth Army and Wilson was appointed C-in-C to the new Persia/Iraq command created in view of the advance of the southern wing of the German armies towards Stalingrad and the Caucasus. His tasks were, first, to safeguard at all costs the oilfields and oil installations in Persia and Iraq from land and air attack and, second, to guarantee oil supplies from Persian Gulf ports to Russia to the maximum extent possible. With no prospect of operations before the spring, Wilson spent the last months of 1942 planning the deployment of the Tenth Army to meet the German threat from Russia. But the Russian counter-offensive in front of Stalingrad changed everything. The Persia/Iraq Command lost its operational importance, and in late January 1943 Wilson was again recalled to Cairo where Churchill told him that he wanted him to take over the Middle Eastern command. Alexander was to be appointed Deputy C-in-C to Eisenhower in North Africa to take charge of operations to capture Tunis.

As C-in-C Middle East, Wilson's tasks were, in order of priority: to maintain the Eighth Army and support its operations until Tunisia was finally cleared of the enemy; to take all measures conforming to the requirements of General Eisenhower for mounting that part of the operation for the attack on Sicily which would be launched from Middle East Command; to make preparations to support Turkey; and to make plans for amphibious operations in the eastern Mediterranean.

In April 1943 Wilson travelled to Ankara to finalize the details of Allied aid to Turkey in the event of a German invasion. It was this sort of quasi-diplomatic role that suited Jumbo Wilson so well. He got on easily with people; he was a 'fixer' and Churchill undoubtedly recognized his talents in this direction. On 16 June Wilson was summoned to Tripoli to meet King George VI who had come to North Africa on a tour of inspection. After lunch on that day Montgomery and Wilson were knighted in the field.

The news of the Italian Armistice on 8 September placed a greater emphasis on resistance movements in Greece, Yugoslavia and Albania. The Italian defection from the Axis left far fewer occupying troops on the ground and larger areas of countryside ripe for guerrilla warfare. Thus the combined Chiefs of Staff laid down on 24 August that 'Operations in the Balkans Area will be limited to supply of Balkan guerrillas by air and sea transport, to minor commando forces and to the bombing of strategic objectives.'[10] Fitzroy MacLean, who spent this period commanding the British Mission to the Yugoslav partisans, was struck by Wilson's appreciation of the potential of guerrilla warfare.[11] He got on well with Tito, guiding difficult meetings in the right direction and, with the aid of the occasional apposite joke, managed to keep those present in good humour.

That autumn Wilson approved the occupation of the Dodekanese Islands, the Italian garrisons of which had – with the exception of one small island – quietly surrendered by 18 September. Churchill, on hearing of Wilson's plan, had sent him a signal on 9 September: 'Personal from Prime Minister to Commander-in-Chief Middle East. Good. This is the time to play high. Improvise and dare.'[12] But the loss of the Dodecanese touched a raw nerve with the Germans, who were stung into counter-action. Kos fell to a German counter-attack on 3 October which the Italian garrison, although stiffened by the Durham Light Infantry, refused to oppose and Leros was retaken on 12 November. The failure of the Aegean adventure was a grave disappointment to Wilson. Churchill had signalled him again on 13 September:

From Prime Minister for General Maitland Wilson. Personal and Most Secret. The Capture of Rhodes by you at this time with Italian aid would be a fine contribution to the general war. Let me know what are your plans for this. Can you not improvise the necessary garrison out of the forces in the Middle East. What is your total ration strength. This is the time to think of Clive and Peterborough and of Rooke's men taking Gibraltar.[13]

There were not, however, sufficient landing craft available at the time in the Mediterranean for such an undertaking. The Dodekanese adventure had always been marginal, Rhodes was out of the question. Wilson would dearly have liked to carry out Churchill's cherished wish to capture Rhodes, but Roosevelt consistently refused to allow any forces to be diverted from Eisenhower and Overlord. The bleeding of the eastern Mediterranean of resources brought Churchill into the most acute differences he ever had with Eisenhower, but at the same time it brought Wilson even closer to the Prime Minister.

Wilson met Churchill in Tunis in December 1943 where the Prime Minister informed him that Eisenhower was to command Operation Overlord the following spring and that he was to succeed Eisenhower as Supreme Allied Commander in the Mediterranean in January 1944. At the time Wilson took over command, two major operations were imminent: the Anzio landings on 22 January and a second operation, codenamed Anvil, against the southern coast of France then scheduled for May. The Anzio bridgehead once established, though secure, failed to achieve the hoped-for break-out. Wilson felt that Allied resources in the Mediterranean could not support two major operations and at the same time hold a reserve in case it was required for Turkey. So he sought a broader directive that required him to contain the maximum number of German divisions in south Europe using the forces earmarked for Anvil. Thus he hoped to continue to concentrate his main effort in Italy but to keep the enemy guessing by posing various potential threats elsewhere. In so doing he was walking a political tightrope: Stalin expected Overlord and Anvil to take place simultaneously in the spring; the French were anxious to have French troops on French soil as soon as possible; Churchill and the British chiefs of staff wanted to kill Anvil stone dead, whilst the Americans wanted to keep it alive. Through all this Wilson was conscious, more than anything else, of being an Allied C-in-C.

On 7 March 1944 he received a three-page signal from Churchill accusing him of being too neutral as an Allied commander and not resolving strategic differences with the Americans sufficiently robustly. It is much to Wilson's credit that he withstood these conflicting pressures and retained the complete confidence of his staff. Churchill failed to understand the delicate balancing act involved in running an Allied staff. Had he fully appreciated the complete fusion of staff and working relationships which Wilson had managed to achieve he would not have objected, as he did in one of the many telegrams he sent to Wilson, to the spelling of the word 'theater' rather than 'theatre' in messages sent out from Allied Forces HQ. Wilson's solution to the conflicting requirements of the Allied governments was to let Anvil die naturally which, without an additional transfusion of landing craft, was going to happen anyway. Once Rome had been taken then it might be advantageous to switch the main thrust elsewhere. Meanwhile Wilson determined to concentrate all his efforts and resources on Italy.

The attempt to break the stalemate in Italy commenced on 11 May 1944 and, after vicious fighting around Cassino, II and IV US Corps drove over the Alban hills on 1 and 2 June to overlook Rome. Allied troops entered the city on 4 June. Wilson, as he had promised, then turned his main efforts to Anvil. The landings by the Seventh US Army on 14 August in the South of France were a testimony to the high standard of teamwork that had been achieved between the three services of Britain and the US – with the added complication of having II French Corps under command. The German Nineteenth Army was severely mauled, some 50,000 prisoners being taken by the end of September. Yet Wilson had firmly opposed Anvil from the outset and Churchill saw it as an extravagant and unnecessary diversion. He, and Wilson with him, would have much preferred to have increased Allied strength in Italy and pressed on up through Austria and Hungary, whilst exploiting Tito's successes in the Adriatic. Anvil prevented this strong thrust into Europe, so keenly sought by Wilson and the Prime Minister. It is interesting to speculate what effect such a strategy might have had on the shaping of postwar Europe.

During the last three months of 1944, Wilson was managing the Eighth and Fifth Armies battling northwards in Italy, the Seventh Army in the South of France, SOE operations in Yugoslavia and special forces operations in Greece. At the end of October, after the German withdrawal from Athens, he returned to Athens and was presented with the Freedom of the City, a city which he had left in very different circumstances three years previously. The fact that he was still in the Mediterranean, indeed had been since 1939, perhaps explains more than anything else why he never caught the public imagination in quite the same way as Monty or Alexander or Alanbrooke or Wavell, all of whom achieved higher-profile roles. Wilson's contribution in the Middle East and Mediterranean was solid rather then spectacular. But that was in keeping with his character and exactly as he would have wanted it described himself.

Wilson handed over command of the Mediterranean theatre to Alexander on 12 December 1944. Churchill's especial trust in the faithful Wilson was exemplified when he appointed him as his personal representative in all military matters to the President of the United States. On 21 November 1944 Churchill had cabled Wilson: 'I can find only one officer with the necessary credentials and qualities, namely yourself.'[14]

Alexander as a field-marshal. His fighting record, good looks and aristocratic sang-froid made him the personifcation of the soldier in the eyes of Churchill, who spared him criticism even during the slowest stages of the Italian campaign.

Wavell, though the most intellectual of Churchill's generals, was temperamentally out of tune with the Prime Minister and had the misfortune to command campaigns where the advantage lay with the enemy.

Above O'Connor in Scotland in 1944 after his return from captivity. His offensive against the Italian army in Libya in 1940 produced the first British victory of the war and established him as one of the army's best liked and trusted commanders.

Left 'Jumbo' Wilson his elephantine size was complemented by a shrewd brain and massive calm, displayed at their best in his management of politico-military relations in the Middle East.

Above right Ritchie (centre) with Generals Norrie and 'Strafer' Gott in the Western Desert. Ritchie had the misfortune to command against Rommel at a low ebb of British fortunes.

Right Cunningham, brother of Britain's leading admiral of the Second World War, achieved outstanding success in defeating the Italians in East Africa but was outgeneralled in the Western Desert by Rommel.

Montgomery and Alanbrooke. Alanbrooke's acute intelligence and high professional competence made him the one military colleague whose authority Montgomery dared not challenge.

Montgomery, in characteristically didactic pose, with war correspondents in Normandy, June 1944. His pedantic attention to detail and lack of self-doubt were among his most important battle-winning qualities.

Hobart, the tank pioneer, advocate of specialized armour and commander of 79th Armoured Division. Temperamentally an outsider, and an impossible subordinate, he made crucial contributions to the success of D-Day.

Percival, before his defeat in Malaya and surrender of Singapore to the Japanese. Official Britain never forgave him for these humiliations.

Slim was, with Montgomery, the most consistently successful of Churchill's field commanders. Unlike Montgomery, he possessed a natural authority and humanity which impressed all who served with him.

Wingate was the strangest of Churchill's generals, a Zionist, a failed suicide, a rebel against convention but a tactical visionary whom Churchill believed might have been a second Lawrence of Arabia.

Churchill surrounded by the grandees of the Anglo-American high command, including Alanbrooke (second left), Alexander (fifth left) and Montgomery (right), North Africa, June 1943. The group also includes Generals Eisenhower and Marshall.

As such he became head of the British Joint Staff Mission in Washington in January 1945. Here he represented Churchill and Attlee in the highest matters of state until early 1947. His main achievement in Washington was the maintenance of a happy and effective working relationship with the Americans. Sending Wilson to Washington was an astute move by Churchill.

What can we make of this great wartime commander whom history has largely passed by? 'Jumbo' Wilson was surprisingly lacking in panache. He seemed to make very little attempt to put himself across to the general public. Instead he simply got on with the series of formidable jobs assigned to him. Not surprisingly he was a product of his generation and, in this respect, held fundamentally differing views to some of the younger wartime generals who had been affected so much by the thinking of Fuller and Liddell Hart. Wilson, it must be remembered, like Churchill had fought in the Boer War. That is not to suggest for a moment that he lacked the capacity for innovative thinking. One only has to look at his desert campaign of 1941 to witness daring initiative and bold decision. But it may account for a certain wisdom and a degree of caution arising from a lifetime of rich and varied experience. Wilson was at his best guiding meetings, cementing relationships, smoothing ruffled feathers, engineering acceptable compromises and persuading the reluctant. He was even, steadfast and cheerful in adversity and a man to be trusted. He made no pretence to be an intellectual and was more impressive in direct confrontation than on paper. He chose his words carefully and was a shrewd judge of character and circumstances. His decisions were on the whole sound, though some of his arrangements for operations in the Dodekanese have aroused criticism.

Churchill undoubtedly had a high regard for Wilson and would have liked to have seen him appointed to command the Eighth Army rather than Cunningham in 1941. It is pointless to speculate what might have been. It is probably fair to say that Wilson was the right man for the difficult, if unspectacular, problems of Syria, the Lebanon, Palestine, Iraq and Persia. He was certainly the right man for command in the Mediterranean and for Washington. Many other senior officers would undoubtedly have been disheartened by what was probably the most enduring theme of his years in wartime command: a continual lack of resources. Wilson was always faced with a more important theatre which had first call on resources: the defence of Great Britain when he was in Egypt, of Egypt when he was in Greece, of the Far East when he was in Palestine, and finally by the strains which Overlord imposed on Italy, Anvil and the Dodekanese.

From his arrival in Egypt in 1939 to his return to England in early 1947 from Washington, Jumbo Wilson spent eight years overseas. Few wartime commanders gave such unstinted and unremitting service. Of all Churchill's generals, his relationship with the Prime Minister was probably the closest. Though he is unlikely to be remembered in history as one of the great wartime field commanders, he deserves to be remembered, like Eisenhower, as a leader who moved nations to work together in a common cause.

NOTES

1 From copy of original report in Wilson Family Papers.
2 Original letter from Wavell to Wilson, Wilson Family Papers.
3 Wilson, *Eight Years Overseas*, p. 66.
4 Text from original signal in Wilson Family Papers.
5 Text from original signal in Wilson Family Papers.
6 Cited in John Connell, *Wavell – Soldier and Scholar* (1964), p. 417.
7 Wilson Family Papers.
8 Cited in John Connell, *Auchinleck* (1959), pp. 285 and 285.
9 Churchill, *Second World War*, vol. III, p. 354.
10 Wilson, *Eight Years Overseas*, p. 179.
11 Fitzroy Maclean, *Eastern Approaches*.
12 Text from original signal in Wilson Family Papers.
13 Text from original signal in Wilson Family Papers.
14 Churchill, *Second World War*, vol. VI, p. 230.

CHRONOLOGY: HENRY MAITLAND WILSON

1881, September 5	Born at Stowlangtoft Hall, Suffolk
1895, September	Starts at Eton
1899, January	Starts at Royal Military College, Sandhurst
1900, March 10	Commissioned into the Rifle Brigade
1901	Serves with 2nd Battalion The Rifle Brigade in South African War
1902	Serves with 2nd Battalion in Cairo
1902, March 18	Promoted Lieutenant
1908, April 2	Promoted Captain
1911, October	Appointed Adjutant, Oxford University Officer Training Corps

1914, October	Appointed Brigade-Major 48 Infantry Brigade (16th Irish Division)
1914, December 1	Marries Hester Mary, daughter of James Digby Wykeham
1915, September 1	Promoted Substantive Major
1915, December	Posted to France with 48 Infantry Brigade
1916, June	Appointed GSO2 41st Division
1917, October	Appointed GSO2 New Zealand Division and awarded DSO
1919, January 1	Promoted brevet Lieutenant-Colonel and attended Staff College
1920, January	Appointed Company Commander RMC Sandhurst
1923, August	Appointed Second-in-Command of 2nd Battalion The Rifle Brigade in Aldershot
1927, January	Appointed Commanding Officer of 2nd Battalion in Landi Kotal, North West Frontier
1928	Moves with 2nd Battalion to Jullunder
1930	Promoted full Colonel and appointed Chief Instructor at Staff College
1934, January 16	Promoted Brigadier and appointed Commander of 6 Infantry Brigade
1935, April 30	Promoted Major-General
1935–37	Spends two years on half pay
1937, August 18	Appointed Commander 2nd Infantry Division
1939, June 15	Promoted Lieutenant-General and appointed Commander British Troops in Egypt
1941, February 22	Appointed Commander of Greek expedition
1941, May 6	Appointed Commander of British troops in Palestine and Trans-Jordan
1941, December	Appointed Commander Ninth Army in Syria and Palestine
1942, August 21	Appointed Commander Tenth Army in Persia and Iraq
1943, February	Appointed Commander-in-Chief Middle East
1944, January	Appointed Supreme Allied Commander in the Mediterranean
1945, January	Promoted Field-Marshal
1945, January 12	Appointed Head of British Joint Staff Mission in Washington DC
1946, March 12	Created 1st Baron Wilson of Libya and Stowlangtoft, County Suffolk
1947, April 23	Departs Washington DC for Great Britain
1947	Appointed President of the Army Cadet Force Association

1955	Appointed Constable of the Tower of London
1960	Retires as Constable
1964, December 31	Dies peacefully at home

10

O'CONNOR

General Sir Richard O'Connor

BARRIE PITT

At the end of October 1940 Mr Churchill was experiencing deep frustration and was thus in a mood of mounting anger. The Battle of Britain had by now passed its crisis point leaving the RAF the undoubted victor, the army which had escaped from Dunkirk was in the process of re-organization and re-equipment as far as was possible and positioned to defend the island's shores should Hitler continue with his plans for invasion; but Britain's only truly professional army, though separated from their enemy by nothing except empty desert, was apparently content to assume a defensive posture, with no intention of taking the initiative against an equally quiescent foe.

Western Desert Force consisting of the 7th Armoured Division and the 4th Indian – the only two divisions in the British Army outside India which could now lay serious claim to a high degree of expertise – was deployed in Egypt doing little, so far as he could see, but use up petrol and vehicle mileage in endless training exercises, and watch the advanced camps of the Italian Tenth Army. The previous month the forward divisions of this 80,000 strong army commanded by General Berti, under the watchful eye of the Commander-in-Chief, Italian Army in Libya, Marshal Rodolfo Graziani (himself continually goaded by Mussolini) had moved ponderously across the Libya–Egypt border, flooded down the Escarpment on to the coast road more by its weight than its energy, and then crept reluctantly eastwards – watched curiously by the British reconnaissance units in the vicinity – until they reached Sidi Barrani.

Here, apparently exhausted by their efforts, they rested, pushing forward only a few miles during the next week as far as Maktila. They then brought up another army but this time of civilians – labourers and engineers who set about constructing a series of fortified encampments on an arc curving south-west from Maktila as far as Nibeiwa nearly twenty miles away, and a second group on top of the Escarpment around Rabia and the Sofafi positions. Along the line of the coast between Sollum and Sidi Barrani they also began the construction of a metalled road and a continuous water pipeline, and soon the former was in use bearing thousands of tons of supplies, brought up and fed into the encampments. It seemed that these were intended to become a permanent feature of the desert scene – and so far as Mr Churchill could see the British Commander-in-Chief, General Sir Archibald Wavell, was prepared to sit still and allow it to happen!

What made the situation even more difficult to accept, was the fact that at Wavell's urgent representations Churchill had himself recently taken the decision to send a supply convoy out to the Middle East carrying over 150 tanks, 100 pieces of artillery, nearly 1,000 machine- and anti-tank guns and as much ammunition as could be crammed aboard – and this at a time when the Battle of Britain had not been won, and men all over England were drilling with pikes instead of guns, armbands instead of uniforms, flags instead of artillery.

Churchill had even overridden Admiralty advice and ordered that the convoy should risk the Mediterranean passage in order that the arms should be at Wavell's disposal as quickly as possible And what was he doing with them? Nothing except make futile gestures against the Italian Empire in Ethiopia (which in Churchill's opinion could well be left to 'wither on the bough') ... and sit and watch Graziani's men consolidate their positions.

In some desperation Mr Churchill had sent the Secretary of State for War, Mr Anthony Eden, out to visit Wavell at the beginning of October to find out what was happening, but when on 28 October Italy invaded Greece, Mr Churchill decided to wait no longer and that the time had come for Draconian measures. If Wavell would not use the men and weapons he had received in the Western Desert, then they should be taken away from him and sent to support the Greeks in their hour of need; and he would brook no argument.

Faced with this ultimatum, Wavell now had no choice but to reveal to Mr Eden that plans were, in fact, well advanced for an attack on the new Italian encampments, but security considerations had made it necessary for the details to be known only to the chief protagonists of the attack, Generals Maitland Wilson and O'Connor.

Relieved, Mr Eden flew home and on 8 November was able to tell Mr Churchill the news – to which the reaction was far better than could have been expected. If slightly put out by Wavell's secrecy, he 'purred like six cats' as the details of the plans were unfolded, ordered a 'Staff study' to be made to ensure that every means of exploitation would be available to follow up any unexpected success, and after assuring Wavell that security on the project would be as strict in Whitehall as it had been in Cairo, sent for the career details of the man who would command the operations on the ground.

Richard Nugent O'Connor was born in 1889, the son of a major in the Royal Irish Fusiliers, was educated at Wellington College and Sandhurst and in 1909 had been commissioned into the Cameronians (Scottish Rifles). He was thus twenty-five years old when the First World War began, and he saw such service on the Western Front and in Italy that when it ended he had been awarded the Distinguished Service Order and bar, the Military Cross, the Italian Silver Medal for Valour, and had been mentioned in despatches nine times. He had also commanded the 1st Battalion the Honourable Artillery Company at Passchendaele as a lieutenant-colonel, a rank he was not to hold again (having reverted to captain at the end of the war) until 1936 when he was given command of the 1st Cameronians; he was almost immediately to be promoted further to take command of the Peshawar Brigade facing the Khyber Pass at a time of some anxiety in the area.

After two years of extremely active service there, he was promoted major-general to command the 7th Division in Palestine, an appointment which also carried the post of Military Governor of Jerusalem. This was the time of the Arab Revolt against ever-increasing Jewish immigration into the country as a result of Nazi persecution, and the role of British troops there was to attempt to keep the peace. They were thoroughly hated by both sides. At the time the northern half of Palestine was garrisoned by the 8th Division commanded by Major-General Bernard Law Montgomery, and between them they exercised such control that both service and civilian casualties were kept to a minimum, and the Jewish settlements at least could expand.

Then in June 1940 Mussolini declared war on Britain. Within twenty-four hours reconnaissance patrols of the 11th Hussars had torn gaps in the wire fencing that the Italians had erected all along the border with Egypt, and captured over fifty astonished Italian soldiers – and O'Connor had received a cable from the commander of British troops in Egypt, Lieutenant-General H. Maitland Wilson, ordering him to proceed immediately to Mersa Matruh, to take command of all forces in the frontier area and undertake the task of protecting Egypt from Italian attack.

These instructions, O'Connor later recalled, he received 'with surprise, and of course pride', adding 'My recollection is that I was given very sketchy instructions as to policy. I did not object, really, as I don't mind being left on my own.'

The two men made an almost ludicrous contrast – Jumbo Wilson massive, heavy in jowl, deep-voiced, slow and almost majestic in gesture, filling his chair and the space to his desk almost to overflowing; O'Connor small, bird-like, sitting nervously on the edge of his chair rather like a shy schoolboy at his first interview with his housemaster. His voice was light and clear, only the medal ribbons on his chest belying his gentle manner and reminding the observer that here was a professional soldier of thirty years' very distinguished service.

A professional soldier, too, of considerable intellectual achievement. The delicate head held a cool and logical brain which saw to the heart of a problem with a certainty and speed which could make other quite sound soldiers appear slow-witted; the slight body had already unconcernedly endured battle in Alpine snows, in Ypres mud and the heat of India, and the gentle manner masked a will and determination as firm as any commander in history. Here was a clear example of the British regular soldier in the mode long ago established by Sir Garnet Wolseley – small, neat and highly professional.

By the middle of June 1940, O'Connor was established at his headquarters at Maaten Baggush, thirty miles east of Mersa Matruh, assessing the forces now under his command, studying the intelligence reports of those against whom his mission was to protect Egypt, and also the land over which he might have to control battles. Three weeks after he had taken command, an astonished subaltern commanding a reconnaissance patrol already fifty miles into enemy country, met his general in his staff car coming from even further west, and when his superior back at base remonstrated with O'Connor, O'Connor apologized; but as his need grew to know even more about the ground which might become his battle area, neither the brigadier's remonstrance nor O'Connor's polite acceptance prevented him from going even deeper into enemy territory whenever he felt it advisable.

Then in September Graziani's elephantine invasion began its ponderous roll forward and O'Connor employed Fabian tactics of withdrawal with his reconnaissance and infantry units, designed to exact the highest possible price for every foot of ground yielded. To the south, he kept the tank squadrons of the 7th Armoured Division out of sight, poised to strike up to the sea and cut the supply and communication lines of the forward Italian divisions when they were sufficiently extended.

The time for this thrust up to the coast, O'Connor considered, would be when the advancing Italians reached Mersa Matruh – surely the minimum target for such a massing of armed force. Then the Italian advance slowed and stopped just past Sidi Barrani, the Italian civilians appeared and work began on the arc of encampments a bare fifty miles into Egypt, and it became obvious that for the moment there was to be no further thrust towards Mersa Matruh, or the continuation of Mussolini's by now much-vaunted Drive to the Nile.

'It was all', wrote General O'Connor as he withdrew the tanks of the 7th Armoured Division and redeployed the Support Group, 'rather a disappointment.'

The task of throwing the Italian divisions back over the border – and even further if possible – was from then on, and despite Mr Churchill's doubts, the overriding objective of Western Desert Force and its commander. The nub of the problem was the disparity in the size of the forces that would be engaged.

Quite soon O'Connor knew that five Italian divisions occupied the camps in front of him; one Blackshirt division in Sidi Barrani, two Libyan divisions divided between Maktila on the coast and the two Tummar camps, a mobile group at Nibeiwa and a Metropolitan division in the Sofafi and Rabia camps. In reserve was a Blackshirt division at Buq Buq, while further back at Sollum, Bardia and Tobruk lay the equivalent of four more divisions; units of the Regia Aeronautica in the region gave them a superiority in numbers of aircraft over the RAF of about five to one.

O'Connor's own forces in the desert consisted of only the 7th

Armoured Division and the 4th Indian, plus 'Corps' troops and the Matruh garrison. In manpower they amounted to some 36,000 men (against 80,000 enemy in the immediate area of attack) but in addition to high morale, these possessed some real advantages. The two armoured brigades of the 7th Armoured could put nearly 200 light and 75 cruiser tanks into battle, and only 60 of the Italian tanks opposite – M11s or M13s – were in any way comparable. The eighty guns of the 1st and 4th batteries of the Royal Horse Artillery with the Support Group of 7th Armoured were all 25-pounders – more than a match for the Italian 75 mms defending the camps; and altogether 7th Armoured and 4th Indian would be putting eleven highly trained infantry battalions into battle, with, of course, all the ancillary engineer, transport, ambulance, recovery and repair services.

But it was with the 'Corps Troops' that the most potent weapon in O'Connor's arsenal lay, for in addition to three more batteries of 25-pounders, one battery of 6-inch howitzers and one of 4.5-inch, they included the 7th Royal Tank Regiment which possessed forty-eight heavy 'I' (Infantry) tanks – the Matildas. The Italians had nothing even faintly comparable and, so O'Connor had every reason to believe, not the slightest inkling of their presence in the Delta. As for air cover, by stripping every available plane from every base in Wavell's command – which stretched from Aden to the Sudan and from Iraq to Egypt – the RAF would be able to put up 48 fighters (two squadrons of Hurricanes and one of Gladiators) and 116 bombers – a mixture of Blenheims, Wellingtons and Bombays – plus two squadrons of reconnaissance aircraft directly under O'Connor's command as Army/Air Co-operation.

Nevertheless, though quality was undoubtedly a high card on O'Connor's side, quantity was so much on Graziani's that two other factors must be brought to play – surprise and exact planning. In pursuit of the first, the RAF wore its pilots to exhaustion and its planes to shreds keeping the Regia Aeronautica away from the area between Maaten Baggush and the border, so that for twenty-four hours a day stores, ammunition and equipment could be moved forward to huge camouflaged Field Supply Depots. As for planning, O'Connor himself and the three senior officers of his staff, Brigadiers John Harding, 'Sandy' Galloway and Eric Dorman-Smith, devised and oversaw exercises both on paper and over ground marked out to resemble the Italian encampments, and gradually evolved a plan to take the fullest advantage of their own strengths and the enemy's weaknesses. The plan was for a 'Five-Day Raid' which would destroy the enemy presence on Egyptian soil, and leave open the possibility of further exploitation if circumstances permitted. The raid would be codenamed Operation Compass, and be launched through the Enba Gap – the space between the bottom of the Escarpment and the Nibeiwa encampment.

By 0100 on the morning of Monday 9 December, the men and the machines were all in place and ready to move off through the gap. From away to their right they could hear the sounds of bombing as the RAF attacked Nibeiwa, and shelling much further away as the Royal Navy attacked Maktila and the northernmost of the Tummar camps. The noise of aircraft was to be kept up all night even when they had run out of bombs, simply to keep Italian attention away from their western approaches.

The orders were given, the long columns crept forwards, 4th Indian infantry and the Matildas curving around to reach the northwestern corner of Nibeiwa by dawn, Support Group infantry and guns atop the Escarpment in a screen to cut off the Rabia and Sofafi garrisons from the battle about to open below them; 4 Armoured Brigade tanks and armoured cars crept north to cut the Sidi Barrani–Sollum road, 7 Armoured Brigade waited in the gap as reserve.

O'Connor and his staff waited and watched from their advanced HQ on the edge of the Escarpment above Bir Enba itself. They could hear no sign of activity of any kind from Nibeiwa or further north, only the sounds of RAF or Royal Navy bombardment coming to them across the desert. Unlikely though it seemed, they had moved over 30,000 men and all their weapons and equipment nearly 100 miles forward from the Delta without the enemy detecting even a concentration of force which might threaten them, let alone an intrusion into their midst of one armoured and one infantry division.

Before dawn the only fully dressed Italian troops in Nibeiwa were the sentries and the cooks preparing breakfast – all shocked out of their minds as the first rays of the sun hit the camp at the same time as a deluge of shells fell among the positions on the eastern face of the camp, directing all eyes that way. As a result, few actually saw the line of Matildas come over a crest half a mile from the main entrance at the north-west corner, to smash their way with almost contemptuous ease through the road-block and the main gates, then fan out across the camp area like avenging furies.

The Italian artillery reacted quickest, but they had first to swing their guns around – for no one among the Italians had dreamed of an attack coming from the rear – and when they did, their shells bounced off the Matildas' armour to howl away into the desert beyond. Impervious and implacable, the tanks ground forward, crushing the gun-crews, knocking the guns off their bases, then when all of them had been silenced, turning their attention to the slit trenches and sunken tents in which the Libyan and Italian infantry were frantically dressing and groping for their weapons. Few had any opportunity to fire them for hard on the heels of the tanks came the Camerons and Rajputana Rifle-men of II Indian Brigade, herding those who surrendered in time back towards the entrance, dealing swiftly with the few who showed any sign of resistance.

Within two hours, Nibeiwa was taken. Dead and wounded lay among the debris and litter of the battle, more than 4,000 officers and men were huddled together in sullen and shaken groups of prisoners, twenty-three Italian tanks, scores of lorries and machine-guns and a positive Aladdin's cave of gorgeous uniforms, bottles of Italian wine, mountains of spaghetti and huge cheeses were there for the victor's taking.

But the victors had other duties to attend to. The battles for the two Tummar camps were tougher than that for Nibeiwa for the supreme advantage of surprise was gone. But in the end the Matildas were as irresistible as ever, the British and Indian infantry as swift and implac-able, and by the time the early dusk had fallen, only one section of Tummar East was still holding out, and they surrendered the following dawn. Maktila and Sidi Barrani were by now surrounded, 4 Armoured Brigade had cut the Sollum–Sidi Barrani road, while to the south at the top of the Escarpment the Support Group still watched the Rabia and Sofafi camps from which there had been no sign of activity all day, and not even much in the way of curiosity about what might be happening to their compatriots below.

To General O'Connor, who had left his HQ soon after the first attack had gone in and been closely attending all phases of the day's actions, it was evident that the highest of his hopes was in the process of being realized; he could now expand his plans for the future. By the evening of 10 December, the main problem posed him by the erstwhile garrisons of the arc of Italian camps from Sidi Barrani down to Nibeiwa was how to feed, water and despatch 38,000 officers and men back towards the Delta and prison-camps while at the same time continuing his own advance to the Egyptian border. First Buq Buq and then Sollum must be taken by the armoured brigades, while the Support Group rounded up the Sofafi and Rabia garrisons. It was while redeploying his forces to bring all this about that O'Connor received an order so unwelcome – indeed, so apparently unrealistic – that he could hardly believe it.

On General Wavell's direct order, 4th Indian Division was to return to the Delta with all its weapons and transport for despatch down into the Sudan, where yet another attempt to invade the Italian East African Empire was to be launched. Their place would be taken as soon as possible by the three brigades of the 6th Australian Division composed of men, the bulk of whom though undoubtedly keen, tough and extremely fit, had hardly been in the army long enough to complete their basic training.

'It was a tremendous shock,' O'Connor was to write later. ' ... I had had no previous intimation of it and it came as a bolt from the blue.'

But it had to be obeyed and as quickly as possible; at least 4th Indian Division's transport could be used to clear some of the enormous build-up in the prison cages.

Meanwhile, the sheer impetus of the success ensured more. The Sofafi and Rabia garrisons – to O'Connor's annoyance – were not cut off from the frontier, but instead, with little more than a token defence of their positions against the Support Group, collected together and trudged away to the west, and very soon it was obvious that other Italian garrisons had the same idea. Soon the garrisons of Sollum, Fort Capuzzo and Sidi Azeiz were all streaming north into the fortress of Bardia and although Sidi Omar was not so quickly evacuated, its defence against two squadrons of RTR and 7th Hussar tanks lasted only ten minutes.

By now the perimeter around Bardia had been strengthened, its garrison had swollen to 45,000 under the command of General Annibale Bergonzoli ('Electric Whiskers') who had already sent to Mussolini the categorical assurance: 'In Bardia we are and here we stay.'

But by 20 December, 16 Australian Brigade had arrived and begun the siege process, a week later 17 Brigade moved up alongside, and twenty-two Matildas circled around to the north of the port with Support Group infantry. At dawn on 3 January, Bangalore torpedoes tore gaps in the chosen sector of the perimeter fence, all Western Desert Force's remaining guns crashed out, and to add to the roar the Royal Navy joined in from the north and east. Australian engineers went in first to check passages through minefields, the huge Australian infantry stormed forward (singing 'South of the Border'), more engineers threw bridges across the ditch and over them waddled the Matildas. Over 400 prisoners were taken in the first twenty minutes – and by noon, the astonished and overworked rear echelons were struggling to cope with 30,000.

The only severe resistance was encountered in the southern section where 17 Brigade, who had marched nearly fifteen miles before reaching the battle area, came up against Italian gunners who fought well, and against whom there were no more Matildas to send. There was some bitter fighting amid the wadies and it was not until the following morning that the last line of defence posts was stormed – but by that time, the Australian thrust in the centre had reached the heart of the fortress around Bardia itself.

At 1100 hours the drive into the town was launched, the six Matildas now left ground forward with Australian infantry alongside and often in front and, with very little in the way of armed resistance, the attackers found themselves with a repetition of what was becoming O'Connor's chief problem. Columns of men marched towards them to surrender, led this time by 'dapper officers wearing swords, pith helmets or "Mussolini caps", knee boots, shaven and scented'. All that now remained was the mopping-up, and by the next morning Bardia was in Australian hands, 40,000 prisoners had been taken and 400 guns captured.

One Italian who was not taken was 'Barba Elettrica' Bergonzoli, who had prudently departed for Tobruk quite early in the proceedings; but it was unlikely that he had arrived in that area much before General O'Connor, whose plan now included an attempt to take Tobruk 'on the bounce'.

He was frustrated by lack of transport. Seven Armoured Brigade had swept through El Adem and cut the western approaches to Tobruk before the last Italians in Bardia had surrendered, and 19 Australian Brigade (not used at Bardia) was sealing in the eastern side of the Tobruk perimeter twenty-four hours later. But it was not until 9 January that enough men and material had been brought up (quite a lot in captured Italian Lancia lorries, driven and maintained quite often by their original drivers who were most willing to help in any way they could) to invest the entire thirty-mile perimeter of Tobruk. It was now evident that a deliberate phased attack would have to be mounted.

It began at 1540 hours on 21 January, and by that evening the Australians of 19 Brigade had taken both Fort Pilastrino and Fort Solaro, while those of 16 and 17 Brigades had driven along the perimeter to take all the defence posts – underground and encased in solid concrete – in the eastern half, and cut and occupied the Tobruk–Bardia road from the eastern perimeter to the central crossroads overlooking the airfield and the port itself. They had also captured the fortress commander, Generale Petassi Mannella and all his staff, but were now so tired that they dropped immediately they stopped moving, and slept where they dropped. Not that the Italians in the neighbourhood bothered them during the night, for they were being beaten not only by Australian vigour and élan, but by their own propaganda. During the previous weeks, in order to avoid having to take more vigorous action himself, Marshal Graziani had repeatedly painted a picture of overwhelming British strength in Egypt – which included one of his more ludicrous flights of fancy, 'the omni-present Camel Corps'. Now the men in Tobruk who had fled there from the previous encounters embroidered their accounts in the same vein. They were unlikely to give accurate numbers to add to their embarrassment, even if they knew them.

The following day when the Australian forward patrols probed down towards the port of Tobruk, quite expecting some form of resistance, the first enemy soldiers they saw ran forward to help them remove a roadblock, and within minutes they were being guided to a large building where Admiral Massimiliano Vietina was anxiously waiting to surrender. Long before noon, the Italian flag had been hauled down from above the headquarters building, and an Australian slouch hat hoisted in its place. Another 27,000 prisoners had been taken and an acceptable number of guns and vehicles – and food and drink in such quantity that for the first few hours many monumental thirsts were slaked with champagne.

Once more, Generale Bergonzoli had vacated the scene early on and was quickly in Benghasi, and General O'Connor was following, urging 7 Armoured Brigade forward into the Djebel towards Martuba, and 4 Armoured to the south to cut the road north from Mechili where an Italian armoured brigade had been reported. As for infantry, three days after the Australian 19 Brigade had stormed through the Tobruk defences, they were driving and marching (for transport was desperately short now and what there was, was worn out) towards Derna where the next line of Italian defences lay, while the other Australian brigades rested and tried to cope with yet another vast batch of prisoners.

During the last week of January 1941 O'Connor was almost totally concerned with the enormous logistical problems which would face an attempt – and he was determined to make one – to press on into the great Cyrenaican bulge and destroy the rest of the Italian Tenth Army there. The Royal Navy were breaking records running petrol and supplies into Tobruk, offloading them and speeding them on their way to the front, and the formation of three more Field Supply Depots was proceeding at Tmimmi for the infantry, twelve miles south for 7th Armoured and one out further to the south-west of Mechili should any attempt to cut along the bottom of the bulge be necessary. By 2 February Brigadier Dorman-Smith had returned from Cairo with assurances from General Wavell that any further advance would receive his blessing and that the required stores – some 3,000 tons plus 1,000 tons of water – would be arriving at their destinations in about twelve days, during which time the troops could enjoy some rest and the tanks could receive some maintenance (though the fifty cruisers left in 7th Armoured Division were all long past their time for complete overhaul, their track mileage having been in some cases exceeded by eighty per cent).

But on the same day the Australians along the coast walked into Giovanni Berta and found no one there to oppose them, a patrol of 11th Hussars probed into Chaulan and found it deserted – and the following day the Australian brigades reported that they were out of touch with the enemy along their entire front. Graziani had lost his nerve and ordered the evacuation of all Italian forces out of the Cyrenaican bulge, back towards Tripoli.

Thus, instead of twelve days, XIII Corps – as Western Desert Force had recently been rechristened – had less than three hours' rest, repair or maintenance. They spent the remainder of 3 February frantically collecting fuel, ammunition, spare tank tracks and as much basic food as they could find, then worked all night repairing their vehicles while their unit commanders studied the orders which O'Connor and his staff dashed off, delivered themselves or sent by despatch rider.

The armoured brigades had concentrated around Mechili (4 Armoured in some disfavour as the Italian armoured brigade – to O'Connor's intense fury – had been allowed to slip away). Their task now was to get their fifty cruisers and ninety-odd light tanks stocked with food and water for two days and as much ammunition as they could cram aboard, and then to put themselves across the coastal road running down the Gulf of Sirte from Benghazi in order to block the Italian army's only escape route. The distance was some 130 miles, the route totally unreconnoitred. It was to prove worse than any of them had ever experienced, with the result that more and more tanks were forced to drop out with every mile covered.

However hard the tank drivers tried to raise the speed, it became obvious that they would never reach the road in time. So the armoured cars were sent off ahead, and after them all the wheeled traffic – infantry lorries, Royal Horse Artillery batteries and scout cars – which could travel faster than the tracked vehicles. The armoured cars of 11th Hussars and King's Dragoon Guards were at Msus by 1500 hours on 4 February to chase an astonished Libyan garrison away. By midnight the leading wheeled vehicles led by Lieutenant-Colonel Jock Campbell of the RHA – with headlights ablaze to avoid danger from Thermos bombs – arrived, and during the morning of 5 February the tanks appeared. One small force was sent due west through Sceleidima towards Ghemines, the rest followed the armoured cars first down to Antelat, then due west to form the block across the road at Beda Fomm.

Incredibly, they arrived in time. The Hussars reached the road just after midday, Rifle Brigade companies filled the gap between the road and the coast by early afternoon, the batteries of the Royal Horse Artillery were in position behind them with their ammunition stacked around them by 1600 hours – and half an hour later the head of what proved to be the leading column of the Italian Tenth Army came bowling unconcernedly along the road towards them.

At the same time as 7th Armoured Division were grinding their way along the base of the bulge, the Australians, by superhuman efforts, were clawing their way around the coast, through Appollonia, Cyrene, Barce, El Abiar – and at last Benghazi came in sight. Their transport was in as bad shape as that of the rest of O'Connor's force, but somehow they manhandled it across broken bridges, over blown and cratered roads, over wadis, through minefields and along the sides of hills, their forward patrols always in danger of ambush by Italian rearguards who would slip away after the first exchange of fire. Only the Australians with their tough physique, coupled with the determination to uphold the military reputation their fathers had won at Gallipoli and their respect for O'Connor, could have covered that awful ground in the time. But they did, and the northern arm of O'Connor's pincer movement closed down on the rear echelons of Bergonzoli's command as they prepared to evacuate Benghazi, and chased them into the maelstrom developing to the south.

The Battle of Beda Fomm was fought on 6 February by a tiny but resolute blocking force, acutely conscious of the fact that they were short of food and ammunition, and were to all intents and purposes out of fuel. They must either win or starve – and starve to death as there was nothing for them to live on in the desert behind them. Fortunately, their antagonists were convinced that they were faced by an enormous force of highly efficient armour and infantry (not to speak of the Camel Corps) equipped with vast numbers of the most modern and sophisticated weapons. The Italians also suffered from the disadvantage of large numbers cramped into a small – and certainly very thin – space; and by the end of that day they were being chivvied from the rear by the fearsome Australians.

Pressure from behind bulged the head of the column, but Italian infantry there were shot flat by the Rifle Brigade companies and the moment Italian armour put in an appearance, they were hammered by Jock Campbell's guns. By the afternoon, the tanks of 4 Armoured Brigade were cruising along their flanks, shooting up any sign of organized resistance. When darkness fell, although the British were worried about their almost empty ammunition boxes and pouches, the Italians were approaching despair at the enormous odds they imagined they faced.

At dawn on 7 February, one more attempt by Italian tanks was mounted. It came perilously close to success did they but know it; but in the end the last five M13s were stopped by the last RHA anti-tank guns – manned by a major, his batman and the battery cook firing their last rounds. And as the exhausted British riflemen and tank crews watched the vast column of men stretching back for miles out of view, wondering what would happen now, a startling change came over the scene. 'First one and then another white flag appeared among the host of men and vehicles. More and more became visible, until the whole column was a forest of waving white banners.' The last of the Italian Tenth Army was surrendering to XIII Corps, commanded by Lieutenant-General Richard O'Connor.

O'Connor and Eric Dorman-Smith had spent the day of the battle organizing and urging on anything they could find in way of supplies. On the morning of 7 February, after breakfasting each on a cold sausage, they drove down in time to watch the Italian surrender, and in due course visited the building where Italian senior officers were being gathered.

'You were here too soon, that is all,' Bergonzoli had said after the capture. 'But we gave battle at once. . . . And always, here as everywhere else, we were grossly outnumbered!'

No one bothered to disabuse him, but the fact was that his Tenth Army had been destroyed by a force which had never exceeded 35,000 officers and men, and had advanced 500 miles in ten weeks in vehicles old and battered before the advance started. Over 130,000 Italian and Libyan soldiers had been taken prisoner, 180 medium and about 200 light tanks, 845 guns and an uncounted number of wheeled and soft-skinned vehicles captured.

In those ten weeks, 500 British and Australian soldiers had been killed, 1,373 wounded and 55 were missing, later posted 'believed killed'.

'I think this may be termed a complete victory as none of the enemy escaped,' O'Connor commented, and later sent a cable to Wavell which began 'Fox killed in the open. ...'

But in O'Connor's opinion it need not end yet. Despite their exhaustion, thirst and hunger, his men were so buoyed up by victory that they could hardly be held back when the whole of Libya, and certainly the port of Tripoli, was surely theirs for the taking. Eighty per cent of their vehicles were in serious need of repair, but if stores came up they would work on them until the wheels turned and if necessary drag them forward. So, giving them his thanks, O'Connor sent Dorman-Smith hot-foot back to Cairo to assure Wavell of their eagerness to advance further, and to ask him to hasten the arrival of the most essential materials.

But when Dorman-Smith arrived at Wavell's office all maps of North Africa had gone and in their place hung a huge map of Greece. Wavell, whose eyes had long been fixed on the Balkans and who never thought North Africa of vital importance, was giving his support to Anthony Eden's wish to send the most powerful force which could be raised across the Mediterranean. XIII Corps would advance no further than El Agheila.

It was a great disappointment to O'Connor, but he organized defensive positions as quickly as he could, then reported back to Cairo where he was found to be suffering from stomach complaints and went into hospital. The front of Cyrenaica was stripped of the most experienced men – including all of the 6th Australian Division – and sent to Greece where in due course they were destroyed in the disaster which followed. And two months later Rommel, who had arrived in Tripoli on the day of Beda Fomm, drove the original units of his Afrika Korps forward at the light screens of British troops at El Agheila, and so rapidly and efficiently did they move that within six days they were approaching Mechili, while chaos reigned throughout the British ranks behind them.

Wavell had himself visited Barce on 2 April, appreciated the disaster which loomed and sent for O'Connor to come as quickly as possible to help General Neame, who was now in command, to sort some order out of the chaos. But it was too late and – tragically for the British – both Neame and O'Connor were taken prisoner by a small striking force Rommel had sent out in advance of his main strength.

As soon as their identities had been established, Neame and O'Connor were flown to Italy, and by 20 April they had both arrived at the Sulmona prisoner-of-war camp in the Abruzzi, east of Rome. Here O'Connor remained until the Italian armistice of September 1943 when he managed to escape from the camp and make his way southwards, disguised in costumes from the wardrobe of the camp dramatic society.

Once home he received the knighthood he had been awarded in 1941, and confirmation of his rank of Lieutenant-General. But his absence from the field during those crucial twenty-six months barred him from the highest command which would certainly have been his otherwise, although he did command VIII Corps during the bitter fighting around Caen after D-Day, later to break through the German defences east of the Orne and reach the Seine. This was the last of his important war-time operations, although he did become Commander-in-Chief of Eastern Command in India, then of the North Western Army. He returned to England in 1946 and spent the last two years of his service as Adjutant-General to the forces.

Honours came to him from his own country and abroad; he was ADC to King George VI from 1946 to 1948 and he was an honorary LLD of St Andrew's University. But he will always be remembered as the man who won the first spectacular victory for British arms of the Second World War.

Although he was in no way bitter about it, O'Connor remained convinced that had Wavell had the vision to see the opportunities that success offered Western Desert Force during the first three days of Operation Compass, and had left 4th Indian Division with him, sending up the Australian 6th Division as reinforcement instead of replacement, then the advance into Cyrenaica would have been that much faster; 4th Indian Division's expertise and especially transport would have lifted them to Benghazi well before the end of January, and they could have been around the corner and on their way to Tripoli before Hitler decided to intervene, let alone actually despatched Rommel and the first of his panzer units.

The Ifs of history are of course imponderable. But one certainty is that the loss, so early, of Richard Nugent O'Connor from the higher direction of Britain's war effort was as unfortunate for us as it was for him.

CHRONOLOGY: RICHARD O'CONNOR

1889, August 21	Born (father Major M.C. O'Connor, Royal Irish Fusiliers)
1903–8	Wellington College
1908–9	Royal Military College, Sandhurst
1909, September	Commissioned The Cameronians (Scottish Rifles)
1914–18	Western Front; commands Honorable Artillery Company Infantry Battalion, Italy; DSO and bar, MC, Italian Silver Medal for Valour, mentioned in despatches nine times
1919–31	Student and Instructor, Staff College, Camberley; Company Commander, RMC Sandhurst; regimental duty
1932–4	GSO2 War Office
1935	Student, Imperial Defence College; marries Jean Ross (d 1959)
1936–8	Commander, Peshawar Brigade, North West Frontier of India
1938–9	Military Governor of Jerusalem; major-general
1939	Commanding 6th Division, Palestine
1940–1	Commander, Western Desert Force; lieutenant-general; CB 1940, KCB 1941
1941, February	Commander, British Troops, Egypt
1941, April– 1943, December	Prisoner-of-war, Italy; escapes
1944–5, January	Commander, VIII Corps, Britain and NW Europe
1945–6	Commander, Eastern and North-Western Commands, India; promoted general, 1945
1946–7	Adjutant-General; GCB, 1947
1948	Retires
1951–4	Colonel of The Cameronians (Scottish Rifles)
1955–64	Lord Lieutenant, Ross and Cromarty; Lord High Commissioner, Church of Scotland, 1964; marries Dorothy Russell, 1963
1971	Knight of the Thistle
1981, June 19	Dies in Scotland

II

CUNNINGHAM, RITCHIE AND LEESE

General Sir Alan Cunningham
General Sir Neil Ritchie and
Lieutenant-General Sir Oliver Leese

MICHAEL CRASTER

Probably the single most famous Army in popular British military history, the Eighth Army has come to occupy a unique place in our military mythology. It overshadows even the Fourteenth Army, a fact sourly recognized in the nickname 'The Forgotten Army' adopted by the latter, and this despite the fact that other Armies in other theatres fought battles of equal skill and savagery and had victories of great consequence. In part the Eighth Army owes its fame to the timing of its most celebrated victory; the Second Battle of El Alamein on 23 October 1942 came at a moment when the fortunes of the Allies appeared to be at their lowest. The Japanese were sweeping all before them in the Far East, the entry of the Americans into the war had not yet been marked by success of arms, and a victory was desperately needed for the sake of national morale. It is a measure of that need that this victory effectively over-shadowed the memory of all that had gone before in the desert, so that to the man in the street there was really only one battle of Alamein; Auchinleck's battle of July 1942 was forgotten.

Above all, however, the fame of the Eighth Army is due to Mont-gomery, the man who commanded it in this historic battle. This was a deliberate policy on Montgomery's part, for publicity was always his forte. The extent to which his image-building came to dominate both official and popular thinking is perhaps best exemplified in the War Office decision, taken after the war, to allow only those who served in the Eighth Army at Second Alamein and after to wear the figure 8 on their campaign ribbon, despite the fact that the Army was formed in September 1941. But if Montgomery built up the fame of the Eighth Army, his success had a less positive effect on the reputations of those officers who preceded and followed him at its head. For the Eighth Army actually had five commanders (six if one includes Auchinleck) in the short years of its existence, from its inception in the Western Desert Force to its final demise as British Troops Austria the day before the entry into Vienna in 1945. Of these five it was Montgomery who came to personify the Army in the public imagination.

Of the remainder three were removed from positions of senior command ('sacked' in popular parlance) in circumstances which have given rise to considerable controversy ever since. Two of them, Cunningham and Leese, had already proved extremely successful commanders in other theatres, while the third, Ritchie, went on to become, subsequently, a very competent Corps Commander in north-west Europe. These were men who were well regarded in their time, and of whom much was expected; failure was not in their vocabulary. In examining their cases therefore it may be possible to draw some lessons from them, to find a common thread that links them together. Thus the purpose of this chapter is not simply to provide a sympathetic rehabilitation but to use their stories to illustrate the pitfalls of high command using the experience of some of Churchill's less celebrated, but none the less able, generals.

The origins of the Eighth Army lie in the Western Desert Force, the troops allocated to the defence of Egypt against the Italian threat from Libya. Already a multinational force, containing British armour and Australian, Indian and New Zealand infantry under the command of Lieutenant-General Richard O'Connor, these were the troops that carried out the astonishing offensive of December 1940 when the Italian Tenth Army under Graziani was driven back from Sidi Barrani on the eastern side of the Egyptian frontier to eventual annihilation at Beda Fomm on 7 February 1941. At a cost of less than 2,000 casualties, of whom 500 were killed, O'Connor with four divisions had defeated an army of ten divisions, capturing 130,000 prisoners, 380 tanks and 845 guns. The offensive was not allowed to continue into Tripolitania because troops were required for the abortive campaign in Greece and O'Connor's were the most experienced and most readily available. Thus a great opportunity was lost: XIII Corps, as the Western Desert Force had been renamed on 1 January 1941, was disbanded, its units and personnel dispersed and a static area command, Cyrenaica Command, set up with new and inexperienced units to defend the recently captured territory.

The failure to allow O'Connor to continue into Tripolitania had allowed the first elements of the German reinforcement for Libya, under Lieutenant-General Rommel, to land unopposed a week after Beda Fomm. British Intelligence assessments considered no German advance would be possible before mid-April at the earliest, but Rommel, never one to be hampered by what others considered as difficulties, attacked on 31 March. By 14 April Tobruk was invested in a siege that was to last 7½ months and by 28 April the British were once more standing on the defensive on the frontier of Egypt. Both Neame, the Area Commander, and O'Connor, recalled by Wavell from his new post as GOC British Troops Egypt to help him, were captured. The Axis forces' shortage of fuel, together with the presence of a lively garrison in Tobruk dangerously close to their lines of communication, led to a lull in the fighting. This lasted effectively until 15 June, when XIII Corps, commanded by General Beresford-Peirse, mounted Operation Battleaxe in an attempt to throw the Axis forces back from the frontier as far as Derna, and so relieve Tobruk. The attack was not a success, largely because of the haste with which it had been prepared; much of the equipment had only just arrived in the theatre, and there had been insufficient time to prepare it for battle and to weld together the new teams that were to man it.

The fact that Battleaxe took place when it did was principally the result of the constant goading of Wavell, the Commander-in-Chief, by Churchill himself. Wavell was having to cope simultaneously with the aftermath of the Greek operation, a pro-German revolution in Iraq that threatened Britain's oil supply, and a planned invasion of Vichy-French Syria. Churchill's eyes were, nonetheless, fixed firmly on the Western Desert where 'a victory ... to destroy Rommel's Army ... would at least save our situation in Egypt from the wreck'. In his bitter disappointment at the failure of Battleaxe Churchill relieved Wavell on 5 July, replacing him with Auchinleck. However, recognizing at the same time how much he had asked of the former, he also sent out Oliver Lyttelton to take care of political affairs and appointed an Intendant-General to oversee the rearward logistics.

Thus in principle the Commander-in-Chief was freed to concentrate upon the matter in hand – the defeat of the Axis in the field. The emphasis from London was still on victory in the desert. The other operations were sideshows in comparison, because until the enemy were driven out of North Africa the Mediterranean was not safe for Allied shipping; until the Cyrenaica airfields at least were in Allied hands air cover could not be provided for the Malta convoys; and Australia was pressing the British government hard for the relief of the Australian Division currently penned up in Tobruk. There were therefore from the outset very strong pressures on Auchinleck's approach to operations in the desert, which made it imperative for him to find the right Commander for his army in the field. His choice fell upon General Alan Cunningham.

General Cunningham had just completed a successful campaign against the Italians in Ethiopia where, with a mixed force of Commonwealth troops, principally South African and East African, totalling approximately 77,000, he had defeated the Duke of Aosta and his force of some 280,000 European and native troops in an advance that had taken him from Kenya to Addis Ababa between February and May 1941, and had culminated in the restoration to the throne of Haile Selassie. A gunner, and the brother of the distinguished sailor Admiral Cunningham – who was at this time Commander-in-Chief Mediterranean Fleet and would subsequently, as Admiral of the Fleet Viscount Cunningham of Hyndhope, become First Sea Lord – General Cunningham had had a fine record in the First World War and a successful career between the wars. From the outbreak of hostilities in 1939 he successively commanded no fewer than three TA divisions before being appointed to succeed General Dickinson in command of the Commonwealth Forces Kenya, in November 1940. His Ethiopian Campaign had been greeted with acclaim by a British public that felt itself starved of military success, and it was the dash and elan that he had shown in East Africa that led Auchinleck to ask for him. There was a feeling that such qualities, so admirably displayed by O'Connor, were essential if the British were to succeed against Rommel – a man in whom the same qualities were all too apparent.

There was nothing, however, in General Cunningham's background, training or experience that particularly equipped him to lead a large armoured force in the desert. In this he was typical of most of the British commanders of his generation, including his Commander-in-

Chief, brought up on the experience of First World War and the small colonial campaigns that had succeeded it. Unlike their opponents the British had never fully grasped the nettle of conversion from horsed cavalry to armoured fighting vehicles. Although British theorists led the world in their discussions of armour and its tactical use, it was pre-eminently the Germans who had put those theories into practice, and had then applied them in war. The results had been experienced in France in 1940, and in the Western Desert in 1941. In effect, O'Connor's campaign in 1940 against the Italians had been merely an extension of the small wars of the colonial era; speed, manoeuvre, and surprise against an ill-coordinated and poorly-sited enemy had enabled him to defeat the Italians in detail and hustle them to the gates of Tripolitania. But unlike his successors, he had not had to face a really well-trained, well-motivated armoured force, whose commander was steeped in both the theory and the practice of armoured warfare.

Not only was General Cunningham thus confronting a new environment and new techniques of which he knew very little, he also had to meet a dauntingly tight timetable. Churchill maintained his relentless pressure on Auchinleck. New equipment was continuing to flow into the Middle East from the factories of Britain. The desert forces were being given top priority for *matériel* and, with his inimitable conviction that equipment once delivered was immediately ready for action and his refusal to accept that time was needed for training and conversion, the Prime Minister was demanding an early offensive. Auchinleck had set the date at November. The operation was to be called Crusader, and Cunningham received his briefing on 2 September. He had two months in which to form and train his army.

The army was to be called the Eighth Army. It was formed officially as such on 26 September. It would have two Corps, XIII to be commanded by General Godwin-Austen, who had been one of Cunningham's divisional commanders in East Africa, and XXX, to be commanded by General Willoughby Norrie. XIII Corps was to be an infantry Corps, containing two Divisions (1st New Zealand and 4th Indian) and a Guards Brigade. XXX Corps was to be an armoured Corps, containing 7th Armoured Division of three armoured Brigades, and a support Group of guns and lorried infantry. There were tanks in the infantry Corps but they were 'I' tanks, designed for infantry co-operation, and considered not suitable for use in decisive tank-versus-tank encounters. In contrast to the German practice of mixed battle-groups of armour and infantry, therefore, the British had opted for the organization put forward by the proponents of the theory that tanks alone could win battles, by being massed in sufficient strength to defeat the enemy's armour and then going on to defeat his infantry and artillery in detail. The problem at this stage in the desert conflict, as Crusader would show, was that the British lacked, at all levels, the training and experience in armoured warfare necessary if theory was to be put into practice.

The task that faced Cunningham was a formidable one. He had to take on the preparation and planning for a major battle that had already been started before he arrived. He had to come to terms with a wholly new environment and a series of military disciplines with which he was completely unfamiliar, he had to take command of a force several times larger than any he had commanded hitherto, and he had to impose his authority upon subordinates whose knowledge and experience of both techniques and terrain were far greater than his own. He had very little time in which to do all this, and the consciousness that the eyes and hopes of everyone at home were pinned upon him increased the pressure immeasurably. It was an unenviable position, but one which Cunningham approached with resolution and energy.

Crusader was timed to start on 18 November, and, as laid down by Auchinleck, had as its main purpose 'to drive the enemy out of North Africa, first by capturing Cyrenaica and secondly by capturing Tripolitania'. One of the principal aims, constantly urged by the Prime Minister, was the relief of Tobruk, now in the seventh month of its siege, the original defenders, 6th Australian Division, having been relieved in September by 70th Division. Rommel's attention at this time was concentrated entirely on Tobruk. He now commanded all Axis forces east of the Cyrenaica bulge; his Panzer Gruppe Afrika consisted of Cruewell's Afrika Korps, containing 15th and 21st Panzer Divisions and Division ZBV (subsequently better known as 90th Light Division), Navarini's XXI Corps of four Italian Divisions, and the Italian Savona Division. Also in Cyrenaica was Gambara's XX Mobile Corps. At the start of the battle Rommel was guarding the frontier with the Savona Division, investing Tobruk with Navarini's Corps, and preparing the Afrika Korps for another attack on the fortress. His desert flank was covered by Gambara's two divisions, the Ariete Armoured at Bir Gubi and the Trieste Motorized at Bir Hacheim. His tank strength was 174 medium tanks in the Afrika Korps, and 146 in XX Mobile Corps. In addition he had 96 of his 50mm anti-tank guns and 12 of the dreaded 88s with the Afrika Korps, and 23 of the 88s with the Savona Division.

The British order of battle has already been described. Cunningham's plan was designed to force Rommel to a decisive tank battle, with the relief of Tobruk as an inevitable, but almost incidental, consequence. To achieve this, Norrie's XXX Corps, with its 491 tanks, was to make a left hook around the frontier defences and occupy Gabr Saleh. The theory was that Rommel would be unable to ignore this threat and would be bound to engage it with the bulk of his armour, thereby bringing on the classic battle of tank fleets. In the meantime Godwin-Austen's XIII Corps would envelop the frontier defences, and await the successful outcome of XXX Corps' encounter after which it would be able to move forward to raise the siege and then continue to drive the Axis back to Tripolitania. It was a plan that was not without its critics; Norrie argued most forcibly that his Corps should not be called upon to halt at Gabr Saleh, a point of no particular significance either strategically or tactically, but should be allowed to push on towards the coast until it made contact with the enemy; Godwin-Austen put forward most strongly the case that his flank must be protected by some at least of XXX Corps' armour. In attempting to meet these objections Cunningham flawed his whole concept by splitting his armour.

The British attack took Rommel by surprise. Concentrating on his own attack on Tobruk he initially refused to believe that he was faced with a major offensive, but allowed Cruewell to send one battle group south to investigate. Initially XXX Corps' advance was unopposed, spirits were high and euphoria ran through the Army. There being no contact at Gabr Saleh, Cunningham allowed Norrie to exploit north. The result was a further fatal division of the armour, as 22 Armoured Brigade became drawn into a battle with the Ariete Division at Bir Gubi and 4 Armoured Brigade remained tied to the flank of XIII Corps, leaving 7th Armoured Division to continue alone to the airfield at Sidi Rezegh, which it reached by 20 November. The perilous consequences of this division were not seen by the army commander, who was greatly cheered by the tank battles of that day, authorizing XIII Corps to start their advance, and 70th Division to break out from Tobruk on 21 November. There was an illusion of victory, marked by an unfortunate press release in Cairo, all too quickly shattered as Rommel and his two Panzer divisions came into the battle, first holding the sortie from Tobruk and then driving the British off Sidi Rezegh on 23 November. On 24 November he mounted his astonishing counter stroke through the rear of XXX Corps' position, driving the British east and south-east, throwing the British command structure into chaos as XXX Corps' HQ took refuge in Tobruk and elements of XIII Corps in disorder started what became known as the 'Matruh Stakes'.

Already on 23 November Cunningham, swinging from the euphoria of victory to the despair of imminent defeat, had asked the Commander-in-Chief to come up to discuss the situation with a view to a possible withdrawal. On his arrival Auchinleck judged that Rommel must be in no less difficult a predicament than the British, particularly because of his logistic situation; accordingly he ordered the Eighth Army to stand fast and continue the offensive wherever possible. At the same time he concluded that Cunningham should be relieved, as he was no longer able to carry on the battle, a view shared by many of the senior commanders and staff officers on the spot. It was not an easy decision, but one that had to be made if anything was to be rescued from the ruins of Crusader. On 25 November, therefore, Major-General Neil Ritchie, the erstwhile Deputy Chief of the General Staff in Cairo, arrived to take over command, and Cunningham flew back to the Delta.

Cunningham was certainly not the first, and equally certainly not the last army commander to be relieved of his command in battle. It was, however, particularly unfortunate that a man who but a short time before had won such a glittering victory should have been exposed to such public humiliation. As has been said, the task that he faced was one of great difficulty. A man who had been fighting a major campaign since February, and who was called upon to take up the burden of Crusader without any respite, would have required great reserves of energy and will-power. Cunningham continued the fight to the finish, but it would appear that his reserves had been exhausted, leaving Auchinleck with no alternative but to relieve him. It was not, however, the end for Cunningham. A fine-looking man, with great charm and authority, he became the Commandant of the Staff College, Camberley shortly after leaving North Africa, and after a number of senior appointments he finally retired from the Army in 1948 having been the High Commissioner and Commander-in-Chief for Palestine.

There has been much discussion as to whether he should have been chosen in the first place, in view of his lack of experience of local conditions, and whether perhaps someone like 'Jumbo' Wilson (who was Churchill's preference) might not have been a better selection. The debate serves to highlight the controversy over Auchinleck's selection of his subordinates. He did not always choose wisely. For him the problem of selection was exacerbated by the fact that, as a product himself of the Indian Army, he had very little personal knowledge or experience of the majority of the senior officers of the British Army. Here was where the strong guidance of the CIGS was needed, but for once it was not forthcoming. Perhaps of greater significance on this occasion, however, was the fact that Auchinleck had great difficulty in accepting that those whom he had chosen were not up to the task that he had given them. It was this very trust and loyalty, given to those who served him, that made 'the Auk' the deeply loved commander that he was; no one would willingly abuse this trust and loyalty, but sometimes they imposed a duty greater than their recipients could perform. It was a mistake that was about to be repeated.

The Eighth Army's second commander, Major-General Neil Ritchie, was in direct contrast to his predecessor. Tall and impressive, he has been described as the image of a British general, and yet (with the exception of a very brief period after Dunkirk when he was charged with the formation of a new 51st Highland Division to replace that captured at St Valery, a period cut short by his being posted to the Middle East to join Wavell's staff) he had commanded nothing larger than a battalion. Commissioned into the Black Watch in December 1914 he had had a distinguished regimental record in the First World War, most of it in the Middle East. He had served on the staffs of Alanbrooke, Wavell and Auchinleck, and was thought of highly by all of them as an 'able and cool-headed staff officer'.

In November 1941, when Auchinleck was looking for a new Army Commander in a hurry, Ritchie appeared to be an excellent choice for a temporary appointment. To appoint one of the Corps Commanders would be to reproduce the problem at a lower level, at a time when all were heavily involved in the day-to-day battle; Auchinleck was no more inclined than before to accept Jumbo Wilson; and he rejected Ritchie's own suggestion that a new man should be sent out from England (pending whose arrival Auchinleck himself would assume command) on the grounds that a new man could not arrive in time and would, in any case, be unfamiliar with the operational situation. The feasibility of this proposition was clearly demonstrated seven months later when Ritchie himself was dismissed and Auchinleck fought First Alamein, but in November 1941 the Commander-in-Chief had other ideas. In any case this was only a temporary appointment to tide the Army over a moment of crisis, after which a permanent commander could be brought in. Ritchie's lack of experience could be made up by Auchinleck himself, as exemplified by his presence at Eighth Army Headquarters for the first ten days of Ritchie's command, when Auchinleck effectively commanded the battle that led to Rommel's withdrawal (starting on 8 December), with Ritchie acting as his deputy.

By Boxing Day Rommel was back at Agedabia, and by 6 January 1942 he was at El Agheila. Cyrenaica was in British hands again, and it was time for a brief period of rest and reinforcement before the offensive was continued. It was time also to consider the appointment of a permanent Army Commander more qualified in age and experience, to take over the Eighth Army. Here, however, there was now a problem; because the Prime Minister in announcing Ritchie's original appointment had not said that it was temporary, it had been accepted by the world at large as permanent, and to return him to Cairo now would cast serious doubts on the achievements of Crusader. And so Ritchie stayed, partly perhaps because Auchinleck, having once reposed his confidence in a man, was very loath to relieve or replace him without the strongest grounds for doing so (and Ritchie's performance so far had seemed perfectly satisfactory); and perhaps partly, it has been suggested, because it gave Auchinleck a direct access to the battlefield, and to the challenges of command in battle, which were more properly denied to him as Commander-in-Chief.

It was indeed only a brief period of respite. To the complete surprise of the British, Rommel attacked again on 21 January, having been reinforced by the acquisition of 45 tanks landed on 19 December, some in Benghazi just before the Axis left the port. British intelligence had totally failed to detect this build-up (a failure which cost the Director of Military Intelligence in Cairo his job), and in the resulting offensive Rommel drove Ritchie right back to Gazala. All the infrastructure that had been building up in the desert in preparation for the British advance into Tripolitania was overrun, while the logistic echelons of the fighting formations streamed back eastwards in the celebrated 'Gazala Gallop' or 'the Second Benghazi Handicap'. In the course of the retreat Ritchie issued tactical orders directly to 4th Indian Division, countermanding those of Godwin-Austen, the Corps Commander (a move for which Auchinleck himself subsequently took responsibility), as a result of which Godwin-Austen asked to be relieved of his command. Auchinleck had flown up to Ritchie when he heard of Rommel's advance and had stayed with him, although on this occasion even he had not been able to stop the Germans. By 4 February, therefore, the Eighth Army found itself back at Gazala – Rommel had been unable to pursue them further, having outrun his supplies – with an Army Commander who had clearly been 'bounced' and who did not appear to enjoy the full confidence of his subordinates. It was a fraught situation. But Auchinleck still could not bring himself to let Ritchie go, despite the urgings of his Chief of Staff, Dorman-Smith, who had been charged by the Commander-in-Chief with visiting the Army and taking soundings.

The campaign in the desert perfectly exemplified that description of war as being long periods of boredom interspersed with brief spells of intense fear. Because of the logistic problems of maintaining an offensive over such a hostile terrain in which every necessity, both personal and military, had to be carried by the participants, the early battles in particular frequently came to a halt because one or other of the combatants had outrun their supply systems. Rommel was particularly vulnerable in this respect, and it was above all Auchinleck's appreciation of his opponent's predilection for operating with a haughty disregard for the niceties of logistic support that enabled him to detect the moment of crisis. There ensued now, between February and May 1942, another of those pauses, as both sides attempted to recoup their losses and prepare for the next round. Ritchie was concentrating on developing the area of Gazala as a springboard for another offensive to recapture Cyrenaica, an offensive for which Churchill back in England was pressing hard. Auchinleck was under a constant bombardment of letters and telegrams, urging action which would take the pressure off Malta. Mindful of the lessons of Crusader and the subsequent withdrawal, as well as of the loss of reinforcements and of some of his seasoned troops and squadrons to the Far East where the war with Japan was proceeding disastrously, the Commander-in-Chief resisted the pressure, urging the need for proper training, a proper supply situation and above all an adequate superiority in armour. He considered that a date around 1 June was practicable, or perhaps August. Churchill was appalled and in the resultant storm Auchinleck was very nearly replaced; faced with an ultimatum to attack in June or resign, he set a date to coincide with the passage of the June dark-period convoy to Malta. All of which came to naught, because by mid-May it became clear that Rommel was himself planning an offensive that would anticipate that of the British. Ritchie therefore turned his attention to the preparation of his army and the Gazala area for a defensive battle.

The Battle of Gazala started on 26 May. In it the Eighth Army was defeated and driven back to El Alamein, and Tobruk was lost. As a result both Army Commander and Commander-in-Chief were replaced.

Ritchie, as Army Commander, has borne the bulk of the criticism, which stems ultimately from the belief (held by Ritchie himself) that in view of his juniority and lack of experience of both the desert and higher command he should have been replaced once the Crusader crisis was over. Much has been written on the subject, most recently in his defence, but there can be no doubt that this is the key to the issue.

Ritchie had laid out his forces in a linear defensive position on the line Gazala to Bir Hacheim, along a thick 'mine marsh' that was covered by the famous 'boxes', each one manned with guns and infantry. Behind it was to be a reserve of armour, able to respond to any breakthrough and ready to move at the critical moment to influence the battle. It has been suggested that this was a particularly dangerous disposition of forces in the desert, and that Ritchie should have adopted instead something approaching the method employed by O'Connor in the early days of the war, when he covered the frontier with a screen of forward patrols and held the bulk of his forces well back. This ignores the fact that Ritchie had been preparing the area for an attack, so that to pull back as suggested would have been to hand over the vast supply dumps at Belhammed and Tobruk, as well as Tobruk itself, to the first serious incursion to be made by Rommel. However, Ritchie did adopt a curious command structure for his defensive line; instead of giving all the static defences to one Corps (XIII) and all the armour and mobile forces to the other (XXX), he simply drew a Corps boundary down the middle of the position and allotted all his forces north of that line to XIII Corps, and all those south of it to XXX Corps, which also commanded all the armour widely dispersed throughout the south of the area. He also ignored the well-tried military axiom that an obstacle that is not covered by fire is no obstacle; there was no possibility that the scattered 'boxes' could cover the full length of the mine-marsh, which would therefore have no more than a delaying effect on any enemy.

In numerical terms the two sides were not ill-matched. Rommel had 561 tanks, of which 280 were German medium tanks. The British had 850, of which 167 were the new Grants that shook the Germans so seriously when they first encountered them. The British Crusader tanks had not been a success, noted for their unreliability above all, and their low track-mileage life which restricted training. Nonetheless it does seem that contrary to popular mythology the tanks were well matched in terms of armour and armament, perhaps even with a slight advantage to the British. Where the Germans scored, and scored heavily, was in their skilful and aggressive use of the ample supply of anti-tank guns which they held, both the 50mm and the 88mm. The British frequently mistook the effects of these guns, deployed forward with the German tanks, for the effects of the tank guns, which gave rise to the prevalent belief in the superiority of the German armour. It was particularly unfortunate that the British never managed to deploy their excellent 3-inch anti-aircraft gun (the direct counterpart to the 88) in the same way.

Rommel's advance on 26 May caught the Eighth Army unprepared. Despite the warnings from Intelligence (perhaps because in the past it had proved so hopelessly inaccurate) the Army was not in its battle stations. Thus wrong-footed on the first day, it never properly recovered its equilibrium for the rest of the battle. Using the Italians to mask the Gazala position the German commander headed south through the desert, hooking round the Free French at Bir Hacheim, and striking north through the rear of the British positions. His route took him through both 1st and 7th Armoured Divisions, but because they were so widely dispersed he was able to engage and defeat their brigades in detail. The speed of his advance was such that at Bir Gubi half the garrison was still at Tobruk, swimming, so that there were insufficient men left to fire all the guns; while the headquarters of 7th Armoured Division was overrun and Messervy, the Divisional Commander, captured (although he subsequently escaped). It was a very confused situation in which the Army Commander, often wildly out of date because of the problems of communications, command and control, found himself quite unable to grip the battle. By the third day Rommel had been brought to a temporary standstill by a combination of the stubborn resistance of the British and his own supply problems, caused by his long and vulnerable lines of communication around Bir Hacheim. He therefore took refuge, with his customary ingenuity, in the shelter of the British minefields, in what became known as the Cauldron. Here he established a defensive position while clearing corridors through the mines to enable him to dramatically shorten his supply lines.

It was a crucial moment, on which Ritchie failed to capitalize. This was a time of interminable committee meetings between the senior members of the Eighth Army. Apart from reaching agreement that Rommel appeared to be beaten these meetings had little constructive result. 150 Brigade, in its 'box' threatening the Cauldron position, was annihilated by the Germans without any effective effort being made for its relief or reinforcement; the counter-attack on Rommel in the Cauldron was ill-coordinated, having two joint commanders instead of a single commander, and signally defeated; the future of Bir Hacheim could not be decided, until eventually after ten days of siege the garrison was ordered to evacuate. By 11 June the situation was critical.

On 12 June, when Auchinleck flew up to visit Ritchie he found the commander calm and resolute. Nonetheless it was not a good day; by that evening Rommel had smashed through both the British armoured divisions north-west of El Gubi, and the British tank strength had now been reduced to seventy. With the evacuation of the Knightsbridge box on the following day the Eighth Army was being pressed steadily back against the coast. Ritchie had had very serious problems of control; given the speed at which events in the desert were moving, every attempt he made to correct the situation or to retrieve the initiative was already irrelevant or out of date by the time that it was implemented. Throughout, however, he had remained steadily optimistic. Now he began to look over his shoulder. On 14 June he outlined to Auchinleck his plan to evacuate the Gazala defences and to establish a new defence in the area west of the Egyptian frontier. This inevitably meant giving up Tobruk, but at this point the Prime Minister intervened once again, with a telegram to the Commander-in-Chief making it clear that Tobruk must be held at all costs.

There is much discussion about the rights and wrongs of what ensued, and Ritchie is commonly blamed both for deceiving Auchinleck and disobeying his orders, although it is clear that Ritchie himself felt that his intentions were known and understood by his superior. In any event Auchinleck's instruction to hold the Tobruk–El Adem line was too late, already overtaken by Ritchie's orders for a general withdrawal, and by 18 June Tobruk was invested once again. This time, however, it was no longer the fortress it had been, many of its defences dismantled, or filled in for the convenience of the base depot it had become and many of its mines lifted to be used in the desert 'mine marsh'. Hastily garrisoned by the 2nd South African Division, and attacked by everything that Rommel could spare or scrape up, Tobruk fell to the Axis on 21 June. On 22 June Auchinleck flew up to visit Ritchie again, and sanctioned a further resumption of the 'Gazala Gallop' back to Mersa Matruh, to give the Eighth Army a chance to regroup and reorganize. But Rommel was never one to give his opponent an opening, and by 25 June he had closed up once again and was offering battle. It was at this point that Auchinleck, for the second time, stepped in and relieved the Army Commander, this time doing what many had argued that he should have done on his previous visit, and assuming command himself.

Ritchie had been a contrast to his predecessor in many ways. Tall, where Cunningham was short, bluff, jovial, the successful staff officer rather than the successful commander, they shared nonetheless the common disability of never fully coming to grips with their command. In Cunningham's case he was the new boy; new to the desert and new to this type of warfare. In Ritchie's case he knew the theatre, and many of the personalities, but he was at the disadvantage of being seen to be the junior, put in to do his master's bidding and never fully succeeding in establishing his authority in his own right. Both Cunningham and Ritchie were members of that select band of British commanders in the first part of the war who had to hold the ring while the country girded itself for total war. As such they had to fight their battles as best they could with what they had and with what they knew. It was with the benefit of their experience that subsequent commanders went on to win. Both Cunningham and Ritchie also were victims of Auchinleck's weakness in the selection of key subordinates – and of that loyalty which prevented him from rewarding perceived shortcomings early on with dismissal, as more ruthless men would certainly have done. But in the case of Ritchie, as with Cunningham, failure in the desert did not mean the end of his career. He went on to be a Corps Commander in Normandy and eventually retired in 1951 as a full General, head of the British Army Staff in the Joint Services Mission to the USA.

Like Macaulay's schoolboy all the world knows that Auchinleck, having relieved Ritchie, took command of the Eighth Army himself, fought Rommel to a standstill in the First Battle of Alamein and was himself then sacked by Churchill at the beginning of August. Montgomery was appointed to take over the Eighth Army, which he did with alacrity, assuming command forty-eight hours early and setting about restoring morale everywhere. In the process he brought in his own men to key positions of influence and authority, among them Oliver Leese.

Commissioned into the Coldstream Guards in 1914, Leese had fought throughout the First World War in France and Flanders, being wounded three times and being awarded the DSO as a platoon commander on the Somme. He returned from being Chief Instructor at the Staff College, Quetta, in time to be the Deputy Chief of Staff to Pownall with the BEF at Dunkirk, and was subsequently appointed in June 1941 to form and command the Guards Armoured Division. It was from this post that he was summoned by Montgomery in early September 1942 to command XXX Corps, one of the three corps in Eighth Army and the one that was earmarked to play the major part in the forthcoming battle, Second Alamein. Leese stayed with Montgomery as Corps Commander throughout the rest of the North African campaign and the invasion of Sicily, finally returning to England with his corps headquarters almost exactly a year later at the end of August 1943. Throughout that period he worked extremely closely with his Army Commander who clearly looked upon Leese as his best Corps Commander, using him to achieve the breakthrough at Alamein, lead the drive to Tripoli and command the British element of the Sicily invasion force. It was therefore hardly surprising, when Montgomery was selected to command 21st Army Group preparing for D-Day, that Leese should have been appointed to take over the Eighth Army from him.

Thus, unlike Cunningham and Ritchie, Leese came to his Army command with the benefit of experience, and experience not only of the theatre in which he was to fight but also of the type of operations that were being undertaken. Admittedly Cunningham had operational experience as a formation commander, but he had not gained it in the Western Desert or armoured warfare. Ritchie had even less relevant experience. Leese was an infantryman who had raised and commanded an armoured division (although not in action), and who had then gone on to command a corps for a year under an extremely successful general, during which time he had fought both armoured and infantry battles in terrain as diverse as the Western Desert and the towns of Sicily. This in itself, however, is not sufficient to explain the success that he enjoyed. The rest must lie in the character of the man. Harold Macmillan, who was at that time Minister Resident Mediterranean, and who liked Leese, wrote of one visit to the Eighth Army when he was being driven by the Army Commander:

Everywhere the general is received with smiles and greetings. He is indeed a very popular figure, and I told him that he conducts the whole affair like an election campaign. It is a remarkable contrast with the last war. Then a general was a remote, Blimpish figure in white moustache, faultlessly tailored tunic, polished boots and spurs, emerging occasionally from a luxurious château, and escorted as a rule in his huge limousine Rolls by a troop of lancers. Now an Army Commander is a youngish man, in shorts and open shirt, driving his own jeep and waving and shouting his greetings to the troops as he edges his way past guns, tanks, trucks, tank-carriers etc, in the crowded and muddy roads, which the enemy may be actively shelling as he drives along.

It is in this perception of Leese, tied to his generalship, that the explanation of his success lies.

Leese took over the Eighth Army on 1 January 1944. Alexander was Commander-in-Chief Allied Forces Italy with two Armies under him, the American Fifth under Mark Clark, and Leese's Eighth. The British Army contained a remarkable diversity of nationalities, numbering among its Corps, in addition to the V (General Allfrey) and XIII (General Kirkman), a Polish Corps (brought out from Persia by General Anders) and a partly trained Canadian Corps; while its Divisions included New Zealanders, Indians, Frenchmen, South Africans and Greeks. It was indeed a true successor to the polyglot army of the desert that found itself bogged down on the line of the River Sangro, on the right of the Allied line. The aim of the German commander, Kesselring, was to hold the Allies on the Gustav Line, of which the pivot was Cassino. To do this he had twenty-one divisions opposing the Allies' eighteen. By the end of February 1944 the second Battle of Cassino had finished in failure, and it was clear that a new approach was needed. The outcome was Operation Diadem, the first of the two major transfers of the Eighth Army across Italy which Leese undertook in complete secrecy, enabling him to hoax the Germans and achieve surprise. By 13 March the entire Army was moved west, to concentrate with the Americans on the breaching of the Gustav and Hitler Lines, and when Operation Dickens, the third Battle of Cassino, also ended in failure on 24 March the planning and preparation for Diadem moved into top gear. The operation started with the fourth Battle of Cassino on 11 May and by 19 May, when Cassino finally fell, the Eighth Army was on the Adolf Hitler Line. On 23 May the Canadians broke through this line also, and the advance was on, with Mark Clark making a beeline for Rome in a move that was to have serious consequences for the subsequent prosecution of the war in Italy, providing the opportunity for the majority of Kesselring's forces to escape the Allied pincer and re-form on the line Florence–Rome. In the reasons that Leese gave for the success of Diadem, in a letter to his old tutor Montgomery, may be found a clue to his own generalship; the operation, he said, was 'carefully prepared ... plenty of time to rehearse, everyone knew what they were doing; maximum concentration of artillery fire and armour'.

Rome had fallen to the Allies on 4 June. By this time it was clear that a strong rivalry was growing between the two Army Commanders. Mark Clark was determined that no opportunity should be missed to enhance the reputation of the Fifth Army, and this led on occasion to friction which hampered co-operation. On 14 July Leese felt impelled to walk out of the French celebrations because of the situation in which he felt his Army was being placed. Tied in with the loss of seven Allied divisions the same month for use in the Normandy landings and in Operation Anvil, the landings in the south of France, and with the switch of popular attention from the Italian campaign to north-west Europe which led to a growing conviction amongst those in Italy that they were being viewed as a sideshow, it became clear by the beginning of August that it was time for a new initiative. The Allies were fighting outside Florence, but it seemed possible that with their reduced numbers they might well have difficulty in achieving the required breakthrough and still have the strength for successful exploitation in the difficult country that lay north of Florence. Leese, in concert with his Corps Commander, Kirkman, therefore put forward a plan that would allow the Eighth Army to use its advantage in tanks, artillery and aircraft by switching its main thrust to the Adriatic coast. This plan eventually came to fruition as Operation Olive.

Conceived as it was by the Army Commander, it took some time to convince Alexander and his staff of the feasibility of the proposal. Prolonged persuasive argument carried the day, however; perhaps not the least attractive aspect of the plan was that it would lead to the separation of the two Armies and their mutually antipathetic commanders. By 12 August, therefore, the Eighth Army had started the second of the switches across Italy for which its commander became so renowned. Once again it was achieved with the minimum of fuss and the maximum of surprise, and when the attack was launched on 26 August it quickly met with success. By 30 August the Eighth Army had closed up to the Gothic Line, and by 19 September the line had been forced and the breakout into the Po Valley had started.

Once again the Army was advancing, but Leese was to see only a little of this phase. On 28 September it was announced that he was to go to South East Asia, to serve under Mountbatten as commander of the army group that was to recapture Burma. It was a fitting climax to an extremely successful tour, in which he had taken over an army bogged down in the memories of its past successes, the realities of the Italian winter and the strength of the Gustav Line, had revitalized it and removed the tarnish that was beginning to gather on its image by restoring to it its self-confidence. His success was marked by the visits of King George VI and the Prime Minister, who were both treated to grandstand views of the operations and who were able to take back a personal knowledge of the real situation, while their presence had an inestimable effect on the morale of the troops. It had been a *tour de force* and was achieved by methods in direct contrast to those of his predecessor, although he always owned to having learned so much from Montgomery. An excellent trainer of men himself, Leese was fully in sympathy with the view that meticulous preparation was the key to success in battle. Italy was a battlefield that lent itself to this approach. Always described as a 'slogging match', the campaign was one in which there was little scope for the Rommel-style lightning sweeps of the desert. Leese had shown himself to be a very competent desert fighter, but it was in the more mundane fighting up the spine of Italy that he finally came into his own as an Army Commander.

It was therefore all the more appropriate that he should have been chosen as the commander of 11th Army Group, and become Commander-in-Chief Allied Land Forces South East Asia (or C-in-C ALF-SEA), as that was a task in which his skill as a manager of resources was sorely needed. It was unfortunate that the environment into which he was thrust was peopled with personalities of a type with which Leese was to find himself unable to come to terms.

Arriving in Kandy, Ceylon, on 10 November 1944, at the headquarters of Mountbatten's South East Asia Command (SEAC), Leese found himself immersed in a world with which he had little sympathy. It seems clear that from the outset he and the Supreme Commander were unlikely to see eye to eye, and it was with a sense of relief that he escaped three days later to his own headquarters at Barrackpore, outside Calcutta. He had taken over the command of 11th Army Group from General Gifford, sacked by Mountbatten after the Battle of Imphal. His command included Fourteenth Army, under the redoubtable Slim, XV Corps under General Christisen, an old friend, Northern Combat Area Command (NCAC) under the American general Sultan, and the Chindits under General Lentaigne. His task was the reconquest of Burma. SEAC's objectives for 1945 were a campaign to establish a presence in central Burma, and the capture of Akyab in the Arakan. The more that Leese considered this the more convinced he became that a great deal more could be achieved provided that sufficient air and sea transport was made available. He therefore set himself the target of 'Rangoon before the Monsoon' and proceeded, with his usual energy, to do everything possible to make it happen. By 3 January Akyab was in British hands, and SEAC was poised for the next step. At this stage Leese was working flat out to ensure that the resources required for the advance on Mandalay and Rangoon were available. In January he arranged that General Browning (Chief of Staff to Mountbatten) should return home to plead – successfully – before the Chiefs of Staff the need for transport aircraft to replace those removed by the Americans in response to the renewed Japanese threat in Chunking. He spent many, many hours in the air himself, gathering together the scattered threads of his enormous command; in one 61-day period he spent thirty-three days flying, during which he covered 36,000 miles in a total of 211 hours. At the same time he brought out many of his old Eighth Army staff to work for him, a move that was not at all popular and did much to alienate the old Far East hands.

The result was a command in total contrast to that which had pertained in Italy. There he had had complete confidence and trust in his superior, and had had the confidence and trust of his subordinates. Now he was trying to force the pace, in accordance with the instructions that he had received in London before travelling out, with a commander whom he neither liked nor particularly trusted, and subordinates who, in some cases, resented the intrusion of this outsider with his desert ways – and staff. Slim in particular, who might have seen himself as a contender for Leese's post although he was never considered for it, was sensitive about what he perceived as the downgrading of the performance of his cherished Fourteenth Army; an inevitable consequence of the introduction of so many of Leese's own men into key posts was a tendency for Eighth Army ways to be introduced.

It was against this background that the advance to Mandalay began on 19 February 1945. By 5 March Meiktila had fallen, but on 16 March Browning came to Leese with a report on Slim's physical condition which led Leese to establish a small Tac HQ of ALFSEA with Fourteenth Army headquarters. On 20 March Mandalay fell, after a remarkable final stand by the Japanese in the fort, reminiscent of scenes from the Indian Mutiny in the nineteenth century. All attention was then turned to the possibility of the capture of Rangoon, and this also fell, on 3 May, in a truly joint services operation that included a parachute drop, a seaborne assault and an attack on land. It was a fitting climax to the career of a general who had now been fighting successfully for two and a half years, but Leese turned immediately to the next task, the capture of Malaya, and it was here that he ran into trouble.

Slim was in need of a rest – indeed he had said as much to Leese in the course of the battle for Mandalay when he had stated that he wanted four months' leave as soon as Rangoon was taken. Leese's view was that someone else should command the Malayan operation, leaving Slim to mop up in Burma; this would mean Slim leaving Fourteenth Army, which Leese considered should be taken over by Christisen. He discussed the idea with Mountbatten who concurred, but said that he thought Leese should convey the message personally. Leese therefore flew up to see Slim, who immediately considered that he had been sacked (although Leese had no authority to take such a course, as Slim must have known) and proceeded to use his not inconsiderable influence to have the decision reversed. When Leese saw Mountbatten on 21 May the Supreme Commander refused to back his Army Group Commander, and asked him to reinstate Slim – and seeing no way out, Leese agreed. Tension between Mountbatten and Leese, which had been growing steadily ever since Leese made it clear that he considered SEAC was not prosecuting the war as efficiently as it might, made the situation impossible, and on 7 June Mountbatten wrote to Alanbrooke, the CIGS, asking for Leese to be sacked. Alanbrooke concurred and on 2 July, while on leave in Kashmir, Leese received a letter from Mountbatten, delivered personally by a member of the supremo's staff, telling him of the decision. Leese returned to England forthwith, handing over his command to Slim who, ironically, found himself thereby forced to relinquish the command of Fourteenth Army.

Leese was an extremely able and charming man, who won the affection and respect of all those who worked for him in Eighth Army. An old-fashioned guardsman, straight as a die, he was not prepared for the more devious world of Kandy and Calcutta and was unable to strike up the same rapport which had smoothed his path elsewhere. In part this was his own fault, the result of the resentment caused by the importation of so many who were seen as outsiders; the other side of the argument is that he would have been most unlikely to have achieved all he did within the timetable he had set himself had he not surrounded himself by those who knew his modus operandi and brought with them, perhaps, a greater sense of urgency. But it was an unhappy episode that reflected little credit on any of those involved – except perhaps Leese himself, who would never discuss the matter, and therefore left the other protagonists to make their own running.

Three generals, therefore, all men of ability and stature, who achieved success in battle but suffered the humiliation of public dismissal. For Ritchie failure was not critical, and he was able to go on and achieve success in a subsequent operational command. For Cunningham, coming immediately on the heels of his Abyssinian triumph, it was more traumatic, but he also recovered and went on to greater things. For Leese, who had risen the highest and had the furthest to fall, it was the end of the line, and after a year as GOC Eastern Command he retired, still a Lieutenant-General.

The careers of these three generals with the Eighth Army are themselves illustrations of the way Britain fought the Second World War. Cunningham and Ritchie were of the old school, the old-style general whose task (carried out successfully) was to hold the ring, making the best of what there was while the country geared itself up for victory. Leese, although of the same generation (he was three years older than Ritchie, and seven years younger than Cunningham, but all had fought in the Great War), was the new breed, fighting with the resources of men and material that had been denied to the others, with an army accustomed to success. Cunningham and Ritchie were overfaced. Their task was too great for them, but had they been given Leese's experience, which amounted to a carefully graduated military education, and the tools of the trade, perhaps they also would have been more successful. Ritchie, for example, went on to be an entirely competent Corps Commander after D-Day.

The moral of their story would appear to be that a commander must choose his subordinates, monitor their progress closely and not be blinded by personal loyalty if they do not match up to the task – this Auchinleck, despite the warning of his staff, could not bring himself to see through to its logical conclusion. The case of Leese shows that high command – really high command – requires a deal of political sensitivity and a strong sense of self-preservation for successful survival. Leese, however, was more concerned with the success of the war effort than his personal career. All three men, therefore, were victims of that peculiarly British vice – the virtue of gentlemanliness; Cunningham and Ritchie above all of Auchinleck's, Leese of his own.

BIBLIOGRAPHY

Barnett, Correlli, *The Desert Generals* (new edition, Allen & Unwin, 1983).
Carver, Michael, *Alamein* (Batsford, 1962).
Macmillan, Harold, *War Diaries* (Macmillan, 1984).

Lewin, Ronald, *Slim* (Leo Cooper, 1976).
Nicolson, Nigel, *Alex* (Weidenfeld and Nicolson, 1973)
Ryder, Rowland, *Oliver Leese* (Hamish Hamilton, 1987).
Warner, Philip, *Auchinleck* (Buchan and Enright, 1981).
Ziegler, Philip, *Mountbatten* (Collins, 1985).

CHRONOLOGY: ALAN CUNNINGHAM

1887, May 1	Born into a distinguished Scottish family
1904	Enters the Royal Military Academy Woolwich
1906, December 20	Commissioned into the Royal Field Artillery
1915	Posted from India to the Western Front, where he serves until the end of the Great War, ending as Brigade-Major RA, mentioned in despatches five times and awarded the DSO and MC
1928, July 1	Promoted brevet Lieutenant-Colonel
1937	Attends Imperial Defence College
1937, December 17	Promoted Brigadier and appointed Commander Royal Artillery 1st Division
1938, September 1	Promoted Major-General, and appointed Commander 5th Anti-Aircraft Division, followed by 66th, 9th and 51st TA Divisions (UK)
1940, October 29	Appointed GOC East Africa, acting Lieutenant-General
1941, May 16	Awarded KCB
1941, September 10	Appointed GOC Eighth Army
1941, November 26	Replaced as GOC Eighth Army
1942, November 11	Commandant Army Staff College
1943, July 23	Promoted Lieutenant-General and appointed GOC Northern Ireland
1944, December 1	Appointed GOC-in-C Eastern Command
1945, November 21	Promoted General and appointed High Commissioner and C-in-C Palestine
1948	Retires; appointed GCMG
1951	Marries
1983, January 30	Dies

CHRONOLOGY: NEIL RITCHIE

1897, July 29	Born in Liss, Hants
1914, December 16	Commissioned into the Black Watch from RMC Sandhurst
1915, September	Wounded at Loos

1917	Awarded DSO in Middle East with 2nd Battalion Black Watch
1918	Awarded MC in Middle East
1937	Marries
1938	Commanding Officer 2nd Battalion The King's Own Royal Regiment
1940	Brigadier General Staff, II Corps, BEF
	Brigadier General Staff, Southern Command
	GOC 51st Highland Division. Major-General
1941	Deputy Chief of the General Staff, Middle East Command
1941, November 26	GOC Eighth Army
1942, June 25	Relieved of command and returned to UK
1944	GOC XII Corps, Europe. KBE
1945	GOC-in-C Scottish Command
1946	General
1947	C-in-C South East Asia Land Forces. KCB
1949	Commander British Army Staff, Washington DC
1951	Retires. GBE
1952	Moves to Canada to work for Mercantile and General Insurance Company of Canada
1983, December 11	Dies in Canada

CHRONOLOGY: OLIVER LEESE

1894, October 27	Born in London
1914, August	Commissioned into the Coldstream Guards from Eton OTC
1914, October 12	Sails for France to join 3rd Battalion Coldstream Guards
1914, October 20	Severely wounded, invalided home
1915	Posted to 2nd Battalion Coldstream Guards, France
1916, September 15	Awarded DSO on the Somme, and severely wounded
1919, August	Adjutant 3rd Battalion Coldstream Guards
1929, November 11	Brigade-Major 1st Guards Brigade
1933, January 18	Marries. Promoted brevet Lieutenant-Colonel
1936, October 1	Commanding Officer 1st Battalion Coldstream Guards
1938, September 29	Chief Instructor Staff College Quetta
1940, May	Promoted Brigadier and appointed Deputy Chief of General Staff BEF
1941, February	GOC 15th Scottish Division. Major-General
1941, June 19	GOC Guards Armoured Division
1942, September 11	GOC XXX Corps North Africa. Lieutenant-General

1943, December 24	GOC Eighth Army Italy
1944, July 26	Knighted in the field by King George VI
1944, November 12	C-in-C Allied Land Forces South East Asia
1945, July 3	Relieved of command
1945, October	GOC-in-C Eastern Command
1946, December 4	Retires
1964, April 30	Wife dies
1965	President of the MCC
1978, January 22	Dies in Wales

12

HORROCKS

Lieutenant-General Sir Brian Horrocks

ALAN SHEPPERD

Brian Gwynne Horrocks, like many young men of his generation, followed his father into the Army. He was born on 7 September 1895 at Ranniket, a hill station in India, the son of Minna and William Horrocks, a surgeon in the Royal Army Medical Corps. William was a man of parts who is best remembered as the Director of Army Hygiene in the First World War, for which he received a knighthood. Brian had a very happy childhood and his schooling followed in the same manner; first to the Bow School at Durham, followed by three years at Uppingham. Here he drifted happily into the Army Class. But games took up most of his time and he passed into the Royal Military College one from bottom. The eighteen months' course ended in the middle of July 1914; for Horrocks this date was particularly significant. While he had joined in many sports, the result of his work was hardly good enough to earn his commission. Furthermore he had been to the races at Gatwick, put his all on an absolute certainty and failed to get back to Camberley on the railway without a ticket. The College authorities were not pleased and Horrocks spent the whole of his last term on restrictions. Now mobilization had taken place on 4 August and all who had completed the course found themselves Second Lieutenants and posted to their regiments.

Within a fortnight Horrocks was in France with a draft for the 1st

Battalion Middlesex Regiment. This was just before the Battle of the Aisne, and soon he was commanding 16 Platoon with Sergeant Whinney in Captain Gibbons' Company. 'Both first class at their jobs,' as Horrocks later wrote, but 'on 21 October at the beginning of the Battle of Ypres, my platoon was surrounded by the enemy and I was wounded and taken prisoner. The war for me was over and my active military career had stopped for four years.' His wounds in the lower stomach for a long time prevented his being able to walk, and in the hospital near Lille the Germans treated the British soldiers in a most inhuman manner, never changing the blankets or the blood-stained garments in which they had been wounded.

Horrocks' experiences over the next four years, the innumerable escape attempts, the constant movement to other and tougher camps, the long periods in solitary confinement are covered in Philip Warner's biography, *Horrocks – The General who Led from the Front.* As Horrocks himself put it, 'I had learnt in a hard school to stand on my own feet and make my own decisions, often in a split second. I had also acquired the useful habit of thinking things out from the enemy point of view so that I might always be one jump ahead.' In addition he had become fluent in French and German as well as acquiring a knowledge of Russian, having lived for several months in a hut with a number of Russian officers. All this in retrospect Horrocks felt was on the plus side. Then there was the innate good humour of the ordinary British soldier, which Horrocks never forgot. 'I always tell young officers there will be moments when your soldiers will drive you almost mad, but never forget this – that we are privileged to command the nicest men in the world.' Nor did he forget what the *Feldwebel* of the Imperial Guard said who escorted him into Germany. 'All front line troops have a respect for each other, but the farther from the front you get, the more bellicose and beastly the people become.'

When the war ended and at the age of twenty-two Horrocks was on leave in England. Young and physically fit he was indeed, but his nerves were in rags. Four years' back pay were spent in six weeks and the only redeeming feature was the attitude of his parents. His wise old father insisted that he should get these four years out of his system in his own way; and how wise he was. Meanwhile the revolution in Russia was reaching its climax, although the British were still involved in helping the White armies against the Bolsheviks. With his knowledge of Russian Horrocks volunteered, and with a party of a dozen officers embarked for Vladivostok.

When they eventually reached this Siberian port they found conditions almost beyond belief, as it was full of refugees who had fled eastwards. Only two British battalions remained to support the two Missions, one at Omsk dealing with equipment and training, the other a railway Mission trying to sort out the chaos on the long lines of communication. With the first-class officers and non-commissioned officers on loan, and the large quantities of surplus equipment, all should have been well. But from the start the White Russian officers were suspicious and resentful of any outside help, an attitude that had already begun to sour relationships with the British. Within three days of landing the party of fourteen officers and a platoon of British soldiers set off for Omsk, some three thousand miles distant, on a train with twenty-seven wagons full of shells. Horrocks was interpreter and records the innumerable attempts by local station masters to remove wagons halted for fictitious repairs. The journey took just over a month and all the wagons arrived intact. Horrocks was sent as second in command of a Non-Commissioned Officers' School in Ekaterinburg (now Sverdlovsk) about 800 miles further west. This charming town was where the Tsar and his family had been murdered. Russian suspicion, however, had grown and it was eventually decided that the Mission must be withdrawn. At their own request Horrocks and George Hayes stayed on as Liaison Officers with the First Siberian Army. In October 1919 they were back in Omsk. Here they joined up with Major Vining and the Mission helping to run the railway. With the front having disintegrated and in the intense cold they joined the milling crowds of refugees trying to get eastwards by rail. In early January 1920 they reached Krasnoyarsk, which it was discovered had fallen days earlier to the Reds.

Horrocks' second period as a prisoner of war lasted for nearly ten months. The British officers refused to work with the Reds and were separated from the White Russians, who were dying by the hundreds each day. Then just as word came that the British were to be repatriated, Horrocks 'began to feel very ill, a high temperature, constant sickness and a burning thirst. This was the blackest moment of my life, for in the anxious eyes of the others I could read one word – typhus.' In the town there were said to be 30,000 cases of typhus – naked corpses stacked on the platforms, frozen bodies piled into sledges on the streets, and in the hospitals patients lying in ranks in their clothes on the floors with the corridors used as lavatories. Horrocks was more than fortunate being able to wake from six days of unconsciousness in an abandoned school, with one heroine of a Russian nurse for 125 patients. Tied down to the bed Horrocks woke to find his friend George Hayes beside him – a brave man who came daily. Somehow Hayes had managed to get milk and white bread, to supplement the black bread and thin soup, which undoubtedly saved his life.

The journey back started in the middle of March, but only reached Irkutsk. Then after two months the party set off for Moscow. Here they were put into the Ivznoffsky Monastery with over 450 other prisoners, and kept on a starvation diet. But for the visits of Madame Carpentier and her daughters, who brought bread and potatoes twice a week, they would have starved. Then news of their repatriation came without any warning, and the next day the British left for Petrograd. 'Our departure,' Horrocks wrote, 'was entirely spoilt for me at any rate, by the sad white faces of our fellow prisoners ... their fate was all too certain.'

It was only when Horrocks reached London and met his parents that he realized how they had suffered through his having disappeared for over a year and literally passed out of their lives. He was now twenty-six years old with little chance of a successful army career, although in retrospect he thought the experiences he had gained were an excellent preparation for the stress and strain of command in war. For the next few years his regiment was busy on security duties before being posted to Aldershot in October 1923. The Army was seriously under strength and forced into the realm of make-believe by the shortage of equipment. Guns were represented by flags and defended posts marked out by white tape, while a marching column was often represented by men carrying poles with flags stretched on to show the space taken up.

Bored with this kind of training Horrocks took up modern pentathlon, which gave him an outlet for his skills as a runner, horseman and shot. Hard training brought success in both the army and national championships, and he was chosen to take part in the 1924 Olympic Games. Here the standard was exceptionally high and he had only modest results.

With the years passing by, his father realized that Brian would soon pass the age of entry to the Staff College at Camberley. And without the magic 'psc' after one's name it was virtually impossible to reach high command in the Army. The proposition was put tactfully but very firmly to Horrocks that promotion was very difficult to get and, without the Staff College, virtually impossible. Horrocks took the advice and worked hard for the examination in 1927. Then shortly before the date of the examination the battalion was ordered to China where General Chiang Kai-shek had established a nationalist government – a very interesting posting for a young officer! Again Sir William stepped in and Horrocks agreed to seek permission to stay behind to take the examination. This he successfully passed, but not high enough to be accepted straight away. In fact he had now to obtain a nomination, and encouraged by his father he attended specialized courses and eventually joined the College for the course of 1931–33.

Meanwhile early in 1927 Horrocks was appointed adjutant of the 9th Middlesex whose headquarters were at Willesden. The life of a territorial battalion was centred on the drill hall headquarters. Training was spread over the Saturdays and other evenings as well, together with the annual camp in the summer. There was little equipment and to attend the rifle range was a rare adventure. What was needed of the regular Adjutant and senior Warrant Officer was endless enthusiasm, combined with a cheerful and imperturbable manner. Horrocks soon found himself at one with his completely new responsibility. After all, in a war, these were the men who in the final analysis win or lose the battle. To know them and work with them gave him an entirely new outlook on the whole question of leadership. This was also the time when Horrocks married a girl who had known him since childhood, Nancy, the daughter of Brook and the Hon. Mrs Brook Kitchin. They were married at the Savoy Chapel early in 1928 and their daughter was born the following year. Philip Warner writes of them,

Both have always been inclined to undervalue themselves, Horrocks because he saw himself as a not very bright philistine who had been lucky to have the success he had, Nancy because she regarded herself as a much less talented person than she was. He was an orthodox though humane Conservative; her views were well to the left of his. But they had much in common.

Joining as a student at the Staff College 1931 course at Camberley, Horrocks was indeed lucky to have as commandant Major-General John Dill, who 'was a man of the highest integrity, great charm and with a first class brain'. He also had a sense of humour. It was Dill who developed the syndicate system of working which still flourishes at Camberley and many other staff colleges. Syndicates are groups of about ten officers who work on a problem together. Eventually a collective view is produced which is then presented by one member, explaining the syndicate conclusion and at the same time summarizing any opposing points that have emerged. It certainly teaches the students to listen carefully to everything that is said and ultimately to present a balanced and rational viewpoint.

On the two-year courses there were senior and junior terms, and although the work was hard and often intensive, there was time for sport and a social life as well. Amongst Horrocks' contemporaries were many officers who later commanded divisions in the war. Of the senior people two names stand out, Captain M.C. Dempsey MC and Captain W. H. E. Gott MC, who both rose to high rank. Horrocks was kept busy, took part in games and did his share in entertaining, rather more than his captain's pay could afford. But the two years were a turning point in his whole career. When the postings came out he learned with some dismay that he was destined for a desk job in the War Office, as Staff Captain in the Military Secretary's Branch. However the work turned out to be stimulating and obviously of importance, as he dealt with promotion of officers up to the rank of lieutenant-colonel. What he did not realize at the time was that such a post in the MS Branch was not given lightly. He had taken over from Myles Dempsey and two years later, in 1936, he took over the post of Brigade Major of 5 Infantry Brigade in 2nd Division in Aldershot from the same officer.

The position of Brigade Major is a coveted appointment for a staff officer and Horrocks now came under the influence of Wavell, who commanded the division. Although not easy to get on with, and regarded by some as often lacking in tact, Wavell had a flair for training his division in highly imaginative exercises. Horrocks regarded him as having the finest brain of anyone he had ever met. Horrocks absorbed much of this and – being an extrovert and close to the soldiers, which Wavell never was – he applied it in his own manner. Horrocks had his own way of getting jobs done, as the Acting Adjutant of one of the battalions in Aldershot recalls. He was sitting in his office one afternoon when he became aware of the Brigade Major's presence. 'What about your mobilization scheme?' enquired Horrocks politely. The Acting Adjutant explained that the Adjutant was on a course and that the scheme was locked in the safe. 'Oh,' said Horrocks, 'that's fine. I should like to have a look at it – perhaps tomorrow afternoon.' The resulting rewrite of a dusty document, produced for the previous occupants of the barracks, solved the problem satisfactorily for all concerned; even if the Assistant Adjutant had to sit up all night to produce it!

Horrocks' next posting came as a complete surprise, as he was sent back to the Staff College as one of the directing staff under the Commandant, Major-General Paget. The date was 1938.

Horrocks later wrote of Paget as having a very strong character and as being one of the most honourable men he had ever met. He also paid great attention to detail. The work was hard and the hours long, and at the outbreak of war the length of the course was reduced to six months and the pressure increased. This was in the first place to cater for Territorial Army officers selected as likely staff officers in the expanding Army; young barristers, schoolmasters and others including five Members of Parliament such as Selwyn Lloyd, later Foreign Secretary, and Walker-Smith, afterwards Minister of Health. Towards the end of his time at Camberley Horrocks became concerned with planning the courses, and the more he knew the Commandant the more he admired his sterling qualities. Then early in May 1940 Horrocks was handing over to his successor, as he had been told verbally that he would get command of 2nd Battalion Middlesex Regiment in France, when news of the German invasion through Holland reached him. This was on the morning of 10 May. Realizing the urgency of reaching France, Horrocks was en route for Southampton in the Commandant's car within a couple of hours.

Three days later he took over the battalion at Louvain. Within an hour or so he was told that the Divisional Commander had arrived at his headquarters. 'I saw a small, alert figure with piercing eyes sitting in the back of his car – the man under whom I was to fight all my battles during the war, and who was to have more influence on my life than anyone before or since.' Montgomery was a controversial figure; his methods of training and command were unorthodox, and although he was regarded as highly efficient, he was often spoken of as a showman. Horrocks felt rather uneasy about the interview, for this was probably what it was, but all went smoothly. The Middlesex Regiment was the division's machine-gun regiment and Horrocks had ample opportunity of getting to know his Divisional Commander. He quickly noticed that throughout the withdrawal to Dunkirk Montgomery had his meals at regular hours and never missed his normal night's sleep.

Horrocks's time as commander of the battalion lasted seventeen days. For the whole of this time the battalion was in action and never once had they been concentrated. Horrocks saw Montgomery every day, often several times and he had his orders direct from the divisional commander. Montgomery's orders were always clear and used the minimum number of words. He himself was always the same, confident, cheerful and apparently quite fresh. He considered that 3rd Division was the best in the Army, and that he was the best divisional commander. By the time Horrocks reached Dunkirk he had come to the same conclusion. Horrocks was now in temporary command of 11 Brigade of 4th Division, but there was little that could be done as the withdrawal over the beaches had already begun. He had his personal share in the adventures of those desperate days and finally reached Ramsgate in a small Dutch cargo boat, in which he had manned the forward anti-aircraft Lewis gun.

Within a few days Horrocks was ordered to take command of 9 Brigade of 3rd Division, and found himself responsible for the coastline from Rottingdean to Shoreham. Horrocks, mindful of his training at the Staff College, found it difficult to believe that the Germans had the experience to mount a seaborne invasion. Yet this was what he had to believe could happen almost at any moment. So he laid plans to get the earliest warning, by having signallers at the end of each pier. Here an experienced officer who actually saw an invasion fleet approaching would signal back by WT and line to his brigade headquarters and fire a white signal rocket. The troops, however, were trained in short mobile exercises so as to keep them alert and active. Horrocks himself slept next to his operations room, and one night the brigade major rushed in to say that a white rocket had just gone up from the end of a pier. 'Shall I send the code word, sir?' Horrocks was in a quandary, but still felt that there must have been some mistake, as there had been no message and the other posts had seen nothing. It turned out that the rocket had been fired by a ship passing in line with one of the piers – a lucky decision, but it owed much to careful planning. Shortly after this the division was withdrawn into a counter-attack role, and it was during the exercises at this time, particularly in the area of Beaminster in Dorset, that the brigade worked with the Home Guard. Horrocks noted their keenness and enthusiasm and his own embarrassment at conferences when he was confronted by rows of be-medalled senior officers serving as privates in the Home Guard.

Then in January 1941 he was appointed Brigadier General Staff of Eastern Command, and in the five months he stayed there he organized large scale exercises. He was, however, delighted to be promoted in June to the acting rank of Major-General in command of 44th (Home Counties) Division. This was a well-established Territorial Division which guarded the area most threatened by German invasion, from the Isle of Thanet to Dover and Folkestone. Also it came under Montgomery. The well-remembered orders that Montgomery insisted upon, banning wives from the operational areas, and his methods of staging conferences after the big training exercises, were marks of this extraordinary leader. Horrocks remarked also on his uncanny knowledge of the personalities under his command, describing how he would often ring Horrocks up to make the most searching enquiries of some second lieutenant he had seen on training. In the end Horrocks was forced to keep a book with all the details of every officer in his division by the phone – something that caused Montgomery great amusement.

On 20 March 1942 Horrocks was cross-posted to take over the 9th Armoured Division. The standard of individual training was excellent but Horrocks knew that he had to make the division into a proper fighting formation, and being an infantry officer this was a tough job. Within a couple of days of his arrival he called the officers to a cinema and addressed them. He told them that he had just had a look at the vehicle parade state and it informed him that only about half of the vehicles were capable of moving at all. 'You', he said, 'know all about mechanical things. As an infantryman, I don't: however in the infantry division I have just come from, almost all the vehicles are serviceable. Perhaps you would care to explain why so many of yours are not.' A Royal Mechanical and Electrical Engineer Officer stood up to answer this question, and was promptly but politely told that perhaps he would be better employed making sure the vehicles would perform, than explaining why they could not.

Many officers had to come to see 'a bloody infantryman whom they had never heard of,' and now were telling each other how lucky they were to have such a spirited general in command. Horrocks made no secret of the fact that these two periods – the time under Wavell in Aldershot and that under Montgomery – were those in which he had learned most of his practical soldiering. Now he was learning about armoured fighting, where all orders were given by WT from a tank – lessons that stood him in good stead later on. At 7 pm on 15 August 1942 the division was training in the north of England when Horrocks got a cryptic message to report to London overnight. Within thirty-six hours he was airborne from Lyneham in Wiltshire as the sole passenger for Cairo. In the Middle East Montgomery had just taken over the Eighth Army at a critical time. What he wanted urgently was someone loyal and reliable, someone whom he knew and who would work directly under him – Horrocks was that man.

Horrocks arrived three days after Montgomery; three days that had seen dramatic changes in the Eighth Army. For Montgomery had issued firm orders that there was to be no more withdrawal and that he would defeat Rommel's attack on ground of his own choosing. Then, and in his own time, Eighth Army would attack and 'we are going to finish with this chap Rommel once and for all.' He gave Horrocks his appreciation of how Rommel would move his Afrika Korps round the southern flank, where the reinforced XIII Corps (commanded by Horrocks) would be holding the Alam Halfa ridge. Here the tanks of two armoured division and all the anti-tank guns would be dug in and the Germans would be trapped and finally driven back.

Montgomery stressed several times that Horrocks must not 'get unduly mauled in the process,' as he then planned to form a strong mobile reserve consisting largely of armoured divisions. Then when this was ready he would 'hit Rommel for six out of Africa'. A factor here was that the Grant tank was only just becoming available. The sixty Grants in 22 Armoured Brigade were the only tanks that could compete with the highly superior Mk III and VIs of which Rommel had 234 tanks. Later some more Grants arrived and were sent to 10th Armoured Division. Although Horrocks's orders were quite clear, he had difficulty with several of the tank commanders who wanted to rush in at the slightest opportunity. At one stage in the battle Horrocks was told to attack into a gap in the German position with 2nd New Zealand Division. Major-General Freyberg, who was a long way senior to the new corps commander, objected, saying that he would use the newly arrived brigade from 44th Division. In the end the attack was launched by the Maori brigade and the British brigade, but suffered heavy losses. On 7 September the battle was over. Hounded by the RAF and continually shelled day and night, the Germans had failed to break through, and XIII Corps had not been mauled.

Before the battle of Alamein, X Armoured Corps was formed of two armoured divisions, 2 Armoured Brigade and the New Zealand Infantry Division. Initially Horrocks had been chosen to command, but his success with XIII Corps where he was popular, combined by his lack of experience in the desert with armour, made him suggest that Major-General Herbert Lumsden, a 12th Lancer with an admirable record, should get the command. Montgomery listened to Horrocks and Lumsden got the command. XIII Corps' part in the battle was to draw off German forces by appearing to be the main thrust in the south, while the breakthrough took place in the northern sector. To begin with all went well, but the clearing of the minefields took longer than expected and the whole impetus seemed totally bogged down. More and more of XIII Corps' troops were switched north, and when the end came and the tanks were through the minefields and into open country with Rommel pulling back, Horrocks was left with a skeleton corps. This situation did not last long, however, as he was given command of X Corps, which during the advance into Libya had been kept in reserve to guard against any Axis breakthrough on the southern flank. When the battle against the Mareth line became bogged down, Montgomery decided to make a sweeping movement round the German flank. Horrocks had his chance. The plan was for X Corps and the New Zealand Division to set off on a 150-mile sweep, ending by an approach through a difficult gap in the mountains. Then they would face the formidable strength of two Panzer divisions and the 164th Light Division. Philip Warner writes:

The Desert Air Force supported it by pounding the Germans on a scale hitherto unknown. A French force under General Leclerc secured a vital pass. The New Zealanders fought like tigers. And the British units pressed on with relentless determination. ... This wide flanking move, pushed through with tremendous drive and tenacity, was one of the most desperate assaults of the war. Assisted by relentless air attacks, it crunched its way through the German divisions, who had been astonished to find this apparently invincible juggernaut bearing down on their flanks.

The battle of Gabes, or rather Wadi Akarit Gap, followed. At first all went well, but when Horrocks tried to take over the breakthrough the leading elements of his X Corps ran into an undisclosed anti-tank ditch covered by 88mm guns and were held up. Eventually the armour got through, but only because the Germans pulled back. Of Horrocks's last battle in North Africa he wrote: 'The next few days were among the most unpleasant of my life.'

Montgomery had already left for Cairo to discuss plans for the invasion of Sicily. Just before he left he had told Horrocks to work out a plan to break through to Tunisia by a strong attack up the coast, taking the view that First Army would be unable to break through from the other direction. Both Freyberg and Tuker of 4th Indian Division hated the idea because it would mean heavy casualties. When Montgomery returned he was in a very irritable state. He didn't like the plans for Sicily and now found nothing had been done in his absence.

Horrocks was hauled over the coals and told to get on with the battle as ordered. Before he left the caravan, however, he pointed out the effect on Eighth Army and suggested that it would be better if the attack was made from First Army's front where the ground was more suitable. Three days later he was called by WT to report at Eighth Army headquarters. Here sitting outside the caravan was Admiral Ramsay, an old friend from the Dover days, who said, 'You are in for a bit of fun, my boy!' Inside Generals Alexander and Montgomery were studying a map. Montgomery turned and said, 'The whole weight of the final attack is being shifted from here round to the First Army front.' To Horrocks's complete surprise he was ordered to take 4th Indian Division, 7th Armoured Division and 201 Guards Brigade and assume command of IX Corps in General Anderson's army. Evidently General Crocker who commanded IX Corps had been wounded and would be out of action for several weeks. So Horrocks was off the same day to a very different kind of army, where moreover there was quite genuine dislike of Eighth Army for having stolen all the limelight. General Anderson cheerfully added 4th British Division and 6th Armoured Division, together with a number of Churchill tanks.

Horrocks decided to attack on a very narrow front with the infantry leading, preceded by the whole of Tedder's Tactical Air Force and an immense weight of artillery. Everything went like clockwork and in two days Tunis had fallen and 6th Armoured Division was on its way to cut off the Germans trying to escape into the Cap Bon Peninsula. As Horrocks pointed out, the final surrender in North Africa was marked by two particularly fitting scenes. The original Desert Rats, the 7th Armoured Division, were in at the final kill and the German 90th Light Division insisted on surrendering to the New Zealanders.

Horrocks had now reached the highest point of his military career. In under four years he had risen from a lieutenant-colonel to a corps commander and lieutenant-general; carrying his map round in Belgium to keep his soldiers in the picture, or getting the twelve matrons of the base hospitals in Tripoli to send their nurses to join in the twice-weekly dances for other ranks only, he had always kept the men under his command in mind. Called out to Egypt by Montgomery he was now firmly established as a commander to be trusted. Moreover he was popular with those under his command, inspiring confidence and focusing their loyalty. Many men he knew by name and wherever he went he was recognized as a commander who believed in his soldiers. Now his corps was detailed to land at Salerno under Mark Clark, and he went to Bizerta to watch 46th Division rehearsing their assault. At the same time a new form of US smokescreen was to be tried out. While visiting the divisional commander the air-raid siren sounded and the party went out into the street to watch the smoke billow over the town. Suddenly a German fighter broke through the smoke with its guns blazing. Horrocks was hit in the chest, and the bullet passed through his lungs and intestines and came out by his spine, while another hit his leg. No one else was touched.

Fourteen months later Horrocks was pronounced fit – or at least he was sufficiently fit to persuade the doctors to mark him fit! He had been lucky not to have been killed, and had survived numerous operations by Colonel Carter, a leading US surgeon in Tunisia, and then Edward Muir at the Cambridge Hospital at Aldershot. Throughout these testing times his ADC, Harold Young, had been with him, proving an invaluable asset. On 2 August 1944 Montgomery sent his aircraft to take him out to France, where he was badly needed to take over XXX Corps. Having struggled through the Bocage country many units were beginning to lose morale and now faced a prominent feature, Mount Pinçon, which completely dominated the countryside. One of Horrocks's former ADCs, Captain R. Denny of the 13th/18th Hussars, leading two troops of tanks, discovered a very narrow track which apparently led to the top of the hill and which seemed undefended. Six tanks succeeded in climbing up and were eventually joined by the 4th Wiltshires, who fought their way up in the dark.

This feat transformed the entire situation and soon the Germans were being forced back through Falaise. The race through northern France and into Belgium began, but Horrocks, having just given his orders for crossing the Seine at Vernon, became ill. Sick and feverish he got back to his caravan and into bed. Efforts to delay a visit from Montgomery the following day only resulted in his turning up within a couple of hours. 'Ah yes, Jorrocks,' he said, 'I guessed something was wrong as soon as I got your message. But don't worry. I shan't invalid you home,' and he gave orders for the caravan to be moved alongside his own at his headquarters. Meanwhile Eisenhower had decided to advance on a 'broad front', and Montgomery was left to thrust up the flank with his own resources.

On 26 August Horrocks was sufficiently well to be given the task of leading the spearhead corps. Montgomery must have felt he had no one else with the necessary dash and experience, certainly no one he could trust to do exactly what he was told. Horrocks now moved into a tank as his tactical headquarters from which to control the advance. By 3 September with XII Corps on his left and an American division on his right he reached Brussels – six days to cover 250 miles. Supply was now a serious problem and Horrocks sent Pip Roberts with 11th Armoured Division to occupy the docks in Antwerp. Had he ordered the division to carry on past Antwerp to cross the Albert Canal and advance some fifteen miles, he would have blocked the Beveland isthmus and cut the German escape route. But Horrocks had his eyes fixed on the Rhine and certainly did not appreciate the cost of clearing the Germans overlooking the Scheldt would cause the Allies 12,800 casualties, half of whom would be Canadians.

Meanwhile Montgomery had launched the battle for Arnhem, with the British and American parachute divisions operating along the long road through Nijmegen. XXX Corps had the task of reaching the British parachutists, who it was expected would capture the bridge at Arnhem. If the Germans had been in full retreat all would have been well. As it was, units were being rushed up to reinforce those already on the ground and progressively everything went wrong for the Allies. Finally by the night of 25/26 September, and despite their heroic efforts, the remnants of the parachutists at Arnhem had to be withdrawn. Struggling forward on the single road, which had been cut several times by German attacks, XXX Corps had failed to reach them in time. It seems almost incomprehensible that the presence of armoured units near Arnhem should not have been known, and to have attempted to advance such a distance on the frontage of the width of a single road now seems crazy. Yet it was a near thing and, in spite of almost everything going wrong, XXX Corps only just failed. Horrocks blamed himself for not having insisted on having a high-ranking Dutch officer at his head-quarters, who might have advised a left hook well west of Nijmegen.

Early in December 1944 XXX Corps was pulled out of the line to prepare for the Battle of the Reichswald, and Horrocks was staying with Queen Elizabeth of the Belgians on the outskirts of Brussels. On 16 December a staff officer from Second British Army rang with the news of the German break-out on the American front in the Ardennes. XXX Corps was moved to cover Brussels and on the 25th Horrocks was sent on leave to England by Montgomery. His first words were, 'Jorrocks, I want you to fly home tomorrow.' Horrocks was completely taken aback. 'May I ask why I am being sacked?' 'Don't be stupid,' Montgomery replied tersely. 'You're not being sacked. I want you to go home and have a rest before a big battle I've got in store for you as soon as we've cleared up this mess here.' Horrocks' protests were useless and off he went on leave. On his return the interrupted preparations for the Battle of the Reichswald were resumed. This was designed to destroy all the German forces between the Rhine and the Meuse, and XXX Corps was lent to the First Canadian Army for the operation. The battle was codenamed Veritable. It lasted from 8 February to 10 March 1945 and Horrocks admitted that it was the greatest battle that he had ever fought.

The battle started with an attack by five divisions through the Reichswald Forest. Away to the right and forty-eight hours later, General Simpson's Ninth US Army were to advance north in a pincer movement. To keep secret the assembly of 200,000 men with 1,400 guns, and to control the forward reconnaissance, required the most rigid planning. To begin with, all the preparations went smoothly. With a severe frost through January the ground was frozen hard and ideal for the launching of armour. Then, disastrously, a heavy thaw set in early in February and turned the ground into a soggy mass. On 9 February the Germans blew a dam which prevented the Americans advancing from the south for fourteen days. Meanwhile the Germans realized that the thrust of XXX Corps was the main attack and had assembled no less than nine divisions against it. Now after a week's bitter fighting II Canadian Corps came in on the left and the battle intensified. Reinforcements of the 11th British and 4th Canadian Armoured Divisions and 43rd Wessex Divisions were brought in, and the Americans finally succeeded in advancing. The German withdrawal across the Rhine (complete by 10 March) brought to a close one of the fiercest battles of the war. First Canadian Army had suffered 15,634 casualties, two-thirds of which were British troops, while the Germans lost about 44,000 men, a half taken prisoner. During the battle Horrocks' sickness had returned, but as a general who was always well forward 'smelling out the battle' he had kept going. None but his senior staff realized what was wrong, and in the mud and rain only his loss of temper showed.

The crossing of the Rhine followed, but this time XXX Corps were not in the lead. Elaborate precautions were again taken to control the forward reconnaissance and to prevent the Germans knowing the crossing points. Finally smoke was used to cover the near bank of the river. The crossing opened on the evening of 23 March and the main difficulty was in building the Class 40 bridges over the 1,500-foot span of water under the inevitably heavy shellfire. Horrocks has described the complexities of building four bridges by 8,000 sappers under the Chief Engineer of XXX Corps. The first, a Class 9, was completed at 0100 hours on 26 March; while the others, all Class 40, were opened by 29 March.

The advance into Germany brought bitter counter-attacks on XXX Corps' front. Every crossroads was contested and every bridge was destroyed. All except one. This was over the River Ems. The bridge had been prepared with marine demolition charges and covered by 88mm guns. Captain Liddell of the Coldstream Guards carried the bridge by running forward alone and cutting the wires connected to the charges. Then still unwounded he waved his company to advance with their supporting tanks. The German garrison lost 40 killed, 10 wounded and 42 taken prisoner. Only one guardsman was killed and four wounded. Horrocks visited the position the next day and got Liddell to show him what had happened. Horrocks put Liddell in for a VC; unfortunately he was killed eighteen days later, before it was awarded.

The capture of Bremen took five days. Horrocks had been not at all enthusiastic about the task and discussed it with Montgomery. Montgomery listened carefully, then told Horrocks exactly what should be done. As Horrocks said, 'The four decisions which he then took cleared up the situation completely, and as far as I was concerned Bremen was finished.' He later wrote, 'It was in Bremen that I realized for the first time just what the Germans had suffered as a result of our bombing. It was a shambles: there didn't seem to be a single house intact in this huge great port.'

Close to Bremen the British had uncovered Sandbostel, one of the horror camps, the discovery of which shocked the whole world. Horrocks was appalled at what he saw, and was physically sick when he visited the survivors at close quarters. He had no love for Germans since his harsh treatment at Lille in 1914; but this was something quite different. He was so angry that he ordered the burgomasters of the surrounding towns and villages to send a quota of women to clean up the camp and look after these unfortunate beings who were dying at an alarming rate. A few days later Horrocks took the surrender of the Germans in the Corps Ems area, and later wrote,

When all was ready I came in and seated myself all alone opposite the two Germans. After issuing my orders for the surrender I finished with these words. 'These orders must be obeyed scrupulously. I warn you we shall have no mercy if they are not. Having seen one of your horror camps my whole attitude towards Germany has changed.' The chief of staff jumped up and said, 'The army had nothing to do with those camps.' 'Sit down,' I replied, 'there were German soldiers on sentry duty outside and you cannot escape responsibility. The world will never forgive Germany for those camps.'

Sydney Jary commanded 18 Platoon of the 4th Somerset Light Infantry through the whole campaign, and has written, 'In close country, forests and street fighting the platoon commander became the linchpin.' After

Bremen, Horrocks caught sight of Jary and hailed him with, 'Glad to see you're still alive, Jary!' Horrocks was a general who knew and respected his men – he was that kind of man.

BIBLIOGRAPHY

Barnett, Correlli, *The Desert Generals* (Allen and Unwin, 1983).

Collier, B., *The Defence of the United Kingdom* (1957).

De Guingand, Major-General Sir Francis, *Operation Victory* (Hodder and Stoughton, 1947).

Ellis, L. F., *The War in France and Flanders 1939–40* (1953).

Ellis, L.F., *Victory in the West*, vol. II (1968).

Horrocks, Lieutenant-General Sir Brian, *A Full Life* (Leo Cooper, 1974).

Horrocks, Lieutenant-General Sir Brian, with Major-General H.E. Essame and Eversley Belfield, *Corps Commander* (Sidgwick and Jackson, 1977).

Montgomery, Field-Marshal Lord, *Memoirs* (Collins, 1958).

Official Histories (all HMSO).

Playfair, I.S.O. and Maloney, C.J.C., *The Mediterranean and the Middle East*, vol. III (1960), vol. IV (1966) and vol. V (1973).

Warner, Philip, *Alamein* (Kimber, 1979).

Warner, Philip, *Horrocks* (Hamish Hamilton, 1984).

CHRONOLOGY: BRIAN HORROCKS

1895, September 7	Born at Ranniket, India
	Educated at Bow School, Durham, Uppingham and Royal Military College, Sandhurst
1914, August 8	Commissioned and joins 1st Battalion the Middlesex Regiment
1914, October 21	Wounded and taken prisoner by the Germans
1919, February	To Russia to help the White Russians
1920, January	Taken prisoner by the Bolsheviks, for ten months

Promotions

1917, January	Captain
1935, January	Major
1937, July	Lieutenant-Colonel
1940, June	Colonel
1940, June	Brigadier
1941, June	Major-General
1942, August	Lieutenant-General

Postings

1927, January–1930, December	Adjutant, TA
1931, January–1932, December	Staff College course
1934, January–1936, February	Staff Captain, War Office
1936, February–1938, January	Brigade-Major, Aldershot Command
1938, July–1939, October	GSO2, Staff College
1939, October–1940, April	GSO1, Staff College
1940, May	Commands 2 Middlesex Regiment, British Expeditionary Force
1940, June	Brigade Commander, British Expeditionary Force
1940, June–1941, February	Brigade Commander
1941, February–June	Brigadier General Staff, Home Forces
1941, June–1942, August	Divisional Commander
1942, August–1943, August	Corps Commander
1944, August–1946, February	Corps Commander
1946, February	GOC, Western Command
1948, March	GOC-in-Chief, BAOR
1949	Becomes sick and is invalided

Later Career

Appointed Gentleman Usher of the Black Rod in the House of Lords, where he remained for seventeen years. He also took up journalism, producing many articles. Horrocks became nationally famous through his television presentations of battles he had taken part in and others as well, and he also took part in sound broadcasts. As an author he wrote *A Full Life*, which was published in 1960, with an extended edition in 1974, and *Corps Commander* in 1977. He also introduced and edited an extensive series of regimental histories. Horrocks became a director of the Bovis Construction Company, and he served on and advised many Service charities.

Sir Brian Horrocks died on 4 January 1985, and a memorial service was held in Westminster Abbey on 26 February 1985.

13

HOBART

Major-General Sir Percy Hobart

KENNETH MACKSEY

Among some random jottings made by Lieutenant Percy Cleghorn Stanley Hobart in 1913 appears in isolation the terse remark: 'Winston Churchill, spiritual kinship with Hobart.' There is nothing to explain why he wrote it. Their paths would not cross for another twenty years. Soldiering, riding and shooting were about their only interests in common – although each could be pretty difficult to cope with when they chose and both were extremely ambitious. Yet Hobart had no pronounced political interests and usually went out of his way to avoid politicians – until the 1930s, that is, when he began to meet Churchill in his Wilderness years when the latter brooded in limbo while Hobart's career seemed to stretch promisingly ahead.

To begin with, Hobart's career was orthodox enough for one of the select Sappers who graduated from the Royal Military Academy to be posted to the élite 1st Bengal Sappers and Miners in India. It was a unit which produced many distinguished officers; more than half of those in his day became generals. But unorthodoxy soon crept in, allied to a considerable intellect, and an abruptness of argumentative manner which daunted those exposed to its fire. Not for nothing was his brother in the Indian Civil Service known as 'the civil' and he 'the uncivil'. Yet he was a picked man whom everybody expected to go far.

The outbreak of war in 1914 almost put a stop to that, for although inadvertently he missed the opening mobile phase in France, he was in the thick of it in March 1915 at Neuve Chapelle. There he demonstrated characteristic ruthless determination to get into the fight and an unlimited courage and resourcefulness, which won him a Military Cross. That was only a beginning. In the next three years the hottest part of the battlefield was wherever 'Hobo' could be found – at Aubers Ridge in May 1915 and Loos in September. By September, however, he had joined the staff of an Indian Army infantry brigade and with them went to Mesopotamia in 1916 to take part in the abortive attempt to relieve the besieged British garrison at Kut al Almara.

In the open desert bounding the River Tigris, Hobart was to absorb the problems of mobile warfare in undeveloped country when logistic support was deficient. He would show immense disgust at the gross mismanagement of the campaign and severely criticize, to their face, senior officers whose tactical handling of troops fell below standards which demanded what he called 'brilliance'. Promoted to Brigade Major, he built a reputation for excellent staff work in the advance to Baghdad in 1917 – and then nearly threw it all away when making an unauthorized flight along the Euphrates in March 1918. Shot down and captured behind the Turkish lines, he was lucky enough, with his pilot, to be rescued by a patrol of armoured cars sent over fifty miles to find him, and to avoid court martial for disobedience. Restored to his brigade in time to take part in General Allenby's masterpiece of an offensive at Megiddo, he was posted as a GSO2 to a British division after an outburst of insubordination which yet again got him into hot water.

In 1923 Hobart took a plunge that only a few officers with prospects were prepared to take. He volunteered to join the newly formed Royal Tank Corps at a moment when, in India, he had been completely rehabilitated to favour by his admirable staff work during the punitive raid on Wana in 1921. In 1919 he had attended the Staff College at Camberley and associated with instructors and students with whom his fate was to be closely linked in the future – with Charles Broad, the future Lord Gort, Henry Maitland Wilson, Alan Brooke and, from the next course, Bernard Montgomery. In 1923, wearing RTC badges, he took up the appointment of an instructor himself at the Staff College, Quetta, where he became responsible for tank matters. There he identified himself with those who belligerently claimed that 'the future lay with the tank', learning from correspondence with Colonel J. F. C. Fuller, the tank's greatest advocate, in England, what limited progress was being made in making the vital experiments upon which that future depended. By the end of his tour at Quetta he had achieved two important goals. He had formulated clear concepts about future tank doctrine. And, scandalizing some members of the military fraternity in 1927, he had appeared as co-respondent in a divorce case in connection with one of his students whose wife, in due course, he would marry.

That same year, when he was posted to England to join 4th Battalion RTC, he also acquired a brother-in-law, Bernard Montgomery, who married his sister. After his own marriage at home and a short spell back in India with armoured cars, he was returned to England in 1931, just in time to take command of 2nd Battalion RTC in revolutionary exercises on Salisbury Plain when Broad commanded an entire tank brigade by voice radio. Hobart's contribution to those exercises and to the series of experiments then going on into mechanized warfare was dynamic and inspiring. It set him apart from the other commanding officers, and was a prelude to his becoming, in 1933, the next Inspector of the Royal Tank Corps with the rank of Brigadier, and thus automatically the commander of the 1st Tank Brigade when it was formally established in 1934.

The 1st Tank Brigade was in the forefront of armoured warfare development on the eve of rearmament by the major European powers when the Germans were in process of creating a secret *Panzerwaffe* (Tank Arm) in contravention of the Versailles Treaty. Intently watched by foreign observers, Hobart was to head the Tank Brigade with distinction and dash throughout the crucial experimental exercises of 1934 during which an Armoured Division of all arms was improvised. It was a period overlain by vitriolic military and political controversy, when the traditional horse- and foot-orientated arms of the Service were compelled by tank enthusiasts, such as Hobart, to come to terms with the inevitability of mechanization. Although soldiers with modern, open minds welcomed the changes that Hobart and his keenest collaborators pressed upon the Army, older diehards resisted him bitterly for all they were worth. In their opposition they were only too happy to bring up against him the scandal of his marriage, as well as his all too frequent explosive outbursts whenever frustrated by bigots and blind conservatives. In 1935, as clear intelligence about the *Panzerwaffe* came to hand and the struggle within the War Office for funds for new tanks (allied to mechanization of the cavalry) was intensifying, Hobart met Churchill at a Tank Corps dinner and formed an association with the man for whom he felt 'spiritual kinship'.

The following year, when Churchill was collecting material for his campaign against Fascism and Nazism, he met Hobart clandestinely to hear about the current state of the tank art. He would have been told about the total lack of modern tanks, and how long it might be before the inferior, cheap models then on order, might be produced. Hobart would have spoken about the slow, thickly armoured tanks for support of infantry and why infantry-minded generals were giving them priority of production over the faster, less well protected cruiser tanks which Hobart (and the Germans) backed as the tools of strategic, deep penetration operations for achieving stunning decisions in the land battle. There is no record of their meeting. But it is almost certain that Hobart would have painted for Churchill a scenario he had presented to the CIGS of playing on the enemy's nerves,

with threats of an armoured force in his rear, near mobilisation centres ... and when the preparations for our main strategic stroke are ready, then we strike in combination with all our forces. Tank thrust in this case will be at a vital point, and pushed really home, i.e. we must accept our losses. But here, as at all times, tanks' true role is to ATTACK WEAKNESS. Use the Line of Least Resistance: Speed; Surprise.

Four years later, after the Germans had demonstrated the devastating effect of this strategy, Churchill was to admit that 'I knew about it but it had not altered my convictions as it should have done'. Churchill spoke for most officers and the generals who stubbornly clung to outmoded technology and techniques and who, at the first convenient opportunity in 1938, shunted off the 'difficult' Hobart with his forcefully argued 'heresies' and his petrol engines to a backwater in Egypt. Effectively removed from the mainstream of combat development philosophy to the arid wastes of the desert, he was tasked to raise an armoured division which, as the 7th in 1940, was to win eternal fame for its brilliance in battle as first of the Desert Rats.

Yet train them as he would to a marvellously high pitch of battle worthiness (despite their obsolete vehicles) and although he established a valid doctrine of mechanized warfare in the desert which was to withstand the test of battle, Hobart never commanded them in action. Instead the same Henry Wilson who had been a fellow student at Camberley in 1919, reported adversely upon him – as one whose 'tactical ideas are based on the invincibility and invulnerability of the tank to the exclusion of the employment of other arms in correct proportion'. 'Being self-opinionated and lacking in stability', he went on, 'I do not consider that Major-General Hobart can be relied on to discard his own ideas and carry out instructions from his superiors in a spirit of loyalty or co-operation.' And the report was endorsed by another old friend, General Sir Archibald Wavell (whose wife was among the ladies who thoroughly disapproved of the Hobart marriage). Wavell sent Hobart back to England where, in 1940, he was forced into retirement – on the very eve of the German victory over France and Britain by means of the strategy and tactics deemed false by Wilson, Wavell and many others.

With the invasion of Britain seemingly imminent in May 1940, Hobart, at the age of fifty-five, was among the first to join the Local Defence Volunteers. He was promoted at once to the rank of Lance-Corporal and charged with the defence of his home village, Chipping Campden. At once Chipping Campden became a hedgehog of bristling defiance, too small for long to hold Hobart, who was soon made a Deputy Area Organizer of what, in due course, would be renamed the Home Guard. But this was a very temporary appointment. For in September Churchill was turning his attention to the tank situation, the poor state of which concerned him deeply. He was looking for a man to put in supreme charge, one who would steer tank philosophy, design and procurement onto the right lines and raise and train the men, the units and formations which would serve them in battle. Convinced by now that it would be armoured divisions on the German model which must be at the core of formations which, one day, would reconquer Europe, Churchill, with his ingrained scepticism of generals, remained to be convinced that those presently in control would tackle the job with radical enthusiasm. Churchill mentioned the difficulty to General Frederick Pile, a Tank Corps officer who was commanding Anti-Aircraft Command at the height of the Battle of Britain.

'I told him', said Pile, 'we had a superb trainer of tanks in Hobart but he had just been sacked. He asked me to get him to come and see him.' This Pile managed to do after resistance by Hobart, who was insistent upon his honour first being reinstated. By the time the meeting took place on 13 October Hobart had prepared, circulated to and received comments from select Royal Tank Regiment (previously Corps) generals on his proposals for 'an Armoured Army'. His aim was to create wholly Armoured Battle Formations which were aggressive 'and not tied to or clogged by Infantry formations'. He wanted ten armoured divisions and 10,000 tanks, a huge training programme under a GOC-in-C Armoured Army who would have the full support of the

Army Council and be a member of it himself. He emphasized the need to train with the RAF and a requirement, as part of an Armoured Army, of mobile anti-aircraft formations, motorized artillery, infantry, engineers and parachutists.

Churchill gave him a good hearing but seems not to have assimilated the proposal for an Armoured Army since, six days later, he was minuting the CIGS, General Sir John Dill, and referring only to command of an armoured division for Hobart. On the other hand he strongly refuted Dill's note setting out 'the case for and against General Hobart', pointing out 'we cannot afford to confine Army appointments to persons who have excited no hostile comment in their career'. A week later, however, when Dill interviewed Hobart and offered him an armoured division he said he would prefer he took on the job of Commander of Armoured Forces, an appointment which fell well short of what Hobart had in mind for a GOC-in-C. For Dill concurred with a brilliant fellow Gunner, General Alan Brooke, that the Hobart proposal, like a similar one for Anti-Aircraft Command previously led by Brooke, was unworkable. Brooke, as GOC-in-C Home Forces, insisted that it was his job to train the Army in Britain and that Dill's preference for a Commander Royal Armoured Corps (CRAC), responsible only for expanding and training the tank formations and units without the scope and sweeping powers Hobart demanded, was correct. Dill asked Hobart to fill this appointment as Lieutenant-General, but Hobart refused and in a further meeting with Churchill in November explained the difficulties of such a job. He declined to take it and suggested either Broad or Pile as the only generals he knew with the necessary qualifications.

In the end, after a round of awkward negotiations, the job of CRAC, without a charter, was given to another Sapper, Giffard le Q. Martel, who had considerable experience of tank technology but, on his own admission, no flair for command. And although Martel was to make the best of a bad job in what he called 'a delicate position' between the War Office, Home Forces and the Royal Armoured Corps, he did indeed encounter most of the difficulties Hobart had foretold until the appointment of CRAC was abolished in 1942. Meanwhile Hobart was given the 11th Armoured Division to raise and train with characteristic fire and purpose – to the chagrin of Martel when they frequently clashed over doctrine and technology.

It is one of the minor tragedies of Hobart's career that he was unable to separate professional differences from personal ones. With Alan Brooke he had been in disagreement over the composition and handling of the so-called Mobile Division (later the 1st Armoured Division) of which Brooke had been given command when it was formed in 1937. Therefore, when Brooke seemed to be at odds with him again in 1940, he took it as a personal grudge. This, in fact, was unfounded – as a very friendly letter from Brooke to Hobart, explaining his reservations about the Armoured Army within the Army, shows. And as would subsequent events. Differences with Martel over policy also produced personal rancour, which surfaced in a number of ways and places, not least in the Tank Parliaments which Churchill founded in 1941 'to consider tank and anti-tank questions'. Martel resented these parliaments as venues where uninformed criticism of the RAC might take root in unwelcome decisions by the Prime Minister. Beforehand he would convene a meeting with the armoured division commanders to settle agreed answers to the matters on the agenda, thus defeating Churchill's aim of encouraging free debate. Martel, in post-war disclosures, made out that it was Hobart alone who refused to comply with this procedure. But it has been made equally clear by others among Martel's generals that they too had misgivings about Martel's competence. For his part, Hobart regarded Churchill as Britain's saviour and was determined to support to the hilt the man who had brought him back to a task for which he was fully qualified and more foresighted than anybody else.

By common consent, Hobart's training of 11th Armoured Division was something apart. This was recognized by Brooke, during large-scale exercises in 1941 and by the chief umpire of one of those exercises who happened to be Hobart's brother-in-law and immediate superior in command of XII Corps, Lieutenant-General Bernard Montgomery. But those who wished to be rid of Hobart, including Martel, still plotted for his removal until, again, the matter came to Churchill's attention and provoked his demand to inspect 11th Armoured Division at short notice. A snap concentration of the division which happened to be spread all over the country when the order came, imposed enormous strain upon so large a formation, but was accomplished in incredible speed and good order. It vastly impressed the Prime Minister, who sent a laudatory message of congratulations. Regretfully Hobart had to admit that it looks 'as if I have become a bone of contention – or rather a symbol of policy – between W.O. and Govt. Rather as it was in 1937'. He noted, too, that he appeared to be 'hanging on to Winston's coat tails', though there was nothing he could do about that since the same people also plotted against Churchill. But it was noticeable how friendly

Brooke was and how Montgomery appeared 'less bumptious' and 'to be growing up and looking towards greater horizons.' A formidable trio was assembling into what would become a great team, although Hobart had two more threats to his position yet to defeat.

In 1942 another attempt was made to unseat him from command of 11th Armoured Division, this time on legitimate medical grounds. But once more Churchill came to the rescue. In a celebrated letter, he wrote:

I am quite sure that if ... I had insisted upon his controlling the whole of the tank developments, with a seat on the Army Council, many of the grievous errors from which we have suffered would not have been committed. The High Commands of the Army are not a club. It is my duty ... to make sure that exceptionally able men, even those not popular with their military contemporaries, should not be prevented from giving their services to the Crown.

Nevertheless Hobart was, with good reason, removed from command of 11th Armoured when it was booked in September 1942 to go to Tunisia. He had been sick and he was fifty-seven, too old for so exacting a job. Bitterly disappointed he had to make do with raising yet another new armoured division, the 79th, the fourth tank formation he had created without so far having seen one fire a shot in anger.

While Hobart's career was again in flux, the war was in transformation and to a large extent at the hand of his principal military mentors as well as Churchill himself. Alan Brooke, who had taken over from Dill as CIGS at the end of 1941, was now firmly in the saddle, playing a dominant role in the formulation of British and Allied strategy. It was he who had managed to send Montgomery to Egypt where, in October 1942, he was to win the Battle of El Alamein and start the Allies on the road to Berlin. And a few months later, as his attention now focused on the prospect of invading Hitler's Fortress Europe, Brooke called for Hobart in response to what he called 'a happy brainwave'.

In March 1943 Brooke was on the verge of disbanding, for lack of resources, 79th Armoured Division – as the last to come, it had to be first to go. But this presented the opportunity to convert Hobart's command into developing and training the specialized armoured devices which, like a siege train of old, would be vital in leading the amphibious assault ashore through the maze of enemy concrete and steel obstacles which barred the way to the green fields beyond. At the same time it would place in a leading role one of the greatest and most forceful armoured innovators and trainers of the day. When after a day's consideration Hobart accepted the CIGS's invitation it was with an impassioned request that the job should be, as well as training, an operational one, to take him overseas into a combat theatre, 'which you seem so anxious to prevent me doing'. And Brooke had laughed and replied that when the new devices were used in the field it would be natural for Hobart to supervise their handling. With that concession Brooke ensured not only Hobart's absolute loyalty in the testing years ahead, but also abolished the need for Hobart ever again to hang on Churchill's coat tails or mistrust the CIGS.

Once given his head, with the well-advertised support of the CIGS, Hobart became an irresistible power-house of creative energy. From the moment his staff and the units which remained or came under his command got to hear under a cloak of deep secrecy what their tasks were to be, his enthusiasm enwrapped them all. But heaven help anybody, such as the Directorate of Research, who stood in the way of progress and Hobart's inflexible determination. The historian of the 4th/7th Dragoon Guards recalled the day Hobart let them into the secret: 'This was a tremendous day. Up to now we have been pushing forward blindly ... life appeared to have no particular object. ... Now in a flash our eyes were opened. We had a goal ... one that would take us all our efforts to attain.'

Their goal, along with many other British, Canadian and American armoured regiments, was to crew swimming tanks (called DDs) which would spearhead the invasion by landing ahead of the infantry. Other regiments would be set the task of manning Crabs and AVREs, which would comprise Specialized Armoured Assault teams tasked to come ashore behind the DDs and clear lanes through the obstacles and mine-fields, at the same time blasting concrete emplacements whose weapons were intended to secure the defences against demolition. The Crabs were ordinary gun tanks fitted with a rotating flail device which beat the ground ahead to detonate mines and pulverize wire. The AVREs (Armoured Vehicles Royal Engineer), which were manned by Hobart's old Corps (and not allowed to forget it), were heavy Churchill tanks equipped with a Spigot Mortar which fired the Petard, an explosive-filled canister used for demolitions. But AVREs were also loaded with all manner of explosive devices and, in addition, could carry externally great bundles of wood (called fascines) to fill anti-tank ditches; twenty-foot assault bridges to span obstacles and a four-inch explosive-filled iron tube, called a Snake, which could be thrust 400 feet into a minefield and detonated for instant lane clearance. There were also Churchill Crocodile flame-throwing tanks of deadly and terrifying effect, which could be used in a number of roles additional to support of lane clearance. And finally the CDL (Canal Defence Light) tank with its thirteen-million candle power searchlight intended to turn night into day and blind the enemy gunners after dark; a machine of great ingenuity but of dubious operational effectiveness which eventually was hardly used at all.

Each of these pieces of specialized armour had to be developed to a high standard of reliability while their crews were trained to a peak in less than a year. At the same time the techniques for employing them had to be worked out with the Royal Navy, whose landing craft would transport them to the beaches, and with the infantry and other arms who would have to work with them intimately in the assault. It was among Hobart's greatest contributions to the success of every operation in which his 'Funnies' took part, that he and his staff managed to work out techniques and drills which, in simplicity and sense, appealed to the Navy and the other arms. It was due to his resolve that only a few staff officers lasted long under his regime, so ruthless was he in sacking those who appeared to fail. But hard as it was to stay with him for long, results were terrific. As each fresh problem was discovered in the course of a never-ending series of experiments, trials and exercises, Hobo would be there sniffing out the difficulties, leading the way in seeking solutions, and badgering the War Office and Ministry of Supply to meet his insistent demands.

By the end of 1943 most of the major problems had been solved and the invasion plan was taking shape. In the New Year there arrived in Britain the commanders who would lead the Allied invasion, including Montgomery to command the initial assault. High among his priorities was a meeting with his brother-in-law to discuss armoured tactics and what the Funnies would do.

'I've been summoned by the Great Man Monty for 11 a.m. on Sat.', wrote Hobart to his wife on 5 January 1944. 'Bowler-Hat? He doesn't like "old" men. (However I think the War Office would want to keep me on in a new job which they are being forced into making, and for which they can't think of anyone with the particular experience).'

He had no need for worry on that score. Montgomery was only too pleased to have Hobart as his Specialised Armour Advisor and, as time went by and their collaboration flourished, would undoubtedly (admit it though he would not) consult his brother-in-law on much else besides. A 79th Armoured Division 'cell' was set up at HQ 21st Army Group where the staff noticed how receptive everybody was to Hobart's ideas and the manner in which they paid attention when a comment was prefaced by: 'My GOC said. . . .' It was furthermore noticed how often Hobart's appreciation of how a battle might be shaped, foreshadowed what actually took place. But the most important aspect of this close accord between the brothers-in-law was the creation of the iron triangle of three of Churchill's most highly favoured generals in key positions on the eve of the great invasion, with Brooke the man at the apex to apply firm handling to Montgomery and Hobart.

Henceforward Hobart could play a hand of even greater strength than when he first took over the Funnies. He was to be found at many great conferences and meetings, for example with all the top American commanders – Eisenhower, Bradley, Hodges – as well as Crerar of First Canadian Army and Dempsey of Second British. To them he would explain and try to sell the various items in what became known by some as his Noah's Ark – and he would be disappointed that the Americans were only interested in the DDs and rejected, to their later detriment, the other 'animals'. Whenever in the closing stages of the run-up to D-Day some crisis would arise (as, for example, the serious problem created by discovery of blue clay on some Normandy beaches into which vehicles would sink) he would instantly form special Wings to find a solution, calling upon the proven, reliable agencies who helped and supplied him throughout the ministries and industry. And when Eisenhower made his brave decision, despite a marginal weather forecast, to attack on 6 June, Hobart was on hand to hear it and give advice to Montgomery.

The rest is history. Where Specialised Armour was used on 6 June in mass in the forefront of the landings, complete success was achieved, regardless of stiff opposition; there deep penetrations inland were made. Where, on the tragic Omaha beach, few DDs managed because of rough seas to swim ashore, the American infantry suffered terribly, nigh unto failure, and only a toehold was purchased. And in the days to come, throughout the grim fighting in the Normandy bocage, it was 79th Armoured Division's Funnies which repeatedly played crucial roles by adapting their characteristics to changing circumstances. The process of educating formation and unit commanders in the correct and profitable employment of specialized armour, which was all too frequently abused by the tank-ignorant – the infantry in particular – was unremitting. Likewise the development and employment of new types of specialized armour was constant – such as obsolete tanks modified to carry infantry safely under armour through the enemy fire to the objective;

and of Buffalo amphibious carriers to lift infantry, supported by DDs, in the amphibious assaults on the islands guarding the River Scheldt and, later, across the rivers Rhine and Elbe. And always the latest gadgets, such as night vision and electronic navigation devices, were being investigated and put to use.

Hobart's path to Berlin was that of 79th Armoured Division's units in the pursuit from Normandy to the Rhine, in the clearing of Brest, the Channel ports and the Scheldt estuary, the fierce fighting in the Reichswald, the crossing of the Rhine and the final pursuit to the Baltic. Always he was commuting between his own headquarters, Montgomery's and the leading formations and units. At times, such as at Boulogne, he was personally involved in the fighting. Inexhaustibly he would visit troops before and after combat, assuring himself they knew their task, probing their experiences, putting right what was wrong, learning fresh lessons, encouraging the efficient and brave, remorselessly sacking those who failed to meet his own standards. In some ways he was a rather lonely man whose contacts with even the élite close staff he assembled was virtually professional only. It was only in his daily letters to his wife that he was able intimately to discuss numerous subjects other than those military.

As Churchill's days as Prime Minister drew to a close, Hobart would arrange with Brooke a way of projecting 79th Armoured Division into the future, earmarking Funnies for the culminating stage of the war against Japan and laying plans for continued research into specialized armour after the war. In a great moment on 26 March he would boat across the Rhine in one of his Buffalos with Churchill, Brooke, Montgomery and Dempsey aboard. 'The old man greeted me warmly but did not say much', he wrote. 'It's difficult to talk against the noise of the craft. . . . Alan Brooke . . . bid me to come to lunch with him when I come over – so perhaps I'll be able to ask if there's any chance of my further employment.' There was, although not as a professor of history at Oxford University despite sponsorship by Churchill, Brooke and Montgomery.

There is no record of whether he met Churchill again after the war or if there were any contacts other than the matter of the professorship. Each would serve in his own way but henceforth in different circumstances to those of their first meeting in 1935. For now it was Churchill whose prospects were good, while Hobart moved into a relative state of limbo as Colonel Commandant of the Royal Tank Regiment before moving into the shades. He died on 19 February 1957, fiercely combative to the end.

BIBLIOGRAPHY

For the most part this chapter is based upon *Armoured Crusader: Major-General Sir Percy Hobart* by Kenneth Macksey, as well as on *The Tank Pioneers* by the same author. Many other books refer to him quite frequently, notably Churchill's *History of the Second World War* and histories of the 7th, 11th and 79th Armoured Divisions.

CHRONOLOGY: PERCY HOBART

1885	Born
1902	At Royal Military College, Sandhurst
1906	Commissioned into the Royal Engineers and posted to 1st Bengal Sappers and Miners
1915–18	Regimental duty in France but on the staff from August 1915 in France, Mesopotamia and Palestine
1919	Staff College, Camberley, and on staff until 1927 in various appointments, including Instructor at Staff College, Quetta
1923	Transferred to Royal Tank Corps
1931	Commands 2nd Battalion Royal Tank Corps as Lieutenant-Colonel
1933	Inspector RTC as Brigadier and thereby also commander 1 Tank Brigade in 1934
1937	DMT as Major-General
1938	Commands Mobile Division in Egypt until relieved of command in 1939 and retired in 1940
1940, May	Joins Home Guard as Lance-Corporal
1941	Commands 11th Armoured Division
1942	Commands 79th Armoured Division
1945	Commands Specialised Armoured Experimental Establishment
1946	Retires
1957	Dies

14

PERCIVAL

Lieutenant-General Arthur Percival

KEITH SIMPSON

At 1810 hours on 15 February 1942 in the Ford factory on Singapore island an exhausted Lieutenant-General A. E. Percival signed terms of surrender with Lieutenant-General Tomoyuki Yamashita of the Imperial Japanese Army which ended the seventy-day campaign in Malaya and Singapore. It was the greatest capitulation of British military arms since the surrender at Yorktown in 1781 during the American War of Independence. At Singapore a British Commonwealth Army of 130,000 surrendered to a Japanese Army of less than 30,000. The campaign had been a series of physical and psychological shocks for the British from beginning to end, starting with the loss of the Royal Navy's capital ships the *Prince of Wales* and the *Repulse* and culminating in the discovery that 'fortress' Singapore was a myth.

Churchill was profoundly depressed by the humiliating circumstances of the surrender at Singapore. It appeared to Churchill that whilst the Americans gave the impression of fighting to the last in the Philippines and the Soviets were waging a total war of defence, a numerically larger British Army had surrendered to a smaller and weaker Japanese force having suffered relatively few casualties. Percival had refused to indulge in any last-minute false heroics and had thus failed to meet Churchill's ultimate test of a military commander. As Churchill later observed, 'I have always followed, so far as I could see, the principle that military commanders should not be judged by results, but by the quality of their effort.'[1] But was Percival responsible for the British defeat in Malaya and Singapore or was he a convenient scapegoat for a wider failure of British leadership and responsibility?

But for the outbreak of the First World War Percival would not have become a professional soldier. In 1914 he was working in the City of London when he volunteered for the Army at the age of twenty-seven. He was a fine athlete, immensely fit and hard working. In 1915 Percival went to France as a lieutenant with the 7th Bedfordshire Regiment, served as a company commander on the Somme and was awarded the Military Cross. In October 1916 he was given a regular commission in the Essex Regiment, and then rejoined the Bedfords, eventually being promoted to the temporary rank of lieutenant-colonel and given command of a battalion in 1917 and then for a brief period a brigade in 1918. Percival ended the war a highly decorated officer, described in his confidential report as very efficient, beloved by his men, a brave soldier and recommended for the Staff College.

In 1919 Percival volunteered for service in north Russia and went as second-in-command of the 46th Royal Fusiliers. In 1920 he served as a company commander and then as an intelligence officer with the Essex Regiment in Ireland fighting the IRA. Percival qualified for the Staff College in 1923, where he was picked out for accelerated promotion. A staff job in Nigeria was followed by regimental service with the Cheshires in 1929, and in 1930 he was sent as a student to the Royal Naval College at Greenwich. A year later Percival was appointed an instructor at the Staff College where he soon came to the attention of Dill, the Commandant. Dill regarded Percival as an outstanding instructor and staff officer and wrote in his confidential report of 1932, 'He has an outstanding ability, wide military knowledge, good judgement and is a very quick and accurate worker.' Significantly, Dill noted, 'He has not altogether an impressive presence and one may therefore fail, at first meeting him, to appreciate his sterling worth.'[2] Lieutenant-General Sir Ian Jacob knew Percival at this time, and later recalled that he was a very pleasant man, highly intelligent, and unquestionably brave, but quiet, 'not the man for a whirlwind'.[3]

During the next ten years Dill was to be Percival's patron, advancing his career through a series of recommendations, and wherever possible appointing Percival to serve on his own staff. After Percival's time as an instructor at the Staff College Dill recommended that he should be sent as a student to the Imperial Defence College. Percival attended the Imperial Defence College in 1935 after two years commanding 2nd Cheshire Regiment. In 1936 whilst Dill was Director of Military Operations and Intelligence at the War Office he helped secure Percival's promotion to Colonel and his appointment as GSO1 Malaya Command. In November 1937 Percival was promoted Brigadier and given command of a brigade at Aldershot, but Dill as GOC Aldershot persuaded Percival instead to accept the appointment as his BGS (Brigadier General Staff).

In 1939 when Dill was appointed to command I Corps in the BEF Percival went with him to France. Although Dill failed to persuade Gort to appoint Percival as MGGS (Major-General General Staff) to the Third Army in February 1940, he did secure Percival's promotion as a major-general and the command of the 43rd (Wessex) Division in England. When in April 1940 Dill returned to England to become Vice CIGS he secured Percival as one of the three Assistant CIGS co-ordinating the Operational and Intelligence Directorates. But in the summer of 1940 Percival asked to be transferred to a field appointment and took command of the 44th Division. He remained with this command until April 1941 when Dill appointed him GOC Malaya in the temporary rank of lieutenant-general, promoted over the heads of many senior and more experienced officers.

Dill's patronage of Percival was based upon a clear assessment of Percival's worth as an efficient and intelligent staff officer who was an indefatigable worker and who, like Dill, was utterly dedicated to his military profession. In April 1941 Percival must have appeared to Dill to be the obvious candidate to be GOC Malaya. The previous incumbent had been short-toured because he was thought to be worn out and had had an uneasy relationship with the RAF and the colonial administration. Dill was aware, therefore, that it was necessary to appoint as GOC Malaya an officer who was tactful and diplomatic, and who could work with the other two services, Commonwealth representatives and the colonial administration. Percival had worked with them all as a student at Greenwich and the Imperial Defence College, and then as GSO1 Malaya Command. Percival's previous experience in Malaya, and the fact that in 1937 he had written an appreciation of the defence of Malaya and Singapore, was another factor influencing Dill. Dill was only too well aware of the inadequate military forces available in Malaya and Singapore and the increasing threat posed by the Japanese. He was unable to persuade Churchill to substantially reinforce Malaya and

Singapore, and Dill probably concluded that the next best thing was to appoint as GOC a first-class staff officer with previous experience of the area. Dill was an intellectual soldier whose *métier* was the staff, and his decision to send Percival to Singapore was in the finest traditions of that model of a modern general staff, the German General Staff. (In 1918 Ludendorff was unwilling to send substantial German reinforcements to bolster the Turkish Army, but he did send Hans von Seeckt, an outstanding staff officer with operational experience, as Chief of Staff to the Turkish Army.)

On 1 December 1941 Dill admitted to Alan Brooke, another of his protégés and his successor as CIGS, that he had done practically nothing to meet the Japanese threat. According to Brooke, Dill told him that 'we were already so weak on all fronts that it was impossible to denude them any further'.[4] In sending Percival to Malaya Dill had sent a clever staff officer, but someone who was totally inexperienced in the command of troops in war at an operational level. Major-General John Kennedy, who worked with both Dill and Brooke as Director of Military Operations, claimed that after Brooke had been appointed CIGS he had 'expressed his concern that officers were being promoted to high command because they were proficient in staff work – which was quite wrong – and urged that fewer mistakes of this nature should be made in the future'.[5]

Percival took up his new appointment with little enthusiasm or confidence, writing in his postwar account : 'In going to Malaya I realised that there was the double danger either of being left in an inactive command for some years if war did not break out in the East or, if it did, of finding myself involved in a pretty sticky business with the inadequate forces. . . .'[6] Sticky business indeed, because when Percival arrived in Malaya in May 1941 he found that his freedom of manoeuvre to influence strategy, the operational deployment of his troops or attitudes of mind was very limited. For the previous twenty years successive British Governments and the three services had debated how best to deter Japan in the Far East and how to defend Malaya and the Singapore naval base. The debate and the decisions taken, or more accurately the decisions deferred, reflected the economic circumstances of the moment, the threat level and fierce inter-service rivalry. The original plan had been to send a fleet to the Far East in the event of a crisis, and the naval base at Singapore was constructed to meet that requirement. Effectively from 1935 it was unlikely that a large fleet would be sent because of the increasing threat posed by the Germans and Italians.

Japanese military expansion in the Far East and the development of air power meant that by 1937 Malaya Command had concluded that to defend the naval base at Singapore the whole of Malaya had to be defended. The RAF claimed that they could defend Malaya against any Japanese air attack and seaborne landings and after 1939 a series of airfields were constructed in north-east Malaya for that purpose.

By the time Percival arrived the defence of Malaya and Singapore was the worst kind of compromise. The primary deterrent of the 1920s had been a fleet sent from Europe, but by 1941 this had dwindled to the deployment of a small force of two capital ships, eventually to consist of the *Prince of Wales* and the *Repulse*. The RAF never had sufficient aircraft to station in Malaya and after 1939 the defence of Britain and the requirements of the Middle East had priority. In December 1941 the RAF had in Malaya 158 obsolescent aircraft instead of the agreed minimum of 336 modern aircraft. The army had always been the poor relation in any defence planning, tasked with local defence of the naval base and internal security. By 1941 it faced the prospects of having to deploy inadequate forces throughout Malaya to defend RAF airfields and potential landing areas, and provide a force to move into southern Siam immediately following any Japanese aggression.

Although the Chiefs of Staff in August 1940 recommended reinforcing Malaya and Singapore, Churchill resolutely opposed them. Churchill's priority was always the Mediterranean and the Middle East, where he believed the war would be won or lost. Churchill was determined to take the offensive in the Middle East and all military resources were to be concentrated in that theatre. This issue by 1941 became one of the main reasons why Churchill was to lose confidence in Dill as CIGS. Churchill underestimated the Japanese, overestimated the deterrent value of a token British naval force, and believed that the existing garrison and 'fortress' Singapore would provide enough time for reinforcements to arrive in the event of hostilities. Churchill's policy was also determined by his strategy of persuading the United States to guarantee the British position in the Far East. American reluctance to give any military guarantees meant that Japan had to be seen to be the aggressor, which further restricted the options facing the military commanders in Malaya.[7]

When Percival took up his command in May 1941 he found that the operational deployment of his troops was determined by three factors. Many of his troops were dispersed to guard static positions, particularly the RAF's exposed airfields in northern Malaya. Secondly, he had to provide a strike force capable of seizing the Kra isthmus in southern Siam after it had been established beyond all reasonable doubt that the Japanese were the aggressors but in sufficient time to prevent them moving south into Malaya. Thirdly, any military preparations he undertook had to cause the least inconvenience and disruption to the Malayan economy, which was crucial to the British war effort. Percival's appreciation of the scale of the problem he faced in 1941 was undoubtedly influenced by the study he had carried out in 1937. Percival was only too well aware of the vulnerability of Malaya and Singapore to Japanese sea and airborne attacks and the failure of London to provide the necessary reinforcements, particularly in tanks, which he had recommended in 1937. As Percival noted after the war, his appreciation made in 1937 'did not differ very materially from that adopted by the Japanese when they attacked Malaya four years later'. Percival also claims that when he had joined Dill at Aldershot in 1938 he had warned him that Singapore, far from being impregnable, 'would be in imminent danger if war broke out in the Far East unless there was an early realisation in high places of the complete change in the problem of its defence which was then taking place'.[8] It is reasonable to assume that Percival's 1937 appreciation at the very least made him pessimistic in 1941 about his chances of successfully repelling a Japanese attack.

As GOC Malaya, Percival found himself a member of a top-heavy civil-military command structure. Since October 1940 the C-in-C Far East had been Air Chief Marshal Brooke-Popham, who was responsible for co-ordinating service policy throughout the Far East. An elderly officer with a somewhat Colonel Blimp image, 'Brookham' had a background as an RAF administrator and staff officer. With a small staff, he had been able to do little to improve the situation in the Far East. In November 1941 he was replaced by Lieutenant-General Pownall, but Pownall never reached Singapore until 27 December, and then the whole command structure in the Far East was re-organized yet again, with Wavell appointed to the ABDA Command and Pownall as his chief of staff. So at a crucial period before and immediately after Japan attacked, Percival found himself with a 'lame duck' C-in-C and then a commander who could only give intermittent direction and advice between his other onerous duties.

Until the Japanese attack the civil authorities could restrict military preparations because of the economic importance of Malaya to the war effort and because they believed the war would never happen. The

Governor of Singapore, Sir Shenton Thomas, was an affable and stolid administrator, but not someone to respond quickly and decisively to a crisis. Percival may have felt uneasy in his company as Shenton Thomas had been Governor in 1937 when Percival had been a staff officer. From the beginning of the war in Europe, relations between the civilians, civil servants and the businessmen and the military was strained. Percival found himself checked at every turn by the civil authorities but appears to have been unwilling to precipitate a crisis over his military requirements. A further complication to civil-military relations had been the appointment of Duff Cooper as Resident Minister in the Far East, sent to improve high-level co-ordination. On the outbreak of war Churchill instructed Duff to form a War Council in Singapore consisting of Shenton Thomas, Brooke-Popham, Percival, Air Vice-Marshal Pulford, Vice-Admiral Layton and Bowden representing the Australian Government. The War Council became another cog in an already cumbersome machine, consuming the time of busy men like Percival and producing inevitable friction. At a service level Percival had good relations with Pulford of the RAF and Layton of the Royal Navy. The irony for Percival was that when he arrived in Malaya both he and the army were very much the junior members of the service team, and yet within the first week of the campaign following the loss of the *Prince of Wales* and the *Repulse* and the effective withdrawal of surviving RAF planes from Malaya to Singapore, his command became almost solely responsible for its defence.

If the civil-military command was top heavy Percival found that his own command left a lot to be desired. By December 1941 the army's strength would rise to some 80,000 men made up of British, Australian, Indian and Malay formations. It was not a homogeneous force and, although well equipped with transport, was short of anti-tank and anti-aircraft guns and was without tanks. Many of the formations were made up of young recruits with little training and the most experienced officers and NCOs had been posted to the Middle East. Apart from the Singapore garrison, Percival had two main field formations in Malaya. The III Indian Corps in the north, deployed to defend the RAF's airfields and coastal landing areas and with the additional task of occupying the Kra isthmus after a Japanese attack, and the 8th Australian Division in the Port Dickinson area. Apart from the considerable geographical distances involved and the difficult nature of the terrain, Percival found he had other problems of command. Radio communications were poor and the telephone system unreliable. Because of the shortage of aircraft

Percival relied upon flying in small privately owned planes or used a car. He found himself acting both as GOC and as army commander with a completely inadequate staff. And then there were his difficulties with Lieutenant-General Heath, commanding III Indian Corps, and Major-General Gordon Bennett, commanding the 8th Australian Division.

'Piggy' Heath had commanded the 5th Indian Division in Eritrea and had been the victor at Keren. A soldier's soldier, he lived for the Indian Army. His relations with Percival were strained from the very beginning. Heath was senior to Percival in age and experience and it cannot have been easy for him to serve as a subordinate. Percival was sceptical about the fighting value and professionalism of Heath's III Indian Corps and believed Heath had an 'Indian Army complex'. After the initial disasters which overwhelmed some of the Indian units Heath urged Percival to withdraw to a position in Johore rather than fighting a delaying battle further north. Percival lost confidence in Heath as a Corps Commander, but lacked the ruthlessness to replace him.

Bennett was a soldier suffering from extreme paranoia who was a rasping, bitter, sarcastic man, given to expressing his views with great freedom. One of Australia's most distinguished citizen soldiers of the First World War, he was prejudiced against regular officers, his own officers, regular or citizen, and disliked and distrusted the British. In fact he was the last Australian officer who should have been appointed to such a sensitive command involving close co-operation with Commonwealth forces. Percival was only too well aware that Bennett, although nominally his subordinate, had a directive from the Australian Government which gave him considerable freedom of action. This combined with his outspoken comments and at times irrational behaviour made him a difficult subordinate for Percival. In turn Bennett found Percival 'unassuming, considerate and conciliatory', which were not qualities likely to impress him. Soon after Percival arrived in Malaya Bennett noted that 'he does not seem strong, rather the Yes man type. Listens a lot but says little.' And later noted in his diary, 'My estimate of him was right. Weak and hesitant though brainy.' Unfortunately, Bennett conveyed these impressions to the press in August 1941 when he said that Percival was 'clever but weak'.[9] Bennett loathed and despised Heath and was to write of him at the height of the crisis in Johore on 27 January 1942: 'He should have been relieved of his command long ago in my opinion but apparently has had some hidden power or influence, as he sways Percival very easily.'[10] When the Australian CGS visited Malaya in August 1941 he asked Percival whether he was satisfied with Bennett. Although Percival was given the opportunity to replace Bennett he decided to let him stay on. Once again Percival appears to have avoided taking an unpleasant but necessary decision.

Shortly after assuming command Percival had been instructed to make a review of the forces required for the defence of Malaya. After undertaking an exhaustive survey of the probable battle area in northern Malaya, Percival submitted his requirements to the Chiefs of Staff in August 1941. He asked for a further seventeen infantry battalions, two tank regiments and two heavy anti-aircraft regiments. The Chiefs of Staff replied a month later saying they were unavailable. With the forces he had available in northern Malaya Percival decided he had no option but to defend the scattered and badly positioned RAF airfields. Percival's dispositions meant that in northern Malaya, astride the trunk road on the west coast, stood only two brigades, less than one fifth of his total force. Furthermore, the 11th Indian Division was given two roles, one offensive, the other defensive. An alternative defence plan would have meant abandoning the defence of the indefensible airfields, putting blocking positions along the trunk road at known bottlenecks, and concentrating most of the infantry for offensive operations. Although Percival was restricted in his freedom of action, he appears to have done little to take obvious defensive measures or prepare for a more aggressive defence of northern Malaya.

Brigadier Simson, the Chief Engineer Malaya Command, claimed that during the summer of 1941 he made a number of specific recommendations to Percival and his staff for the construction of defences in northern Malaya, including training in anti-tank and jungle warfare, all of which were ignored.[11] It is difficult to explain Percival's attitude except that he was representative of most senior officers and colonial officials in believing that it was vital not to disrupt the Malayan economy and that construction of defences would affect native morale, and in a general underestimation of the Japanese. What struck Brigadier Simson as Percival's most serious mistake was the presumption that the Japanese could not land on the east coast of Malaya between November and March because of the northeast monsoon.[12] Percival admits that this fallacy had already been exposed in his own 1937 study, but he had, nevertheless, concluded that it was 'unlikely that the Japanese would select a date for their attack during the period December–February when the monsoon is at its height as it would involve running considerable risks'.[13] And Percival was not a commander who would run risks, so he was unlikely to imagine a potential enemy commander doing so.

From 6 December 1941 the military authorities in Singapore were aware Japanese convoys were heading from Indo-China towards Siam and Malaya. But over the next forty-eight hours the British military authorities were paralysed by their own caution. Brooke-Popham was very conscious of his instructions from London not to use military force until the Japanese had demonstrably been proved to be the aggressor, which of course gave them the initiative. Brooke-Popham finally cancelled the plan whereby the 11th Indian Division would have moved into Siam to occupy the Kra isthmus. Instead it was ordered to occupy a defensive role at Jitra on the west coast road.

Within seventy-two hours of the initial Japanese landings in Siam and along the north-east coast of Malaya the British had suffered three major defeats. By the evening of 10 December the Japanese had destroyed the bulk of the RAF's planes in northern Malaya and Pulford withdrew his surviving aircraft to Singapore. The two Indian brigades defending the airfields were forced to abandon them to the Japanese after being badly mauled. With the effective withdrawal of the RAF the army was to fight the rest of the campaign in Malaya without proper air support. On 9 December Churchill's naval deterrent, Force Z, the *Prince of Wales* and the *Repulse*, were sunk by Japanese aircraft off the eastern coast of Malaya. This was a tremendous psychological shock to everyone in Singapore and London and gave the Japanese control of the seas off the eastern coast of Malaya which, combined with their air superiority, enabled them to carry out further seaborne landings. The third disaster for the British was the effective destruction by the Japanese of the 11th Indian Division. The Japanese foiled a British attempt using a small force from the 11th Indian Division to block them at the Ledge in southern Siam. The Japanese then pushed south with tanks and penetrated the defensive positions of the 11th Indian Division, and over the next twenty-four hours the division retreated in some chaos.

The initial Japanese successes were based on their aggressive tactics and offensive spirit. In comparison, the British appeared lethargic and pedantic, always literally on the defensive. Percival in Singapore had great physical difficulty in commanding and controlling the battle in northern Malaya. Heath's III Indian Corps headquarters at Kuala Lumpur was two hundred miles away, and the Siam border was another two hundred and fifty miles further north. Neither Percival nor Heath could really influence the battle, and at the height of the battle for

Jitra Heath was in Singapore. Following the series of disasters in northern Malaya Percival was forced to reconsider his strategy. Pulford and he decided that the Japanese had to be held as far north as possible to enable the remaining RAF airfields to be protected, which would allow the surviving RAF planes to give air cover to the reinforcements which would be arriving by sea. As Percival was to write after the war, 'I held the view that the first step towards recovery of any sort was to regain control of the air and that this could only be done by bringing in more fighters. I was prepared to make almost any sacrifice to get these fighters in safely and to get them into the air.'[14] This influenced Percival's decision to keep two of his brigades in eastern Malaya where they were supposed to protect the remaining airfields. This turned out to be a waste of resources and in retrospect Percival should have used these two brigades to reinforce his position in the west.

Percival's strategy depended upon a number of assumptions. The Japanese had to keep their advance to the tempo of the gradual British withdrawal – they didn't. Heath's III Indian Corps had to fight a carefully co-ordinated withdrawal slowing down the Japanese and inflicting the maximum number of casualties – they didn't. Sufficient reinforcements had to arrive in time, properly equipped and trained to be used in a decisive counter-stroke against the Japanese before Singapore itself was invested – they didn't. After the defeat at Jitra Percival found that Heath disagreed with the strategy of gradual withdrawal, preferring instead to break contact with the Japanese and withdraw much further south to a prepared defensive position. Percival lost confidence in Heath and later recalled: 'all the way down the peninsula, I had a feeling that unless I issued definitive orders as to how long such and such a position was to be held, I should find that it had been evacuated prematurely.'[15] The Japanese were able to advance faster than the British could reinforce Singapore, or Percival could deploy troops and aircraft to stop them. Instead of being able to concentrate sufficient forces for a counter-stroke, Percival was forced to feed reinforcements into his existing formations in a piecemeal fashion. Despite the seriousness of the situation in the Far East Churchill bent all his energies into winning the war in the Mediterranean. From 18 November Churchill had concentrated on Operation Crusader, Auchinleck's offensive in North Africa, and he was then distracted by Rommel's counter-offensive. Although Churchill did sanction reinforcements for Malaya, he appears to have adopted a policy of damage limitation.

Whilst Heath's III Indian Corps was withdrawing south, Percival was preparing his defensive positions in Johore. But according to Brigadier Simson, Percival refused to allow the construction of defensive works, telling Simson on 26 December that 'Defences are bad for morale – for both troops and civilians.'[16] At a conference of senior commanders on 5 January 1942 it was decided that III Indian Corps would withdraw into a defensive position in Johore after denying the Japanese the airfields at Kuala Lumpur and Port Swettenham. Bennett had proposed that his 8th Australian Division should hold the position in the west, but Percival's plan was that III Indian Corps would be responsible for the defence of western Johore whilst Gordon Bennett's 8th Australian Division would be responsible for the east.

Percival's carefully constructed plan was thrown into confusion on 7 January when the Japanese attacked with tanks at the Slim River and virtually destroyed the 11th Indian Division. On the same day Wavell arrived in Singapore and on 8 January he visited the front. Wavell was more impressed with Bennett than he was with Heath or Percival, and was encouraged by Bennett's plan for a vigorous defence of Johore. On the evening of the 8th Wavell summoned Percival and without any discussion handed him the new plan for the defence of Johore. The plan was effectively Bennett's original proposal and it must have shocked Percival, indicating as it did that he had lost Wavell's confidence. Pownall noted in his diary for the 8th that Wavell was 'not at all happy about Percival, who has the knowledge, but not the personality to carry through a tough fight'. Pownall hoped that 'it won't mean that I have to relieve Percival *pro tem*, until someone tougher than he can come from elsewhere. But it might so happen.'[17]

Percival had the unenviable task of implementing a plan imposed on him by Wavell, and entrusting its execution to a subordinate in whom he lacked confidence. Furthermore, Wavell's plan involved a messy exchange of forces, with Bennett temporarily losing a brigade of his 8th Australian Division but leaving the 9th Indian Division and an Indian Brigade placed under his command. Bennett's command, known as Westforce, was deployed to defend north-west Johore with III Indian Corps to the rear. Percival was forced to act directly as an army commander. 'As our area of manoeuvre was becoming so restricted, I felt that the time had now come to exercise more direct personal control of the operations than had previously been possible.'[18] This was the last thing Percival was capable of doing, and in just over a fortnight from 14 to 31 January the Japanese took the initiative, and after a series of seaborne landings down both the west and east coasts, and by penetrating the British defences and outflanking them, forced Percival to withdraw from Johore onto the island of Singapore. Bennett misappreciated Japanese intentions in the west, and on 15 January Japanese troops turned his left flank at Muar. In order to take direct control of the battle Percival was forced to motor long distances to conferences in the forward area, combining his duties as GOC Malaya with those of an army commander. At these conferences Percival arrived tired and worn out and usually failed to take control. As the British official historian Woodburn Kirby noted, 'Bennett would then take the floor putting forward impracticable proposals until Heath would break in with a sensible suggestion based on sound military considerations, which Percival would accept and act upon.'[19]

Percival appears to have been unwilling to consider in advance any plan for a withdrawal of his forces from Malaya onto Singapore island or to take the necessary measures for the defence of the island. Wavell took the initiative from 10 January, prodding Percival in a series of letters and meetings. Although Percival claimed in his postwar account that he had issued orders as early as 23 December to establish defensive positions on the north of the island, little seems to have been done. Wavell met Percival at Singapore on 20 January to discuss with him how the island should be defended if the battle for Johore was lost.

Wavell had concluded that the eventual Japanese attack would be made on the north-west coast and suggested positioning there the freshest troops, but Percival, despite his postwar claims to the contrary, was to remain convinced that the Japanese would land in the north-east. Wavell decided to defer to the judgement of the commander on the spot, which seems rather inconsistent given his earlier decision to over-rule Percival's plan for defending Johore.[20] As the troops were withdrawn from Malaya across the causeway onto Singapore island on 30–31 January, they moved straight to the areas Percival had allotted them for the defence of the island. Percival had decided to conduct a forward defence, with Bennett's division holding the coast along the north-west of the island and Heath's III Indian Corps with the recently landed 18th Division holding the north-east coast. Percival allocated only one brigade as his reserve and the troops deployed along the coast had to prepare their own defences. There was considerable chaos, confusion and panic on the island, which had suffered badly from Japanese air raids, and the morale of the civilian population was low. Commanders and troops were tired and dispirited and whilst the military believed that the civil authorities had done little to prepare for a siege, the civil authorities felt the military had misled them and failed in their duty.

The Japanese began the assault on Singapore on the night of 8 February in the north-west against Bennett's 8th Australian Division. For the next eight hours the Japanese were able to exploit their landings and penetrate the Australian position. Percival later explained that his inactivity was due to a reluctance to use his only reserve brigade before he was certain that he was not facing a Japanese feint whilst the main attack took place in the north-east. 'I had learnt on exercises we had held in England not to commit your reserve until you are quite certain you are dealing with the real thing.'[21] Unfortunately for Percival the Japanese attack was the real thing and due to a series of errors Bennett's 8th Australian Division abandoned a defensive position to its rear, which allowed the Japanese to penetrate to the centre of the island. Percival found himself coming under pressure from Churchill, who sent Wavell a signal on 10 February calling for a fight to the finish. By 12 February Percival was forced to withdraw all his troops to a defensive perimeter around Singapore city. On 13 February Percival held a conference with his military commanders to discuss the shortages of water and food and the poor morale of the troops. Both Heath and Bennett advocated capitulation, but Percival decided to keep fighting, heeding Churchill's instructions and Wavell's orders. But at a final conference on 15 February Percival once again canvassed the opinions of his military commanders and having put everyone on record decided to capitulate.

By the criteria of what makes an effective military leader, Percival was a failure. His physical appearance was unprepossessing, being described at the time as 'a tall thin person, whose most conspicuous characteristics were two protruding rabbit teeth'.[22] His friend and biographer John Smyth has admitted that 'It is probably the case, too, that appearances in a higher commander are important. If the commander looked the part, as Bill Slim did with his jutting jaw and bull-dog build, or as Monty did ... then the effect on the troops was psychologically good. Percival lacked these superficial qualities. ...'[23] Pownall described Percival as someone 'who has the knowledge but not the personality to carry through a tough fight,' and thought he was 'an uninspiring leader and rather gloomy. ...'[24] Ian Morrison, a journalist, observed Percival throughout the campaign in Malaya and thought that he was

a man of considerable personal charm, if one met him socially. He was an able staff officer with a penetrating mind, although a mind that saw the difficulties to any scheme before it saw the possibilities. But he was a completely negative person, with no vigour, no colour, and no conviction. His personality was not strong, and as a leader he did not appeal either to the troops (to whom he was unknown except by name) or to the general public.[25]

In his diary and private correspondence Bennett was very critical of Percival, who he thought had 'quite a good brain and sound judgement but very weak. . . . He wants the army to fight and to stop retreating, but lacks the personality to make it fight or even to remove officers who lack the fighting spirit.'[26] In his account of the campaign published later in the war, which was an apology for his own behaviour in leaving Singapore without permission just before the capitulation, Bennett was more generous, writing : 'In my opinion, the system was more to blame than the individual. General Percival had a brilliant career. He was very active and energetic, playing a good game of tennis which would be the envy of many younger men. . . . He knew Malaya and its problems and was probably the best selection for the appointment to command the land forces there.'[27]

Percival appeared on numerous occasions to be unable to come to a decision or propose decisive action, particularly vigorous counter measures against the Japanese. Bowden, the Australian Government's representative on the War Council, observed that Percival had 'no answer to Japanese infiltration tactics but to retreat, and I do not remember his ever proposing any counter-offensive action. Other incidents have suggested lack of decision.'[28] Shenton Thomas gives an account in his diary of a meeting of the War Council on 14 December 1941 at which Percival circulated a memorandum setting out the arguments for and against withdrawal from Penang but with no final conclusion or recommendation. To Shenton Thomas, 'defend to the last' meant exactly that, but Percival qualified it with 'but to the best of our ability' although well knowing that his ability could not be sustained.[29] Major Wild, one of Heath's staff officers, observed Percival during the final days on Singapore. 'I had become inured during the past week to seeing General Percival's painful inability to give a decision, and on three occasions to make any reply whatever, when points of operational importance were referred to him. . . .'[30]

There was always something of the perpetual Staff College instructor about Percival even when he was supposed to be exercising operational command. Duff Cooper told Churchill that Percival wasn't a leader, 'he cannot take a large view ; it is all a field day at Aldershot to him. He knows the rules as well and follows them so closely and is always waiting for the umpire's whistle to cease-fire and hopes that when the moment comes his military dispositions will be such as to receive approval.'[31] Bennett watched Percival undertake a reconnaissance in Johore on 10 January 1942 : 'This recce reminded me of peace-time army exercises without troops. There was much walking about from one point of vantage to another, much discussion on the relative fields of fire etc.'[32] Contemporaries agreed with Woodburn Kirby, who thought that Percival as a military commander had 'neither the drive nor the ruthlessness which was needed. . . .'[33] Harrison, the GSO1 of the 11th Indian Division, told Smyth in 1970 that Percival 'lacked the quality of ruthlessness', and Thyer, the GSO1 of the 8th Australian Division, concurred : 'He lacked that ruthlessness that a commander needs in a tight place. A man of the highest principle, he was a wee bit too tenderhearted.'[34]

Percival's self-effacement, modesty and even timidity is revealed in his postwar account of the campaign. He was unwilling to criticize the authorities in London and Delhi for their part in the disaster. Discussing the muddle and hiatus in the higher direction of the war in December, when Pownall replaced Brooke-Popham followed by the appointment of Wavell, Percival diffidently wrote : 'I have no wish to suggest that any of these changes were wrong or that things should have been arranged otherwise, but it cannot be denied that the general effect was far from healthy.' Commenting on the untrained reinforcements of 45 Indian Brigade, which arrived at the end of December, Percival hastily qualified his criticism by writing, 'In making these statements I have no wish to blame anybody for sending these troops to Malaya. After all it was better than having none at all.' And again at the end of January, with reference to Indian and Australian reinforcements, 'I have no wish to blame the authorities either in India or in Australia for sending these untrained men.'[35]

Percival was physically brave, physically fit, and a first-class staff officer in peacetime but without experience of command in war. He was uninspiring, gloomy, with a personality that saw difficulties rather than opportunities ; weak and hesitant and at times unable to reach a decision ; lacking the necessary aggressive qualities and ruthlessness to be a military commander in war. Percival failed to meet Wavell's criteria for military leadership, spelt out in the first of his Lees Knowles lectures at Cambridge in 1939 : 'I hold to be the first essential of a General, the quality of robustness, the ability to stand the shocks of war. .... All materials of war, including the General, must have a certain solidity, a high margin over the normal breaking strain.'[36]

In apportioning blame for the events in Malaya and Singapore which culminated in the eventual capitulation, contemporary participants and witnesses at all levels speak and write of its 'inevitability'. Pownall made a judicious assessment ten days after the surrender:

There is no doubt we underestimated the Jap. But suppose we'd made a better shot and got the Jap at his true worth, would it have made any real difference? I very much doubt it. Our policy was to avoid war with Japan as long as we could (or make America cause it, if it was to happen) and we gambled on that policy succeeding (or if it didn't succeed on America bearing the brunt). With all our other commitments I don't believe that however highly we had rated the Japs as fighters we could have caused thereby to improve the condition of our services in the Far East. We just hoped it wouldn't happen and it did.[37]

Ultimate responsibility for this strategy lay with Churchill. Ronald Lewin, the military historian and biographer of Wavell, almost exonerates Percival for his role in the disaster. 'Nobody can carp with any justice at an officer who is posted to a position for which he is not suited : the responsibility lies with his superiors or the military secretariat ... and it was cruel fate that put him in charge of Singapore's defences.'[38]

Percival cannot be held responsible for the strategic, political and military decisions taken with regard to the defence of Malaya and Singapore, but he can be criticized for his failings as a military commander. Once the campaign had begun, the Japanese advantage in sea-power and airpower was overwhelming, but at no time did the Japanese have more than one third of the ground forces that were at Percival's disposal. For the Japanese the campaign until the very final moment of the British capitulation was a close-run thing, and it is possible that a military commander of Montgomery's or Slim's calibre might have prolonged the defence of Malaya permitting the necessary build-up of reinforcements in Singapore for a decisive counter-stroke. Pownall admitted that 'We were frankly out-generalled, outwitted and out-fought.'[39] In the opinion of Woodburn Kirby, Percival failed to take the only two decisions which might have bought the time required for sufficient reinforcements to reach Singapore. He failed to concentrate his forces in the vital area west of the central range in Malaya, and he failed to construct field and anti-tank defences at bottlenecks along the north–south communications and to cover the three approaches to Johore Bahru with permanent defences on which to retire.[40] Another military historian, Major-General Sixsmith, censored Percival for his inability to make up his mind on what he wanted to do or to impress his will on the battle.

There is no evidence that he ever directed his commanders' minds towards any plan that might regain the initiative, or to any area in which a decisive battle might be fought. Instead the only plan in their minds was to hold on as long as possible. . . . In the record Percival gives of his conversations with his subordinate commanders it is noticeable that the suggestions always came from them. It was never that he told them what to do but that they told him what they must do.[41]

Dr Norman Dixon has attempted a psychological explanation of Percival's failure as a military commander. He believes that Percival had pathological-achievement motivation which is associated with a weak ego and feelings of dependency and that he was driven by the fear of failure. According to Dixon, such personalities 'are so to speak, driven from behind rather than pulled from in front. They have to achieve not for the satisfaction which achievement brings but because only by doing so can they bolster up their constantly sagging self-regard'. Dixon suggests that if Percival had gone ahead and erected defences in Malaya or Singapore it could have meant admitting to himself the danger in which he stood. He concluded that Percival's refusal to prepare defences in Johore and Singapore was the behaviour of someone who tried to avoid the unpleasant consequences of failure by not really trying.[42]

Percival neither had the temperament, the experience, the ability nor the necessary robustness to meet the appalling challenge he faced in 1941 as GOC Malaya. The Chiefs of Staff had regarded the Far East as a dormant theatre and as such had sent the second eleven to fill command appointments. As Wavell told Shenton Thomas on 10 February 1942, he had considered after his previous visit whether to relieve Percival, but had concluded, 'it's not easy to get leaders nowadays'.[43] Percival remained in command to the bitter end, and after other senior commanders had left, including those from the Royal Navy and RAF, he took the responsibility of surrendering to a numerically inferior and racially despised enemy.

NOTES

1 Winston S. Churchill, *The Second World War*, vol. IV, *The Hinge of Fate* (1951), p. 128.
2 Sir John Smyth, *Percival and the Tragedy of Singapore* (1971), p. 259.

3 Raymond Callahan, *The Worst Disaster : The Fall of Singapore* (1977), p. 111.
4 Arthur Bryant (ed.), *The Turn of the Tide 1939–1943* (1957), p. 277.
5 Sir John Kennedy, *The Business of War* (1957), p. 198.
6 Lieutenant-General A. E. Percival, *The War in Malaya* (1949), p. 27.
7 For the background to the British debate over the defence of Malaya and Singapore and Churchill's policy, see Major-General S. Woodburn Kirby, *Singapore: The Chain of Disaster* (1971); Callahan, *The Worst Disaster*; Louis Allen, *Singapore 1941–1942* (1977) and H. P. Willmott, *Empires in the Balance : Japanese and Allied Pacific Strategies to April 1942* (1982).
8 Percival, *War in Malaya*, pp. 17 and 23.
9 A. B. Lodge, *The Fall of General Gordon Bennett* (1986), p. 48.
10 Ibid., p. 119.
11 Ivan Simson, *Singapore : Too Little, Too Late* (1970), pp. 30, 33–8, 42, 54–6.
12 Ibid., p. 48.
13 Percival, *War in Malaya*, p. 57.
14 Ibid., p. 207.
15 Percival, 'Comments', 30 November 1953, Percival Papers, Imperial War Museum.
16 Simson, *Singapore*, p. 69.
17 Brian Bond (ed.), *Chief of Staff : The Diaries of Lieutenant-General Sir Henry Pownall*, Vol. 2, *1940–1944* (1974), p. 76.
18 Percival, *War in Malaya*, p. 21.
19 Woodburn Kirby, *Singapore*, p. 205.
20 See Woodburn Kirby, *Singapore*, pp. 220–1 and Lodge, *The Fall of General Gordon Bennett*, pp. 135–7.
21 Percival, *War in Malaya*, p. 272.
22 Ian Morrison, *Malayan Postscript* (1942), p. 158.
23 Smyth, *Percival*, p. 258.
24 Bond, *Chief of Staff*, p. 76.
25 Morrison, *Malayan Postscript*, p. 159.
26 Lodge, *The Fall of General Gordon Bennett*, p. 181.
27 Lieutenant-General H. Bennett, *Why Singapore Fell* (1944), p. 21.
28 Lodge, *The Fall of General Gordon Bennett*, p. 181.
29 Brian Montgomery, *Shenton of Singapore : Governor and Prisoner of War* (1984), p. 94.
30 Lodge, *The Fall of General Gordon Bennett*, p. 181.
31 Callahan, *The Worst Disaster*, p. 249.
32 Bennett, *Why Singapore Fell*, p. 102.
33 Woodburn Kirby, *Singapore*, p. 129.
34 Smyth, *Percival*, p. 261 and Lodge, *The Fall of General Gordon Bennett*, p. 181.
35 Percival, *War in Malaya*, pp. 187, 207 and 235.
36 Field-Marshal Lord Wavell, *Soldiers and Soldiering* (1953), pp. 14–16.

37 Bond, *Chief of Staff*, p. 92.
38 Ronald Lewin, *The Chief: Field-Marshal Lord Wavell, Commander-in-Chief and Viceroy, 1939–1947* (1980), p. 165.
39 Bond, *Chief of Staff*, p. 85.
40 Woodburn Kirby, *Singapore*, pp. 251–4.
41 Major-General E. K. G. Sixsmith, *British Generalship in the Twentieth Century* (1970), p. 271.
42 Norman Dixon, *On the Psychology of Military Incompetence* (1976), pp. 234–48.
43 Montgomery, *Shenton of Singapore*, p. 131.

CHRONOLOGY : ARTHUR PERCIVAL

1887, December	Born
1902–6	Educated at Rugby School
1906–14	Clerk in an iron-ore merchants office, City of London
1914	Volunteers for the army, Inns of Court OTC
1915	Captain 7th Bedfordshire Regiment, France
1916	Military Cross, Regular Commission, Essex Regiment, temporary major
1917	Second-in-Command 7th Bedfordshire Regiment
1918	Acting Lieutenant-Colonel, CO 2nd Bedfordshire Regiment, temporary brigade commander, awarded DSO
1919	Second-in-Command 46th Royal Fusiliers, North Russia, bar to DSO
1920–22	Company Commander and Intelligence Officer 2nd Essex Regiment, Ireland
1923–4	Student at the Staff College Camberley, promoted major in the Cheshire Regiment
1924–8	Staff Officer, Nigeria, brevet Lieutenant-Colonel
1929	Company Commander 2nd Cheshire Regiment
1930	Student at the Royal Naval College, Greenwich
1931–2	Instructor at the Staff College
1932–4	Lieutenant-Colonel commanding 2nd Cheshire Regiment, Malta
1935	Student at the Imperial Defence College
1936–7	Colonel and GSO1, Malaya Command
1938–9	Brigadier, General Staff, Aldershot Command
1939–40	Brigadier, General Staff, I Corps, BEF
1940, February–April	Major-General commanding 43rd (Wessex) Division, UK
1940, May–July	Assistant CIGS

1940, August– 1941, April	Major-General commanding 44th Division, UK
1941, April– 1942, February	Temporary Lieutenant-General, GOC Malaya Command
1942, February– 1945, August	Prisoner of war
1946	Retires from the Army with honorary rank of Lieutenant-General
1949	Publishes *The War in Malaya*
1950–55	Colonel of the Cheshire Regiment
1966, January 31	Dies

15

WINGATE

Major-General Orde Wingate

JOHN W. GORDON

The news, flashed to London, managed to be tragic even in that wartime season of death. Patrols had finally reached the jungle crash site. Their reports confirmed the worst: at the age of forty-one Orde Charles Wingate – major-general and leader of the daring 'Chindit' special operations behind the Japanese lines in Burma, and previously missing – was dead, killed in the crash of his American B-25 bomber on 24 March 1944.

To Winston Churchill, Wingate's death was a blow that deprived British arms of a 'man of genius who might have become a man of destiny'. In a theater in which the defeat-retreat cycle had so far been the bitter rule, he had to Churchill seemed the one commander able to hit back at and best a jungle-wise and seemingly unstoppable enemy. Indeed, by early 1944 he appeared to some a sort of 'new Lawrence' – this time 'of Burma'. The admirers of this new Lawrence (Wingate was in fact distantly related to T. E. Lawrence 'of Arabia') also included some Americans: President Franklin D. Roosevelt and members of the US Joint Chiefs of Staff. These men, meeting Wingate for the first time at the Quebec (Quadrant) Conference in August 1943, had detected flashes of brilliance and they liked the fiery intensity with which this British soldier briefed his new plan for Burma. And so, as Churchill was left to conclude, Wingate had been rather more than merely a theorist of small, long-range raiding units. With his death, a 'man of the highest quality ... [had been lost and] a bright flame ... extinguished'.

Something close to this view prevailed out in the jungles of central Burma and deep in the enemy's rear. With the monsoon rains soon to blow in, the 20,000 British, Gurkha, and West African soldiers comprising Special Force – the Chindits – felt their own sense of loss. Deployed in their fan of separate columns or holding a series of strongpoints sustained by air-dropped supplies, these troops could only speculate as to what might follow the death of the chief by whose ideas they were inspirited, forged into an operational force, and brought to battle. And at least to some degree these thoughts were shared by their American comrades-in-arms of Operation Galahad (to give it its codename) – the brigade-sized US Army force, officially the 5307th Composite Unit (Provisional) but labelled in the press as 'Merrill's Marauders'.

A rather different picture of Wingate obtained, however, among the more conventionally minded staff and command elements at headquarters from army corps up to theater level. To these, Wingate seemed an arrogant, out-of-control visionary whose ideas about warfare in the enemy's rear were unworkable. Short in stature and wiry, almost simian in appearance, Wingate glared out at those who questioned his theories from baleful blue eyes. His trademarks were famous – and, to many, offensive. The Old Testament beard, the Wolseley-era pith helmet (which even the theater commander, Admiral Lord Louis Mountbatten, pronounced as having come either 'from a museum or an ancestor'), the studied, deliberate casualness about hygiene (it was suggested that he had a particular jungle-filthy uniform that he saved for special occasions) all seemed too much a part of a cultivated image of ascetic toughness, too much playacting.

Most of all, however, Wingate's unorthodoxy was dangerous. He was unstable: it was known that he had tried to kill himself in Egypt two years before. Thereafter, as his fortunes improved, his direct access to and ability to influence first General Sir Archibald Wavell, at that point the theater commander-in-chief, and then the Prime Minister himself, had succeeded in diverting men and resources away from the conventional formations that really counted. Events had shown in stark clarity, it was argued, that his long-range penetration scheme consumed men at an appalling rate. The numbers spoke for themselves. Of his First Chindit operation only two-thirds of the force had actually managed to make it back to friendly lines ; of these, riddled with dysentery, typhus and malaria, only a fraction could be declared fit for duty again.

But the dilemma posed by these two conflicting views – Wingate as brilliant eccentric leader of unconventional operations on the one hand, or dangerous maverick on the other – transcends the contentious personality and theatrics which sparked animosity in others. The problem is a larger one. It touches on the whole issue of the special-operations approach as a way of dealing with a distant and difficult theater, to which the Allies were increasingly reluctant to send resources in demand elsewhere. Finally, to look at Wingate is also to look at the British style of warfare. For, while virtually all major combatants in World War II experimented to some degree with so-called 'special forces', it was the British experiment with them that holds pride of place both as to scale and expectations. Moreover, if that war in so many respects was a golden age for the employment of special forces, Orde Wingate must be seen as Winston Churchill's paramount theorist and most committed advocate of their use. This is not to suggest that there was any lack of leaders who excelled at the conduct of these sorts of operations. Certainly none could exceed in daring and flamboyance the leader and founder of the Special Air Service, David Stirling. Only Wingate, however, both planned and then carried out behind-the-lines special operations at the level of general officer. To do so he had made and won his case before not just the Allies' highest planning apparatus, the Combined Chiefs of Staff, but also the two leaders of that successful coalition, Winston Churchill and Franklin Roosevelt.

Wingate's family background and early career were largely conventional. Born in India in 1903, Wingate was fourth-generation military; his father, maternal grandfather, and great-grandfather all having served as officers in the British or the Indian service. He attended Charterhouse as a day student and, at the age of eighteen, entered the Royal Military Academy, Woolwich. Bored by team sports and the structured curriculum, his cadet career at Woolwich was little more distinguished than his schoolboy one at Charterhouse. He was commissioned – after a first-year incident in which he successfully stared down upperclassmen bent upon hazing him – into the Royal Artillery in 1923. The example of his eminent colonial-soldier cousin, General Sir Reginald Wingate, former Sirdar or Commander-in-Chief of the Egyptian Army, Governor-General of the Sudan and High Commissioner for Egypt, helped

to spark youthful ambition. Wingate followed up a course in Arabic
by assignment as a company commander in the Sudan Defence Force.
This gave him the chance to participate in a Royal Geographical Society-
sponsored expedition in search of the 'lost oasis' of Zerzura, a legendary
place believed to exist somewhere in the vastness of the Libyan Desert.
Wingate's quest to find Zerzura was unsuccessful; indeed, no such
oasis was ever found. He had also bucked the tide of progress by insisting
upon the use of camel transport, whereas Major Ralph Bagnold and
other British explorers had already shown the superiority of motor
vehicles in such desert penetrations. On the other hand, the effort won
Wingate a brief moment of glory and whetted his appetite for more.

Now thirty-two, Wingate returned to England, married eighteen-
year-old Lorna Paterson and settled down to prepare for the qualifying
examination for the Staff College. When he passed but failed to gain
admission, he resolved to take drastic measures. It was his boldness
in confronting the Chief of the Imperial General Staff that secured
for him not the Camberley billet but the next best thing: a general-staff
appointment in 1936 with the British forces attempting to maintain order
in Palestine.

This was Wingate's first big break and the point of departure for
his advance into the arena of unconventional operations. Such advance
would proceed in a kind of three-phase progression through the last
eight years of his life, 1936 to 1944. But the first phase was Palestine.
In it would come his first meeting with Wavell, the future commander
who would ask for him in the Middle East and in India, and with
Winston Churchill, who would ensure that Wavell's plans for Wingate
were supported at all levels. In short, Palestine, because it changed
Wingate's thinking and gave him the opportunity to show what he could
do, was the key to much that happened later. Present as well were those
elements which would reappear: frequent trouble with his superiors
and their staffs, a willingness to jump the chain of command should
it suit his purposes to do so, and an acute sense of military politics
and of the nature and realities of irregular operations.

Almost from his arrival he was won over to the Zionist cause. This
conversion was attributable neither to Jewish ancestry (there was none)
nor to the odd religious streak that stemmed from his evangelical Plymouth Brethren upbringing. Rather, it was his belief that it was his
destiny to lead some wronged and beleaguered people to victory, that
must account for it. He soon commenced organizing and training and
then leading into combat a force of special patrols. These were called

the Special Night Squads : along with the Haganah and the Palmach, they are the rootstems of the present-day Israeli Army. His charter to employ them came from Wavell, only recently appointed commander in Palestine, who had already given thought to the potential of 'motor guerrilla' and other irregular forces. In the months that followed, raids and ambushes carried out by the Special Night Squads became successful to the point that they turned the tide of Arab attack. Arab harassment of Jewish settlements fell off drastically, and sabotage of the Haifa oil pipeline all but stopped.

This work won Wingate a DSO, mention in dispatches and trouble with his superiors. Leave in London gave him the opportunity to submit a paper on unconventional operations to Basil Liddell Hart, military theorist and defense correspondent of *The Times*, who in turn passed it on to Winston Churchill. Wingate's first meeting with the future Prime Minister came at a dinner party late in 1938. Already journalists and others familiar with Wingate's role in Palestine professed to be 'struck by his resemblance to Lawrence of Arabia', and Wingate's first-hand accounts easily held Churchill's attention. All in all, the evening could not have hurt the cause of establishing Wingate's credentials as a promising leader of unconventional operations.

Thus Wingate's conduct and abilities in Palestine had won him the favorable attention of Wavell and Churchill. It was these two figures, more than any others in the British command, who were about to play the crucial early role in guiding their nation's experiment with special-operations forces. Two decades before, both had known Lawrence well – Wavell as a staff officer to Allenby had been an observer of Lawrence's role in 1917–18, and Churchill as Colonial Secretary during the Iraqi troubles of the early 1920s had appointed Lawrence a special advisor. But if Wavell and Churchill saw him as playing a Lawrentian role in some future campaign, it did little to comfort Wingate during a period of considerable frustration. Even after the outbreak of war in 1939, adversaries – who hinted that he had 'gone over to the Jews' – kept him tied down in dead-end assignments.

Certainly the slowness to employ Wingate in a role better suited to his demonstrated abilities cannot be attributed to any reluctance on the part of the British Army to experiment with unconventional operations. Not only was there the 'Lawrence legend' – the example of T. E. Lawrence as a master of guerrilla operations and the 'only old-style hero' of the 1914–18 war. There was also the existence of staff plans that considered the potentialities of unconventional operations. Even after the abrogation of the 'Ten-Year Rule' (that there would be no major war in Europe following 1918), the legacy of the era of 'imperial policing' and the long absence of a clear-cut Continental mission made the British Army receptive to ideas for peripheral ventures. These attacks-on-the-cheap did not fail to weigh the use of guerrilla activities. In 1935, for example, after the Italian invasion of Ethiopia, British military authorities in Egypt had commenced development of a plan for fostering a 'desert revolt' among Libya's disaffected Senussi tribesmen. The idea was to divert Italian forces away from a putative invasion of Egypt. Known as the 'Arab "G" Expansion Scheme', the plan probably owed more than a little to the fact that Lawrence's book, *Seven Pillars of Wisdom*, was published that year and instantly proved a bestseller. Three years later, a General Staff Report, 'The Raising of Insurrections : Possibility of Guerrilla Activities', looked at such operations as applied to Europe. At the same time a process of reformation of the infantry arm was also under way. The result was to give small units of infantry far greater effectiveness. They acquired greater operational flexibility through the use of 'fire and maneuver' tactics, and more firepower through the adoption of portable automatic weapons and lightweight explosives. A decentralization of command and control was effected through radio communications and the enhancement of the role of junior leaders – a development initiated by the Germans in World War I. Although overshadowed by the process of mechanization and the building of an armored arm, these infantry developments were crucial to the advent of special forces.

Wingate's participation in this process began in autumn 1940, with the arrival of orders taking him to the Middle East. This step – and the start of Wingate's second phase of involvement with the special-operations process – was once again the work of Wavell, by now Commander-in-Chief Middle East. Indeed, by the end of summer 1940, the British experiment with these operations was about to get under way in serious fashion, and Wavell's ideas regarding its direction were clear and well formed. As he envisioned them, special-operations forces – or simply 'special forces', to use the term that now came into vogue – were to raid, harass, operate with indigenous guerrillas, or gather intelligence on the flanks or in the rear of the enemy. The assumption was that such operations, difficult and hazardous, particularly when carried out in depth or in exotic terrain such as jungles, mountain or desert, fell outside the normal range of capabilities expected of a conventional unit. Moreover to take a standard unit and give it the additional training and equipment necessary to perform the specialized mission seemed a bad bargain, since to do so would pull it away from regular duties. On top of that there was a powerful elitist factor present: in the wake of Dunkirk, and with perhaps a psychological need to out-tough a militaristic and obviously competent foe, it was argued that only the best – the fittest, the toughest, the wiliest – could successfully endure the rigors and dangers of special operations. Special forces were seen, then, as being both élite and special: élite because of their highly selective recruitment and arduous training; and special in the military sense that they performed deep-penetration tasks not regularly assigned to conventional units.

The Germans, not the British, had been first to try their hand at special forces in this war. Certainly Nazi ideology appeared to glorify the notion of war as conducted 'by small teams of young heroes, airmen, tank-crews, [and] stormtroops ... "supermen" who would [win] by daring and violence. . . .' But the so-called 'Brandenburg' units which the Nazis formed and employed in Poland in 1939 were essentially saboteurs operating in civilian clothing. Rather than uniformed soldiers carrying out direct-action missions, the Brandenburgers remained part of the *Abwehr* or intelligence establishment. German faith in the blitzkrieg and its balanced, all-arms taskforce approach as the decisive element in ground combat ruled out any substantial expansion of the special-warfare effort until after Axis military fortunes began to decline.

From the beginning, the British effort was far larger and of a fundamentally different character. It commenced in June 1940 on a two-pronged basis two thousand miles apart. One prong was in Britain itself and centered around the seaborne light-infantry raiding forces called Commandos; the other was in Egypt, where forces able to penetrate and exploit the desert were formed. The formation of the Commandos owed much to Churchill's backing and the 'lessons' which he drew from Pitt's 'conjunct operations' in the age of sail. Churchill also labored under the misconception that German success in the Battle of France had been due to the role of élite 'stormtroops' which had ranged against rear areas, sowing demoralization. With the Battle of Britain about to begin, he decried his generals' 'dull mass' military constructism and demanded special units, made up of picked men of the 'hunter class', who could mount hit-and-run raids against the Axis-held coasts of Europe. The removal to these units, which were given the Boer War term 'Commando', of some of the most promising junior officers and soldiers, only fuelled the animosity with which conventional soldiers regarded the greater publicity and separate establishment accorded these special forces. Churchill also formed the Special Operations Executive (SOE), intended as an instrument for fostering resistance movements within the Axis-occupied countries. Its purpose, in the Prime Minister's view, was to make 'stabbing attacks ... between the chinks of the enemy's military and economic armour' – in short, sabotage. (Two years later, the SOE would serve as a model for the creation, under General William J. Donovan, of the US Office of Strategic Services (OSS), units of which Wingate would encounter in Burma.) Thus, Churchill envisioned in his first weeks as Prime Minister a full and active program of special operations, ranging from Commando raids to sabotage operations.

But it was the other locus of the special-operations effort, the Middle Eastern one, that Wavell called Wingate to join. By that time, in Egypt, where an Italian invasion from Libya appeared imminent, Wavell had already given his powerful support to desert-explorer Bagnold's plan to form a special unit called the Long Range Desert Group (LRDG). These operations in the desert campaign were to prove very successful, most famously 'L' Detachment, Special Air Service, under Major David Stirling. But all that was in the future. What Wavell needed to do now was to add to Italian difficulties in Africa by any means possible. One of the most immediately available was to expand an already successful special-operations program under way in Libya. At about the same time that Wavell directed the LRDG to switch over from intelligence-gathering to an aggressive campaign of 'beat-ups' against enemy outposts in the interior of the Libyan desert, the necessary steps were completed to bring about a native guerrilla war against the Italians in Ethiopia.

This was to be a British-fostered partisan revolt along the lines of the Arab 'G' Expansion Scheme of five years before. The difference was that the arena was not Libya but Ethiopia, and the leader not some Senussi sheikh but the exiled Emperor of Ethiopia, Haile Selassie. The essence of Wingate's role in this was to be the military advisor and leader of a guerrilla campaign – in his words, a 'patriot revolt' – centered around Haile Selassie. The plan was classically simple. While two British forces thrust into Italian East Africa from opposite sides, Wingate with the Emperor would take a column of guerrillas across the Sudanese border and into Ethiopia. Wingate's immediate goal was to establish a lodgement in the mountains by which to rally the native tribesmen. When these had flocked in sufficient numbers to join their emperor, the whole array would descend upon the capital, Addis Ababa, compounding Italian problems as it proceeded.

The execution of the plan taxed Wingate to the fullest. A cadre of British officers and NCOs arrived to help train the native irregulars. But Wingate himself had little real authority, the logistical support was meager, and a bitter rivalry soon developed between Wingate himself and the other principal British leader.

His campaign commenced in January 1941. Its prospects improved considerably when news arrived of the dramatic British successes in the desert campaign far to the north, and Italian morale in East Africa began to plummet. Wingate's greatest single success occurred when he, by audacity, determination and considerable logistical improvisation, employed his Gideon Force to baffle and disrupt the enemy garrisons blocking the road to Addis Ababa. One by one their key outposts were abandoned, and the Italians fell back. This effort – not without its analogies to Lawrence's campaigns of 1916–18 in which, at more than one point, more enemy troops were involved in trying to hunt down the guerrillas than were actually facing the main British army – helped open the way for British conventional forces to take back Haile Selassie's capital from the Italians. When the triumphal re-entry came, early in May 1941, the fighting for East Africa was largely concluded, although here and there mopping up continued into the summer.

This triumph preceeded the lowest point of Wingate's life, a point when he came close to ending his life. Given leave in Cairo (and reduced from acting colonel back to major), he wrote a blistering report in which he exposed all the organizational shortcomings that had so hampered Gideon Force. Not unexpectedly, the report produced a small but powerful upheaval at GHQ Middle East. Even Wavell, ever Wingate's friend, took him to task for the intemperate and bitter tone of the document. Nor did Wingate's idea for a thrust from the Tibesti Mountains and north into Libya gain support. In fairness, the plan was not without its technical flaws. As Wingate explained it to desert explorer Bagnold, the idea was to use RAF support to sustain a brigade-sized force as it moved up through the desert. Bagnold pointed out that the air force lacked the numbers of aircraft needed to make such a plan work. And although he himself had already sent an LRDG raid into the region, and General LeClerc's Free French (with LRDG support) would push into it as the desert campaign drew to a close two years later, there was no way that Wingate's plan was at that moment supportable.

In any case, Wavell's own days in the Middle East were now at an end. In June 1941, hard on the heels of the failure of his efforts to smash Rommel and the German reinforcements sent to shore up what remained of Mussolini's African empire, Wavell was reassigned by Churchill to become Commander-in-Chief India. Wingate's patron was gone, removed to a distant theater by order of his other patron, the Prime Minister. To Wingate's feelings of despondency, rejection and despair must be added his physical condition. On top of the intense mental and physical strain of Ethiopia, Wingate was also suffering from malarial fevers that pushed his temperature up to 104 degrees. Rather than report to sick-bay and receive the proper attentions of a military doctor, Wingate chose instead to visit a private physician – on the grounds that he had to avoid at all costs being shunted off to convalescence in some rear area. The result was that he greatly exceeded the normal dosage of atabrine (quinacrine hydrochloride). For whatever reason, alone in his hotel room, he finally stabbed himself in the throat with a sheathknife. He was saved because he fell unconscious before he could finish the job and, when help arrived, the bleeding was stopped before it was too late.

Months of recuperation followed, during which he was sent home to England. By the time a medical board declared him fit for duty again, his career was once more on its positive slope of fortune. He gave invited lectures on the Ethiopian campaign (for which he received a bar to the DSO he had won in Palestine), and was touted for a slot with the SOE. Friends gained the Prime Minister's promise to make sure that Wingate received fair treatment from the Army in his next assignment. They need not have worried. In December 1941 there occurred the event which propelled him into the last phase of his special-warfare progression and to the final campaign that would claim his life : Japan's entry into the war. In the weeks ahead, the forces of Imperial Japan, having smashed the US Pacific Fleet at Pearl Harbor and gone on to take Guam, Wake and other important points, moved forward towards the conquest of Malaya and the Philippines with seemingly inexorable momentum. Singapore fell in February 1942. The week before, Wavell had sent the War Office a radio signal requesting that Wingate be assigned to his command.

If the subject of that signal, Wingate, had regarded the command structure for Ethiopia as complex and convoluted, his arrival in this new theater in March must have given him pause. To begin with, there were the very different goals of the two principal allies involved, the United Kingdom and the United States. The chief British objective, as the Japanese continued to expand westward onto the Asian mainland, was to ensure the security of India. The Americans, on the other hand, entertained notions that Chiang Kai-shek could be made into a full partner and his Nationalist Chinese army an effective fighting force. This might draw enemy forces away from the US Marines spearheading the central Pacific drive as originally laid out in War Plan Orange, and might make it possible to use China as a base from which to mount operations against Japan itself.

But any clash of strategic views was as nothing compared to the clash of personalities. Were Wingate altogether the egotist and offbeat eccentric his enemies made him out to be, then his arrival into this new arena put him in good company. Topping the list was the chief American representative, Lieutenant-General Joseph W. Stilwell. At the age of sixty, Stilwell was fluent in Chinese and an 'old China Hand' of long standing. He was also a first-rate tactician whose utter lack of tact placed him among the poorest choices when it came to the diplomatic task of waging coalition warfare. His dislike of the British approached the pathological. Moreover, 'Vinegar Joe' inherited an unworkable command structure that put him in charge of (to use the US designation) the vast China–Burma–India Theater (or CBI). In addition to his CBI responsibilities (split between the British headquarters at New Delhi and the Chinese one at Chungking), Stilwell also had simultaneously to serve as Chiang's chief of staff, administer all US lend–lease aid, and ensure construction of the Ledo–Burma road as a supply line for same. Almost from the outset he proved unequal to the task of coping with high-level administration. He was at his best when in the field inspiring Chinese soldiers to fight. He did not get on well with Wavell, before the war regarded as one of the most innovative thinkers in the British Army but whom Stilwell regarded as being 'tired' and unwilling to push aggressively against the enemy. The American general affected an outdated campaign hat and a primitive 'field-soldier' style of living that transcended even Wingate's. His predilection for spending excessive amounts of time in the field inspiring Chinese units led one American officer to complain that Stilwell was 'the best three-star company commander in the whole damn theater'.

Eventually, in reaction to problems with Stilwell and the Chinese and the shifting strategic fortunes of the theater, the British created an entity called Southeast Asia Command or SEAC, of which Stilwell became the deputy. By then Wavell had, of course, been replaced by General Sir Claude Auchinleck (with whom Churchill had already replaced him once before, in June 1941, in Cairo) as Commander-in-Chief India. Wavell was made Viceroy. As C-in-C, Auchinleck's responsibility was to train and equip the Indian Army for combat. The actual conduct of operations against the Japanese was vested in SEAC. The Supreme Allied Commander for SEAC in 1943 was Admiral Lord Louis Mountbatten. Although nearly twenty years younger than his American deputy, the two generally got on well together, Mountbatten being – along with Wingate – one of the few British officers that Stilwell permitted himself to respect. But all that was in the future. For the moment, the CBI theater was one in which the Japanese were on the attack, and the various high-level figures involved, American and British, were desperate to sort things out and find some means of stopping them.

Thus when Wingate arrived in March 1942, his orders from Wavell were to report to the Bush Warfare School and take over guerrilla operations against the Japanese. He was also restored to his temporary rank of colonel. Despite its name, the Bush Warfare School was less a school than an organization for mounting unconventional operations. Wingate briefly contemplated the insertion of cadres of its British personnel into China, for the purpose of leading indigenous guerrillas against the Japanese. Indeed, five years before, a US Marine Corps major, Evans Fordyse Carlson, had been the first Western officer to slip through the Japanese lines and reach Mao Tse-tung's force of Chinese Communist guerrillas. Carlson's detailed report, which reached President Roosevelt, not only inspired interest in guerrilla schemes in China but also assisted Carlson's proposal to form special battalions of Marine Raiders (of which he commanded one, with the President's son, James, as his executive officer). British and American guerrilla cadres, under SOE, OSS and Naval Group-China auspices, would over the next two years undertake operations in China.

But the immediate and essential requirement was to stop the Japanese in Burma. In the wake of the fall of Rangoon and just before the disastrous retreat of British and Chinese forces (two divisions under Stilwell) from Burma in May, Wingate carried out a detailed reconnaissance of as much of the country as he could. This reconnaissance became the basis of Wingate's theory of how to beat the Japanese. His thinking at this point was a logical extension of his experiences with the Special Night Squads and Gideon Force. It also reflected an important shift: he no longer wanted control of mere guerrilla operations conducted behind enemy lines; he wanted instead to create special long-range penetration forces that would slip into Burma to maraud, ambush and stir up trouble in enemy rear areas. These 'Long Range Penetration Groups', as he contemplated them, would like guerrillas rely on the tactic of hit-and-run. The units themselves, however, would be made up not of guerrillas, with their free and easy ways, but of soldiers acting with the discipline, training and reliability of regular formations.

Wingate recognized that possession of Burma gave the Japanese not just access to the world's largest rice exports, but also drove a wedge between India and China. But Burma's geography looked promising for the sort of operation he had in mind. Three principal north-south river systems drained south out of valleys cut in mountain and hill-range ramparts: in the east, closest to China and to Thailand, the Salween; in the center the Irrawaddy; and in the west, closest to India, the Chindwin. One aspect of all this seemed particularly obvious to Wingate: any Japanese effort to effect a major breakthrough along the 700-mile India-Burma front would have to be fed by supply lines that used these river valleys; these supply lines were therefore vulnerable provided they could be reached. To put together a force capable of operating deep in enemy rear areas meant, however, removing men and resources from the conventional effort; there was resistance. Wingate's ability to persuade Wavell, still the C-in-C and as supportive of unorthodoxy as ever, proved the essential element in overcoming opposition. In the end he got most of what he wanted. The Long Range Penetration Groups were the result. They were given the formal title of 77 Indian Infantry Brigade, with Wingate as their brigadier.

These 3,000 men were the troops that eventually became known as the 'Chindits' – an anglicized mispronunciation of the term for the statuary lions that guarded Burmese temples. Wingate's original idea was that his unit should be made up solely of volunteers. When it proved impracticable to man his entire force in this way (although volunteers from the Bush Warfare School did form the nucleus), he accepted existing units and set out to meld them into one organization. In this way he took a battalion each from the Burma Rifles, the Gurkhas, and the King's Liverpool Regiment. Wingate spent the summer of 1942 training this force for an operation originally intended for the late autumn. It was Stilwell's intention to push the Chinese to attack down into north Burma, while at the same time British sea, air and land forces would attack into the central and southern zones of Burma. The role of the Chindits would be to support both the Chinese and the British efforts by disrupting the Japanese lines of communication. Wingate divided his force into separate columns, conditioned them to the jungle's harshness by a relentless program of forced marches, and practiced the radio co-ordination and receipt of the air-dropped supplies by which each column would be sustained behind the lines.

By the time he was ready to go, the operation was on the back burner. There were a variety of reasons: Chiang's heel-dragging; the lack of progress of the British offensive into south Burma; and the claims of Stilwell's supposed subordinate, Major-General Claire Chennault, USAAF, famous as the founder of the 'Flying Tigers', that airpower rendered a ground offensive unnecessary. In two hours of discussion, however, Wingate persuaded Wavell to let him go ahead with the Chindit part of the plan. In the final analysis, it was his argument that such an attack would divert the enemy and help to buy time that carried the moment.

And so, early in 1943, the Chindit columns, supported by pack mules and even elephants, began slipping into enemy territory. Three months later (and some eight hundred men fewer) they returned, having molested the Japanese all the way to the far side of Burma's second river, the Irrawaddy. The key rail line linking Mandalay to the interior town of Myitkyina was cut in a number of locations. Not only was that important artery severed (if only briefly), but a full program of ambushes, mines implanted, and sudden attacks plagued the whole Japanese road-and-trail network through which it ran. When the enemy set off in pursuit, the Chindit columns – their moves co-ordinated by Wingate by radio – slipped off into a new part of the jungle. At the point when they had crossed the Irrawaddy, however, luck and the men's strength began to wane. Hunger, thirst and disease rather than enemy action at last forced Wingate to order the move back to India. Only by breaking up into small groups and swimming first the Irrawaddy and then the Chindwin was the enemy cordon evaded. Those too sick or too wounded to keep up were – in accordance with the Chindits' hard rule – left behind in the jungle.

Wingate, emaciated, bearded, wearing his battered pith helmet and lugging a rifle and a map case, emerged from the jungle to find himself and his men heroes. Press coverage gave full play to these men who had raided deep into enemy territory and survived to tell the tale. The Prime Minister was so taken with Wingate's feat that he wanted him made the commander of the whole British offensive into Burma. Wingate, he said, 'is a man of genius and audacity ... and no mere question of seniority must obstruct the advance of real personalities to their proper stations in war'. And while the CIGS and his staff finally dissuaded him from making such an appointment, they could only acquiesce in Churchill's insistence that Wingate be flown back immediately for a private meeting.

This was the immediate backdrop to Churchill's decision to take Wingate to Quebec in August 1943. When Wingate got back to London and had his meeting, so powerful was the impression he made that the Prime Minister decided on the spot that the Chindit leader must be taken to the Quadrant Conference so that the Americans could see him. Arrangements were made forthwith so that Mrs Wingate could accompany her husband as part of the official party travelling across the Atlantic aboard the *Queen Mary*. On the sea journey Wingate honed his new plan for an expanded long-range penetration effort in Burma. This time the Chindits would vault over the enemy, flying in by transport plane and glider rather than walking in as before. His idea was to insert behind the enemy eight full brigades, which would use their engineers to clear jungle airstrips. A line of strongholds, kept fed and munitioned by airdrop, would be established in Burma's river valleys. These positions would be held against enemy counter-attack; other groups of Chindits, lurking outside the barbed-wire perimeters, would be available to fall upon the Japanese from behind even as they attacked. By the time the party arrived at Quebec, Wingate, put through his paces by the CIGS and other senior officers, had evolved his plan to the point that he was more than ready to take on any doubters in the American camp.

For that reason – and because his plan seemed a good compromise between Churchill's proposal for a thrust towards Singapore and the Americans' counterproposal for retaking Burma to secure land communications with China – Wingate's briefing met with success. His plan also appeared to provide a way of waging warfare on the cheap, when both allies increasingly felt their resources being drawn to other fronts. The Americans pledged themselves to provide the bulk of the aircraft and gliders needed to support the airborne component of Wingate's concept. They committed themselves as well to providing a 'good faith intention' ground element. This was the force, of brigade size, that was designated 'Galahad' and later called the 5307th Composite Unit and, later still, 'Merrill's Marauders'. It would be organized and trained by Chindits along Chindit lines, and sent into combat in early 1944. As to the air component which the Americans promised to provide, this comprised, in addition to the glider-towing C-47s and light liaison aircraft, an actual close-support striking element – thirty P-51 Mustang fighter-bombers and twenty B-25 Mitchell medium bombers. The whole force, consisting of nearly 300 aircraft, was designated No. 1

Air Commando, US Army Air Forces. Its commander was a fighter pilot with experience in North Africa, thirty-year-old Colonel Philip Cochran.

Cochran, who had been handpicked by the USAAF's chief, General Henry H. Arnold, did not meet Wingate in person until a month after Quadrant. He was at first suspicious of the Chindit leader. A short, cocky 'hot pilot', Cochran had sung in a dance band during his fraternity days at Ohio State University; he initially affected trouble understanding Wingate's 'exaggerated' British accent. In subsequent meetings, however, the two achieved a meeting of minds that produced a rare harmony of co-operation between air and ground efforts. The importance of the Air Commando to Wingate's fortunes was immense. Without the planes his force remained essentially light infantry raiders with nothing in the way of hitting power beyond the weapons they carried in their own hands. With them, the Chindit columns had at their disposal a flying artillery which could be radioed down to fall upon any Japanese position that stood in their way.

Wingate, meanwhile, set about preparing his ground force for the push into Burma; 77 Brigade remained the nucleus of this expanded effort. Joining the original Chindits were some six additional brigades as well as separate forces or detachments; the whole, supported by artillery and the USAAF No. 1 Air Commando, became officially 'Special Force', or 3rd Indian Infantry Division. In view of the expanded size of the Chindit enterprise, Wingate was given the rank of an acting major-general. He divided the command-and-control apparatus of Special Force into Rear, Main, Launching, and Tactical Headquarters elements, of which this last, the Tactical Headquarters, would of course go into Burma with the columns.

Wingate's Second Chindit expedition was set for spring 1944. It was to be one part of a three-part operation. In the north, Stilwell's Chinese divisions (X Force) were to thrust into Burma from India, covering engineers who constructed both a road and an oil-carrying pipeline. In the south, the British XV Corps, commanded by Lieutenant-General William Slim (soon to be elevated to command of the Fourteenth Army), would push into the Arakan, and the British IV Corps would advance across the Chindwin. The role of Special Force was to support both Stilwell and Slim by the establishment of air-supplied strongholds astride the key Japanese supply lines. Other forces would fan out to raid and disrupt. Galahad, initially under the control of Special Force, was to be passed to Stilwell, who would likewise use it in Chindit-like missions on his own front. The main goal of Special Force was to establish a force in the enemy rear, one that, because of its air resupply, could be sustained against even the most concerted enemy counter-attacks. It was Wingate's contention – anathema to the ears of more conventional soldiers – that the Chindit presence, permanently maintained rather than merely hit-and-run raiders and so deep in the vitals of the enemy, would engender paralysis. Overall control of the whole offensive, including X Force, Galahad, Chindits and the two army corps, would be carried by Admiral Lord Louis Mountbatten, newly arrived as Supreme Allied Commander, SEAC.

In the event, while these preparations were being made, the Japanese themselves gave thought to offensive operations. Concluding that Wingate's First Chindit expedition of the previous spring had been only the preliminary move to a British offensive to retake Burma, the Japanese decided to mount a spoiling attack into north-west India. Such an attack would buy time and perhaps also stoke the fires of the Indian nationalist movement. Another Japanese offensive would thrust up from Burma towards the east China air bases from which Chennault's bombers were now able to threaten Japan itself.

The Allies' second offensive into Burma opened in February 1944. Three months later, Galahad – or what was left of it – took the airfield at Myitkyina. Three months later still, the Japanese finally evacuated the town of Myitkyina itself, after some of the hardest fighting of the campaign. In this grand climax to the campaign, Stilwell had won his objective. And in those same months, while the Chindits were airlifted into establishing their strongholds in Myitkyina, endured privations, fought the Japanese in a score of battles, and reached and then far exceeded the agreed limit for time spent in the jungle, the Japanese themselves mounted two offensives. One objective, far to the north, was Chennault's forward airfields in eastern China; those they easily reached. The other objective was Imphal, just across the Indian border from Burma. Slim, now Fourteenth Army commander, used a kind of draw play to lure the Japanese into the flat terrain around the town. He was able to use his superiority in supporting areas to fight battles of annihilation. In the hard fighting for Imphal and Kohima to the north, the Japanese wasted their strength; in the end, they had to withdraw back into Burma. This made possible new Allied offensives, one against the Burma Road itself, and, early in 1945, Slim's push to retake Mandalay and then Rangoon itself. These various battles resulted in the annihilation of an entire Japanese field army. By that time, of course,

Stilwell had been relieved, both the Chindits and Galahad been disbanded, and Wingate was long since dead, killed just three weeks after Special Force had commenced its airlift.

Given the controversy that Wingate so often attracted, what, in the end, had his contribution to this final outcome really been? First of all, as the general who achieved the victory in a theater often forgotten by the people at home, it would seem reasonable to begin with the assessment provided by Field-Marshal Sir William Slim. Commenting some years after the war on the whole issue of special forces, Slim stated that 'The last war [had] spawned a surprising number of special units and formations ... each trained, equipped, and prepared for some particular type of operation. These did not give, militarily, a worthwhile return for the resources in men, material and time that they absorbed.' Such groups became 'super-soldiers'; they consumed good men, scarce equipment, and generous amounts of training time, yet carried out only a limited number of operations. This induced a kind of cult of special forces and jealousy in non-special ones, and reinforced the notion that only units of this type could be used for certain operations. The overall effect was 'undoubtedly to lower the quality of the rest of the army – both by skimming the cream off it, but [also] by encouraging the idea that only specially equipped corps d'élite could be expected to undertake ... those most obviously demanding and hazardous missions, such as long-range penetration.'

Slim's words have been more or less accepted as the last word on the subject ever since. And yet they would seem to overlook several specific contributions of Special Force and its Chindits. Wingate's forces successfully forced the Japanese, at least for a time, to keep their forces divided. His First Chindit campaign in 1943 managed to tie down the best part of two Japanese divisions. In 1944, his Special Force, plus the actions of the Chinese and Galahad in the north, kept a full enemy division busy and not available for the thrust towards Imphal. And if Slim first turned the tables on the Japanese when he lured them into the offensive against Imphal, it must be remembered that they had the year before resolved to make such attack only when the First Chindit thrust into Burma had convinced them of the need for a pre-emptive strike.

Moreover, many of the methods and tactics which Slim used in the attainment of a victory by his conventional forces had been evolved

and practiced by Special Force. Special forces are useful labor.
for tactical experimentation; what works for them may prove to
application on a wider basis. Both the air resupply effort which so ar
Slim around Imphal, as well as the techniques for coping with Japane
roadblocks, had earlier been perfected and practiced extensively by the
Chindits.

In addition, the First Chindit campaign did much to break the spell
of Japanese invincibility in the jungle. The standard formation, it was
true, had to learn to beat the enemy on their own terms, but the overall
effect of the Chindits was to encourage the whole army. Special Force
was an early means of bringing troops to bear on the enemy, when
the geography and road network of Burma offered no other alternative.

This was possible because Wingate had achieved a workable application of special operations to the jungle environment of Burma. His
thinking had passed through the evolutionary stages of the Special Night
Squads, Gideon Force in Ethiopia, and come to the situation in Burma.
He grasped that the need was less that of using indigenous partisan
groups, such as were employed by the SOE and OSS units which supported Special Force; instead, the need was to have standard units
carry out guerrilla tactics. Wingate sensed that the Japanese Army, only
partially mechanized in the European fashion, had perfected in its long
bitter campaign in China a robust light-infantry approach which it had
successfully adapted to jungle warfare. At the same time, its frugality
did not free it altogether from the tether of its supply lines. Just as
Lawrence in the desert against the Turks had seen that '[a]rmies were
like plants ... firm-rooted, nourished through long stems ...', so
Wingate saw that the Japanese 'long stems' ran up through Burma's
river valleys. In the First Chindit operation he had raided against these.
In the Second, his thinking had progressed to a much larger role. Sustained by air, Special Force would set its barbed-wire fortresses in the
jungle astride these enemy supply routes and strangle them.

No other special operations endeavor of the war rivalled in scale
or ambition the one that Wingate successfully argued before presidents
and prime ministers. No other special force leader achieved the rank
of general officer and controlled twenty thousand men in the field and
in the enemy's rear. What Wingate put together gave the Allies an expansion of capability. It made central and northern Burma into an additional
arena, rather than keeping Allied operations restricted to the immediate
India–Burma front.

What Wingate did cannot be measured merely in numbers of Japanese tied down or in tonnages of supplies intercepted on the enemy's of communication. His role was greater; it might have been greater had he not been killed. Among the components of Wingate's generalp were detailed planning, the ability to get the plan across and inspire en to risk their lives in carrying it out, and a vision of how to employ a radio-based command-and-control system that made full exploitation of Allied airpower. Where Wingate was flawed was at the level that military officers today usually refer to as the 'operational art' – the level, that is, between tactics, with its focus upon a single battle or engagement and the employment of relatively small forces, and the overall level of strategy, with its focus upon the playing out of the war within a particular theater. The operational art, rather, concentrates upon specific campaigns and the employment of forces larger than a single division in order to achieve outcomes useful to the overall strategy. It is thus a sort of bridge between tactics and strategy. The reason that Wingate's generalship must be regarded as being flawed at the operational level is that he fundamentally misjudged Japanese vulnerabilities to his plan for 1944. There is no evidence to suggest that Japanese operational capabilities were terminally crippled by the very costly insertion of Special Force so deep in their rear.

Where Wingate's generalship approached genius was at the strategic level of seeing and contributing a way whereby the Japanese could be made to fail. The fact that conventional military means eventually triumphed over the Japanese suggests that Wingate's approach, with its high demands in resources and men, will always remain a controversial one. His special gift was the combination of clarity of vision, character, and charm (often reserved only for the powerful) that enabled him to put his ideas across forcefully and persuasively in the highest circles. His ability to think in terms of employing special forces to achieve strategic ends, and to exert command of those forces in the field, has not since been matched.

CHRONOLOGY : ORDE WINGATE

1903, February 26	Born at Naini Tal, United Provinces, India
1916	Enters Charterhouse School
1921	Enters Royal Military Academy, Woolwich
1923, August	Commissioned into Royal Artillery
1926, October	War Office-sponsored Arabic language course, School of Oriental Studies, London

1928, April	Company commander, Sudan Defence Force
1929, June	First-class interpretership in Arabic
1932, February	Royal Geographical Society camel expedition to find 'lost oasis' of Zerzura in Libyan Desert
1935, January	Returns to England. Marries Lorna Paterson
1935, December	Adjutant, 71 Field (Artillery) Brigade, Territorial Army, Sheffield. Passes examination for Staff College but fails to gain admission
1936	Joins British forces in Palestine. Organizes Special Night Squads. DSO and mentioned in dispatches
1938, November 30	Meets Churchill for first time
1940, November	Appointed military advisor and leader of guerrilla campaign in Ethiopia
1941, January	Ethiopian campaign begins. Wingate employs Gideon Force
1941, May 5	Victorious entry to Addis Ababa. Receives bar to DSO
1941, July 4	Attempts suicide, Continental Hotel room, Cairo. Returns to England for medical recuperation
1942, March 22	Arrives in Burma, with rank of Colonel, to begin unconventional operations training at Bush Warfare School, Maymyo
1942, July	77 Indian Brigade formed (later known as Chindits), with Wingate as Brigadier
1943, February	First Chindit expedition commences (three months behind Japanese lines)
1943, August	Awarded second bar to DSO
1943, August 5	Churchill takes Wingate to Quebec for Allied conference (Quadrant) and presentations before Roosevelt, Marshall, Mountbatten and Combined Chiefs of Staff
1943, September	In charge of Special Force, including enlarged Chindit forces; made acting Major-General
1944, February 5	Second Chindit expedition begins, one part of a three-part operation with Stilwell and Slim
1944, March 24	Killed in jungle air crash behind Japanese lines

16

SLIM

Field-Marshal Lord Slim

DUNCAN ANDERSON

While he was Governor-General of Australia Field-Marshal Lord Slim wrote *Defeat into Victory*, an account of the Burma campaign of 1942–45. It was a publishing sensation. The first edition of 20,000 sold out within a few days. *Defeat into Victory* was quite unlike the memoirs produced by other generals in the aftermath of 1945. The reader looked in vain for a 'Great Captain' striding across the stage of history, deploying his divisions in accordance with some brilliantly conceived and implemented masterplan. Instead he encountered an ordinary man, one often assailed by self-doubt, who made mistakes (sometimes with near-disastrous consequences) and did not consider himself particularly brave. Slim attributed his success to others. He claimed that he had simply had the good fortune to lead an exceptionally able 'team' – by which he meant the entire Fourteenth Army.

After its publication in 1956, *Defeat into Victory* was accepted as the classic account of the Burma campaign. Despite, or perhaps because of, his characteristic modesty and understatement, Slim was rapidly elevated to the status of military hero. The Official History of 1958 pronounced Slim almost solely responsible for the victory of 1945. James Lunt, a veteran and recent historian of the Burma campaign, went one step further by comparing Slim favourably with Cromwell. Slim had all the latter's military virtues but 'certainly more humour, and I suspect, more humanity'. Comparisons of a similar order have been made by Sir Geoffrey Evans and Ronald Lewin, both of whom wrote full accounts of Slim's career. Slim possessed all the qualities that the ancient Chinese philosopher Sun Tzu had outlined for his 'Heaven-born captain' – the ever-victorious general.

Slim would probably have been embarrassed by the hagiographic tendencies of his later biographers. He is now so thoroughly enshrined in the pantheon of great generals that it becomes hard to square his present reputation with the lukewarm reception he met with on his return to England in 1945. Montgomery and Alexander were the men of the moment, elevated in the popular imagination by a sustained publicity campaign. When Alfred Wagg's *A Million Died* appeared in 1943 – the first book on the Burma campaign – Slim warranted no more than an amusing passing anecdote, but an entire chapter was devoted to Alexander as the proclaimed hero of the retreat. Wagg's book established a pattern of historical interpretation. There were books on Stilwell, Mountbatten, Wingate and the Chindits, but none on Slim, who appeared only as a footnote to the lives of others. The film industry followed suit. During the first fifty minutes of *Burma Victory*, screened in November 1945, familiar faces flash onto the screen – Mountbatten raises morale, Wingate plays hob with the Japanese communications, Stilwill takes Myitkyina and builds the road, Leese plans the offensive. Slim makes a brief appearance in the film's last ten minutes, but the producer has felt it necessary to supply a potted history explaining just who Slim is and the role he played in Burma. Returning veterans of the Fourteenth Army sitting in the audience were puzzled by what they felt was a complete distortion of the scenes they had actually witnessed, not least by the minor walk-on part ascribed to Slim. They knew from their experiences that Slim had been the vital presence responsible for the real-life 'Burma Victory'.

The celluloid industry is notorious for its distortions of historical reality, but *Burma Victory* merely mirrored the interpretation of events accepted in the corridors of power. On 6 April, just after Slim had won a crushing victory at Meiktila, Churchill wrote to his wife that 'Dicky, reinforced by General Oliver Leese, has done wonders in Burma.' A not unreasonable tribute, apart from the fact that one very obvious name was missing. Churchill had arrived at a fixed view of the Burma campaign, in which Slim played little part. Alexander had brought the Army out of Burma in 1942, Orde Wingate had breathed life and fight into it in 1943 and 1944, and 'Dicky' Mountbatten and Oliver Leese had planned and executed its brilliant offensives in 1945. For much of the war Churchill had been only dimly aware of Slim's existence – and what he did hear was probably not particularly favourable. He had thought highly of Wingate, whom he had selected for high command in the Far East, and took the news of his death on 24 March 1944 very badly. 'This is a very heavy blow to me, for you know how much I have counted on this man of genius, who might well have been a man of destiny.' His opinion of the far less flamboyant Slim was very different. The following summer, when Alanbrooke proposed that Slim should be promoted to command ALFSEA, Churchill replied, with a quip redolent of Samuel Johnson: 'I cannot believe that a man with a name like Slim can be much good.' It was said in jest, but revealed a certain state of mind. Slim had not been one of Churchill's generals.

It was one thing for a general to escape popular recognition, another for him to be overlooked by the very man responsible for keeping his finger on the pulse in wartime Britain. To understand Slim's low profile at this time we need, however briefly, to reject the perspective of *Defeat into Victory*: here Slim, writing with hindsight, tended to view his early disappointments and failures as the necessary prelude to his later success, part of the learning process which ultimately made him the general that he became. It is all too easy to forget that when Wingate was killed in March 1944 Slim had only one victory to his credit, a minor action against the Vichy French in Syria in July 1940, and that the list of his defeats was very long. Slim's personal faith in his Army was more than counterbalanced by the serious doubts voiced in Whitehall: and when success finally did come, it was easier for the government to attribute that success to the new men they had appointed – Leese and Mountbatten. Only one anecdote survives from Slim and Churchill's first meeting in the summer of 1945. In a mood of post-lunch expansiveness, Churchill was holding forth on his chances in the forthcoming general election when Slim punctuated his speech with the laconic comment, 'Well, prime minister, I know one thing. My army won't be voting for you.' Churchill had been sufficiently impressed by the man not to allow party politics to interfere with his judgement, and went on to appoint him C-in-C Allied Land Forces South East Asia. But his recognition of Slim's qualities had come very late in the day.

Slim was very different from Churchill's other generals. Unlike Alexander, Alanbrooke and Auchinleck, he was not a scion of the Anglo-Irish ascendancy, nor could he trace his singularly unimpressive family name back into the annals of the Norman conquest, as could Montgomery and Wavell. His father was a Birmingham ironmonger, and Bill Slim, like many a bright son of a lower-middle-class family with aspirations, gained a scholarship at the local grammar school. His first job was that of teacher in an elementary school in the slum districts of Birmingham, followed by a post as junior clerk in a metal-tubing firm. It was precisely the wrong kind of background from which to embark on an army career. Had he been higher up the social scale, Sandhurst and a commission as an officer would have been a natural and well-worn path to tread. Had he been a working-class lad, he could have joined up as a private soldier. But although young men from the respectable lower-middle class had little to do at this time with the regular army, many of them did have an intense interest in military affairs. Slim, like many of his peer group, had been brought up on popular military histories, had served in his school cadet corps and had continued part-time military activity almost as a matter of course in a territorial unit – in Slim's case Birmingham University's OTC. Slim, and the hundreds like him, greeted the outbreak of war in August 1914 with enthusiasm. War meant temporary commissions as second lieutenants and escape from the deadly routine of the junior clerk. Most of Slim's contemporaries in the OTC did not survive the war: those who did were usually so sickened by the experience that they severed all connections with the army.

Slim was fortunate in having a 'good' war. In July and August 1915 he had seen eighteen days' intense fighting with the Warwicks at Gallipoli, had been severely wounded, and had been laid up in England until the autumn of 1916. He had then been sent to Mesopotamia and saw another four months' active service until in March 1917 he was wounded in an action for which he was awarded the MC. He was then invalided to India where he spent the war as GSO3 at Army HQ with the rank of acting captain. Slim had acquitted himself well in combat, but the periods of action, although intense, were not prolonged. Moreover, he had been at Gallipoli when morale was still high and victory seemed attainable. He had arrived in Mesopotamia just at the point at which the new commander General Sir Frederick Maude was getting a grip on an army demoralized by the fall of Kut-el-Amara. Slim later wrote: 'Maude was in charge and there was not a man in the Force who did not feel the renewed energy and hope that were vitalizing the whole army. To watch an army recovering morale is enthralling; to feel the process working within oneself is an unforgettable experience.' Once again victory seemed within reach, and it was. Maude went on the offensive on 13 December 1916, Kut was retaken on 23 February and Baghdad fell on 11 March. It had been a very different experience from the bloody stalemate of the Western Front.

Slim had proved a good junior officer. His physical courage was amply demonstrated by leading his men in headlong charges against heavily defended Turkish positions. The injury he received at Gallipoli by rights should have crippled him for life, but, as his biographer Ronald Lewin points out, his year-long struggle to overcome his debility attests to both his physical and moral stamina. Slim also revealed a natural talent as a manager of men. The first story in his *Unofficial History*, 'The Incorrigible Rogue', gives the reader some insight into Slim's techniques. Many officers would have dismissed the 'rogue', the ex-tramp Richard Chuck, as a hopeless case. He does the bare legal minimum of work and presents an exterior of dumb insolence and stupidity, to the extent that his platoon commander wants him discharged as mentally deficient. But Slim perseveres with the man: he recognizes that Chuck is playing a clever game in order to secure a medical discharge, and lets him know he is on to him. From this point a mutual respect develops – there are many similarities between them. Both men loathe military 'bull', both have a profound contempt for staff officers whose rigid adherence to routine makes the proper business of the soldier more difficult, and Slim turns a blind eye to Chuck's numerous infractions of military discipline. Chuck is never a 'good soldier', but Slim creates in his company the conditions in which Chuck can emerge as a first-rate fighting man. There was many a Richard Chuck in Slim's company – unwilling conscripts who had no desire to fight. Slim's management of them was an excellent testimony to his qualities as a junior officer.

All this was impressive, but scarcely exceptional. At the end of the war there were hundreds of gallant and competent junior officers like Slim who had come from non-military backgrounds and who now wished to continue with military careers. Many were to be disappointed. In 1916 as a means of staying on in the post-war Army Slim had transferred to the West India Regiment, the only regular unit in which it was reported an officer without means could live on his pay. But Britain had another Army, the Indian, in which this was also possible; here advancement might be secured even by an officer from the lower middle classes of Birmingham. In March 1917, after being wounded for the second time, Slim had been invalided to India, and had been employed as GSO3 on the staff. He had worked professionally, had impressed his superiors, and in February 1919, in the face of War Office objections as to its impropriety, he transferred to the Indian Army.

The next twenty years can be quickly summarized: 1920–26 Adjutant 6th Gurkhas; 1926–28 student at Staff College, Quetta; 1929–33 Staff Officer, Army HQ; 1934–36 Indian Army DS Staff College, Camberley; 1937 student, Imperial Defence College; 1938 lieutenant-colonel 7th Gurkhas; 1939 commandant, Senior Officers School, Belgaum. How should one interpret this career? It contains three different kinds of postings: regimental, staff and education, both as a student and an instructor. Slim's appointment to the 6th Gurkhas was the longest period of regimental soldiering in his career. It served to integrate him into the Indian Army – he learned its languages and customs. Operations on the North West Frontier, although of little apparent relevance to modern warfare, also gave him valuable additional combat experience. The periods on the staff (adding up to more than seven years if one includes his employment during the closing phases of the First World War) gave him a profound insight into administrative problems. Unlike many successful generals who seem to take administrative and logistic support for granted, Slim in later years always took pains to ensure that his staff officers knew that their contributions had been invaluable. In his educational appointments Slim was both a good student and a good teacher – he could absorb large quantities of information and analyse it with subtlety. But although he had a good analytical mind, there is no evidence that Slim was at the forefront of military innovation during the 1920s and thirties. His biographer, Ronald Lewin, mentions that Slim met the armoured warfare theorist Percy Hobart at Quetta in 1926, but the recollections he records of contemporaries at Camberley and later at the Imperial Defence College would suggest that Slim was viewed as a something of an old-fashioned traditionalist. What does emerge is once again Slim's ability to manage men – this time in the role of communicator. Even those who regarded his lectures on warfare on the North West Frontier as outmoded still praised the style of their delivery. Slim was less interested in the theory than the reality of war; less concerned with speculating how he might employ future developments in military equipment than with making the best out of what was currently available.

Despite a solid and impressive track record, Slim's lieutenant-colonelcy came late in the day. He was already in his forty-seventh year and only the intervention of General Sir John Coleridge, whom Slim had first met at Army HQ in 1917 and who was now GOC Northern Command India, swung the board in his favour. Other officers in the Indian Army with exemplary First World War records had achieved as much, and perhaps more than Slim – men such as Christopher Maltby, Lewis Heath, John Smyth and Arthur Barstow. But their careers had ended less fortunately; Maltby and Heath languished in Japanese captivity, Barstow had been killed during the retreat to Singapore, and Smyth had been relieved of command after the disaster at the Sittang bridge.

Slim's relatively slow career progress, paradoxically, proved ultimately lucky. Those of his contemporaries who enjoyed rapid promotion found themselves suddenly facing the onslaught of a first-rate enemy, whereas Slim, during the first thirty months of the war, was consigned to backwaters. His opponents – the forces of the Italian and French empires, and the Persian Army – were reluctant to fight. Although a number of actions occurred – Ethiopia between November 1940 and January 1941, Syria in July 1941, and Persia a month later – they were not of sufficient seriousness to jeopardize the outcome of war. Mistakes could be made without serious consequences, and these thirty months proved an invaluable training exercise.

Slim's first command was the newly formed 10 Brigade, destined to become part of 5th Indian Division. After eleven months' basic training at Jhansi in Uttar Pradesh, in August 1940 10 Brigade was ordered to the Sudan. Three months later it launched the first British offensive of the war, an attack to retake the fort of Gallabat, captured by the Italians back in July, and to capture the neighbouring fortress of Metema, just inside the Ethiopian border. For Slim it was a vitally important battle in every respect. This was the first time he had overall control. Anthony Eden, Secretary of War, had personally wished him luck while on a recent visit to Khartoum, and Slim, still an obscure brigadier, felt the full psychological pressure of his new responsibilities.

Things went badly wrong. Serious mistakes were made – not least by Major-General Lewis Heath, the divisional commander, who insisted on replacing an Indian battalion by a British battalion in each of his brigades. Slim found himself commanding the 1st Essex, who lacked the experience of training alongside Indian forces and were unable to shake off the attitudes acquired by years of colonial policing. At first success seemed possible: a surprise aerial attack by the available handful of Wellesley bombers and Gladiator fighters was backed up by a twelve-tank squadron which advanced to take Gallabat. But even this success was deceptive. Nine of the twelve tanks were knocked out by mines or hidden boulders – something which could have been avoided by a proper reconnoitering of the ground in advance. Several tank crew members were shot by the advancing Garhwalis, who were unfamiliar with the tankers' uniform and mistook them for the Italian enemy. Slim's armoured force had been put out of action by his own infantry.

The assault on Metema was the next phase of the operation. When the 1st Essex moved forward and crowded into Gallabat, the fort became a sitting target for Italian bombers and fighters – a possibility Slim should have anticipated. His own aircover, sporadic at best owing to poor liaison with the RAF, was rapidly wiped out. Despite Slim's efforts to keep his men together, Essex battalion panicked and fled. Bitter recriminations followed. Slim had relieved the commanding officer, but Essex officers blamed the battalion's dishonour on Slim's poor planning and bore him a long-lasting grudge. Slim accepted full responsibility. He blamed himself for lacking the initiative to attempt a further assault on Metema with his two remaining battalions: Metema garrison, he reasoned, was probably just as badly shaken as the Essex and hence vulnerable to attack. As he later pointed out, he had 'taken counsel of his fears' at this time. On learning that Metema garrison had been on the very point of surrendering, he resolved to be more bold in the future.

The disaster at Gallabat might have ruined Slim's career once and for all – but within the space of six months he found himself acting major-general in command of his own division. His promotion was the result of a series of fortunate accidents, set in train by a near disaster. In mid-January 1941 Slim was wounded in an Italian strafing attack. He was evacuated back to India and relegated, as he saw it, to the staff, where he was employed in preparing contingency plans in the event of Iraq's defection to the Axis. The crisis came on 2 May when elements of Iraq's Army loyal to the pro-Axis prime minister attacked the British base at Basra; an expeditionary force under Lieutenant-General Quinan was despatched from India, and Auchinleck chose Slim to act as his chief of staff. Within days of Slim's arrival the commander of one of Quinan's divisions, the 10th Indian, fell ill, and on 15 May Quinan appointed Slim to the unexpected vacancy.

Slim commanded the 10th Indian Division for a little over ten months. It was a happy time for him. There were no repeats of Gallabat, and his former humiliating experiences at the hands of Italian colonial troops the previous November had taught him to adopt a more aggressive approach in battle. Within six weeks of his appointment he led the 10th in a successful attack on the Vichy French colonial garrison at Dier-ez-Zor in eastern Syria. Working closely with his brigade commanders he devised a daring two-pronged assault – a thrust from the south against the most heavily defended sector of the town, while another column made a wide sweep through the desert and attacked the less heavily defended northern side. Communication with the column proved difficult and logistics were nightmarish. At a critical moment the column actually ran out of fuel and movement was only maintained by draining petrol from vehicles on the lines of communication. In the event the attack went in later than planned but was completely successful. Resistance was light – so light, in fact, that the daring manoeuvre was probably unnecessary. But it served to restore Slim's self-confidence and provided useful experience for the next campaign, the occupation of Iran, which proved to be a perfect training exercise. Slim's division carried out its objective – the seizure of the Pai Tak pass and the occupation of Kermanshah – with exemplary efficiency, and raced on to occupy Hamadan before the Russians, advancing from the north, could reach it. Although there had been little actual fighting Slim had learnt how to move a division rapidly through mountainous country, experience which was to prove useful in the very near future.

By the spring of 1942, Slim and 10th Division were back in Iraq – consigned to backwaters, so it seemed, for the foreseeable future. But Slim's abilities had not passed unobserved in higher quarters, where various proposals were being made for his future employment. Wavell, now C-in-C India, put forward Slim's name, along with that of another officer, as possible candidates for his Chief of Staff. But Auchinleck, now C-in-C Middle East, demurred, arguing that neither officer had 'the reputation, personality, and experience which would give the Indian Army full confidence in their ability'. To Auchinleck, Slim seemed nothing more than a competent second-division player. Meanwhile in now embattled Burma, Major-General Bruce Scott and Major-General 'Punch' Cowan, former officers of the 6th Gurkhas, were trying to persuade their newly-arrived army commander, Lieutenant-General Harold Alexander, to ask Whitehall to appoint Slim as Burma Corps commander.

It was an appointment one would not have wished on an enemy, let alone an old friend. So far the campaign had already destroyed the career of one commander, Lieutenant-General Tom Hutton, and looked certain to destroy others. On the eve of his departure to take over command of the Army, Alexander himself had been warned by Mountbatten in no uncertain terms of the dangers which lay ahead. 'You must tell Winston that you will go out to Burma and fight as hard as you can, but that in your opinion there is no way of halting the advance until it has petered out in the gateway to India ... if they [Whitehall] regard this as a defeat for which you are responsible, it will damage you irretrievably.' These considerations were far from Scott and Cowan's minds when they pressed for Slim's appointment. They had first-hand knowledge of his abilities, and knew that if anyone could retrieve the situation, it would be Slim. Alexander acted on their advice and on 11 March 1942 Slim flew into Magwe.

Burma was a peculiarly fitting trial for Slim's abilities, calling into play all the skills he had acquired during his military career. He had already experienced the problems of operating over long distances – in the Middle Eastern theatre, supply lines of over a thousand miles had not been uncommon. He was also used to managing without air cover, adequate equipment, reliable intelligence or proper supplies. The problems posed by an unfriendly, often hostile population, were not new to him, nor were the stresses of working in a primitive, undeveloped environment. Many other British Army officers would have been daunted by a situation which Slim regarded as commonplace. However, he was faced by two factors which were new to him – a defeated and demoralized Army and a first-rate enemy which had the initiative.

Slim had ideas on how to deal with both these difficulties. He needed to convince the troops of Burma Corps that there was now someone in control who could win. Within hours of his arrival he was visiting Scott's and Cowan's units, talking to as many officers and men as he could – something he continued to do throughout the campaign. The memoirs of many Burma veterans attest to the impact of Slim's presence. A few words could have the most extraordinary effect on morale. Slim intended to consolidate Burma Corps and launch a counter-attack at the first opportunity, but first of all he needed reliable intelligence. His solution – the Pegu Yoma intelligence service, a force of improvised cavalry patrols – came straight out of the nineteenth century. Slim also collected as much information on Japanese methods of operation as he could, not only from his own officers but also from his Chinese allies. His first visit to Alexander's headquarters was spent in earnest conversation with a Chinese general who had fought at Changsa in 1938, the only defeat the Japanese had suffered until that time. From these sources Slim devised a plan for countering the classical Japanese attack of wide outflanking movements through the jungle. Units were to be deeply echeloned. When the Japanese got behind the first echelon, the second would launch an attack on the rear of the Japanese positions. The British were, as he was painfully aware, at a profound disadvantage: they were road-bound, whereas the lightly equipped Japanese could move across the country at amazing speeds. As yet it was a problem which he had neither the time nor resources to overcome.

Slim acted on Burma Corps like a tonic. His diagnosis of its problems was correct, his remedies were sound. Yet even after his arrival, the corps continued to stagger from defeat to defeat. Slim was only a corps commander, subject to confusing and often contradictory orders issued by Alexander's headquarters. Any thoughts about the relationship between the two men in this tense situation must remain tantalizingly speculative. It is perhaps not insignificant that both Slim's and Alexander's memoirs are brief and oblique in their respective comments. Alexander makes only a passing reference to Slim, while *Defeat into Victory* contains only two anecdotes relating to Alexander, both describing his reckless courage when under fire – a quality admired but not exactly approved by Slim. The tributes to leadership which one might expect are conspicuous by their absence.

Alexander's handling of the campaign at Army level proved little short of disastrous. Only a few days before Slim arrived, Burma Corps had almost been trapped through his insistence on holding Rangoon in the face of overwhelming odds; luck rather than good generalship had averted disaster. Admittedly, Alexander's task was not easy – Wavell proved a hard master, and he was faced with the often incompatible demands of two difficult allies – Chiang Kai-shek and General 'Vinegar Joe' Stilwell. Yet as army commander it was his job to resist pressure and to make finely tuned and often difficult decisions. Instead he tended to waver and delay, allowing the campaign to drift. As corps commander Slim desperately needed clear and attainable objectives. Was he to attack the enemy, retain territory, or keep Burma Corps intact and withdraw to India? Such clear direction was never given.

Time and again Slim saw his carefully laid plans for counter-attacks rendered impotent by directives from Army HQ. On 30 March he was ordered to launch an offensive down the Irrawaddy Valley south of Prome, in order to relieve pressure on the Chinese who were under attack at Toungoo in the Sittang Valley. Slim knew his corps wasn't ready. He predicted that the attack would end in failure, and it did. The only hope he had of stemming the Japanese advance was to keep the two divisions of Burma Corps together, but Alexander's capitulation to Sino-American pressure meant that units were constantly being detached to support the Chinese. As late as 20 April Slim was still hoping to launch a Napoleonic master-stroke – an offensive by his entire corps and a Chinese division down the Irrawaddy Valley to halt the Japanese advance, followed by a rapid change of axis across the Pegu Yomas to fall on the rear of the Japanese in the Sittang Valley. The Chinese withdrew before the offensive could be launched. The retreat continued, and on 25 April Alexander finally issued the order for a withdrawal to India, which, in the acid words of Burma veteran James Lunt, was 'the only far-reaching decision Alexander made'.

Alexander's responsibility as army commander now lay in maintaining the efficient functioning of the rear areas for as long as possible, supervising an orderly withdrawal, and ensuring the successful demolition of access routes. It was Slim's task to keep the frontline forces intact and conduct rearguard operations. The conduct of these two aspects of the retreat is instructive. The rear areas rapidly fell apart, the administrative troops degenerating into bands of pillaging brigands. Confusion reigned supreme. Major Michael Calvert waited for days for Alexander's order to demolish a vital railway bridge – an order which never came. Conversely, Major Tony Mains, acting under Alexander's explicit orders, destroyed a stockpile of fuel outside Mandalay which was almost essential for the successful withdrawal of Slim's 7 Armoured Brigade. Years later Slim had still not forgiven the unfortunate Mains.

The retreat of the frontline forces, however, proceeded with almost clockwork precision. A brilliant rearguard action at Kyaukse delayed the Japanese, and at Monywa and Shwegyin, Slim extricated his forces from near disaster with considerable skill. Once contact was broken with the Japanese at Shwegyin, the retreat became as much a race against the monsoon as against the advancing Japanese. Slim marched back with his exhausted and now disease-ridden columns up the Kebaw Valley to the relative safety of Tamu on the India–Burma border. Thin and ragged as they were, they still carried their weapons like soldiers.

By rights, Slim's conduct of the two-month retreat should have earned him recognition in the highest quarters as a general of first-rate ability. Yet in the event it was Alexander as army commander whom the waiting press men interviewed, Alexander who was the hero of *A Million Died*, Alexander whom the BBC extolled as 'a bold and resourceful commander, [who] has fought one of the great defensive battles of the war'. Stilwell knew better. He had seen both generals under stress and knew that 'good old Slim' rather than 'Alex [who] has the wind up' was the real hero of the piece. 'Vinegar Joe' lived up to his name in his acerbic dismissal of Alexander's BBC publicity as 'crap'.

Alexander gave Slim no share in the praise. We have no record of his feelings about Slim after the retreat: but it seems no accident that both Lieutenant-General Noel Irwin, the commander on the India–Burma border, and Churchill himself, with whom Alexander subsequently stayed, seem to have formed a very low opinion of Slim without having met him personally. By May 1942 a pattern had emerged which would dog Slim until the end of the Burma campaign. Although he was held in the highest esteem by the officers and men he commanded, others took the credit for any achievements there had been while passing the blame for the many disasters onto his shoulders. Irwin, who from April onwards had watched the rabble of rear-echelon units enter Burma, held Slim responsible, and told him so in no uncertain terms on their first meeting. Their relationship never really improved from this point. It is perhaps not without significance that Irwin had been an officer in the 1st Essex. Slim angrily denied the charge of incompetence and rounded on Irwin with a counter-accusation of negligence towards the men of Burma Corps, who were at that time bivouacked on the hillsides without any cover during the monsoon season. Fourteen years after the event in *Defeat into Victory* Slim did nothing to hide the anger he still felt.

The next year was one of the most difficult in Slim's life. After convalescing, Wavell appointed him to command XV Corps, but had also appointed Irwin to command Eastern Army. Slim's corps, which during the summer of 1942 was responsible for the seaward defences of Calcutta, was shortly transferred westwards to the Ranchi Plateau for training. Irwin evidently had little confidence in Slim's ability as a commander on the battlefield. In September 1942, when Wavell ordered Eastern Army to advance into the Arakan and recapture Akyab, Irwin determined that Slim would have no part in the operation, and instead commanded it himself from Eastern Army HQ in Barrackpore. At first the operation proceeded smoothly, if uninspiringly. Major-General Lloyd's 14th Division advanced slowly down the Arakan against negligible opposition until on 10 January 1943 it ran into a strongly defended Japanese position at Donbiak. At Irwin's insistence Lloyd proceeded with piecemeal frontal attacks, all of which were beaten back. Finally on 10 March Irwin sent Slim to the Arakan, not to take command but merely to report on the situation.

To Slim, the problems were immediately apparent. Lloyd's divisional headquarters was trying to command nine brigades – clearly a corps headquarters was needed. Morale was low, the troops were jumpy, and the sporadic assaults were doomed to failure. Irwin ignored Slim's report, sent him back to Ranchi, and continued to fight the battle on the pattern he had established. On 24 March the Japanese, moving north through supposedly impenetrable mountains around Lloyd's flanks, burst onto the coastal plain to the rear of his positions. Lloyd ordered his brigades to retreat northwards. Irwin's patience at last snapped. He countermanded Lloyd's withdrawal order, sent him back to India, and he himself took command of the Arakan front, in the meantime ordering Major-General Lomax to advance with a reserve division. On 3 April, shortly after Irwin handed over operational command to Lomax and returned to Barrackpore, the Japanese struck again, cutting off two British brigades. The situation was now desperately serious, with a full-scale disaster in the offing. On 5 April Irwin finally ordered Slim's XV Corps HQ to Chittagong, but with instructions not to take over administrative control and to assume operational control only when ordered to do so. The situation was absurd. Slim was sorely tempted to intervene, but, impressed with Lomax's handling of the battle, refrained. It was not until 14 April that Irwin finally conferred operational control on Slim.

The Arakan campaign was now beyond redemption. It had degenerated into a grim struggle to rescue British battalions now hopelessly scattered amidst Japanese troops along the coastline. Irwin had been responsible for this shambles, but with shameless effrontery he now attempted to blame Slim for the disaster. On 8 May he wrote caustically to his corps commander: '17 Bns. have been chased about by possibly 6, a sad but realistic commentary on the present fighting'. On the same day Irwin informed Wavell that the 'commanders are far from being much good'. By 12 May Slim had successfully extricated the British troops, who were now back in the positions they had occupied nine months earlier. Two weeks later, Slim received a final shaft from Irwin – a letter severely criticizing his conduct of the battle and intimating that he would be relieved of command.

Twenty-six May 1943, the day Irwin's letter arrived, was the most significant in Slim's career. For a short while it looked as if that career was now in shreds. But Irwin had lost touch with events. In far-away Washington, Wavell (recently recalled from India), Churchill and Alanbrooke were in conference, planning a major shake-up of Eastern Army.

Irwin, rather than Slim, was blamed for the Arakan disaster, and later that day he received a telegram informing him of his dismissal. Irwin, who, despite all his faults, could take it on the chin, immediately sent a telegram to Slim: 'You're not sacked – I am.'

Slim had survived, but for some months continued to regard himself as a commander under sentence. But by now the nadir of the campaign had been reached, and during these months Slim's position steadily improved. Irwin's replacement, General Sir George Gifford, was very much like Slim in temperament and outlook. Five months later, when Lord Louis Mountbatten arrived to take over as supremo of a new South East Asia command, Gifford became Commander-in-Chief of 11th Army Group. Mountbatten had clear ideas about how the campaign should be fought. He stressed offensive action, and announced that in future fighting would continue during the monsoon season. Many Burma veterans were horrified by the suggestion, but Slim was not, and his support won him promotion to command of the new Fourteenth Army. It was well deserved. After suffering a series of defeats by the Japanese, Slim may not have rated himself highly as a military strategist. But there are defeats and defeats. Once he had taken command of the retreat in March 1942 there continued to be defeats, but there were no more disasters.

Arakan, where Slim transformed potential disaster into orderly defeat, was merely the prelude to an extraordinary metamorphosis virtually unparalleled in military history. Many armies have risen, phoenix-like, from the ashes of defeat – the Prussian Army after 1806, the US Army after 1861 – but none so spectacularly as the Eastern Army in the summer of 1943. Within a short space of time an utterly defeated and demoralized army went on to win a series of remarkable victories, all the more outstanding given that circumstances could scarcely have been less favourable. Slim confronted one of the world's most forbidding theatres of operation – seven hundred miles of virtually trackless, disease-infected jungle-clad mountains, swamped for half the year by the monsoon rains. The Eastern Army came at the bottom of the priority list for supplies and manpower. Exceptional ingenuity was required to function at all under such conditions. *Defeat into Victory* amply testifies to the resourcefulness of Slim's crew, who managed to bring under control tropical diseases such as amoebic dysentery and malaria (which at one stage laid low eighty per cent of some units, including Slim himself) and who bulldozed the jungle to create roads, airfields and bases. Slim stood behind this achievement, partly because he knew how to pick the right men for the job, more significantly because he fostered the right atmosphere for determined endeavour. Manpower and other resources might be short, but Slim remained absolutely inflexible in his insistence on adequate medical supplies, viewing physical health as the key to morale and success. Although his troops shunned anti-malarial drugs with the common suspicion that they caused impotence, Slim ruthlessly enforced their administration. 'God helps those who help themselves' became his and their motto. Jute was transformed into parachutes, 'bithness' – strips of locally manufactured and bitumized hessian – became their effective substitute for an all-weather road surface. And later the banks of the Chindwin were transformed into an ad hoc boatyard for the construction of a sizeable flotilla of wooden barges and gunboats.

Admittedly, other armies were at the same time testifying to the triumph of the human will over circumstance in equally daunting locations – for example the Americans and Australians in the steamy jungle-clad terrain of the south-west Pacific. Yet few generals can ever have had to bind together a more heterogeneous and less enthusiastic army than the one Slim found himself commanding, where the British rubbed shoulders with Indians, Gurkhas, East and West Africans. Most of the British were homesick conscripts, unwilling to risk their necks for an empire in which they had long since lost faith. Few Indians felt any residual loyalty to the Raj, and were scarcely keen to help the British reimpose their rule over Burma. The East and West Africans can have had even less motivation to fight.

It was here that Slim revealed his greatest strengths as a general. Morale was the key – he needed to convince his Army both that the Japanese could be beaten, and should be beaten. In some ways the first task was the easier. Once his Army had become used to living and operating in jungle territory, the myth of the invincible Japanese jungle-warrior was soon exploded. From the autumn of 1942, when XV Corps had moved to Ranchi, Slim set up a highly realistic training programme: units were sent into the jungle for weeks at a time and learned to fight in it. In jungle warfare, everyone was in the front line. Slim's men learnt Japanese tactics of jungle attack rather than British tactics of defence: they were to get behind the Japanese first and surround them.

Training could inspire confidence, but not motivation. From past experience, Slim had learned that the best approach was the most simple and direct – to talk to as many troops as he could, man to man, cutting through the traditional barriers of military hierarchy. It was also the most time-consuming. Slim reckoned that this exercise took up a third of his time. But it was time amply well spent. Virtually alone amongst British generals of the Second World War, Slim possessed the common touch – the ability to communicate high ideals in simple language. He convinced his soldiers, whether Hausa riflemen, Harijan Pioneers, or British gunners, that they were all integral and essential parts of a great war machine – the Fourteenth Army. The aim of this Army was neither the protection nor the reconquest of an empire, but the destruction of the embodiment of human evil – the Japanese Army. It was a goal in which all the various races and religions of Fourteenth Army could bury their differences.

When it came to putting theory into practice, Slim took things steadily and carefully. Failure at this stage would have been psychologically disastrous, and his initial limited attacks, often deploying entire brigades against single Japanese companies, were designed to ensure success. Once confidence had been built up, patrols could subsequently be sent ever further into Japanese-controlled areas. By the end of 1943, troops in the Far East were feeling far better about themselves than they had six months earlier. The rate of sickness had fallen, rations had improved, and the jungle and the Japanese no longer seemed quite so formidable. Although still virtually unknown in England, the man who had orchestrated this transformation was now known throughout Fourteenth Army as 'Uncle Bill', a nickname which combined both affection and respect.

Slim was responsible for the Army's revitalization but ultimately had little say in its large-scale deployment. By the autumn of 1943 various plans were on the table in Delhi, London and Washington: they boiled down to a choice of one or two approaches – either an overland advance from north-east India or a maritime attack somewhere on the south-west coast of Burma. Slim, like most of the strategic planners, favoured the latter course – but the necessary shipping would not be available for months to come. By autumn two limited operations were under way – an advance by the three divisions of Slim's XV Corps into the Arakan, and an advance by Stilwell's Sino-American force in the north-east to take the city of Myitkyina and eventually link up with the Burma Road. But the Japanese commander, Lieutenant-General Shozo Kawabe, also had plans afoot. The autumn months saw Lieutenant-General Renya Mutaguchi's Fifteenth Army building up its strength to four divisions containing over 100,000 men in all. They were preparing for a large-scale invasion of north-east India via the British bases of Imphal and Dinapur. If successful, this new Japanese assault would not only destroy Slim's forces in the area, the IV Corps of Fourteenth Army, but would also cut Stilwell's lines of communication with India. It might also provide the spark which the Japanese still hoped would ignite an explosion of nationalist, anti-British sentiment throughout the subcontinent.

Between December 1943 and March 1944 opposing Allied and Japanese plans produced three overlapping campaigns – Stilwell's drive for Myitkyina, the second Arakan, and the struggle for the Imphal plain – all conducted more or less simultaneously along a 700-mile front. Slim's capacity was now tested to the limit as he flew from one area to another dealing with crisis upon crisis. Each area imposed different burdens. Stilwell was in charge of battle in the north-east, and Slim had complete confidence in his abilities. The problems came from a different quarter. Major-General Orde Wingate, at Wavell's personal request, had arrived in the Far East early in 1943 to form and command the Chindits, a long-range penetration group which, by the summer, had started to operate behind Japanese lines. Slim was singularly unimpressed: like the cavalry raids of former centuries, the Chindits were all flash and dash, but produced no long-term results. But Wingate had found a powerful backer in Churchill, whose taste for the heroic almost guaranteed his approval of Chindit tactics. By late 1943 the Chindits had risen in strength to six brigades, the equivalent of three infantry divisions. Wingate, by this stage entertaining delusions of grandeur, envisioned the Chindits elevated from a minor supporting role to that of star of the show: transported and supplied by air, they would sweep through south-east Asia and singlehandedly retake Singapore. On 4 December he demanded that Slim transfer one of Fourteenth Army's reserve divisions to his command, threatening political repercussions if he did not comply. Slim stood his ground and Wingate backed down. A more ambitious and less determined general than Slim might have given way at this point: the subsequent drain on the overstretched resources of Fourteenth Army could well have tipped the balance in favour of the Japanese in the battles at Imphal and Kohima. Slim consigned the Chindits to a far more reasonable and limited role, supporting Stilwell's forthcoming offensive.

On 5 March 1944, the eve of the Chindits' airlift into northern Burma, Slim and Wingate once again confronted each other – for the last time – in a brief encounter which speaks volumes about their respective qualities. A last-minute intelligence report, indicating that the Japanese had detected the Chindits' landing zones and were preparing ambushes, threw Wingate into a state of near-hysteria. He insisted on the postponement of the operation, but Slim, whose long experience had rendered him both less credulous and more daring, ordered the operation to proceed. As he had suspected, the report was inaccurate. Within a few days Wingate was dead – killed in an aircraft crash. His place in the pantheon of great Second World War generals was now secure. It might have been less secure had not Slim, only a few days earlier, made his last major decision for him.

Meanwhile, Slim's problems on the other two fronts had multiplied. By 4 February, 5th and 7th Indian Divisions had advanced nearly forty miles into the Arakan and had reached the Moungdow–Buthidaung road – the scene of very heavy fighting the previous year. The Japanese now struck. A 6,000-strong task force moved ten miles north-east around the British left flank and then wheeled south, striking deep into the British rear areas. To an onlooker, it must have seemed ominously like a replay of last year's catastrophe. But this time British morale was high and Slim was in control. Though the speed and force of the Japanese assault took him by surprise, Slim quickly got a grip on the situation: he ordered units to hold their positions and to wait for air supplies. From 6 to 24 February Japanese attacks repeatedly targeted in on the British headquarters area at Sinzweya, the so-called 'administrative box'. Now Slim's earlier insistence that rear-area troops – office workers, clerks, babus – should be trained to fight with the same facility as front-line units, paid off. The box held, two fresh British divisions advanced from the north, and the Japanese were crushed, losing more than 5,000 men. Slim was elated, viewing it as 'a victory about which there could be no argument'. This was true enough, but retrospectively it was scarcely the kind of victory on which one could rest one's laurels. Slim had committed four divisions to a battle which the Japanese had intended primarily as a diversion. The Imphal front was now left dangerously weak, and it was here that the Japanese launched their main thrust.

Since December 1943, intelligence reports had been piecing together a fairly accurate picture of Japanese intentions. Slim predicted that the Japanese would strike across the Chindwin, and he planned to fight a defensive battle on the Imphal plain, where IV Corps' superiority in armour and artillery would be telling. Timing was all. A rapid withdrawal to the plain of IV Corps' divisions, currently spread out in the mountains to the south, would soon signal to the watching Japanese that he had divined their plans. If he left the withdrawal too late, there was every chance that the outlying divisions might be cut off and defeated. Here Slim once again erred on the side of caution – as he himself confessed

in *Defeat into Victory*. The Japanese attack came far earlier than anticipated – on the 4th, rather than the 15th, of March. Three separate battles
quickly developed. Seventy miles south of Imphal, 17th Indian Division
was soon cut off on the Tiddum road, and fighting for its life as it
withdrew northwards. Meanwhile fifty miles east of Imphal, Japanese
troops were pressing back the 20th Indian Division along the Tamu
road. The most serious threat of all developed fifty miles north of Imphal.
The Japanese 31st Division was closing in on the lightly defended village
of Kohima. Dimapur, the rail-head and supply base of the Fourteenth
Army, only thirty miles to the east, now lay within striking distance.
On 29 March the Japanese finally cut the Imphal–Kohima road, isolating
IV Corps in Imphal. Things looked bad for the British. A year earlier,
defeat would have seemed inevitable, but now the Japanese faced an
enemy made formidable by both training and leadership under an astute
general. Slim's strategy was simple – consolidation of his troops on
the Imphal plain to await reserves. The Japanese would waste their energies in a battle of attrition. The plan worked, and Kohima was held,
but it was a close-run thing. Between 5 and 20 April, Japanese attacks
were fierce and unrelenting. The day was saved by the arrival at Dimapur
of XXXIII Corps, who advanced south and broke into the town. Fifty
miles south of Kohima, the siege of Imphal continued into the last
week of June, when XXXIII Corps were finally able to hack their way
through the last remaining road-blocks. By this time the Japanese supply
situation had become desperate. They had failed to capture any of the
British bases, and with the breaking of the monsoon in mid-June, their
own supply chain through the mountains from the Chindwin had become
untenable. On 5 July, retreating under British counter-attack, they were
forced to withdraw to the Chindwin.

For the Japanese the battle had been a disaster. One hundred thousand
men had crossed the Chindwin in March: July witnessed the sorry
return of only 35,000, all of them emaciated by hunger and tropical
disease. It was the greatest land defeat as yet suffered by the Japanese,
and their generals paid the price in full, dismissed wholesale, from
General Kawabe all the way down through the chain of command.
Yet Japanese resilience seemed unlimited. By the autumn of 1944 they
had rebuilt their armies in Burma to a strength of more than 250,000
men. The new commander, General Kimura, deployed relatively small
armies on the north-eastern and Arakan fronts, and concentrated his
forces in central Burma to crush Fourteenth Army when it came south
of the Chindwin. Kimura intended to impose upon Slim essentially

the same sort of battle as Slim had imposed on Kawabe. Rather than holding the southern banks of the Chindwin, Kimura pulled his forces back behind the half-mile-wide Irrawaddy. As the British advanced, he reasoned, their supply lines would fail, and their already weakened divisions would now thoroughly exhaust themselves in the conflict. Kimura had already devised a name for this climactic confrontation: 'The Battle of the Irrawaddy Shore'.

For Slim the battles of Imphal and Kohima had at last brought recognition of a sort. In December 1944 he and his corps commanders were knighted. But this recognition had been tardy. In London the command of Fourteenth Army continued to be criticized for unimaginative and over-cautious tactics. Slim was viewed as a reliable general, one who could stave off disaster but who lacked the foresight and flair to carry off a decisive and exciting victory. Changes had also been afoot in the organization of British Army command – changes which did little to aid Slim's task. In November 1944 General Sir Oliver Leese, the former Eighth Army commander, took over from General Gifford. Slim and Gifford had got on well together, but the relationship between Slim and Leese bordered on the openly hostile. Slim's final operations were carried out with scant regard for both Leese and the Eighth Army men who now filled the offices of SEAC HQ.

Slim almost fell into Kimura's trap. By this stage, he had reached the point where he could second-guess Kawabe's tactics, unaware that Kawabe had been replaced by Kimura in the high-command shake-up. He was preparing himself for a climactic battle on the plains between the Chindwin and the Irrawaddy around Shewbo on the supposition that the last thing the Japanese would do was give up ground. Their forces would be approximately equal – some five divisions apiece. Although Fourteenth Army had technically twice the strength of the Japanese forces, only a small proportion, even with air supply, could be maintained south of the Chindwin. Superior air power and armour would win the day.

Slim's suspicions grew as the spearhead of IV Corps, 19th Division, advanced rapidly south against unexpectedly light opposition. By 16 December suspicion had hardened into certainty. Over the next forty-eight hours, without consulting Leese, Slim changed tactics in a last-minute and brilliantly daring operation. Leaving a dummy IV Corps headquarters near Shewbo to maintain radio contact with 19th Division, which continued to advance towards the Irrawaddy, Slim secretly moved the bulk of IV Corps 100 miles to the west; during the next two months he sent it down a bullock-cart track which ran 150 miles south-east to Pakokku on the Irrawaddy, nearly 50 miles south of the main Japanese defences, and only 50 miles west of Meiktila, the main Japanese supply and communication centre in central Burma. In the meantime, 19th Division, supported by XXXIII Corps, had closed in on the northern bank of the Irrawaddy in the Mandalay area. On 12 February it carried out a series of bloodily contested crossings. The Japanese, obsessed with the danger to Mandalay, dismissed a report of massive columns moving through the jungles on their left flank as nothing more than yet another Chindit-style long-range penetration raid. On 13 February IV Corps struck. It crossed the Irrawaddy with negligible opposition, and by 4 March its armoured columns had taken Meiktila. General Kimura, already hard-pressed around Mandalay, rushed forces south to deal with the new threat, and two separate battles developed – a house-to-house struggle for Mandalay, which fell to 19th Division on 21 March, and the battle to retake Meiktila, which the Japanese gave up on 28 March after suffering heavy losses.

Slim's brilliant manoeuvre had shattered the Japanese defences in central Burma, and the remnants of their divisions now withdrew in confusion along the Irrawaddy. Slim did not give them time to consolidate. From 1 April to 1 May, Fourteenth Army spearheads raced southwards, slashing through the Japanese rearguards. Kimura's last and sole hope lay in the onset of the monsoon, which might break and slow down the British advance before it reached Rangoon. Heavy rain set in on 2 May while Fourteenth Army was still fifty miles north of the city, but by this stage it no longer mattered. On the previous day, XV Corps had landed south of Rangoon and the Japanese had evacuated the city. On 6 May Fourteenth Army and XV Corps linked up a few miles north of the city. To all intents and purposes, the Burma campaign was now over.

Slim's revitalization of the Army had proved him to be a general of administrative genius; his conduct of the Burma retreat, the first and second Arakan, and Imphal–Kohima, had shown him to be a brilliant defensive general; and now, the Mandalay–Meiktila operation had placed him in the same class as Guderian, Manstein and Patton as an offensive commander. Given the pattern of Slim's career, there was a certain predictability that his achievements would be followed, not by recognition, but by dismissal. On 7 May, Leese flew into Slim's HQ at Meiktila with the astounding news that he was to be relieved of command of the Fourteenth Army and transferred to a much smaller residual force tasked with mopping-up operations. Slim chose not to accept the post, viewing it for what it was – effective dismissal. Over the next two weeks, as news spread throughout Fourteenth Army, a storm of protest erupted. Troops became mutinous, officers threatened to resign, and Leese, who backtracked in embarrassment, found himself dismissed instead. On 1 July, shortly after his first meeting with Churchill, Slim was appointed to the now vacant position of Commander-in-Chief, Allied Land Forces SEAC. At long last he had achieved a position from which no one, not even Field-Marshal Montgomery, could relegate him to the wings. He had now become one of Churchill's generals.

BIBLIOGRAPHY

Allen, Louis, *Burma: The Longest War 1941–45* (London, 1984).

Barker, A. J., *The March on Delhi* (London, 1966).

Brett-James, Antony, *Ball of Fire: the Fifth Indian Division in the Second World War* (London, 1951).

Brett-James, Antony and Evans, Lieutenant-General Sir Geoffrey, *Imphal* (London, 1962).

Callahan, Raymond, *Burma 1942–45* (London, 1978).

Calvert, Brigadier Michael, *Slim* (London, 1973).

Connell, John, *Auchinleck* (London, 1959).

Evans, Lieutenant-General Sir Geoffrey, *Slim as Military Commander* (London, 1969).

Fraser, David, *Alanbrooke* (London, 1982).

Gilbert, Martin, *Winston S. Churchill*, vol. VII, *Road to Victory 1941–1945* (London, 1986).

Jackson, General Sir William, *Alexander of Tunis as Military Commander* (London, 1971).

Kirby, Major-General S. W., *The War Against Japan* (5 vols, London, 1957–69).

Lewin, Ronald, *Slim: The Standardbearer* (London, 1976).

Lunt, Major-General James, *A Hell of a Licking* (London, 1986).

Mains, Lieutenant-Colonel Tony, *The Retreat from Burma* (London, 1986).

Masters, John, *The Road Past Mandalay* (London, 1961).

Moon, Penderel (ed.), *Wavell, The Viceroy's Journal* (London, 1973).

Nicolson, Nigel, *Alex* (London, 1973).

North, John (ed.), *The Alexander Memoirs 1940–45* (London, 1962).

Perrett, Bryan, *Tank Tracks to Rangoon* (London, 1978).

Slim, Field-Marshal the Viscount, *Defeat into Victory* (London, 1956); *Unofficial History* (London, 1959); *Courage, and other broadcasts* (London, 1957).

Tulloch, Major-General Derek, *Wingate in Peace and War* (London, 1972).

CHRONOLOGY: WILLIAM SLIM

1891, August 6	Born at 72 Belmont Road, Bishopston, Bristol
1908, September	King Edward's School, Birmingham
1909	Uncertified elementary teacher working in various Birmingham slum schools
1911	Junior clerk at Stewarts & Lloyds, Ltd, Birmingham (manufacturers of metal tubes)
1912	Enrols in Birmingham University OTC
1914, August 22	Gazetted 2nd Lieutenant 9th Battalion Royal Warwickshire Regiment
1915, August 8	Wounded at Gallipoli – evacuated to England
1916, September 2	Gazetted temporary Captain – posted to Mesopotamia
1917, March 11	In advance guard which captures Baghdad – in subsequent operations north of city Slim is awarded MC
1917, March 29	Wounded again – evacuated to India
1917, November	Appointed GSO3 Army HQ India
1918, November	Appointed GSO2 – temporary Major – Army HQ India
1919, May 31	Transfer from British to Indian Army and gazetted Captain Indian Army
1920, March 27	Posted Captain 1/6th Gurkha Rifles
1926, January 1	Marries Aileen Robertson, daughter of Rev. John Anderson Robertson, minister of Church of Scotland
1926, February	Student at Staff College, Quetta
1928	Staff, Army HQ, India
1933, May 19	Gazetted Major
1934	Indian Army Instructor, Staff College, Camberley
1937	Student, Imperial Defence College
1938, May 2	Gazetted Lieutenant-Colonel – appointed to command 2/7th Gurkhas
1939, April	Appointed to command Senior Officers School at Belgaum
1939, September	Promoted to Brigadier – posted to command 10 Indian Brigade at Jhansi
1941, January	Wounded yet again by Italian aerial attack in Eritrea – evacuated to India
1941, June 1	Promoted acting Major-General – operations in Iraq, Syria and Iran
1942, March 14	Promoted acting Lieutenant-General – appointed to command Burcorps
1942, May	Appointed to command XV Corps in India

1943, October	Appointed Commander-in-Chief Eastern Army (name changed to Fourteenth Army)
1944, December 15	Knight Commander of the Bath
1945, July 1	Promoted General
1945, August	Appointed Commander-in-Chief Allied Land Forces South East Asia
1946	Commandant of Imperial Defence College – created GBE
1947	Deputy Chairman of British Railways
1948	Chief of the Imperial General Staff
1949, January 4	Promoted Field-Marshal
1952	Created GCMG
1953, May 8	Sworn in as Governor-General of Australia
1954	Created GCVO
1956	First publication of *Defeat into Victory*
1959	Created Knight of the Garter
1960	Elevated to peerage as Viscount Slim of Burma
1963	Constable and Governor of Windsor Castle
1970, December 14	Dies in London

17

CARTON DE WIART AND SPEARS

*Lieutenant-General Sir Adrian Carton de Wiart
and Major-General Sir Louis Spears*

G. D. SHEFFIELD

The military careers of Adrian Carton de Wiart and Louis Spears offer many points of comparison. They came from similar backgrounds. Both achieved high rank and a degree of fame at an early age, and both served as the head of a military mission. Above all both Spears and Carton de Wiart enjoyed the trust and confidence of Winston Churchill, who during the 1939–45 war appointed them to positions of some responsibility; positions to which, however, they were not entirely suited.

By the evening of 2 July 1916, the second day of the Somme offensive, the British 19th Division had succeeded in capturing most of the village of La Boisselle, which the Germans had turned into a miniature fortress. At 6 pm on that day, the Divisional commander, Major-General Tom Bridges, visited the front line and appointed the commander of the 8th Gloucesters, Captain (temporary Lieutenant-Colonel) Adrian Carton de Wiart DSO, to command the troops of 57 Brigade in the village, the other three battalion commanders having either been killed or incapacitated. La Boisselle was under intense enemy artillery fire, and on the morning of 3 July the Germans began to mount heavy counterattacks.

323

By 12:30 Carton de Wiart's men were having to contend with 'probably the most intense fighting the Division had up to that moment experienced'. The British had been forced to give ground before the advancing Germans, until they were deployed behind a hedge running through the approximate centre of the village. It was later stated that 'It was owing in great measure to his [Carton de Wiart's] dauntless courage and inspiring example that a serious reverse was averted.'

Carton de Wiart was a striking-looking man, who wore a black eye-patch and was missing one hand. He strode up and down the line under heavy fire encouraging his men, apparently oblivious of the danger. At one juncture, he counter-attacked a potentially serious German thrust with all his available reserves, which amounted to a sergeant with half a dozen men. The principal weapon in such close-quarter fighting was the Mills bomb. Carton de Wiart could be seen leading parties of bombers, pulling out the firing pins with his teeth and hurling them with his good hand. The German attack was checked at the hedge. By mid-afternoon on 4 July, after a prolonged struggle to bomb the German defenders out of the ruins of the village, La Boisselle had once more passed back into British hands. For this action, Carton de Wiart was awarded the Victoria Cross.[1]

The fight of 3–4 July 1916 is an excellent illustration of Carton de Wiart's methods as a commander and a soldier. He was outrageously brave and believed in 'leading' in a literal sense; not for him were the comforts of so-called 'château generalship'. His impressive list of wounds (variously numbered as eight or eleven) testify to the risks to which he regularly and willingly exposed himself. Carton de Wiart was, in short, a fighting general. It was ironic that most of his post-1918 military career was to be spent in a series of quasi-diplomatic posts in which abilities other than those of courage and leadership were to be required.

Adrian Carton de Wiart was born in Brussels on 5 May 1880, and his early childhood was spent in Egypt. He was educated in England. On the outbreak of the Boer War in 1899 he abandoned his studies at Oxford and enlisted as a trooper in Paget's Horse, a newly raised regiment of volunteers. In the Boer War, 'Trooper Carton' – he used a *nom de guerre* to surmount the problems of being under-aged, and having foreign nationality – first revealed his almost suicidal courage. Although he was badly wounded in a skirmish and was temporarily invalided out of the Army, Carton de Wiart ended the war as a subaltern in a regular cavalry regiment, the 4th (Royal Irish) Dragoon Guards. The next twelve years were spent in peacetime soldiering in England, India and South Africa. In 1914 he applied for secondment to the Somali Camel Corps, for his father was unable to continue to pay him an allowance, and thus he could no longer afford to live the far from inexpensive life of a cavalry subaltern in England. On 23 July 1914 Carton de Wiart left England. While he was at sea war broke out with Germany, and he arrived in Somaliland to join a collection of disgruntled subalterns all desperately trying to get back to Europe. In the meantime, there was a campaign to be fought against Mahomed bin Abdillah Hassan, the 'Mad Mullah'. On 18 November 1914 he was hit four times while leading a group of Somali troops in an assault on an enemy-held fort. The future Lord Ismay, who was also present, recalled that Carton de Wiart ran towards the fort, but was hit in the arm and the ear, having already been wounded in the eye, but he 'did not check in his stride'. For this action Carton de Wiart was awarded the DSO, although he modestly omitted any mention of his decorations from *Happy Odyssey*, his autobiography published in 1950.[2]

Carton de Wiart returned to England, where, in a nursing home in Park Lane, his left eye was removed in January 1915. This hospital was to become very familiar to Carton de Wiart over the next four years; he was wounded so often that, as he was to write, he 'became one of their most regular customers ... even silk pyjamas with my name on were reserved for me'. In February 1915 he joined the 4th Dragoon Guards in the trenches near Ypres, where they were serving as infantry. Three months later, on the night of 10–11 May 1915, he was wounded once again, this time in the hand. Carton de Wiart reinforced his reputation for utter fearlessness by pulling off two of the fingers on his shattered hand, after a surgeon at the dressing station had refused to amputate them. Later his hand was removed altogether. Nonetheless, the one-handed and one-eyed Carton de Wiart had returned to the front in time for the opening of the Battle of the Somme in July 1916.

Although he survived the fight for La Boisselle unscathed, given Carton de Wiart's style of leadership it was inevitable that sooner or later he would again be wounded. On 23 July 1916 he was hit in the head by a machine-gun bullet at High Wood. He had a spell recovering in the Park Lane hospital before returning to France. This was to be the pattern for the rest of Carton de Wiart's Great War career; a bout of active service would be temporarily interrupted by a more or less serious wound, which would be followed by his return to France, where the cycle would begin again. His talent for leadership was recognized by promotion to Brigadier-General, and he commanded 12, 105 and 113 Brigades in 1917 and in 1918. Despite his elevation Carton de Wiart retained the mentality of a front-line soldier and he continued to add to his collection of wounds.[3]

By the end of the First World War, Carton de Wiart was a celebrity in the Army, admired by men ranging from Sir Hubert Gough to the soldiers of the 8th Gloucesters (who nicknamed him 'Nelson'). Carton de Wiart's eyepatch and missing hand enhanced his dashing appearance rather than detracted from it and he looked every inch a hero. Not surprisingly, he was lionized by Society. In 1916, Cynthia Asquith noted in her diary that she had called on Tom Bridges and his wife, Florrie, 'and with them – great excitement – was the hero of the war, Carton de Wiart'.[4] Thus it was not altogether surprising that Carton de Wiart should come to the attention of Winston Churchill, the Minister of War in Lloyd George's peacetime coalition, although the two men did not actually meet until the end of 1919. A man of Carton de Wiart's stamp was just the type to appeal to Churchill, and Carton de Wiart was appointed as second-in-command, and later head, of the British Military Mission to Poland.

In the years immediately following the First World War Churchill was obsessed with the idea of opposing the Bolshevik regime in Russia which threatened to spread revolution to the rest of Europe. Churchill's aim was to use Poland as a weapon against Lenin. His plans met considerable opposition, not least from the Prime Minister, Lloyd George. Indeed, on 25 January 1920 the British Government took a decision not to provide Poland with military aid that could be turned against Russia.[5] One is tempted to see the dispatch of such a well-known 'fire-eater' as Carton de Wiart as a substitute for more tangible assistance. Certainly, a man of his personality and reputation 'possessed all the qualities which were best designed to appeal to the Polish officers among whom he was sent. He was wealthy, aristocratic, cosmopolitan, Catholic, heroic, and indefatigably foolhardy . . . . According to the ethos of the day, he was more Polish than the Poles.'[6]

Carton de Wiart arrived in Warsaw on 12 February 1919, by his own admission almost totally ignorant of Poland. He soon discovered that Poland was engaged in five wars: against the Germans, the Bolsheviks, the Ukrainians, the Lithuanians and the Czechs. As might be expected, Carton de Wiart managed to get involved in the fighting. Among other adventures, he was on board a train when it was attacked by Cossacks, and was involved in two plane crashes. During the decisive battle of Warsaw, he commuted back and forth from the front line every day.

However, the British Military Mission had little or no influence over the course of the war. Clearly, Carton de Wiart found the British attitude embarrassing, and he attempted to persuade his political masters to throw their weight behind the Poles. On one occasion, just before the Cabinet's fateful decision of January 1920, he claimed in the course of the same argument that the Poles were capable of both capturing Moscow and coming to terms with the Bolsheviks.[7] The best that can be said is that Carton de Wiart's charm, charisma and courage helped to counterbalance the generally unfavourable perceptions of Britain held by men such as Pilsudski and Paderewski at a time when Britain seemed to be pursuing an Eastern European policy that was consistently anti-Polish. One unexpected result of Carton de Wiart's time in Poland was that he fell in love with the country. He left the British Army in 1924 and settled on an estate in the Pripet Marshes. There he lived the feudal existence of a Polish landowner, indulging to the full his love of shooting. Except for an annual visit to England, he remained in Poland until 1939.

On the eve of the Second World War Carton de Wiart was once again appointed as head of the British Military Mission to Poland. On 24 August 1939 he had an interview with the Polish Commander-in-Chief, Marshal Smigly-Ridz. Carton de Wiart had a low opinion of Smigly-Ridz's ability, and on hearing the outlines of his strategy, he reacted with some alarm. As he recalled in his memoirs, 'I found myself in strong disagreement with his proposal to fight the Germans as soon as they had crossed the frontier into Poland.'[8] Carton de Wiart had even suggested that the Poles should abandon the Vistula river line and the capital, Warsaw, in order to defend the line of the Bug. What both the Poles and Carton de Wiart failed to reckon with was the power of the German blitzkrieg.

In his memoirs, Carton de Wiart interpreted Smigly-Ridz's strategy in a curiously simplistic way, stating that the marshal feared he would be accused of cowardice if he decided to fight in the interior of the country. In fact, as a recent work has demonstrated,[9] Polish strategy was inspired by a mixture of economic, political, diplomatic and military motives, the basic concept being to hold the Germans on the frontier in order to buy time for mobilization. That Carton de Wiart should offer such a naïve interpretation is perhaps evidence of his unsuitability for a role which took him away from the environs of the battlefield and demanded a grasp of the higher direction of war, although Carton de Wiart's judgement was coloured by what he described as Smigly-Ridz's 'decision to desert his Army'[10] in September 1939, when the Polish commander crossed into neutral Romania.

The Poles were in an unenviable position in September 1939. They were outnumbered and outclassed by the German armed forces, and had to face the possibility of attack from four directions. The Poles' only real hope of survival lay in a prompt Franco-British offensive against Germany's western frontier. In late August 1939 Carton de Wiart found the Polish population excessively optimistic about the outcome of the war, but as the campaign began to go badly, Poles began to ask what had happened to the promised Allied offensive. Thus, for the second time in twenty years, Carton de Wiart found himself in the invidious position of acting as the military representative of a power friendly to Poland but unwilling to provide anything more than moral support. His instructions from London made this very clear: 'In view of the difficulties of rendering direct military support by British Armed Forces to the Poles, the question of inspiring confidence is of the greatest importance. ...' This task was made no easier by the behaviour of the British government; they did not declare war until forty-eight hours after the German invasion began on 1 September, and then made only the feeblest of military responses. On 5 September Carton de Wiart signalled that the events of the last few days had

caused the greatest mistrust of our intentions and this will continue to exist until positive action is taken by the British forces to relieve pressure on the eastern frontier. The dropping of pamphlets by British bombers in [sic] Germany has caused considerable concern in Poland as they see no useful purpose and they feel we are not serious in our intentions and are merely waiting until Poland is overrun when we shall agree to some kind of peace.[11]

For the British Military Mission, the campaign was a nightmare of retreat under heavy air attack. Forced to move out of Warsaw in the first week of the campaign, Carton de Wiart was unable to write a formal letter until 16 September. By then his staff had swollen to 63 strong, and as they made their way towards the Romanian frontier they were impressed by two things: the efficiency of the enemy intelligence service, and the devastating impact of the Luftwaffe. The wife of one of his staff was killed in an air raid. For Carton de Wiart, this was one of the events which led him to believe that he had seen 'the very face of war change – bereft of romance, its glory shorn, no longer the soldier setting forth into battle, but the women and children buried underneath it.'[12]

On 17 September Soviet forces crossed into Poland. Typically, at the moment when any remaining illusions as to the outcome of the campaign were finally dispelled, Carton de Wiart made a serious offer to stay with Smigly-Ridz and fight on with him on Polish soil. Britain might have deserted Poland in its hour of need, but Carton de Wiart's personal code of honour would not allow him to follow suit. Smigly-Ridz's abandonment of his army, while condemned in the roundest terms by Carton de Wiart, almost certainly saved the latter from a pointless death. Carton de Wiart eventually returned to Britain via Romania.

The British Military Mission were able to draw some accurate lessons from the Polish campaign. Aside from the shortcomings of Polish strategy and communications, it was the fearful potency of armoured and mechanized forces, and above all, airpower that made a deep impression on Carton de Wiart and his staff. In a letter of 16 September he wrote: 'The dominant factor is the air superiority of the Germans, which quite apart from the material damage it has done, has severely shaken [Polish] morale ... that of GHQ included.'[13] The depth of Carton de Wiart's respect for the Luftwaffe was to be revealed in Norway, in the spring of 1940.

In April 1940 Carton de Wiart was faced with the greatest challenge of his career : an independent command of troops on active service. Carton de Wiart might appear an unlikely choice for command of 'Mauriceforce', the Central Norwegian Expeditionary Force. He was aged sixty, had never been to Staff College, and his last experience of command had been in 1918, when he had been only one brigadier in an army of sixty divisions. He did, however, have two factors in his favour ; a formidable reputation and personal experience of German operational methods. As GOC of Mauriceforce his path once again crossed with that of Winston Churchill, the First Lord of the Admiralty, who as Chairman of the Military Co-ordination Committee bore a large measure of responsibility for planning the campaign.

On 9 April 1940 the Germans invaded Norway and Denmark. The Allies responded by landing troops of their own in Norway. The most important objective was Narvik in the north of the country, but preparations were also made to seize Trondheim, the 'strategic key' to central Norway. Carton de Wiart, who was at that time commanding a Territorial division, the 61st, was appointed to command Mauriceforce on 12 April. Operation Maurice was intended to secure the Trondheim area, in particular road and rail communications. The British naval action off Narvik on 13 April gave the impression that the German garrison of the port was demoralized and that one brigade, half of the British force intended to capture it, could be sent south to Namsos, 60 miles north of Trondheim, to co-operate with a third force. This was Morgan's 148 Brigade, which was landed at Andalsnes to the south of Trondheim, and it was intended that the city would be taken by an attack from the flanks. This was to be combined with a naval assault on Trondheim itself.[14]

Carton de Wiart arrived to take up his command in his usual spectacular fashion. As his Sunderland flying boat arrived off the Norwegian coast on 14 April, the aircraft was attacked by German fighters. Repairing to the destroyer HMS *Somali*, he met the noted writer Colonel Peter Fleming, and the explorer Captain Martin Lindsay, who had already reconnoitred Namsos. Their report was not encouraging. Deep snow would make movement from the port difficult, and there was little possibility of concealing large bodies of troops from aerial reconnaissance. In order to minimize the threat from the air during disembarkation, the troop-ships were sent 100 miles north to Lillesjona. Mauriceforce assembled over the next few days in Namsos, as parties were landed under the cover of darkness. Up to this point, Namsos had not been subjected to heavy air attack but on 19 April General Audet's newly arrived brigade of French *Chasseurs Alpins* revealed their presence by opening up on German aircraft with machine-guns. To Carton de Wiart's fury, this alerted the Luftwaffe to the Allied presence, and at 10:15 German aircraft re-appeared. As bombs rained down onto Namsos, the General coolly lit a cigarette and gave vent to his feelings about the *Chasseurs*: 'Damned Frogs – they're all the same. One bang and they're off!' The raid had two consequences. Namsos was badly damaged, which posed difficulties of resupply and reinforcement, and from that point onwards Mauriceforce received constant attention from the Luftwaffe.[15]

Carton de Wiart's original instructions had been to attack Trondheim in co-operation with a direct assault on the town from the sea, and accordingly he pushed Phillips' 146 Infantry Brigade forward to Verdal and Steinker, 50 miles from Trondheim, which they reached on 19 April. The ill-equipped *Chasseurs Alpins* were left at Namsos. The British were scarcely better off in terms of equipment and the men and their officers were inexperienced, although Carton de Wiart had great respect for Brigadier Phillips. Worst of all, air cover could only be provided spasmodically from British aircraft carriers, ensuring that Carton de Wiart's men were subjected to seemingly ceaseless pounding from the air. Sickleforce fared little better. Consisting of two brigades under

Major-General Paget, it was landed at Andalsnes, south of Trondheim, on 18 April. They found themselves under pressure from German forces advancing from the Oslo area which prevented them from performing their role as the southern arm of a pincer movement. Unfortunately, the achievements of Paget and Carton de Wiart were overestimated in London. On 19 April Churchill proposed the effective abandonment of the direct naval assault on Trondheim (Operation Hammer), largely in the light of 'The considerable advance made by Carton de Wiart [and] the very easy landings we have had at Andalsnes. ... [sic]'[16] It was now proposed that the two arms of the pincer movement would constitute the main assault on Trondheim. To Carton de Wiart, although there was delay in informing him of the abandonment of Hammer, it had become increasingly clear that his chances of taking Trondheim were minimal. On 21 April Carton de Wiart's men, extended south to Verdal, were attacked by German naval and ground forces and forced to withdraw. On the 22nd he signalled that he had ordered Phillips' Brigade to 'retire by the Steinker–Namsos road', rather than let them endure the ordeal of shelling and air attack any longer. He had taken a deliberate risk in pushing Phillips south, but it was a risk worth taking.

I had hoped by pushing Phillips' Brigade south as far as I did and [sic] if a heavy raid on Trondheim had taken place I might have made a dash for Trondheim but now I clearly cannot do this – and I must try to extricate Phillips. When I get them back to Namsos there is cover nowhere for them. I should be grateful if you will let me know what your policy will now be. I much regret to give you such a gloomy view of the situation but it is a true one.[17]

Carton de Wiart was a man of renowned courage and coolness, not given to panic. His constant repetition of the aerial threat and his recommendation of evacuation can only have underlined the seriousness of the situation to the authorities in London. On 27 April the decision was made to pull out and, in three hours on 2 May 1940, Carton de Wiart's force was evacuated by the Royal Navy.

Carton de Wiart emerged from the Norwegian campaign with his reputation largely intact. His personal example had been superb. His demeanour under air attack was as calm as it had been under shellfire on the Somme twenty-four years earlier. Carton de Wiart had failed to take his objective, but there is little doubt that his only chance of capturing Trondheim had rested in a combined attack with Hammerforce or Sickleforce. Since neither materialized, it is unfair to apportion him more than a small share of the blame. Carton de Wiart emerges with considerable credit for his reiteration of the unpalatable facts – that the expedition had been cobbled together and was ill-prepared, and that in the face of German air superiority the British cause was doomed. To some extent, his war record protected him from accusations of faint-heartedness, but it took considerable moral courage for a man of his type to insist from the very beginning that the campaign was unwinnable. Most importantly, Carton de Wiart retained the confidence of Churchill, who was notoriously intolerant of failed generals.

Norway proved to be Carton de Wiart's last active military command, but in April 1941 he was appointed to head the British Military Mission to Yugoslavia. While flying over the Mediterranean his aircraft crashed off the North African coast, and for the next two years Carton de Wiart was a prisoner of war of the Italians. He was thrown into the company of other captured British generals, and on 25 March 1943, at the age of sixty-three, he escaped through a tunnel, and remained at large with Sir Richard O'Connor (the victor of Operation Compass in 1940) for eight days. Despite being recaptured, Carton de Wiart was not destined to remain a prisoner for long. In August 1943 General Zanussi, the principal assistant to the Italian Chief of Staff, was dispatched to Lisbon, to speed up the process by which Italy was to conclude an armistice with the Allies. Carton de Wiart accompanied him as a token of good faith. As has often been remarked, the choice of the easily recognizable Carton de Wiart for a supposedly clandestine mission was a somewhat strange one. One inevitable result of this episode was a reinforcement of the Carton de Wiart legend; it was widely supposed that he was the mastermind behind the Italian armistice.[18]

In October 1943 Churchill appointed Carton de Wiart as his personal representative to the Chinese leader, Chiang Kai-shek, a task to be combined with that of acting as liaison officer between Chiang and Mountbatten (Supreme Commander South East Asia). Carton de Wiart's mission was not to prove an easy one. China was a diplomatic battle-ground between British and US interests. In 1939 Britain had been the Western power with the greatest influence in China, although under some pressure from the US. The following five years saw a dramatic reversal in this relationship, with the US assuming the role of the dominant Western power in China. This was mirrored by the differing British and American perceptions of the importance of China to the war effort against Japan. Broadly speaking, the US regarded the operations in Burma mainly from the point of view of providing bases for the supply of China, while the British were dedicated to the re-conquest of a part of their Empire. However, it was recognized that in order to harmonize inter-Allied relations, the British had to pay something more than mere lip service to the importance of keeping Chiang in the war. Thus in August 1944 we find Churchill sourly commenting on British troops being 'misemployed' in Burma, fighting 'under the worst possible conditions' to protect the American air route over the 'Hump' 'into their very over-rated China'.[19] American suspicions of British imperialistic designs added a further dimension to the problem.

The situation demanded someone who could both work with the Americans and protect British interests from American encroachment. An example of the weakness of the British position, which added to Carton de Wiart's difficulties, is the fate of a proposed operation by SOE to train pro-British guerrillas in the Hong Kong area. This, it was hoped, would facilitate the re-imposition of British rule in the Crown Colony in the aftermath of a Japanese surrender. Carton de Wiart had been given a role in the co-ordination of the plethora of British sub-conventional activities carried on in China, but he concurred in a decision taken jointly with the Ambassador and GOC China to abandon this plan on the grounds that 'our military position in China is now so precarious' that Chinese and, above all, American sanction was necessary for both military and political reasons. Carton de Wiart's transport problems might serve as a parable of the decline of British influence and independence in China. He was provided with a series of British Wellingtons, which crashed with monotonous regularity. Eventually he was given an American Dakota aircraft; this gave two years of perfect service.[20]

Carton de Wiart's stance towards Chiang was generally favourable. In late 1944 he was alarmed by the Japanese offensive which appeared to put Kunming, with its vital airbase, and possibly even Chungking, at risk. Thus he sided with the Americans against Mountbatten over the issue of withdrawing Chinese troops from Burma.[21] If this can be seen as the judgement of the man 'on the spot' of the magnitude of the Japanese threat, his casual dismissal of the importance of Mao Tse-tung and the Chinese Communists might be seen as confirmation of one historian's judgement that Carton de Wiart was 'almost as politically naive as he was brave'. Carton de Wiart had a rather simplistic view of Communism and dismissed Mao simply as a Moscow-trained fanatic. In January 1945 he reported in person to the British War Cabinet. His report, which lasted for only six and a half minutes, ignored the Communists altogether and was, according to one who was present, uninformative.[22] Carton de Wiart, like Churchill himself, was essentially a

Victorian, a man whose opinions were formed during the heyday of Empire. Before 1943 he had never visited China and his knowledge of the country can be judged by the fact that he had imagined it as being 'full of whimsical little people with quaint customs who carved lovely jade ornaments and worshipped their grandmothers'. The appointment of Carton de Wiart as his personal representative in China was one of Churchill's more eccentric decisions.[23]

Edward Louis Spiers (he changed the spelling of his surname in 1918) was born in Paris on 7 August 1886 and he spent much of his childhood with his grandmother in France. Young Louis grew up to be bi-lingual, and, like Adrian Carton de Wiart a few years earlier, had to learn the ways of an English schoolboy when he came to England to be educated. Spears decided on a military career, and entered the British Army through the Militia in 1903. In 1906 Spears was gazetted into the 8th King's Royal Irish Hussars, and four years later he transferred to the 11th Hussars. Spears's interests were not confined to those traditionally associated with cavalry subalterns. He translated and expanded upon a French manual which was published as *Cavalry Tactical Schemes* (1914). He also translated a study of the Russo-Japanese War, and became keenly interested in the use of modern weapons. Spears's unusual linguistic talents were recognized by the War Office when he was seconded from his regiment and employed to devise bi-lingual codes.[24]

On the outbreak of war in August 1914, Spears was initially attached to the *Grand Quartier Général* (French High Command), but on 14 August he was attached to General Lanrezac's French Fifth Army. Spears's task – that of liaising between Lanrezac and Sir John French, Commander-in-Chief of the British Expeditionary Force (BEF) – was of the utmost importance. The German Schlieffen Plan aimed to encircle the French armies and destroy them in a classic *Kesselschlacht*, or 'cauldron battle'. The position of Fifth Army and the BEF on the Allied left flank placed them opposite the line of march of von Kluck's German First Army, on the extreme right flank of the German Army; in other words, the BEF was deployed in the most important, and vulnerable, sector of the front. Spears's problems in co-ordinating the two armies were greatly increased by the relationship of the two army commanders. At a meeting on 17 August, Lanrezac quickly concluded that French was an unreliable fool. As Spears wrote in his reminiscences of the campaign, 'It was of course the armies that paid the penalty. They were incalculably weakened in the trials they were so soon to face together, by the understanding between their leaders.' The two armies, who depende their very survival on their close co-ordination of effort, thus set to fight an enemy without 'a single will and a closely knit plan'.[25] T gulf between the two armies had to be bridged largely through the effort of Spears. It was an awesome responsibility for so junior an officer.

On 23 August this mutual suspicion and misunderstanding almost resulted in the destruction of the BEF at Mons. Although the BEF had not yet been fully engaged, events on Fifth Army's other flank had left Lanrezac dangerously exposed. French travelled to confer with Lanrezac, expecting the latter to take the offensive. On the way, he met Spears. In a peasant's cottage, against a background of domestic activity, Spears tried to impress on French that the Intelligence Bureau of Fifth Army believed that the BEF was about to be outflanked by the Germans, and 'Unless the French armies, by a vigorous offensive, interfered with this manoeuvre, its full force would fall on the British Army....' Unfortunately, in Spears's opinion, Lanrezac was highly unlikely to carry out an offensive move. To his horror, French decided to abandon his attempt to reach Lanrezac. 'Perhaps I was not emphatic enough', wrote Spears years later, 'I was only a subaltern, and much intimidated at having to deal with such important people.'[26]

Spears was able to assuage his conscience later that day after he discovered that Fifth Army was retreating along the length of its front. Faced with the strong possibility of envelopment and destruction, Lanrezac's decision to withdraw was a sensible one. What was inexcusable was his failure to take prompt action to inform the British, or even grant Spears an interview. Fortunately Spears was briefed by Fifth Army's intelligence chief and, at about 7 pm, Spears set off for French's HQ at Le Cateau. There he gave French the grim news that the BEF were now marooned some nine miles ahead of Fifth Army. French retired with Murray, his Chief of Staff, and a period of agony began for Spears. He could clearly see that if French persisted with his plan to advance, 'the British Army would be engaging in a Balaclava adventure on a huge scale' with Spears himself cast as Nolan. Spears's relief can be imagined when Murray emerged to say that French had cancelled his orders for an advance to the north.

The next twenty-four hours was to see the BEF win a defensive victory at Mons, but strategically the Germans remained on the offensive. On the night of 23 August Lanrezac decided to continue his retreat. Spears was horrified at the implications for the BEF. 'To retire without

...ing them was to abandon them to certain destruction. Yet that ...pparently exactly what he [Lanrezac] was proposing to do.' Once ...n Spears was the bearer of bad news to Sir John French, having ...hed by motorcar over to Le Cateau ; once again, the BEF was ordered ... retreat. Spears was to play an important role in many of the battles on the Western Front, but none of his interventions were quite as vital as those during the Battle of Mons. 'The British Army was saved by the skin of its teeth, more, perhaps, by the efforts of Spears, a subaltern, than by any other single man.'[27]

Spears continued in the capacity of a liaison officer for the next three years with the French Tenth and Sixth Armies. In January 1917 he was appointed as liaison officer between GHQ and Franchet d'Esperey's *Groupe des Armées du Nord*. In his two volumes of memoirs of the 1914–18 war, he discussed the role of the liaison officer. He considered that the liaison officer lived a more interesting life than that of the average trenchbound subaltern. He was required to have a sound knowledge of a whole range of subjects, from logistics to grand strategy, and rubbed shoulders with the mighty. But liaison work also had its disadvantages. It was a physically gruelling and lonely job, and the liaison officer could easily become unpopular, regarded as too pro-French by the British and too pro-British by the French. The job of a liaison officer was a highly responsible one. He might be called 'upon without warning not only to explain a situation but to interpret it, to foretell how a general would act, what the result of an operation was likely to be.' This constituted a heavy burden. One of the worse experiences of Spears's life occurred on the night before the beginning of the Nivelle Offensive in April 1917, when he was irrationally tortured by guilt at his contribution to a plan which he, correctly, foresaw would end in disaster. It should not be forgotten that at this time Spears was only thirty-two years old, and less than three years before had been a lieutenant.[28]

Spears ended the war as a Brigadier-General and head of the British Military Mission to Paris, a position which he held until 1920. This represented a move away from the battlefield to a diplomatic role, liaising between the British and French Ministers of War. Not the least of the benefits that Spears gained from the First World War was the friendship of Winston Churchill. They had met socially before the war, but their friendship was sealed in December 1916, when Churchill visited the Front just after having been excluded from office. Spears was 'entirely captivated' by Churchill, and quickly became a confidant. In return, Churchill greatly admired the courage and achievements of the younger

man. In October 1916, after hearing that Spears had again been v
he wrote to him in typically Churchillian, but nonetheless sincere,
'You are indeed a Paladin worthy to rank with the truest knig.
the great days of romance.'[29] This was to prove a lasting friend.
which had the profoundest effects on Spears's life and career.

With the encouragement of Churchill, Spears left the Army in 192
and devoted himself to politics and business. Spears proved to be a
sturdily independent MP, championing some unpopular causes. He was
chairman of the Anglo-French Committee of the House of Commons,
and came to be regarded as an apologist for the French, becoming
known as 'the Member for Paris'. Although Spears remained deeply
attached to Churchill he was accepted by the wider circle of anti-appease-
ment MPs who regarded Churchill with suspicion.[30] On the outbreak
of war in September 1939 Spears found it difficult to obtain active
employment, his contribution to the war effort being confined to the
clandestine training of liaison officers. However, fifteen days after the
arrival of Winston Churchill in 10 Downing Street Spears found himself
in Paris as the Prime Minister's personal representative to Paul Reynaud,
the French Prime Minister.[31]

In June 1940 Spears was forced to witness the death of a country
he knew and loved. In the process, many of his deeply held convictions
about France and the French were challenged. Shortly after his arrival
in France on 25 May 1940 he attended a meeting of the French War
Committee. Spears was aware that the military situation was poor: that
a strong German armoured force had attacked through the supposedly
impenetrable Ardennes and had raced to the coast, cutting off the Anglo-
French forces that had advanced into Belgium. As an experienced liaison
officer Spears was not surprised when Reynaud complained that 'British
Generals always made for harbours', but he was not prepared for the
stark evidence of defeatism in the French Army, which extended up
to the highest levels. A staff officer from Blanchard's army group in
Belgium concluded a report with the categorical statement that he
believed 'in an early peace'. This was followed by a bitter 'monologue'
from Weygand, the French Commander-in-Chief, which ended with
a proposal that Blanchard should abandon his attempt to break through
to the south through the German cordon, and instead fall back on the
Channel ports. Spears successfully argued against this course of action.
However, the fact that Weygand had suggested the cancellation of a
major action on the basis of the unsubstantiated report of a junior officer
produced 'real doubts concerning Weygand's capacity' in Spears's mind.

⸳ found the contrast between the present situation and 1914–18
⸳th sharp and poignant. In both the first and last years of the
War the Allies had been placed in perilous positions. Then the
⸳o resist had been evident. But in 1940 Spears was faced with alarm-
evidence of the low morale and poor performance of large sections
⸳ the French Army. He had greatly admired the French poilu of the
Great War, and the seemingly effortless German triumph in 1940 'had
been to me very like a personal humiliation'.[32]

On the evening of 26 May, the defeatists in the French War Committee
won a further victory, when the possibility of an early peace was discussed. Spears's tactics were to counter anti-British feeling and to support Reynaud against the defeatists by convincing all and sundry of
Britain's determination to fight on, and that France's best hope of ultimate survival lay with continuing the war, from the French Empire,
if not in metropolitan France. Spears had a difficult task. Liaison between
the BEF and French forces was extremely poor, and both sides suspected
that the other was not pulling its weight. Naturally, Spears found this
situation extremely galling; little notice appeared to have been taken of
his experience of liaison work in the First World War. The British
evacuation from Dunkirk and the refusal to commit greater numbers of
fighter aircraft to the Battle of France were understandable and sensible
from London's point of view. The French, naturally, did not see these
British decisions in such a favourable light. Spears made his own contribution to Anglo-French mistrust by making tactless remarks: for
instance, on 6 June he replied to Weygand's criticisms of the RAF with
a scathing comment on the total absence of French pilots from the skies.[33]

Spears's role in the events that led to the break-up of the Anglo-
French alliance was that of a minor actor and major chronicler. At
the vital conference between Churchill and Reynaud at Tours on 13
June 1940 Spears was shocked by what he saw as Reynaud's collapse
of will. Reynaud asked that France be released from an earlier agreement
not to make a separate peace. Churchill, while making clear his opposition to this course, was still reluctant to give a categorical refusal.
On Spears's prompting, the British adjourned for a walk in a garden
to discuss the proposal. When they returned Churchill again missed
the opportunity to express his complete refusal to countenance such
a move. Paul Baudouin, Secretary to the French Cabinet, was thus
able to spread his version of the meeting, which was that Britain *had*
given consent to France making a separate peace. In part this was based
on a deliberate misunderstanding of Churchill's (admittedly erratic)

French. On learning of this from de Gaulle, Spears cha̶̶̶̶
Minister to the airport and 'got from him an absolute an̶̶̶̶
confirmation' of his opposition to France making a separate pe̶̶̶
ever, it was Baudouin's version which was widely believed. ̶̶̶
too, cannot be excused from some of the blame as he consistentl̶̶̶
to refute Baudouin's tale.[34]

If Spears had effectively countered Baudouin's distortion, the ρ̶̶̶
of Anglo-Vichy relations might have been somewhat smoother. On ̶̶̶
June the British gave their assent to the French concluding an armistice,
but only on condition that the French fleet sailed to British ports. Campbell (the British Ambassador) misunderstood his instructions and made
it appear that assent had been superseded by the extraordinary British
offer of union with France made later that day. (Spears played a minor
role in this stage of the drama; he held the paper on which Reynaud
took down details of the offer, which de Gaulle, Under-Secretary in
the Ministry of National Defence since 5 June, telephoned through from
London.) However it appeared to the French that 'the British position
had moved from assent on 13 June to categorical refusal on 16 June,
whereas in fact it had moved in that time from refusal to conditional
assent'. This further 'evidence' of British perfidy strengthened the hand
of the French defeatists. Pétain emerged at the head of a new government, which made peace with the Germans. The relationship between
Britain and the Vichy regime, which was always going to be a difficult
one, began on a note of exceptional bitterness and distrust.[35]

As early as 11 June Spears had begun to look upon de Gaulle as
the only man who offered hope for the future of France. On 16 June
de Gaulle told Spears that he, de Gaulle, feared he would be arrested
on Weygand's orders. As a result Spears made the decision which was
to constitute his greatest contribution to the struggle against Hitler.
He decided to help de Gaulle escape to England. In doing so he was
taking a gamble. De Gaulle was no longer a minister, simply a very
junior brigadier; technically, if he issued a call for resistance while
Pétain was negotiating an armistice, he would be in rebellion. It was
by no means clear whether de Gaulle would receive a friendly welcome,
and in fact the British attitude towards the Free French and the Vichy
regime was to be highly ambivalent over the next two years.[36] However,
Spears decided that 'To help de Gaulle ... was the only way of pursuing
the mission the Prime Minister had entrusted to me.' After considerable
cloak-and-dagger activity, de Gaulle went to the airport on 17 June
1940, ostensibly to bid Spears farewell. At the last moment, Spears pulled

ard. As Churchill wrote, de Gaulle 'carried with him, .eroplane, the honour of France'.[37]

cariousness of de Gaulle's position on arrival in London .1elps explain the storminess of his relationship with Spears. s role in promoting and establishing de Gaulle in the summer .o can hardly be overestimated. It was Spears who was instrumental ersuading Churchill to reverse the Foreign Office's decision to ban c Gaulle from broadcasting to France. On 28 June 1940 Spears was appointed head of the 'Spears Mission' to liaise with de Gaulle. For a man who believed that 'France cannot be France without greatness'[38] and who regarded himself as the upholder of French honour, the position of being a pensioner of the British, and protégé of Spears, was an embarrassing and humiliating one. Incidents such as the failure to inform him in advance of the British attack on the French fleet in July 1940 reinforced de Gaulle's consciousness of his ignominious position. De Gaulle's policy was dedicated to establishing himself as the leader of a sovereign state, the theoretical equal of Britain and the USA. In order to make this pretension credible, he needed to establish his control over as much of the Vichy-controlled French Empire as possible.

However, de Gaulle had more than merely short-term aims; he also had an eye on France's post-war position. In particular, he had grave reservations about British intentions towards the Levant, suspecting that Britain was preparing to use war-time conditions to seize these French mandates.[39] This paranoia about the threat of British imperialism blinded him to other, more important factors, such as the strength of anti-French feeling among the Levantine natives, but de Gaulle's fears about the British had some basis in reality. The British were committed to pursuing two policies that were mutually incompatible. On the one hand, they were committed to supporting the Free French, and maintaining French presence in the area; on the other hand, they were also committed to a Free French declaration of independence for the Levant, given in 1941 in an attempt to create an anti-Vichy fifth column. The French had established two republics that were only nominally independent, but the British, for reasons of sentiment and the desire to maintain good relations with the Arabs, wanted to give the republics real power – which would inevitably be at the expense of the French. De Gaulle was dedicated to countering any British moves in the Levant that he considered detrimental to French interests, and in July 1941 this led him into a headlong clash with Spears.

July 1941 was the turning point in Spears' relations with de Gaulle,

and in his whole attitude to France. Overnight Spears turn[...]
if not violently, francophobe'. The roots of Spears's dis[...]
with de Gaulle went back at least to the spring of 1941, when[...]
to suspect that the Frenchman was more concerned about esta[...]
the Free French position in the Levant than in contributing to the [...]
Allied cause. By June he was able to write that 'the Cross our C[...]
manders have to bear is the Cross of Lorraine'.*[40] However, it v[...]
the affair of the Syrian Armistice that brought Spears's simmering dis[...]
content to a head. Since the Fall of France in 1940 the Vichy administration in the Levant had observed a precarious neutrality, and until
June 1941 the overstretched British had left Syria and Lebanon alone.
During the Iraqi campaign of May 1941, the Vichy government had
allowed Iraq-bound German aircraft to refuel in Syria. Spears had previously warned of the danger of a Levantine 'Trojan Horse' in the
British rear and had forcefully demanded that Wavell, the British Commander-in-Chief, take some form of preventative measures. Iraq
brought the dispute between Spears and Wavell to a head. Spears took
his case to Churchill, who ruled against Wavell. Operation Exporter,
the invasion of the Vichy territories by British Empire and Free French
forces, began on 8 June 1941.

Spears's victory over Wavell was in many ways a pyrrhic one. In
the short term, Spears 'succeeded in alienating just about everybody
in Cairo' including Wavell, and the Prime Minister reinforced Wavell's
authority by ordering that all communications 'should in future go
through the Commander-in-Chief if they touched military matters'.
Spears took this decision from Churchill badly, regarding it not only
as a blow to his prestige and authority in the Middle East but also
as an unexpected slight from an old friend. Spears even went as far
as to consider resigning.[41] The campaign also dealt a fatal blow to his
relationship with de Gaulle. On 14 July General 'Jumbo' Wilson, the
commander of the expedition, signed an armistice with the Vichy authorities at Acre which virtually ignored the Free French and, in de Gaulle's
words, 'amounted to a pure and simple transference of Syria and Lebanon to the British'. As Dr Gaunson has argued, the Acre agreement
was the result of 'an unhappy coalition of circumstances and human
limitations' rather than a deep-laid British plot. De Gaulle did not
see it in these terms.[42]

---

* The cross of Lorraine was the symbol of the Free French. This comment is often
erroneously attributed to Churchill.

, considered the terms of the armistice 'quite preposterous' eed in June succeeded in getting Wilson and de Gaulle armistice terms. These had been rejected, officially because as trespassing on Wavell's territory in acting as an intermediary, o because Spears's tactless behaviour had offended Middle East mand. In meetings on 20 and 21 July 1941 the incandescent de ulle let his frustration boil over in interviews with Spears and Oliver ,yttelton, the Minister of State. Perhaps the low point of Anglo-Free French relations was reached when de Gaulle handed Lyttelton a paper 'which could only be read as terminating alliance between Free French and Great Britain'. This 'ingratitude' was for Spears the final straw. That very afternoon he was party to a decision that the British should be prepared to replace de Gaulle and possibly even incarcerate him.[43]

What had triggered this 'conversion'? Gaunson has suggested that throughout his life Spears had been a dedicated Francophile. His disgust at the moral decay he saw in 1940 had been temporarily counter-balanced by de Gaulle's heroic and lonely stand against the Nazis. But the realization that de Gaulle's ambitions for France, if not for himself, took priority over everything else, caused a violent revulsion against his former idol.[44] A more prosaic explanation might be that Spears was offended that his protégé, the man he had physically rescued from the defeatists in June 1940, had chosen to take an independent path. Spears's feelings for de Gaulle were fully reciprocated. The Englishman rose 'to the top of de Gaulle's rather crowded private demonology'. It is clear that de Gaulle believed that, detestable as Spears was, ultimately his policies were dictated by Churchill. On 2 June 1945, de Gaulle gave a press conference in which he attacked British policy in the Levant, slipping in a bitter reference to his former friend: '[Spears] has represented his country at Beirut for three years. It is difficult for me to imagine that during those three years he followed any policy but that of his government.'[45]

The breach between Spears and de Gaulle exacerbated, rather than created, the Anglo-French tension over the Levant. Spears's behaviour towards both de Gaulle and Catroux, the Free French Delegate-General in the Levant, was on occasion extremely high-handed. Since de Gaulle was able to match Spears blow for blow in bitterness and tactlessness this gave inter-Allied relations an edge which would otherwise have been missing. Spears's enthusiastic espousal of the Arab cause in the summer of 1941 gave the personality clash an ideological element. Arabism replaced Francophilia as the driving force behind Spears, who seems to have been unhappy without a 'cause' to support. This lethal brew of personal animosity and deeply held conviction helped to produce one of the most serious inter-Allied clashes of the Second World War.

It would be wrong to see Spears's role as purely destructive. He was firmly convinced that his policy of promoting Arab independence was in the national interest, given that the official British policies were in practice unworkable. Too often, he was placed in the position of Solomon, adjudicating between the French and the natives. Thus it was inevitable that he would alienate one side or the other. His decisions were not invariably in favour of the natives. In March 1942 he declined to support a Syrian anti-colonialist body. As Kersaudy comments, the Free French would have been amazed had they known of this: 'To them, the name of Spears was the very synonym of anti-French agitation in the Levant'.[46] Spears was able to justify his general policy by referring to Churchill's somewhat ambiguous statements of British policy, and by the fact that his knighthood and promotion to Minister to the Republics in 1942 implied official approval of his policies. While his friendship with the Prime Minister shielded him from his (British) enemies many, including the Foreign Office, regarded him as an obstacle to the improvement of relations with de Gaulle. In November 1943 the Lebanese parliament in effect declared the French mandate at an end, and the French responded by overthrowing the government of the Republic. The hand of Spears was (probably justifiably) seen behind the Lebanese move. Harold Macmillan attributed the problems in part to the fact that 'Spears is out for trouble and personal glory'.[47]

On several occasions, notably in October 1942, Spears had come close to dismissal. Finally, in November 1944 Churchill, who had recently returned from the Liberation parade in Paris intoxicated by the revival of his old love for France, removed Spears as Minister. Spears's friendship with Churchill had undoubtedly protected him in previous years, and Churchill came to regret his dismissal, which soured, at least for a time, their relationship. Whatever damage Spears had done to Anglo-French relations, and it has been suggested that de Gaulle's 'non' to British membership of the EEC in 1967 was in part a legacy of the bitterness of these years, the impact on Spears himself is plain. A member of his family was to write: 'His experience in the Middle East was so traumatic, and his disillusionment with the French (and in particular with de Gaulle) so profound, that the wounds he suffered between 1941 and 1944 never properly healed.'[48]

Having been present at the naval bombardment of Sabang and the sur-

:ender of Singapore in 1945, Carton de Wiart was retained by Attlee as the Prime Minister's representative in Chungking until 1946. Carton de Wiart then returned home and lived in retirement in Ireland until his death in 1963. He married twice, in 1908 and 1951, and had two daughters by his first marriage. Spears lost his parliamentary seat in the Labour landslide of 1945, and concentrated on his business career, playing a major role in the formation of the Institute of Directors. In 1918 he had married Mary Borden, a successful American novelist, who was to run an ambulance service in both world wars. Spears married for the second time in 1969 and died in 1974.

Spears and Carton de Wiart were both somewhat short-tempered, peppery individuals, not perhaps ideal material for diplomats. The title of Carton de Wiart's autobiography, *Happy Odyssey*, gives a fair indication of his attitude to war. In many ways, his military values belonged to a century earlier than the twentieth. John Keegan's description of the style of leadership of the quintessential Heroic general, Alexander the Great – 'exemplary, risk-taking, physical, passionate' – seems equally applicable to Carton de Wiart. To borrow another phrase from Keegan, Carton de Wiart's 'wound history is a sort of shorthand index of his style of leadership'. Ismay recalled a conversation in which Carton de Wiart ascribed his wounds to bad luck rather than excessive risk-taking, but as Ismay commented, 'The men whom he led told a different story'.[49] A style of leadership which led to him being wounded four times while in command of a brigade did not easily adapt to the very different demands of diplomacy. While his physical courage and martial prowess may have been useful in Poland in 1920 when his role was in effect limited to impressing the natives, rather different skills were needed in China in 1944–46. Carton de Wiart was glad that Churchill gave him an active role in the war effort but there is no doubt that he would have preferred a field command, a position for which, if not for his age, he would have been better suited.

The lasting monument to Carton de Wiart is probably the character of Ritchie-Hook in Evelyn Waugh's *Sword of Honour* trilogy. Spears is likely to be remembered for his volumes of memoirs, which remain some of the most useful and well written to have emerged from the two world wars. Unfortunately, his literary successes were not entirely matched by diplomatic triumphs. Unlike Carton de Wiart, Spears was frustrated in his desire to command men in battle, and appears to have transferred his aggression to the diplomatic arena. Even while remembering that Spears was faced with the problem of operating within the parameters of ill-thought out and contradictory British polic. that de Gaulle would have been a troublesome and cantankero no matter who had been British representative, it is clear that S was the wrong man to have in the Levant after July 1941. Spears offe extremism when compromise, or at least fudge, was needed, and o. is forced into the conclusion that Churchill would have been wise. to have removed Spears from his position as soon as Spears fell out with de Gaulle. Ultimately, one must question Churchill's wisdom in placing and maintaining both Spears and Carton de Wiart in positions to which they were temperamentally unsuited.

NOTES

(All books published in London unless stated.)

1 A. Carton de Wiart, *Happy Odyssey* (Jonathan Cape, 1950), pp. 70–4; T. Bridges, *Alarms & Excursions* (Longmans, 1938), pp. 156–60; E. Wyrall, *The History of the 19th Division 1914–18* (Edward Arnold, n.d.), pp. 40–9, 246.

2 Carton de Wiart, pp. 47–53; Lord Ismay, *The Memoirs of Lord Ismay* (Heinemann, 1960), pp. 25–6.

3 Carton de Wiart, p. 54; obituary, *The Times*, 6 June 1963.

4 H. Gough, *Soldiering On* (Arthur Barker, 1954), p. 149; Wyrall, p. 239; C. Asquith, *Diaries 1915–18* (Hutchinson, 1968), p. 244.

5 N. Davies, 'Lloyd George and Poland 1919–20', *Journal of Contemporary History*, vol. 6, No. 3, 1971, pp. 140–1.

6 N. Davies, *White Eagle Red Star* (Macdonald, 1972), p. 94.

7 M. Gilbert, *Winston S. Churchill*, vol. IV, Companion, Part 2, *Documents July 1919–March 1921* (Heinemann, 1977), p. 994.

8 Carton de Wiart, p. 155.

9 S. Zaloga and V. Madej, *The Polish Campaign 1939* (New York: Hippocrene Books, 1985), pp. 24–7.

10 Carton de Wiart, p. 159.

11 Public Record Office (PRO) WO 216/47; WO 202/114.

12 Carton de Wiart, p. 156.

13 PRO WO 202/125.

14 For Norway 1940, see T. K. Derry, *The Campaign in Norway* (HMSO, 1952) (British Official history); D. Macintyre, *Narvik* (Evans Bros, 1959).

15 Carton de Wiart, pp. 168–9; D. Hart-Davis, *Peter Fleming – A Biography* (Jonathan Cape, 1974), pp. 225–6.

16 W. S. Churchill, *The Second World War*, vol. 1, *The Gathering Storm* (Cassell, 1953 edn), p. 565.

17 PRO WO 168/97.

18 Carton de Wiart, pp. 180–234; J. Hargest, *Farewell Campo 12* (Michael

h, 1943); H. Macmillan, *War Diaries 1943–45* (Macmillan, 1984), p.

Gilbert, *Winston S. Churchill*, vol. IV, *Road to Victory 1941–45* (Heinemann, 86) p. 936. For the background to the Anglo-American struggle for influence in China, see C. Thorne, *Allies of a Kind: The United States, Britain and the War Against Japan 1941–45* (Hamish Hamilton, 1978).

20 Thorne, pp. 557–8; Carton de Wiart, pp. 247–8.

21 Thorne, p. 557; P. Ziegler, *Mountbatten* (Fontana edn, 1985), p. 289.

22 Thorne, p. 560; Carton de Wiart, pp. 268–71; D. Dilks (ed.), *The Diaries of Sir Alexander Cadogan 1938–45* (Cassell, 1971), p. 694.

23 Carton de Wiart, p. 235.

24 For Spears's early life and personal details, see E. L. Spears, *The Picnic Basket* (Martin Secker and Warburg, 1967) and his obituary in *The Times*, 28 January 1974.

25 E. L. Spears, *Liaison 1914* (Heinemann, 1930), pp. 73–9.

26 Ibid., p. 135.

27 Ibid., pp. 148, 172; J. Terraine, *Mons: Retreat to Victory* (Pan edn, 1972), p. 89.

28 Spears, *Liaison 1914*, pp. 51–2, 117–20, 340–1; E. L. Spears, *Prelude to Victory* (Jonathan Cape, 1939), pp. 47–50, 482.

29 M. Gilbert, *Winston S. Churchill*, vol. III, *1914–16* (Heinemann, 1971), p. 600; vol. III, Companion, Part 2, Documents, p. 1578.

30 N. Nicolson (ed.), *Harold Nicolson's Letters and Diaries 1930–39* (Fontana, 1970), pp. 371–2.

31 C. Andrew, *Secret Service* (Heinemann, 1985), p. 457; E. L. Spears, *Assignment to Catastrophe* (Reprint Society edn, 1956), p. 178.

32 Spears, *Assignment*, pp. 182, 189–96, 376.

33 Ibid., p. 388; B. Bond, *France and Belgium 1939–40* (Davis-Poynter, 1975), p. 132.

34 Spears, *Assignment*, pp. 504–22; M. Gilbert, *Winston S. Churchill*, vol. VI, *Finest Hour 1939–41* (Heinemann, 1983), pp. 526–38.

35 Spears, *Assignment*, pp. 584–92; R. T. Thomas, *Britain and Vichy: The Dilemma of Anglo-French Relations 1940–42* (Macmillan, 1979), pp. 18–22.

36 See Thomas, *Britain and Vichy*.

37 Spears, *Assignment*, pp. 608–11, 619.

38 C. de Gaulle, *War Memoirs*, vol. 1: *The Call to Honour 1940–42* (Collins, 1955), p. 9.

39 For Anglo–Free French rivalry in the Levant, see A. B. Gaunson, *The Anglo-French Clash in Lebanon and Syria, 1940–45* (Macmillan, 1987) and F. Kersaudy, *Churchill and de Gaulle* (Collins, 1981).

40 E. L. Spears, *Fulfilment of a Mission* (Leo Cooper, 1977), p. 292; Gaunson, pp. 27, 29.

41 Gaunson, pp. 193–5.

42 de Gaulle, p. 194; Gaunson, pp. 44–5.
43 Spears, *Fulfilment*, pp. 123, 134; C. de Gaulle, *War Memoirs*, vol. *Call to Honour 1940–42, Documents* (Collins, 1955), pp. 190–1; Spears, *Fulfilment*, pp. 137–8.
44 Gaunson, pp. 66–8; E. L. Spears, *Two Men Who Saved France* (Eyre a. Spottiswoode, 1966), p. 144.
45 Kersaudy, p. 192; C. de Gaulle, *War Memoirs: Salvation 1944–46, Documents*, p. 260.
46 Kersaudy, p. 195.
47 Macmillan, p. 295.
48 D. Hart-Davis, Editorial note in Spears, *Fulfilment*, p. xi.
49 J. Keegan, *The Mask of Command* (Jonathan Cape, 1987), pp. 77, 61; Ismay, p. 353.

CHRONOLOGY: CARTON DE WIART

1880, May 5	Born in Brussels
1899, June	Goes up to Balliol College, Oxford
1899 (late)	Enlists as trooper in Paget's Horse
1900	Wounded in South Africa
1901	Commissioned into Imperial Light Horse
1901, September 14	Commissioned into 4th (Royal Irish) Dragoon Guards
1901, March	Joins regiment in India
1904–8	ADC to Sir Henry Hildyard, Commander-in-Chief South Africa
1908	Marries Countess Frederica, daughter of Prince Fugger Babenhausen
1910–14	Adjutant of a Yeomanry regiment, the Royal Gloucestershire Hussars
1914, July 23	Sails to join Camel Corps in Somaliland
1914, November 17	Takes part in action against Dervishes for which he is awarded the Distinguished Service Order
1915, January 3	Left eye removed as a result of wound received on 17 November 1914
1915, February	Joins 4th Dragoon Guards near Ypres
1915, May 9	Wounded during 2nd Battle of Ypres
1915, December	Left hand amputated as a result of wound received on 10 May 1915
1916, July 2	Commanded 8th Gloucesters at La Boisselle in an action for which he is later awarded the Victoria Cross
1916, September	Wounded at High Wood
1917, January 11	Appointed to command 12 Brigade
1917, November 23	Wounded

...ril 7	Appointed to command 105 Brigade
...pril 20	Wounded
...November 19	Appointed to command 113 Brigade
..., February 12	Arrives in Warsaw as Head of British Military Mission to Poland
...923, May 1	Placed on half-pay
1924	Mission to Poland ends. Retires from the Army and settled in Poland
1939, July	Appointed Head of British Military Mission to Poland
1939, August 24	Interview with Smigly-Rydz
1939, September 1	German invasion of Poland commences
1939, November 29	Appointed to command 61st Division
1940, April 14	Arrives in Norway as Lieutenant-General commanding Central Norwegian Expeditionary Force
1940, May 5	Arrives back in England after evacuation of CNEF from Norway
1940, May 14	Reappointed to command of 61st Division
1941, April 5	Ordered to fly to Yugoslavia as Head of British Military Mission but later shot down and captured by Italians
1943, March 25	Escapes from POW camp with Lt.-Gen. Sir Richard O'Connor. They remain at liberty for eight days
1943, August 28	Arrives in England from Lisbon after release by Italians
1943, October 18	Sets out from London to take up position as Churchill's personal representative to Chiang Kai-shek
1944, July 25	Present at naval bombardment of Sabang
1944, December	Reports to War Cabinet on situation in the Far East
1946	Retires from post in China
1949	Wife dies
1950, July	Published memoirs, *Happy Odyssey*
1951	Marries Mrs Joan Sutherland
1963, June 5	Dies in County Cork, Eire

CHRONOLOGY: EDWARD SPEARS

1886, August 7	Born
1903, November 14	Joins Kildare Militia (3rd Battalion Royal Dublin Fusiliers)
1906, May 23	Gazetted into 8th Hussars
1906	Publishes *Lessons of the Russo-Japanese War*
1910	Transferred into 11th Hussars because of ill-health
1914	Publishes *Cavalry Tactical Schemes*
1914, August 5	Temporary Captain

1914, August–1917, May	Liaison officer with French Army
1917, May 5	Appointed Head of British Military Mission in Paris
1918, January 1	Brevet Lieutenant-Colonel
1918, January 23	Temporary Brigadier-General
1918, March	Marries novelist Mary Borden
1919	Awarded CBE
1920	Retires from Army
1921	Awarded CB
1922–4	National Liberal MP for Loughborough Division of Leicester
1930	Publishes *Liaison 1914*
1931–45	Conservative MP for Carlisle
1939	Publishes *Prelude to Victory* (memoir of 1917 Nivelle Offensive)
1940, May 25	Arrives in France as Churchill's representative with Paul Reynaud, French Prime Minister
1940, May 26	Promoted to Major-General
1940, June 17	Returns to England with de Gaulle
1940, June 28	Appointed Head of British Mission to de Gaulle
1940, September 23	Present with de Gaulle at Dakar fiasco
1941, April 1	Arrives in Cairo with de Gaulle
1941, July	Head of Spears Mission, Syria and Lebanon
1942, March 21	Returns from London as First Minister to the Republics of Syria and Lebanon
1942, March	Knighted
1944, December 5	Resigns as First Minister in the Levant
1945	Honorary Major-General
1945, July	Loses parliamentary seat in General Election
1953, July 1	Created 1st Baronet
1953–4	President, Institute of Directors
1954	Publishes *Assignment to Catastrophe*, his memoir of the French campaign of 1940
1966	Publishes *Two Men Who Saved France*, a study of Pétain and de Gaulle
1967	Publishes *The Picnic Basket* (volume of memoirs and essays)
1968, December 2	Wife dies
1969	Marries Nancy, daughter of Major-General Sir Frederick Maurice and Spears's long-serving secretary
1974, January 27	Dies
1977	*Fulfilment of a Mission*, Spears's account of his Middle East sojourn, is published posthumously

INDEX

Adam, Sir Ronald, 20, 37
Addis Ababa
  Ethiopian campaign (1941), 203
  Wingate's patriot revolt, 284, 285
Aerial warfare
  Chindits, support for, 291–2
  Cyrenaican airfields, 203
  Ethiopian campaign, in, 304, 305
  Habbaniya, attacks on, 80, 173
  Ironside's views, 23
  Malayan airfields, 260
  Malta convoys, cover for, 203
  Norway, aerial threat (1940), 330, 331
  Tunis, in battle for, 236
  Western Desert, cover in, 188, 189
Afrika Korps
  all-purpose spearhead, as, 153
  component forces in 1941, 205
  El Agheila, advance on, 197
Akyab, 83, 218, 219, 310
Alam Halfa, battle of
  forces in, 234
  strategy, 154
Alamein, battles of, see El Alamein, battles of
Alanbrooke, Viscount, see Brooke, Alan
  Francis, 1st Viscount Alanbrooke
Albanian front, 169

Alexander, Harold, 1st Earl Alexander of
  Tunis (Field-Marshal)
  appointments and career
    Athens, service in (1944), 124
    Burma, command in (1942), 110
    Dunkirk (1940), 109–10
    Field-Marshal (1944), 123
    First World War service, 106, 107
    Latvia, service in, 107
    Lt.-Colonel (1922), 108
    Mediterranean Supreme Commander, 124
    Middle East C-in-C, 95, 112
    North Africa, Ground Forces
      Commander, 113
    North-West Frontier, service in 1938, 108
    Staff College, at (1926), 108
  chronology of life of, 128
  Churchill, relations with, 11, 111
  criticisms of, 108, 110
  military strategy and experiences
    American troops, view of, 111, 114
    Anglo-American force in Italy, view of, 121
    Burma withdrawal, 309
    decorations, 106, 107
    diplomacy with Allied forces, 111
    HQ, Macmillan's description of, 115–16
    Imperial Defence College, at, 9
    Italian campaign, 115–23

...old, 1st Earl Alexander of
...d-Marshal) – *cont.*
...ategy and experiences – *cont.*
...constraints, 117, 118
  ...and evacuation, art of, 109
  ...of command, 104–5, 122
  ...cal skills, 109
  ...unis and Bizerta victories, 115
  ...ner generals, contacts with
    Brooke, 112
    Clark, 123
    Eisenhower, 113
    Montgomery, 112–13, 116–17, 157
    Patton, 157
    Slim, 308
  personal life
    artistic activities, 8, 105
    birth and education, 105
    character, 11, 105–6, 125
    common sense, reputation for, 108, 109
    languages, command of, 8
    political career post war, 125
Aliakmon Line, 79, 170
Amphibious assaults
  Akyab, 83
  problems of, 159
  vehicles and training (1943–4), 250, 251, 254
  see also Anzio; D-Day; Salerno
Andalsnes, Norway, 26, 330, 331
Anderson, Sir Kenneth Arthur Noel (Lt.-
  General), 156, 236
Anglo-American alliance
  Alexander's view of American troops, 111, 114
  American view of British attitude to
    European invasion, 96, 98
  British generals in favour with Americans,
    145
  China, diplomatic differences over, 332
  Chindits, US support for, 291
  Far East, plans for
    in 1942, 286–7
    in 1944, 98–9
  Greece, effect of British action in, 172
  Italian campaign, 117, 121
  Middle East war strategy, 124, 141
  Montgomery, US relations with, 145, 157
  North African landings, 95
  Operation Anvil/Dragoon, *see* Anvil/
    Dragoon, Operation
  Operation Overlord, *see* Overlord,
    Operation
  Operation Torch, *see* Torch, Operation
  Southern and Western Europe, conflicting
    priorities, 98
  'Vienna alternative' plan, 98
Anglo-French alliance (*see also* France), 338
Anvil/Dragoon, Operation

Allied views on mounting, divergent, 98,
  123, 177
  effect of, 178
  Mediterranean forces, use of, 119
  postponement, purpose of, 159
Anzio landings, 119, 120–21
Arab revolt against Jewish immigration, 185
Arabs, British relations with (1940), 340
Arakan campaign
  Japanese assault (1944), 316
  Slim's advance (1943), 314
  Slim's assessment, 310–11
  Wavell's plan, 83
Archangel, Allied expedition to (1918), 18
Ardennes
  German breakthrough (1940), 337
  German offensive (1944), 162, 163, 238
Armoured Army, Hobart's proposal for,
  247–8
Arnhem, battle for, 100, 162, 238
Atlantic sealanes, 93
Auchinleck, Sir Claude (Field-Marshal)
  appointments and career
    England posting (1940), 134
    Field-Marshal (1946), 143
    IV Corps, command of, 134
    V Corps, formation of, 136
    Home Guard, organization of, 136
    India, C-in-C (1940), 130, 137
    India, Deputy CIGS (1935), 133
    Middle East, C-in-C (1941), 137
    Norway, GOC-in-C (1940), 134–5
    Peshawar Brigade, command of, 133
    Quetta, student at Staff College, 133
    Southern Command, GOC, 136
  bibliography, 145
  chronology of life of, 145–6
  Churchill, relations with
    Auchinleck's stoicism, effect, 131
    Auchinleck's failure to satisfy Churchill,
      130, 135
    Middle East situation, misunderstanding
      over, 139
    revision of Churchill's opinion, 137
  criticisms of, 140, 141
  India, experience in
    accepted for Indian Army, 131
    C-in-C (1943), 142
    modernization of Indian Army, 133
  Middle East field headquarters, 140
  military strategy and experiences
    anti-invasion policy (1940), 136
    'boxes' plan at Alamein, 154
    French and English troops, opinions of, 136
    Indian Army, training and equipment of,
      287–8
    Mesopotamia, lessons learned in, 133

Middle East, preparation of army for war in, 139
Sandhurst, career at, 131
subordinates, selection of, 207–8
other generals, contacts with
Montgomery, 140, 141, 152, 153
Wilson, 208
Wingate, 142
personal life
birth and education, 131
diplomacy, shortcomings as to, 138
linguistic ability, 8, 131
peerage, refusal of, 144
personality, 144–5
stoicism, origins of, 131
troops, relations with, 132
Australian forces
Divisions
6th Division, 77, 191, 197, 205
7th Division, 173
8th Division, 269
Brigades
16th, 191
19th, 192, 193, 195
Western Desert Force, in, 201

Baghdad, 244, 301
Bagnold, Ralph Alger (Major), 74, 168, 284, 285
Balkans, operations in, 169–72, 176
Baltic Landeswehr, 107, 108
Bardia, 191, 192
Barrackpore, 218, 310
Basra, 132, 305
Battle of Britain, 75
Battle of the Atlantic, 97
Battleaxe, Operation, 202
Baudouin, Paul, 338–9
Beda Fomm, battle of, 195, 201
Beirut, 173
Belgium
course of fighting in 1944, 162–3, 237
Gamelin's 'Plan D', 40, 42
Benghazi, 194, 195, 209
Bennet, Gordon (Major-General), 263, 270
Beresford-Peirse, Lt.-General, 80, 202
Bergonzoli, Annibale (General, Italian Army), 191, 192, 193, 195
Billotte, Gaston (General, French Army), 38–9, 42, 43
Bir Gubi, 212
Bir Hacheim, 212
Bizerta, fall of, 115
Bletchley, code and cypher school, 4
Bradley, Omar (General, US Army), 158–9, 161
Brandenburg units in Poland, 283

Bremen, capture of, 240
British Army
civil/military relations (1939), 37
class consciousness tradition, 109
diversity of nationalities within, 216
imperial policing duties, benefits of, 9–10, 108
mechanization, see Mechanization of British Army
officers contrasted with German officers, 9
personnel, character valued above intellect, 106
pre-war unpreparedness, 19, 37
special operations, see Special forces
British Army, formations of (see also Indian Army)
Army groups
11th Army Group, 218, 312
21st Army Group, 158, 162
First Army, 156, 236
Second Army, 158, 159, 160, 162
Fifth Army, 120, 178
Seventh Army, 178
Eighth Army, see Eighth Army
Ninth Army, 175
Fourteenth Army (Eastern Army), see Fourteenth Army
Corps
IV Corps, 134, 317, 318
V Corps, 136
X Corps, 153, 234, 235
XII Corps, 152, 237
XIII Corps, 194, 233, 234
XV Corps, 292
XXX Corps, 154, 215, 238, 239–40
XXXIII Corps, 317, 319
Royal Armoured Corps, 248
Royal Tank Corps, see Royal Tank Regiment
Divisions
1st Armoured Division, 108, 109, 249
2nd Division, 166
3rd Division, 151, 231
4th Division, 232, 236
5th Division, 42
6th Armoured Division, 236
7th Armoured Division, 168, 183, 187, 188, 189, 190, 191, 206, 236; see also Desert Rats
8th Division, 151, 185
9th Armoured Division, 233
10th Armoured Division, 234
11th Armoured Division, 248, 249
14th Division, 83, 310–11
19th Division, 319
44th Home Counties Division, 154, 232
46th Division, 236
79th Armoured Division, 250, 252, 254

Army, formations of – *cont.*
...ons – *cont.*
...ards Armoured Division, 215
...gades
  ..st Tank Brigade, 245
  4th Armoured Brigade, 189, 190, 196, 206
  5th Infantry Brigade, 230
  6th Infantry Brigade, 166
  7th Armoured Brigade, 192, 193
  10th Brigade, 304
  17th Brigade, 192
Regiments
  Cameron Highlanders, 190
  Cameronians (Scottish Rifles), 185
  4th/7th Dragoon Guards, 251, 325
  Kings Dragoon Guards, 195
  Durham Light Infantry, 176
  11th Hussars, 186, 194, 195
  Prince of Wales Leinster Regiment, 53
  Royal Horse Artillery, 188, 195
  Royal Scots Fusiliers, 1
  Royal Tank Regiment, 168, 188, 191, 244,
    245, 254
  Royal Warwickshire Regiment, 150
Territorial Army, 37, 231, 232
British Expeditionary Force
  France, service in 1914, 334–5
  France, service in 1939/40, 152, 338
British Somaliland, 75, 76
Broad, Charles, 244
Brooke, Alan, 1st Viscount
  Alanbrooke (Field-Marshal)
  appointments and career
    CIGS (1941), 89
    not given Supreme Allied Command, 101
    rejection of command of Desert Army, 11
    Southern Command (1940), 29
  bibliography, 101–2
  chronology of life of, 102
  Churchill, relations with
    functions, respective, with regard to
      strategic planning, 92–4
    Norway, Churchill's plan for campaign, 94
    partnership with Churchill, importance of,
      11, 92, 101
    resentment, Brooke's grounds for, 90–92
    shared backgrounds, 89–90
  military strategy and expertise
    exceptional grasp of, 10
    Italian campaign, view of, 97–8
    Montgomery, support for, 95, 99
  other generals, contacts with
    Alexander, 112
    Dill, 65
    Hobart, 248, 249–50
  personal life
    birth and education, 89

character, Montgomery's assessment, 10
  personality, views of friends, 100–1
Brooke-Popham, Robert (Air Chief
  Marshal), 261, 262
Burma
  Chinese armies offered for defence of, 81
  geography of, 289
  Wingate's reconnaissance, 288
Burma campaign
  A Million Died (Alfred Wagg), 309
  Allied forces deployed in, 278
  British view of, 332–3
  Churchill's view of, 299, 333
  ending of, 319
  Japanese retreat, 99
  Leese's service under Mountbatten, 217
  Long Range Penetration Groups, 289; *see
    also* Chindits
  Sino-American pressure, effect of, 309
  special operations, Wingate's application of, 295
  strategies, conflict between Churchill and
    Brooke, 98–9
  US view of, 332–3
  Wavell's strategy, 82–3
  withdrawal to India (1942), 309
Burma Corps, 307, 308
Bush Warfare School, 288

Cabinet Ministers, *see* War Cabinet
Caen, 159, 160
Campbell, Jock (Lt.-Colonel), 195
Canadian Army
  Hitler Line breakthrough, 216
  Normandy landings, 158
  Reichswald, Battle of the, 238–9
Carton de Wiart, Sir Adrian (Lt.-General)
  appointments and career
    Brigadier-General (1917), 326
    China, missions to (1943), 332–3
    Chiang Kai-shek, Churchill's
      representative to, 332
    Chungking, Attlee's representative in 1945,
      344
    decorations, 324, 325
    Norwegian Expeditionary Force, command
      of (1940), 329
    Poland, Military Missions, 326, 327, 328
    Yugoslavia, Military Mission, 332
  chronology of life of, 347–8
  Churchill, relations with, 326, 332
  Italian armistice negotiations, in, 332
  liaison officer duties, 332
  military strategies and experiences
    Burma campaign, view of, 333
    courage, reputation for, 324, 325, 331
    First World War service, 323
    leadership, style of, 324, 344

mechanization of German forces,
assessment of, 329
prisoner of the Italians (1941), 332
service between wars, 324
Somali Camel Corps, 325
South African war service, 324
strategic naiveté, 327
wounds, 325
personal life
appearance, 324, 326
autobiography, 344
birth and education, 324
character, 15
marriages, 344
Poland, in, 326, 327, 328
political naiveté, 333
Casablanca Conference, 113
Cassino, battles of, 120, 178, 216–17
Catania, 116, 117
Chiang Kai-shek, 308, 332, 333
China
armies offered by Chiang Kai-shek, 81
British and US interests in, 332
US views on role of, in Far East theatre,
286–7
Chindits
first expedition
casualties, 278–9
component forces, 289
course of, 290, 294, 295
name 'Chindit', origin, 289
role of, 289
second expedition
aerial support, 292
component forces, 291
planning, 291, 291
Slim's view of, 315
strength of, in 1943, 315
Chindwin River, 289, 317
Churchill, Sir Winston
American view of, 96
Bolshevik regime in Russia,
opposition to, 326
Chiefs of Staff, relationships with, 10–11,
59–60
Curragh incident in 1914, 71
France's separate peace in 1940,
attitude to, 339
generals, relationships with individual
Alexander, 11, 111
Auchinleck, 130, 130, 135, 137, 139
Brooke, 10–11, 60, 89–90, 94, 100
Carton de Wiart, 326, 332
Cunningham, 204
Dill, see under Dill
Gort, 11–12
Hobart, 245, 247, 254

Ironside, 21, 29–30, 26–7
Montgomery, 12–13, 152
Percival, 14
Slim, 14, 300
Spears, 15, 336–7, 341, 343
Wavell, 12, 71, 76, 77, 80
Wilson, 174, 178–9, 180
Wingate, 13–14, 277, 281
generals, relationship with, collectively
disputational style, 58, 59
First World War experience, effect of, 148
House of Commons behaviour, influence
of, 56
Hitler
methods contrasted with, 7
opposition to, 2
literary works, 2
military career, 1–3
Minister of Defence, as, 6
Nazism, opposition to, 246
personality
breadth of vision and romanticism, 92
Brooke contrasted with Churchill, 91–2
Roosevelt, relationship with, 93
Singapore surrender, depression at, 256
war strategy
Boer War experiences, influence of, 5
British Army as principal war-waging
instrument, 6
Burma campaign, view of, 14, 299–300
command, style of, 7
Far East, opposition to Brooke, 98
Malaya and Singapore, 260, 272
Middle East and Singapore, priority
question, 55–6
papers written in 1941, 93
plenary authority, requirement of, 15
rationalization of machinery for directing
war, 6–7
Scandinavian strategy, 24–5
'set Europe ablaze' instruction, 5
SOE, setting up of, 5
tank warfare, influence of Hobart, 246
view of war, 4–5
Churchill tanks, 236, 251
Clark, Mark (Lt.-General, US Army)
Alexander, relationship with, 123
Leese, rivalry with, 217
Salerno, landings at, 118
seizure of Rome as objective, 121, 122, 216
Cochran, Philip (Colonel, US Army Air
Force), 292
Colville, Sir John (biographer of Gort), 34,
47
Commandos, 283, 284
Committee of Imperial Defence, 6
Compass, Operation, 77, 189

...tle for, 79
...r, Operation
...ive of, 205
...ning, start of, 174
...paration, 204, 205, 206
...nks, British strategy involving, 206
withdrawal after, 210
Cunningham, Sir Alan (General)
  chronology of life of, 222
  Churchill, pressure exerted by, 204
  desert warfare, no preparatory experience,
    204
  Ethiopian campaign, 203
  personal qualities, 207
  relieved of command in battle, 207
Cyrenaica
  British/Italian offensives and counter-
    offensives, 168–9
  Cyrenaica Command, establishment, 202
  Italian forces, components of (1941), 205
  O'Connor, strategy of, 193–4
  Operation Crusader, see Operation
    Crusader
  recapture, plans for (May 1942), 210
  removal of troops from, to Greece, 197
  Rommel in (1941), 171

D-Day landings, see Overlord, Operation
Damascus, 173
De Gaulle, Charles (General)
  ambitions for France, Spears' view of, 342
  escape to England (1940), 339
  Jerusalem, in, 173
  Levant, opposition to British moves in, 340
  policy after escape from France, 340
  Spears' relationship with, 15, 340, 342
  Syrian armistice, 342
  Vichy French empire, need to control, 340
  Wilson's dealings with, 174
Dempsey, Sir Miles (General), 159, 160, 162
Denmark, German invasion, 134, 329
Desert Rats (7th Armoured Division)
  North Africa, at final surrender in, 236
  Operation Crusader, in, 206
  Support Group, 188, 189, 190, 191
  Western Desert Force, in (1940), 168, 183,
    187
Desert War, see Western Desert Campaign
Diadem, Operation, 120, 122, 216
Dickens, Operation, 216
Dill, Sir John (Field-Marshal)
  Americans' view of, 66, 67–8
  appointments and career
    Boer war service, 54–5
    CIGS, 14, 51–2, 56–60
    early war years (1939–40), 55
    Vice-CIGS, 27, 55

Washington, diplomatic posts in, 53, 60–68
bibliography, 68
chronology of life of, 68
Churchill, relations with
  communication difficulties, 59
  criticisms of Dill, 14, 52, 57
  generals, Dill's support for, 58
  unsatisfactory nature of relationship, 51–2,
    56,59
  strategy, differences as to, 57–8
Harry Hopkins, dealings with, 61
Hore-Belisha, relationship with, 55
Marshall (American Chief of Staff),
  relations with, 14, 63–5
other generals, contacts with
  Auchinleck, 138
  Brooke, 61
  Hobart, 248
  Horrocks, 229
  Percival, 257–8
personal life
  birth and education, 53
  marriages, 54
  Washington, service in, 52–3, 60–68
Dinapur, 314, 317
Dixon, Dr Norman, 273
Dodecanese Islands, 176
Dorman-Smith, Eric (Brigadier), 193, 197
Dragoon, Operation, see Anvil/Dragoon,
  Operation
Dunkirk, experiences at
  Alexander, 109–10
  Horrocks, 231–2
  Montgomery, 152, 231
Dyle Line, 40, 43, 109, 152

East African Campaign, 78, 285
Eastern Command
  Horrocks (1941), 232
  Ironside (1936), 19
Eden, Sir Anthony, 1st Earl of Avon
  Slim, support in Khartoum, 304
  Wavell, support for, and visits to, 77, 168,
    169, 184
Egypt
  defence against Italian threat from Libya,
    186, 201
  political activity in 1939, 167
  special operations forces of British Army,
    283
  Turkish invasion threat, 132
  Wilson as C-in-C British Troops, 1939, 167
Eighth Army
  Auchinleck as GOC, 111
  Catania, landings at, 116
  commanders, sequence of, 201
  component forces, 204

Crusader offensive, 139; *see also* Crusader, Operation
El Alamein campaign ribbon, 201
El Alamein second battle, fame resting on, 200
function in Middle East, 95
Gott, appointment and death of, 11, 95
Gustav Line breakthrough, 121
Italy in 1944, 178
Leese in command (1943), 158
Montgomery in command (1942), 141, 149, 154
Operation Vulcan, 115
origins of, in Western Desert Force, 201, 204
popular perception of, 200
Eisenhower, Dwight D. (General)
  Alexander, relations with, 113
  Italian campaign, planning of, 117
  Montgomery, relations with, 16, 100, 145, 162
  Operation Overlord, command of, 16, 101, 158, 176–7
  Sicilian campaign, plans for, 156–7, 175
El Agheila, 77
El Alamein
  Eighth Army retreat to, after Gazala, 210
El Alamein, first battle
  Auchinleck as commander, 200, 208
  course of battle, 139
El Alamein, second battle
  course of, 154–5
  start of, October 1942, 112–13
  victory, 141
Ems, River, crossing of, 239–40
Enfidaville, 115, 156
Enigma radio traffic, 4; *see also* 'Ultra'
Escaut Line, 22–3
Ethiopian campaign
  British development of desert revolt, 282, 284
  Cunningham against Italians, 203

Falaise, 159, 160, 161
Far Eastern theatre of war
  Allied Command, creation of, 81
  Anglo-American divergence on strategy, 286–7
  Brooke and Churchill, conflicting strategies of, 98–9
  divergence of resources to, on entry of Japan, 175
Field Force, the, *see under* France
Finland, invasion, 24, 26
Fourteenth Army (Eastern Army)
  Burma campaign, final stages of, 319
  'Forgotten Army', as, 200
  Irwin in command (1942), 310

Japanese forces, compared with, 318
  name changed to Fourteenth Army (?) 322–3
  objective of, in Far East, 314
  revitalization under Slim, 312–13
  SEAC, in, 218
Fourth Indian Division
  Horrocks, under command of, 236
  Italian East African campaign, in, 77, 190
  Nibeiwa battle, in, 189
  XIII Corps, in, 204
  Western Desert Force, in, 168, 183, 188
Fox-Davies, Harry (Lieutenant), 74
France (*see also* Vichy French)
  armistice in 1940, British view of, 339
  British relations with Vichy French and Free French, 340
  conflicting strategies in 1940, 338
  Field Force, British (1939)
    aims of, 22
    C-in-C appointment, confusion, 21, 38
    communications, shortcomings in, 39
    Gort as commander, 21
    Ironside's visit to, 24
    movements in 1940, 26
    invasion by Allied forces, *see* Overlord, Operation
    morale of senior commanders in 1940, 43
    Normandy battle, effect on France, 161
    Operation Anvil/Dragoon, *see* Anvil/ Dragoon, Operation
    Scandinavian strategy (1940), 25, 42
Free French forces
  Bir Hacheim, at, 212
  de Gaulle, support in Levant, 341
French Army
  Chasseurs Alpins, 25, 330
  morale of, in 1940, 337, 338
French North Africa, *see* Torch, Operation
Freyberg, Sir Bernard (Lt.-General, New Zealand Army), 12, 234, 235
Fuller, J. F. C. 'Boney' (Colonel), 18, 244

Gabes, 235
Gabr Saleh, 206
Galahad Force, 291, 291, 293
Gallabat, 304, 305
Gamelin, Maurice (General, French Army)
  Belgium, proposed advance into, 40
  Gort's deference to, 38
  Panzer corridor, action to cut (1940), 44
Gazala, battle of, 210–14
Generals (British Army)
  Churchill's appointments, general comments, 15
  Churchill's treatment of, 56, 58, 59, 148
  comparisons of characters, 7, 8

British Army) – *cont.*
    ...n and military training, 8
    ...orld War generals, character of, 8
    ...ssional lives, similarity, 8–9
    ...ond World War generals, character of, 8
    ...man Army
    ...ommunication systems in Europe in 1943,
        96–7
    Cyrenaica, forces in (1941), 205
    Divisions, 90th Light Division, 205, 236
    mechanization, 204, 329
    mixed battle groups, practice as to, 204–5
    Norway 1940, movements in, 331
    Panzer Gruppe Afrika, 205
    prevention of build-up of, before D-Day,
        96–7, 98
    special forces, use of, 283
    surrender in North Africa, 236
German invasion of England, threat of
    defence plans, 28–9, 136
    Horrocks, service on South coast, 232
Germany, Allied advance into, 239
Gideon Force, 285
Gifford, Sir George (General), 312
Godwin-Austen, Henry (Lt.-General)
    British Somaliland, in, 76
    Crusader, part in, 206
    Ritchie, conflict with, 209
    XIII Corps, command of, 204
Goodwood, Operation, 160
Gort, John, 6th Viscount Gort (Field-
    Marshal)
    appointments and career
        CIGS, 20, 36
        early army career, 35
        Field Force, with the, 21, 23
        Gibraltar, Governor of, 46
        Inspector-General of Training, 45
        Malta, Governor of, 46
        Military Secretary, 19
        Palestine, High Commissioner, 46
    chronology of life of, 49
    Hore-Belisha, relations with, 37, 40
    Ironside's view of, as CIGS, 20
    military strategy and views
        continental commitment of army (1939), 36
        mechanization, failure to support, 38
        Territorial Army, support for, 36
        Western Front, service on, *see* Western
            Front campaign *below*
    personal background
        austere lifestyle, 35
        birth and education, 34
        courage, reputation for, 8, 34
        enjoyment of war, 38
        marriage, 36
        nicknames, 35

obsession with detail, 39–40
personality, 47
Western Front campaign
    Allied chain of command in 1940, place in,
        42
    Belgium, actions on invasion of, 42
    criticisms of leadership, 39, 42
    French generals, encouragement for, 43, 45
    French orders, under, 38–9
    Gamelin, relations with, 38, 40, 44
    German advance, actions to counter, 44
    Government decisions, communications
        breakdown, 42
    Montgomery critical of, 39
    return to England from Belgium, 45
    Weygand Plan, response to, 44
Gothic Line, 123, 217
Gott, W. H. E. (General 'Strafer'), 11, 95, 112,
    140, 153
Graziani, Rodolfo (Marshal, Italian Army),
    183, 187, 188, 193, 194
Greece
    British assistance to Greek Army in 1941, 77
    British guarantee of Greek independence in
        1939, 78, 169
    campaign in, effect of, 77, 172–3, 201
    evacuation of Imperial forces in 1941, 172
    German declaration of war, 170
    Greek army, plan for withdrawal from
        Macedonia, 170
    Italian invasion in 1940, 77, 184
Gustav Line
    attack on, 119
    construction, 118
    Eighth Army penetration, 121
    Kesselring's strategy, 216

Habbaniya, 80, 173
Haile Selassie, 284
Hammer, Operation, 331
Heath, Lewis, 304
Hitler, Adolf, 2, 7
Hitler Line, 121, 216
Hobart, Percy (Major-General)
    appointments and career
        Camberley, student at, 244
        capture by Turks in 1918, 244
        decorations, 244
        early military career, 243
        Egypt, Commander Mobile Division,
            246–7, 249
        11th Armoured Division, 248, 249
        First World War service, 244
        Local Defence Volunteers, 247
        Quetta, instructor at, 244–5
        Royal Tank Regiment, Colonel
            Commandant, 254

79th Armoured Division, raising of, 250
bibliography, 255
chronology of life of, 255
Churchill, relationship with, 243, 245, 247
military strategies and expertise
  conferences in 1944/5, attendance at, 253
  contact with troops in action, 254
  invasion strategy and tactics in 1944, 252–4
  mobile warfare, introduction to, in 1916, 244
  specialized armoured vehicles and devices, development of, in 1943–4, 250–4
  tank warfare, emphasis on, 244–8
other generals, contacts with
  Brooke, 248–9, 250–51
  Dill, 248
  Montgomery, 250, 252
  Wavell, 247
  Wilson, 244, 246–7
personal life and character
  argumentative manner, 243, 244
  marriage, 245
Home Guard, 136, 247
Hong Kong, 333
Hopkins, Harry, 61–2
Hore-Belisha, Leslie, 1st Baron Hore-Belisha
army appointments by, effects of, 19
army reform, efforts toward, 36
Dill, relationship with, 55
Gort, relations with, 21, 36, 37, 40
Ironside, attitude to, 18, 19
Liddell Hart, reliance on, 19, 37
'pill-box' incident, 40–42
resignation from War Office, 24, 41
Secretary of State for War, appointed, 19
Horrocks, Sir Brian (Lt.-General)
appointments and career
  Aldershot in 1923, 228
  Eastern Command, Brigadier General Staff, 232
  5th Infantry Brigade, Brigade Major, 230
  First World War service, 226
  44th (Home Counties) Division, Major-General, 232
  4th Division, 11th Brigade, temporary command, 231
  4th Indian Division in 1942, 235
  Middlesex Regiment, 2nd Battalion, command of, 231
  9th Armoured Division, command of, 233
  9th Middlesex Regiment, adjutant (1927), 229
  Staff College, on staff (1938), 230
  X Corps, command of, 235
  3rd Division, 9th Brigade, command of, 232

XIII Corps commandant, 233
  War Office, post at (1934), 230
bibliography, 241
biography (Warner), 226, 229
chronology of life of, 241–2
military strategies and experience
  armoured fighting, lessons in, 233
  Dunkirk, 231–2
  Normandy and Belgium, in (1944), 237
  relations with troops, 230, 236
  summary of early military career, 236
  wounded, 236–7
other generals, contacts with
  Dill, 229
  Montgomery, 231, 233, 235–6
  Paget, 230–31
  Wavell, 230
personal life and character
  birth and education, 225, 228
  linguistic ability, 8, 226
  marriage, 229
  sporting activities, 225, 228
Russia, adventures in, 226–8
summary of later career, 242
Husky, Operation, 115, 116

Imperial Force, North Africa (1941), 170
Imphal
  campaign for Imphal plain, 315–17
  early objective in Burma offensive, 293
  Japanese plans for invasion of India from, 314
  siege of, 317
  Slim's defence plans, 316
India
  independence, events leading to, 143
  Japanese plans to attack, 293, 314
  Second World War, Indian views at outbreak of, 134
Indian Army
  Arakan, advance into, 316
  Auchinleck as C-in-C, 130
  First World War, Divisions fighting in, 132
  independence, splitting of army at, 143–4
  modernization of army under Auchinleck, 133
  Western Desert Force, infantry in, 201
Indian Army, formations in
  Corps
    III Indian Corps in Malaya, 262
  Divisions
    3rd Division, 134
    4th Division, see Fourth Indian Division
    5th Division, 304, 316
    6th Division, 132
    7th Division, 316
    11th Division, 264, 265, 267

formations in – *cont.*
 – *cont.*
  ...sion, 317
  s
    ...fantry, 173
    ...d Infantry, 83
    ...shawar Brigade, 133
  ...egiments
    62nd Punjabis, 131, 132, 133
    6th Rajputana Rifles, 190
Intelligence (*see also* 'Ultra')
  Burma campaign, in, 307, 315, 316
  Gazala, failure at battle of, 212
  Wavell, Italian information available to, 76
Invasion of Western Europe, *see* Overlord,
  Operation
Invasion threat (England), 28–9, 136, 232
Iraq
  Iraq campaign in 1941, 341
  Mesopotamia campaign (First World War),
    132
  Rashid Ali rebellion (1941), 137
Iraqi Army
  Basra, attack on (1941), 305
  Germans, collaboration with, 173
  Habbaniya siege, 173
Ironside, Edmund, 1st Baron Ironside (Field-
  Marshal)
  appointments
    Commandant at Staff College in 1922, 18
    CIGS (1939–40), 18, 21–8
    Gibraltar, Governor of (1938), 20
    Home Forces Commander, 29
    Inspector-General of Overseas Forces, 20, 21
    Poland, mission in 1939, 21
    summary of military career, 18
    unsuitability of appointments, 19
  Archangel expedition, 18
  chronology of life of, 32
  Churchill, relations with, 21, 26–7, 29–30
  military strategy and experience
    air warfare strategy, views on, 23
    defences against German invasion of
      England, views on, 28–9
    Escaut Line, views on proposed advance
      to, 22–3
    France, role in battle of, 27–8
    German generalship, views on, 27
    Middle East, view of strategic importance
      of, 20
    Norway, evacuation of, 27
    RAF tactics, views on, 23
    Scandinavia, strategy involving, 24–6
    South African war experiences, 17
    strategic priorities, view at outset of war,
      22
  War Cabinet, relations with, 21, 27

personal life and character
  early life, 17
  linguistic ability, 17
  nickname, 17–18
  politicians, attitude to, 18
  popular reputation, 21
  temperament and character, 18
Irrawaddy River, 289, 318–19
Irwin, Noel (Lt.-General), 83, 310–12
Israeli Army, 280–81
Italian Army
  Benghazi (1941), 196
  Nibeiwa battle, 189
  Sidi Barrani, 169
  Western Desert, campaign in, 168, 169, 183,
    187
Italian Army formations
  10th Army, 183, 196
  Corps
    XXI Corps, 205
  Divisions
    Ariete Armoured Division, 205, 206
    Savona Division, 205
Italian campaign
  Alexander's part in, 117–23, 124–5
  Anglo-American alliance in, 116–18
  Leese's part in, 123, 216–18
  Montgomery's part in, 157–8
  removal of Allied forces for other
    operations, 217
Italy
  armistice in 1943, 176
  armistice negotiations, 332
  declaration of war in 1940, 75, 186
  Egypt, diplomatic activity (1939), 167
  Ethiopian campaign, *see* Ethiopian
    campaign
  Mediterranean campaign, effects of, 97
  Wilson's strategy as to, 177–8

Japan
  entry into war, events following, 175, 286
  strategies toward defeat of, 99
  surrender of, 99
Japanese Army
  annihilation after battles in Burma, 293–4
  Arakan, 316
  attacking tactics in Burma, 307–8
  India, planned offensive into, 293, 314
  Malaya, strategy in, 265, 268
  rebuilt armies in 1944, 317
  Singapore, assault on, 269
Japanese generals
  Kimura, 317–18, 319
  Renya Mutaguchi, 314
  Shozo Kawabe, 314, 317
Johore, 267, 268

Kasserine Pass, 114
Kesselring, Albert (Field-Marshal, German Army), 118
Kipling, Rudyard
quoted on Alexander, 106, 107
Kirke, Walter, 20
Kohima, 293, 317, 318
Kos, island of, 176
Kra Isthmus, 261, 262
Kyaukse, Burma, 309

Lanrezac, Charles (General, French Army) 334, 335, 336
Latvia, Alexander in, 107
Lebanon, Vichy French in, 173, 174
Leese, Sir Oliver (Lt.-General)
appointments
Eighth Army command, 158, 215, 216
Fourteenth Army, 318
S.E. Asia, under Mountbatten, 217, 218–20
XXX Corps, command of, 154, 215
chronology of life of, 223
military strategy and experience
Alam Halfa, in battle of, 154, 155, 156
First World War service, 214
infantry experience, 215
Operation Diadem, 216
Operation Olive, 217
other generals, contact with
Clark, 123, 217
Montgomery, 215, 218
Slim, 219, 318
personal character, 215–16, 220
Levant
Anglo-French tension (1941), 342
Free French declaration of independence in 1941, 340
Spears, policy of, 342–3
Lewin, Ronald, 302
Libya
British forces, strength in 1941, 169
Italian forces in (1940), 168
special operations in, 284
Wavell's plans in desert war, 76
Libyan forces
prisoners in Western Desert, 196
Sidi Barrani, Divisions near, 168, 187
Liddell Hart, Basil Henry (Captain), 18, 19, 20, 37, 281
Lloyd, W. L. (Major-General), 310
Local Defence Volunteers, 136, 247
Long Range Desert Group
Bagnold's plan to form, 284
formation in 1940, 74
precursors of, 168
Luftwaffe, 330

Lumsden, Herbert (Major-General), 155, 234
Lyttelton, Oliver, 202, 342

Maaten Baggush, 186
Macedonia, 170, 171
Maktila, Egypt, 168, 184, 189
Malaya
airfields, construction, 260
airfields, defence of, 262, 264, 266
civil authorities, restrictions on military by, 261–2
communications problems in 1940, 262–3
defensive works, 264, 267, 272
Japanese attacks on, 265, 267
military forces in, inadequacy of, 258
withdrawal of forces to Singapore, 268
Malta convoys, 203, 210
Mandalay
capture (1945), 219, 293, 319
Chindit operations, 290
Manstein Plan, 27
Maori Brigade, 234
Mareth Line, 156, 163, 235
Market Garden, Operation, 100, 162, 238
Marshall, George C. (General, US Army), 14, 63–5
Martel, Sir Gifford (Lt.-General), 248, 249
Matilda Tanks, 189, 190, 191, 192
Maurice Force, 329, 330
Mechanization of British Army (see also Tanks and tank warfare)
controversy in 1930s, 245
Gort, failure to support, 38
Hobart's tank campaign, 244–8
Ironside, support of, 18
slowness of most generals to adapt to, 204
Wavell, experimental work, 73
Medenine, 156
Mediterranean theatre of war (see also Western Desert campaign)
Alexander as Supreme Commander, 124
Churchill's plans for, 93, 97
Churchill's priority, 260, 266
Operation Torch, 94, 111, 153
opposing policies of Churchill and Brooke, 94
supply convoy (1940), 184
Meiktila, Burma, 219, 319
Merrill's Marauders, 291–3
Mersa Matruh, 186, 187, 213
Mesopotamian campaign, 132
Metema, Ethiopia, 304, 305
Middle East (see also Mediterranean theatre of war)
Dill's comments on strategic importance, 57

...st – *cont.*
...Army, importance of, 95; *see also*
...th Army
...rals, reshuffle of, in 1942, 185
...paration of Eighth Army under
  Auchinleck, 139
priority attached to, in 1940, 136–7
Wavell as GOC (1939), 74–5
Wilson as C-in-C (1943), 175
Military academies
  British and German systems contrasted, 9
  British generals, training of, 8
  Camberley Staff College, syndicate system,
    229
Minefields
  Chindit operations, 290
  El Alamein, clearance before, 234
  training in clearance, desert war, 155
Mohmand, Operation (1935), 133
Monte Cassino, *see* Cassino, Battles of
Montgomery, Bernard, 1st Viscount
    Montgomery of Alamein (Field-Marshal)
  Americans, relationship with, 100, 161–2
  appointments and career
    decorations, 150
    Eighth Army, command of, 11, 95, 141, 149
    Palestine, Major-General in, 151
    Royal Warwickshire Regiment,
      commissioned in, 150
  bibliography, 163
  chronology of life of, 163–4
  Churchill, relationship with, 12–13, 152
  criticisms of, 99, 155–6, 162
  military strategies and experience
    alternating thrusts strategy, 163
    anti-invasion (of England) policy, 136
    casualties, attitude to, 160–61
    caution and calculation, emphasis on, 149,
      151, 158
    desert warfare plans, 154–5
    El Alamein victory, 141, 155–6
    First World War service, 150–52
    image with troops, 157
    Italian campaign, 157–8
    morale, emphasis on, 152, 158
    Normandy landings strategy, preparation
      of, 158–60
    Operation Market Garden, 162
    Operation Vulcan, 115
    Palestine, peacekeeping force (1939), 185
    preparation of 3rd Division in 1939, 152
    Rommel, strategy against, 233–4
    strict routine, adherence to, 152, 231
    training, excellence at, 151, 152, 155
  other generals, contacts with
    Alexander, 112–13, 116–17
    Auchinleck, 152, 153

Brooke, 152
Eisenhower, 16
Gort, 39
Hobart, 250, 252
Horrocks, 231
Leese, 215
personal life and character
  birth, 149
  education, 150
  publicity, skill in, 200
  Sandhurst, misdemeanour at, 150
  tactlessness, 157, 163
  wound suffered in 1914, 8, 150
  political talents, 142
Moungdow-Buthidaung road, 316
Mountbatten, Lord Louis, 1st Earl
    Mountbatten of Burma (Admiral)
  Leese's service in Burma under, 217–20
  second offensive into Burma, 293
  Stilwell, relations with, 288
  views on prospects for Burma campaign, 307
Myitkyina, Burma, 290, 293, 314, 315

Namsos, Norway, 330
Narvik
  Allied Norwegian campaign, 25–6, 135
  German seizure, in 1940, 134, 329
Neame, Philip (Lt.-General), 197–8, 202
New Zealand forces
  Alam Halfa, 154, 234
  Eighth Army, in, 204
  German surrender to, in North Africa, 236
  Greece, in, 172
  Western Desert, in, 154, 156, 201
New Zealand formations
  Corps
    X Armoured Corps, 234, 235
  Divisions
    1st New Zealand Division, 204
    2nd New Zealand Division, 156, 234, 235
  Brigades
    4th and 6th, 172
    Maori Brigade, 234
Nibeiwa
  Italian forces at, 184, 187
  Operation Compass, 189–90
Nijmegen, 238
Normandy Landings, *see* Overlord,
    Operation
Norris, Sir Willoughby (Lt.-General), 204,
    206
North African campaign (*see also* Torch,
    Operation; Western Desert Campaign)
  Churchill's plans for, 93, 94
  course of, 96, 236
  reshuffle of generals in 1942, 175
  Wavell, strategy of, 75

Norway
  Carton de Wiart in expedition to, 15, 329–31
  German invasion, 134, 329
Norwegian campaign
  Anglo-French operations, 26
  armaments ship, loss of, 135
  Auchinleck, appointment of, 134
  Chamberlain's conduct of, 3
  Churchill's plan for, 94
  effects elsewhere of operations in, 42
  evacuation, 27, 135, 331

O'Connor, Sir Richard (General)
  appointments
    Cameronians, commissioned into, 185
    decorations, 8, 185
    India, C-in-C Eastern Command, 198
    knighthood, 198
    Palestine, command of 7th Division in, 185
    Peshawar Brigade, command of, 185
  chronology of life of, 198–9
  military strategy and experience
    capture and escape, 197, 202, 332
    Cyrenaican strategy, 193–4
    First World War service, 185
    Libya, with Wavell in, 79
    Normandy, action in, 198
    Sidi Barrani victory, 77, 189
    Western Desert campaign, 187–97
  personal life and character
    birth and education, 185
    character, 186
    Wilson, contrasted with, 186
Olive, Operation, 123, 217
Overlord, Operation
  conditions deemed necessary for success, 96–7
  course of, 99–100
  Eisenhower as commander, 177
  German generals, conflicting policies of, 136
  priority for, Roosevelt's insistence, 176–7
  strategy and planning, 158–60
  tanks, role of, 252–4

Paget, Sir Bernard (General)
  chief of staff to Ironside, 29
  Horrocks, relations with, 230–31
  Sickleforce, commander of, 330–31
Palestine
  peace-keeping force in (1939), 151, 185
Panzerwaffe (German Tank Arm), 245
Patton, George (General, US Army)
  campaign in Sicily, 117, 157
  desert war strategy, 114
  Normandy landings, part in, 159, 161
Pearl Harbor, 52, 81
Pegu Yoma intelligence service, 307
Percival, Arthur E. (Lt.-General)

  appointments and career
    decorations, 8
    First World War service, 257
    France, service in 1939, 258
    Greenwich Royal Naval College, 257
    Ireland, service in 1920, 257
    Malaya, GOC, 258, 260, 261
    Russia, service in, 257
  chronology of life of, 275–6
  Churchill's attitude to, 14
  criticisms of, 270–71, 273
  Dill, relations with, 257–8
  Malaya, service in
    communications problems, 265
    defensive works, attitude to, 267
    Japanese landings, view of likelihood, 264
    officers, difficulties with, 263
    review of forces required for defence, 264
    Singapore surrender, 14, 269
    strategy, failures in, 266
    withdrawal, no advance plans for, 268
  personal life and character
    appearance, 269
    personality, 257, 258, 269–72
    psychological explanation of character, 273
    Russian speaker, 8
Pétain, Henri Philippe (Marshal, French
  Army), 339
Phillips, Brigadier, 330, 331
Pile, Frederick (General), 247
'Pill-box incident', 41–2
Poland
  Brandenburg units in, 283
  British government stance in 1920, 326–7
  Carton de Wiart as head of British Military
    Mission, 1919–24: 326–7; 1939: 327–9
  Churchill's policy against Lenin, 326
  German forces, strength of, in 1939, 328
  Ironside's visits to, 21
  Polish war strategy in 1939, 327
  Soviet invasion in 1939, 329
Pownall, Sir Henry (Lt.-General)
  Director of Military Operations and
    Intelligence at War Office, 21, 36
  Gort, chief of general staff to, 38
  Ironside, opinion of, 18, 21, 26
  Malaya and Singapore, comments on, 272
  'pill-box incident', involvement in, 39–41
  Scandinavian policy, views on, 24, 42
  Singapore, service in, 261
Prince of Wales, sinking of, 256, 260, 265
Prince of Wales' Leinster Regiment, 53
Prisoners of war
  Italians in Western Desert, 190, 191, 192, 193,
    196
  Reichswald, Battle of the, 239
  Sidi Barrani action, captured in, 201

Conference, Quebec, 84, 277, 291

donment (1942), 82, 83
ance on, and capture (1945), 219, 293
exander at, 111, 308
ashid Ali, 173
Regia Aeronautica, 187, 188
Reichswald, Battle of the, 238–9
Repulse, sinking of, 256, 260, 265
Reynaud, Paul
  criticism of Gort, 34
  Spears as Churchill's representative to in
    1940, 337
  strategy for French army in 1940, 338
  Tours conference with Churchill, 338
Rhine, River, crossing of, 239
Rhodes, plan to capture, 176
Rifle Brigade, 166, 196
Ritchie, Sir Neil (General)
  chronology of life of, 222–3
  Cyrenaica, planned offensive to recapture,
    210
  Eighth Army commander, 208
  Gazala, loss of command after, 210–11
  Joint Services Mission to USA (1951), 214
  Normandy, service in, 214
  personal qualities, 214
Rome, Allied entry, 121–2, 178, 216
Rommel, Erwin (Field-Marshal, German
  Army)
  Afrika Korps, use of, 153
  desert offensive in 1942, 95
  El Alamein, withdrawal from, 155–6
  Kasserine Pass action, 114
  Libya, advance in 1941, 79, 202
  offensive toward El Alamein, 139
  tanks available to, 234
  Wavell's book, reader of, 74
Roosevelt, Franklin D.
  Churchill's meetings with in 1941, 93
  Operation Overlord, insistence on priority
    for, 176–7
  Stalin, attitude to, 96, 98
Royal Air Force
  air warfare strategy, Ironside's views, 23
  Greece, in (1941), 170
  Habbaniya siege, 173
  Malaya, withdrawal from, 265
  Malayan airfields, construction, 260
  Singapore, withdrawal from Malaya to, 262
  Western Desert (1940), 187, 188, 189
Royal Navy
  Maktila, attack on, 189
  Norway, evacuation of force from, 331
  Operation Overlord, landing techniques,
    252

Singapore, inter-service relations in (1940),
  262
Tobruk, supplies to, 193
Salerno landings, 118, 236
Sandbostel camp, discovery of, 240
Scandinavia
  Churchill's strategy in 1940, 24, 42
  German invasions, 134, 329
Shewbo, Burma, 318
Shingle, Operation, 119, 120–21
Sicilian campaign
  Middle East command, launched from,
    175
  Operation Husky, 115, 116
  plans for campaign, 156–7, 235
Sickleforce, 330
Sidi Barrani
  Allied troops, composition of, 201
  British capture of, 77, 201
  Italian advance to, 76, 184
  Italian forces in area, strength of, 168, 187
  O'Connor's campaign, 189, 201
Sidi Rezegh, 206–7
Simson, Brigadier, 264
Singapore
  army strength, multi-national forces in,
    262
  Churchill's policy toward, 260
  defences, 268
  Dill's view of strategic importance, 56
  fall of, 65, 256, 269, 286
  inter-service relations in 1940, 262
  Japanese assault on, 268–9
  military forces, inadequacy, 258
  naval base, defence of, 259
  War Council in, 262
  withdrawal from Malaya to, 268
Sinzweya, Burma, 316
Sixsmith, E. K. G. (Major-General), 273
Slim, William, 1st Viscount Slim of Burma
  (Field-Marshal)
  appointments and career
    between-wars career, 303
    Burma Corps Commander, 307
    XV Corps, command of, 310
    First World War service, 301
    Fourteenth Army, command of, 312
    Indian Army, transfer to, 303
    Mesopotamia, service in, 301
    SEAC, C-in-C Allied Land Forces, 320
    10th Brigade, command of, 304
    10th Indian Division, command of, 305
    West India Regiment (1916), 302
  bibliography, 320
  biographers, 299, 302, 303
  Burma Victory (film), 299
  chronology of life of, 322–3

Churchill, relations with, 14, 300
Defeat into Victory, author of, 298, 308, 310
military strategy and experience
  Arakan campaign, 310–11
  assessment of generalship, 319–20
  Burma campaign, command of, 307, 308
  early military career, 301, 302
  Eastern Army, revitalization of, 312–13, 319
  Far Eastern campaign, 14
  Japanese tactics, methods to counter, 307–8
  management of men, 303, 304, 307, 310, 314
  medical supplies in Burma, securing of, 313
  morale, emphasis on, 313
  recognition after Burma battles, 318
  special forces, postwar view of, 294
  Syria, operation against Vichy French, 305
  training programme for jungle warfare, 313
other generals, contacts with
  Alexander, 308
  Irwin, 310–12
  Leese, 219, 318
  Wingate, 315–16
personal life and character
  background, 300–1
  journalistic activities, 8
  languages, command of, 8
  nickname, 314
  wounds, 301, 302, 305
public reputation and low profile, 299, 300
Unofficial History, author of, 302
South African forces
and South African division at Gazala, 213
South East Asia Command
creation of, 287–8
Southern Command
Alexander as successor to Auchinleck, 137
Auchinleck, formation under, 136
Montgomery as subordinate to Auchinleck,
  152
Wavell as GOC in 1938, 74
Spears, Sir Louis (Major-General)
appointments and career
British Military Mission to Paris,
  (1918–20), 336
de Gaulle, head of British Mission to, 340
entry into British Army, 334
Hussars, gazetted into, 334
Member of Parliament, 337, 344
Reynaud, Churchill's representative to,
  337–9
Syria and Lebanon, Minister to, 343
Arab cause, espousal of in 1941, 342–3
chronology of life of, 348–9
Churchill, relations with, 15, 336–7, 341, 343
de Gaulle, relations with, 339–40, 340–41,
  342
departure from Army in 1920, 337

diplomatic shortcomings, 346
First World War service, 334–6
France, changing attitudes to, 338–42
French armies, service with in 1914, 334
French army morale in 1940, view of, 337,
  338
liaison duties, 334–5, 336
linguistic ability, 334
literary works, 334
military strategies and experience
  modern weapons, interest in, 334
  Mons, intervention in battle of, 334–6
  training of liaison officers, 337
personal life and character
  birth and education, 334
  character, 15, 344
  marriage, 344
  wounds, 337
Wavell, relations with, 341
Special Air Service, 139, 279, 284
Special forces (*see also* Chindits)
  British Army experience of, 281–2
  Churchill's belief in, 5
  controversy surrounding value of, 282–3,
    294–5
  German Army, use by, 283
  Libya, in, 284
  'Special Force', 292–3
  Wingate's theories, 279, 281
Special Operations Executive, 5, 284, 333
Spiers, *see* Spears
Staff colleges, *see* Military academies
Stalin, Joseph
  Churchill's wish to impress, 141
  expectations as to Allied actions in 1943, 177
Stalingrad, 175
Stilwell, Joseph (General, US Army)
  Alexander, relations with, 308
  attitude to British, 111, 145, 287
  Burma withdrawal, assessment of, 309–10
  Galahad Force, command of, 292–3
  India/China land communications plan, 83
  Mountbatten, relations with, 288
  Myitkyina, drive for, 315
  Wavell, relationship with, 82, 287
Stirling, David, 279, 284
Strike, Operation, 115
Sweden
  iron ore fields as objective in 1940, 24–6
Syria
  defence of Middle East, Wilson's activities,
    174–5
  Syrian armistice, 341–2
  Vichy French in, 173, 174

Tanks and tank warfare
  Allied armies' resources in 1944, 251

...nk warfare – *cont.*
...ny's attitude to tank warfare in
...05
...51
251, 254
...th Army, tanks in, at formation of, 204
...Alamein, at battle of, 141
...thiopian campaign, 304
'Funnies', 252, 253, 254
Gazala, opposing strengths at battle of, 211
German anti-tank guns at Gazala, 211–12
German *Panzerwaffe*, 245
German tanks in Western Desert, 205, 234
Grant tank, 234
Hobart's enthusiasm for, 244–50
Japanese tanks in Malaya, 265, 267
Macedonia, in, 171
Malaya and Singapore, Allied shortages in
(1941), 261, 262
Martel as CRAC, 248
Matildas in Western Desert, 189, 190, 191,
192
Middle East tanks, priority for in 1940, 136–7
O'Connor's tactics in 1940, 187
Operation Crusader, strategy in, 206
Rommel, captured tank of, studied, 138
technical equipment in 1944, 254
types of tanks in 1930s, 246
types of tanks in 1944 invasion of Europe,
251–2, 253–4
Wavell's reinforcements, Middle East, 75
Western Desert Force, in, 194, 195, 196
Wilson's recognition of tanks' importance,
168, 174
Thermopylae Line, 171
Thomas, Sir Shenton (Governor of
Singapore), 262, 270
Tobruk
actions leading to Allied capture, 192–3
Battle of Gazala, 210, 213
Italian forces in, 187
Operation Crusader, 205, 206
relief by Eighth Army, 139
Rommel, taken by, 95
siege of (1941), 202
Torch, Operation
Alexander as task force commander, 111
Anglo-American views on plan, 94
Montgomery, role of, 153
Tripolitania
Allied failure to advance into (1941), 197,
201–2
British advance into (1942), 209
Operation Crusader, *see* Crusader,
Operation
Trondheim, 329, 330, 331
Tummar, battles for camps, 187, 190

Tunisian campaign
Anglo-American differences as to strategy,
96, 97
end of, 115
Operation Vulcan, 115
planned breakthrough in 1942, 235
tactical problems of Tunisia, 113
Tunis and Bizerta, fall of, 115
Turkey
Allied aid to in 1943, 175
Egypt, potential invasion of, in 1915, 132
Ironside's assessment of strategic
importance in 1939, 22

'Ultra'
Bulgaria, information on German
movements into, 169
Churchill, daily quota of, 4
desert campaign, information in, 76, 80, 138
Greece, threat to, 78, 79
Middle East Command, information
available to, 76
Montgomery, action on information in
desert war, 156
United States of America (*see also* Anglo-
American alliance)
Far Eastern campaign, 99
war strategy, conflicting views, 94, 97–8,
286–7
US Army, formations of
12th Army Group, 158
Armies
First Army, 159
Second Army, 162
Third Army, 159
Fifth Army, 158
Seventh Army, 178
Ninth Army, 239
Corps
II Corps, 114
VI Corps, 120
Valmontone, 121, 122
Veritable, Operation, 238–9
Vichy French
Anglo-Vichy relations, 339
armistice at Acre in 1941, 341
attacked by Slim in Syria, 306
Habbaniya, support for German attack on,
80, 173
Lebanon, resistance to Allied troops in, 173
Levant, neutrality in, 341
surrender in Syria and Lebanon, 174
Syria, support to Germans in, 173
'Vienna alternative', Alexander's, 98
Vulcan, Operation, 115

Wadi Akarit, 156, 235
War Cabinet

formation under Churchill, 3
Ironside's relations with, 22, 23, 27
pre-war unpreparedness, 19
Washington, D.C.
Churchill and Dill, diplomatic activity of, 60–68
Wavell, Archibald, 1st Earl Wavell (Field-Marshal)
appointments and career
Black Watch, commissioned into, 72
Boer War service, 72
dismissal from desert campaign, 80
Field-Marshal, 85
First World War service, 72–3
India, ordered to, in 1941, 80–81
intelligence section at War Office in 1914, 72
Lees Knowles lectures, 71, 72, 74
Middle East GOC, 74–80
Palestine, GOC, 73–4
Russia, service in, 72
Southern Command, GOC, 74
Staff College successes, 72
Supreme Allied Commander, South West Pacific, 81
Viceroyalty of India, 84
bibliography, 86
chronology of life of, 86
Churchill, relationship with, 12, 58, 71–2, 76, 77
nell as biographer, 71
ediates between W. and Churchill,

rategy and experience
offensive, 83, 84
ampaign, 83
ns, list of, 85
its, support for, 84
hinese, relations with, 81
Compass operation, 77
desert war strategy, 75, 185
East Africa in 1941, 78
Field Service Regulations, contributor to, 71
Greek campaign, 78
infantry, support for, 73
Libyan offensive, plans for, 76
officers supported and promoted by, 74
planning, belief in, 79
Sidi Barrani victory, 77
Singapore withdrawal, plans for, 82
Tobruk, holding of, 79
other generals, contacts with
Horrocks, 230
Spears, 341
Wingate, 74, 278, 281, 282, 285
personal life and character
academic career, 70–71

accident in Singapore visit, 82
aerial mishaps, 75
interests outside army, 70
literary works, 8, 70–71, 74
nickname, 72
political views, 85
self-assessment, 70
taciturnity, 20, 71
temperament, 12
Weichs, Maximilian von (General, German Army), 171
Western Desert campaign
air cover, 188, 189
Alexander and Montgomery, relationship between, 112–13
Anglo-American relations, 113–114
army preparation under Wilson, 167–8
'boxes' system, 213
Brooke's rejection of command, 11
casualties, 196
Italian prisoners, provision for, 190
logistical problems, 210
London emphasis on, in 1941, 203
long-range patrols under Wilson, 168
offensives urged by Churchill, 94
Operation Crusader, see Crusader, Operation
planning of campaign, 169
tanks, disposition of, 187–8
termination of campaign, 197
Wavell, strategy of, 75
Western Desert Force (see also Eighth Army)
components of, 168, 183
Eighth Army, origins of, 201
objectives in 1940, 187
renamed XIII Corps, 79, 194, 202
Western Front
communications problems in 1940, 39, 42–3
German advance in 1940, 44
Scandinavian operations, neglect during, 42
Weygand Plan, 44, 45, 337
Wilson, Henry Maitland, 1st Baron Wilson (Field-Marshal)
appointments
Aldershot, command of 2nd Division, 166
Athens, freedom of city, 178
Cairo, C-in-C British Troops in Egypt (1939), 167
Greece, command of British Imperial Force in, 169–71
knighthood, 175–6
Middle East C-in-C (1943), 175
Palestine and Transjordan, command in (1941), 173
Sixth Infantry Brigade, command of (1934), 166
South African War service, 166

...ry Maitland, 1st Baron Wilson
  ...Marshal) – *cont.*
  ...ments – *cont.*
    ...College senior instructor, 1930, 166
    ...shington, head of British Mission 1945,
      ...79
...ronology of life of, 180
Churchill, relations with
  closeness of relationship, 178–9, 180
  Eighth Army appointment, Churchill's
    support for, 174, 179
  first meeting, 175
  Greece, cooling of relations over, 172
de Gaulle, dealings with, 174
Hobart, relations with, 244, 246–7
military strategies and experience
  Greek campaign, view of, 172
  Italy, strategy regarding, 178
  Ninth Army, command of, 175
  Operation Overlord, part in, 177
  surprise, insistence on, in desert, 168
  Syria's involvement in defence of Middle
    East, 174
  training, emphasis on, 167, 168
  'W' force, 170, 171, 172
  Western Desert campaign, planning of, 169
personal life and character
  appearance, 167
  birth and education, 166
  character, assessment of, 179
  diplomacy, talent for, 167, 174, 175, 176, 179
  O'Connor, contrast with, 186
  personality, 167
Vichy French, signing of Syrian armistice
  with, 341–2
Wingate, Orde (Major-General)

appointments and career
  Bush Warfare School, Burma, 286, 288
  Palestine, general staff appointment in
    1936, 280–81
  Sudan Defence Force in 1928, 280
Churchill, relations with, 13–14, 277, 291
Cochran (US Army Air Force), relations
  with, 292
chronology of life of, 296–7
Lawrence of Arabia comparison, 277, 281
military strategy and experience
  controversial views of other officers, 278, 279
  Ethiopian campaign lectures, 286
  generalship, assessment of, 294–5, 296
  long-range penetration scheme, 278,
    288–9; *see also* Chindits
  unorthodoxy, 278
  Zionist cause in Palestine, 280
other generals, contacts with
  Auchinleck, 142–3
  Slim, 315
  Wavell, 74, 278, 281
personal life and character
  appearance, 278
  Arabic speaker, 280
  background, 13, 279
  birth and education, 279
  death, 277, 294, 316
  suicide attempt, 285, 286
special operations involvement, 280–82
Wingate, Sir Reginald (General), 279

Yugoslavia
  campaign in, effect of, 172
  German declaration of war again...
  guerrilla warfare, 176

Warner now offers an exciting range of quality titles by both established and new authors. All of the books in this series are available from:
Little, Brown and Company (UK) Limited,
Cash Sales Department,
P.O. Box 11,
Falmouth,
Cornwall TR10 9EN.

Alternatively you may fax your order to the above address. Fax No. 0326 376423.

Payments can be made as follows: Cheque, postal order (payable to Little, Brown and Company) or by credit cards, Visa/Access. Do not send cash or currency. UK customers: and B.F.P.O.: please send a cheque or postal order (no currency) and allow £1.00 for postage and packing for the first book, plus 50p for the second book, plus 30p for each additional book up to a maximum charge of £3.00 (7 books plus).

Overseas customers including Ireland, please allow £2.00 for postage and packing for the first book, plus £1.00 for the second book, plus 50p for each additional book.

NAME (Block Letters) ....

ADDRESS..

....

☐ I enclose my remittance for _____

☐ I wish to pay by Access/Visa Card

Number ☐☐☐☐☐☐☐☐☐☐☐☐☐☐☐☐☐☐

Card Expiry Date ☐☐☐☐